The Georgics of Virgil

THE GEORGICS
OF VIRGIL

A CRITICAL SURVEY

L. P. WILKINSON

Brereton Reader in Classics in the
University of Cambridge and
Fellow of King's College

CAMBRIDGE
AT THE UNIVERSITY PRESS
1969

Published by the Syndics of the Cambridge University Press
Bentley House, 200 Euston Road, London N.W. 1
American Branch: 32 East 57th Street, New York, N.Y. 10022

Library of Congress Catalogue Card Number: 75–79058
Standard Book Number: 521 07450 9

Printed in Great Britain
at the University Printing House, Cambridge
(Brooke Crutchley, University Printer)

To

PETER BURBIDGE

Contents

CONTENTS

CONTENTS

Preface

My debts are numerous, and most gratefully acknowledged. My friends Messrs D. W. Lucas, W. A. Camps and A. G. Lee read the whole typescript, and Prof. K. D. White that of chapters ix and x. From them I adopted many useful suggestions, and they are in no way responsible for my errors. Prof. Erich Burck of Kiel nobly lent me his own copy of his doctoral dissertation, *De Vergilii Georgicon partibus iussivis.* For help of various kinds I am indebted to Dr R. R. Bolgar, Prof. M. L. Clarke, Prof. P. de Courcelle, Mr E. P. M. Dronke, Mr G. E. Fussell, Mr J. S. L. Gilmour, Prof. F. J. H. Haskell, Mr E. J. Kenney, Dom David Knowles, Prof. J. Perret, Prof. A. T. Phillipson, the late Dr F. J. E. Raby, Dr M. L. Ryder, Prof. W. H. Thorpe and Prof. J. H. Waszink.

Acknowledgement must also be made to Doubleday and Company and Jonathan Cape Ltd for permission to quote from Mr C. Day-Lewis's translation of the *Georgics*, and to the Clarendon Press, Oxford, for permission to quote from Mr T. F. Higham's translation of *Works and Days* in the *Oxford Book of Greek Verse in Translation*.

Finally I must thank for their usual skill and care the University Typewriting Office, Cambridge, and the staff of the Cambridge University Press, whose production of my last book, *Golden Latin Artistry*, was awarded a gold medal at the Leipzig Fair, and particularly Mr Peter Burbidge to whom this one is gratefully dedicated.

L. P. W.

Cambridge
August 1968

Note

Superior figures in the text refer the reader to the Index of References beginning on p. 332, which is preceded by a list of abbreviations used for some modern works.

A list of modern works cited will be found on p. 343, an index of passages cited from the *Georgics* on p. 360, and an index of proper names on p. 351.

I · *Introduction*

The *Georgics* is a splendid poem (I use the singular advisedly), even if it may not be, as Dryden roundly called it, 'the best Poem of the best Poet'. Yet there is no book in English devoted to it. Sellar, eloquent and judicious as ever, did it admirable justice in so far as it was understood and appreciated in the last century.[1] But since then our books on Virgil in general have tended to concentrate on the *Aeneid*. Thus in T. R. Glover's lively *Virgil* (1904) the *Georgics* claimed little more than half a dozen pages out of more than 300, and there are only scattered references to it in W. H. Jackson Knight's *Roman Vergil* (1944). Turning to America, Tenney Frank's *Vergil: A Biography* (1922), absorbed in building castles of sand on the basis of apocrypha, allotted it only one chapter of fifteen short pages. H. W. Prescott's *The Development of Virgil's Art* (1927; reprinted 1963) allowed it twenty pages out of 481. In fact the sole general treatment of the poem in English in this century, apart from the lively, impressionistic survey in E. K. Rand's *The Magical Art of Virgil* (1931), is the chapter, valuable if sometimes fanciful, in Brooks Otis' *Virgil: a Study in Civilized Poetry* (1964); and there are major aspects which he would not claim to have dealt with at all.* The collection of essays entitled *Virgil* and edited by Professor D. R. Dudley (1969) barely touches on the *Georgics*, through no fault of the editor.

On the other hand, it is a significant fact that three translations in English appeared during or just after the Second World War. Cecil Day-Lewis published in 1940 a delightful version in loose six-beat lines, distinguished by fresh and sensitive phrasing—a true poet entering into the experience of another; R. C. Trevelyan produced a blank-verse translation, restrained and faithful, in 1944; and L. A. S. Jermyn another in blank verse, which did not

---

* The standard Conington–Nettleship–Haverfield edition (1898) is good on points of scholarship, less good on husbandry. T. E. Page's edition of Virgil (1898) is best on the *Georgics*. He was a Lincolnshire man. There is a useful new edition of Books 1 and 4, intended for schools and General Degree students, by H. H. Huxley (1963).

appear until 1947. There were others elsewhere: a French translation in unrhymed Alexandrines by S. Hubaux and A. Tomsin was published at Liège in 1947, and one in *vers libre*, made by P. A. Nicolas in German-occupied North Africa, at Paris in 1948.[2] It was surely a yearning to escape from the horror and chaos of a distracted generation into the timeless peace and routine of agriculture that drew these to the *Georgics* in that crisis. Virgil himself, living in an age of violence and 'displaced persons', had expressed the contrast by an inspired asyndeton and change of rhythm (*G.* 2. 510–13):

gaudent perfusi sanguine fratrum,
exsilioque domos et dulcia limina mutant
atque alio patriam quaerunt sub sole iacentem.
agricola incurvo terram dimovit aratro.

Day-Lewis has described how he felt as he worked at his version in the West Country (at a time when bombs were beginning to rain on our cities): 'I felt more and more of the kind of patriotism which I imagine was Virgil's—the natural piety, the heightened sense of the genius of the place, the passion to praise and protect one's roots, or to put down roots somewhere while there is still time, which it takes a seismic event such as a war to reveal to most of us rootless persons.'[3] Jermyn's experience is still more significant; for his version was a *cura invigilata* that kept him alive during years when, an elderly civilian caught in Singapore, he was interned by the Japanese in Changi gaol and Sime Road prison-camp. For most of the day he was too weak through under-nourishment to do anything. But the evening meal contained a small meat-content which gave him strength to devote half an hour every night to building up his honeycomb:

tantus amor florum et generandi gloria mellis.

Wordsworth, writing in 1805 (*The Prelude*, XII), testified to having found refuge in Nature from 'these distracted times':

In Nature still
Glorying, I found a counterpoise in her,
Which, when the spirit of evil reached its height,
Maintained for me a secret happiness.

I. INTRODUCTION

In the matter of recent exposition and interpretation of the *Georgics* the German-speaking world has been far better served. K. Büchner's monumental article 'P. Vergilius Maro' for the *Real-Enzyclopädie* (VIIIA, 1955), published separately in 1956, extends to nearly 500 columns, giving a full survey of recent scholarship along with personal interpretation. W. Richter's edition with commentary (1957), in spite of what may seem some errors of judgement (and beware of misprints!), is a most valuable garner of wide learning. And F. Klingner's running commentary *Virgils Georgica* (1963) is a masterpiece of sensitive criticism which includes material already collected by him from his earlier work in *Römische Geisteswelt*.

The French have now a Budé edition of 1956 by E. de Saint-Denis, and a compact and suggestive chapter in J. Perret's *Virgile: l'homme et l'œuvre* (1952). As to Italian, I much regret that I have been unable to consult Castiglioni's *Lezioni intorno alle Georgiche di Virgilio* (1947) or E. Paratore's *Introduzione alle Georgiche di Virgilio* (1938); but I have been able to read Paratore's *Virgilio* (1961). Book 3 has now been edited by A. Marsili (1965).

The literature about Virgil is so vast, and the origin of any idea about him so hard to locate, that I have followed in the main text the sensible example of Professor Otis, making general acknowledgements, indicating particular debts only when I am specially conscious of them, and leaving documentation of recent controversies on various topics to appendixes.

In the hope that this book may be readable by those whose Latin is rusty, or even non-existent, I have translated most of the passages I quote, and sometimes explained terms, for example *aition*, which are familiar to classical scholars.

The chief obstacle to appreciation of the *Georgics* has been its ostensible *genre*: it was deceptive and has abundantly deceived.* This is no more a didactic poem than Ovid's *Ars Amatoria*: it simply masquerades as such. From the very beginning, in Hesiod,

---

* 'A didactic poem . . . giving practical advice to farmers on the cultivation of crops' (H. H. Scullard, *From the Gracchi to Nero*, 2nd edn. 1963, p. 245).

didactic poetry contained passages designed for relief; till finally, in the best genuine example of the *genre*, the *De Rerum Natura*, the non-technical part has become a main object: τὸ πάρεργον κρεῖττον τοῦ ἔργου. If the *Georgics* has to be assigned to a *genre*, it is Descriptive Poetry. This seems to have been realised by the young Addison, who wrote the perceptive Essay prefixed to Dryden's translation.* 'This kind of Poetry I am now speaking of addresses itself wholly to the Imagination . . . It raises in our Minds a pleasing variety of Scenes and Landskips whilst it teaches us, and makes the dryest of its Precepts look like a Description.' It was not in the nature of the Roman poet to invent a new *genre*—*Graecis intactum carmen (pace* Lucilius); and the *Georgics* is so rich in import that Virgil may not have been fully aware of what was his principal aim. But taken as a whole the pleasure it conveys is that which, for some mysterious reason, we derive from vivid poetic description. To quote Addison again: 'We find our imaginations more affected by his descriptions than they would have been by the very sight of what he describes.'

The fact that description in poetry can give pleasure was appreciated already by Homer, witness his similes, which elaborate far beyond the point of comparison.† *Iliad* 8. 555–61 is a well-known example:

> ὡς δ' ὅτ' ἐν οὐρανῷ ἄστρα φαεινὴν ἀμφὶ σελήνην
> φαίνετ' ἀριπρεπέα, ὅτε τ' ἔπλετο νήνεμος αἰθήρ·
> ἔκ τ' ἔφανεν πᾶσαι σκοπιαὶ καὶ πρώονες ἄκροι
> καὶ νάπαι· οὐρανόθεν δ' ἄρ' ὑπερράγη ἄσπετος αἰθήρ,
> πάντα δέ τ' εἴδεται ἄστρα, γέγηθε δέ τε φρένα ποιμήν·
> τόσσα μεσηγὺ νεῶν ἠδὲ Ξάνθοιο ῥοάων
> Τρώων καιόντων πυρὰ φαίνετο Ἰλιόθι πρό.

---

* That it had been he who wrote it was revealed by Dryden in the Preface to his translation of the *Aeneid*. See also L. P. Wilkinson, 'The Intention of Virgil's Georgics', *G. & R.* (1950), pp. 20, 26–8. Michael Grant, in his *Roman Literature* (1954), deals with the *Georgics* under the heading of 'Descriptive Poetry', and J. Perret in his *Virgile* (1959) calls 'one of the few successful descriptive poems that man can find in his age-long archives' (p. 79).

† See also his descriptions of an uninhabited island (*Od.* 9. 116–41) and of the gardens of Alcinous (*Od.* 7. 112–32).

I. INTRODUCTION

In Tennyson's translation:

> As when in heaven the stars about the moon
> Look beautiful, when all the winds are laid,
> And every height comes out, and jutting peak
> And valley, and the immeasurable heavens
> Break open to their highest, and all the stars
> Shine, and the shepherd gladdens in his heart:
> So many a fire between the ships and stream
> Of Xanthus blazed before the towers of Troy.

Nor was it only a matter of describing pleasant things. Hesiod's starkly realistic description of winter is one of the best passages in the *Works and Days* (504–35). But its counterpart, Summer (582–96), was perhaps more influential; for Hesiod was a master to the Hellenistic Age, which was also the age of Pastoral.

Ἦμος δὲ σκόλυμός τ' ἀνθεῖ καὶ ἠχέτα τέττιξ
δενδρέῳ ἐφεζόμενος λιγυρὴν καταχεύετ' ἀοιδὴν
πυκνὸν ὑπὸ πτερύγων, θέρεος καματώδεος ὥρῃ,
τῆμος πιόταταί τ' αἶγες καὶ οἶνος ἄριστος,
μαχλόταται δὲ γυναῖκες, ἀφαυρότατοι δέ τοι ἄνδρες
εἰσίν, ἐπεὶ κεφαλὴν καὶ γούνατα Σείριος ἄζει,
αὐαλέος δέ τε χρὼς ὑπὸ καύματος· ἀλλὰ τότ' ἤδη
εἴη πετραίη τε σκιὴ καὶ βίβλινος οἶνος,
μάζα τ' ἀμολγαίη γάλα τ' αἰγῶν σβεννυμενάων,
καὶ βοὸς ὑλοφάγοιο κρέας μή πω τετοκυίης
πρωτογόνων τ' ἐρίφων· ἐπὶ δ' αἴθοπα πινέμεν οἶνον
ἐν σκιῇ ἑζόμενον, κεκορημένον ἦτορ ἐδωδῆς,
ἀντίον ἀκραέος Ζεφύρου τρέψαντα πρόσωπα,
κρήνης τ' ἀενάου καὶ ἀπορρύτου, ἥτ' ἀθόλωτος,
τρὶς ὕδατος προχέειν, τὸ δὲ τέτρατον ἱέμεν οἴνου.

> When the cardoon flowers and the loud cicada sings
> perched on a tree, pouring from under his wings
> a flood of shrillest music time and again:
> when summer is ripe, and the heat a burden of pain,
> then are the she-goats fattest, and wine is best
> and women most fair; but men are languidest,
> for Sirius parches the heads and the knees of men
> and burns their bodies with drouth. O give me then
> the shade of a rock, with Biblis' wine set by,

5

and bread of the best, and the milk of goats drained dry!
Then be a heifer chosen to make my meat
that has not calved but feeds in the greenwood yet,
and firstling kids! Bright wine for my plenishment
I'd drink, in the shade, when food has brought content;
and then, as I sit, briskly the West should blow
meeting my brow; and from the unsullied flow
of some spring-water for ever running past
three cups to the gods I'd pour: of wine a last.*

True, this is more a description of pleasure than scenery, but is it not the ancestor of the famous description at the end of Theocritus' *Thalysia* (7. 135–47)?

πολλαὶ δ᾽ ἄμμιν ὕπερθε κατὰ κρατὸς δονέοντο
αἴγειροι πτελέαι τε· τὸ δ᾽ ἐγγύθεν ἱερὸν ὕδωρ
Νυμφᾶν ἐξ ἄντροιο κατειβόμενον κελάρυζε.
τοὶ δὲ ποτὶ σκιεραῖς ὀροδαμνίσιν αἰθαλίωνες
τέττιγες λελαγεῦντες ἔχον πόνον· ἁ δ᾽ ὀλολυγών
τηλόθεν ἐν πυκιναῖσι βάτων τρύζεσκεν ἀκάνθαις.
ἄειδον κόρυδοι καὶ ἀκανθίδες, ἔστενε τρυγών,
πωτῶντο ξουθαὶ περὶ πίδακας ἀμφὶ μέλισσαι.
πάντ᾽ ὦσδεν θέρεος μάλα πίονος, ὦσδε δ᾽ ὀπώρας.
ὄχναι μὲν πὰρ ποσσί, περὶ πλευραῖσι δὲ μᾶλα
δαψιλέως ἁμὶν ἐκυλίνδετο· τοὶ δ᾽ ἐκέχυντο
ὄρπακες βραβίλοισι καταβρίθοντες ἔραζε·
τετράενες δὲ πίθων ἀπελύετο κρατὸς ἄλειφαρ.

Dangling above our heads hung canopies
Of whispering elms and rustling poplar-trees;
Near us the water of the sacred well
Dropped from the Nymphs' cave, tinkling as it fell;
On every twig in shadow sat with glee
The sunburnt crickets, chattering busily;
And murmuring afar off in solitude,
Bowered in the deep thorn-brake, the turtle cooed.
All rich delight and luxury was there:
Larks and bright finches singing in the air;
The brown bees flying round about the well;
The ring-dove moaning; everywhere the smell

* Tr. T. F. Higham, in *The Oxford Book of Greek Verse in Translation* (1938), pp. 144–5.

6

I. INTRODUCTION

Of opulent summer and of ripening-tide:
Pears at our feet and apples at our side
Rolling in plenteousness; in piles around
Branches, with damsons burdening to the ground,
Strewn for our feast; and from the full wine-tun
Wax of a four-years-aged seal undone.*

This is the sort of poetry that Keats was concerned to write in his *Ode to Autumn*. It is, I believe, only the modern craze for finding symbolism in everything that sees in that poem a praise of the autumn of life, or of maturity in general. Here is what the poet had to say about its composition, in a letter to J. H. Reynolds: 'How beautiful the season is now—How fine the air. A temperate sharpness about it. Really, without joking, chaste weather—Dian skies—I never lik'd stubble-fields so much as now—Aye better than the chilly green of Spring. Somehow a stubble-plain looks warm—in the same way that some pictures look warm—This struck me so much in my Sunday's walk that I composed upon it.'[4] And that is all. The only symbolic quality suggested (unless you count warmth) is chastity; but the poem is hardly about that. 'The storms in Vergil are not easy to interpret', says Jackson Knight. 'Bad weather seems in general to be for him as for Shakespeare a kind of cosmic accompaniment and signal of a failure in human love and friendliness.'[5] This can hardly apply to the one in the Prognostics or Weather-signs (1. 356 ff.), simply elaborated from Aratus. Why should everything have to be *interpreted*?

The Hellenistic taste for the picturesque, and also for realism, made descriptive passages a common feature of both poetry and history. Ἐκφράσεις, critics called them. Orators had to be warned not to drag them into forensic speeches: verdicts would not depend on a description of a storm.[6]

One might imagine that Virgil developed his faculty for landscape-painting through his study of pastoral poetry. But read through the *Eclogues* in search of pictorial glimpses and you may be surprised. The most individual, perhaps, is 9. 7–10, but that

* Tr. Walter Headlam in *A Book of Greek Verse* (1907), p. 213.

7

may be intended as a recognisable piece of Mantuan territory concerned in the appeal against evictions (see p. 33). The best examples are in *Eclogue* 1. Lines 46–58 describe the farm restored to Tityrus, large enough for him though liable to flooding by the river and therefore partly consisting of bare patches of stones or rushy swamps. Here, sitting in the shade among the streams he can listen to the buzzing of his bees, the singing of the hedger, his farmyard pigeons and the turtle-dove in the elm. Not perhaps a picture this; but at least line 76, admired by Wordsworth,

> dumosa pendere procul de rupe videbo,

evokes a vivid image of goats that seem from a distance to hang on a hillside; and the poem ends with a justly famous landscape which gives the impression of originating not in literature but in the poet's own observation:

> et iam summa procul villarum culmina fumant,
> maioresque cadunt altis de montibus umbrae.

And now smoke is rising from the farmhouse roofs far off, and longer shadows are falling from the high mountains.

The list of flowers and fruits presented to Alexis in 2. 45–55 hardly counts for this purpose; nor do the various trees and shrubs, the stage properties of pastoral, which are casually mentioned throughout. The lovely line (7. 45)

> muscosi fontes et somno mollior herba

borrows its magic from Theocritus' ὕπνω μαλακώτερα (5. 51), used of a fleece.* For the rest, there are only some conventional scenes such as (10. 42–3),

> hic gelidi fontes, hic mollia prata, Lycori,
> hic nemus.

This seems to have been suggested by Theocritus 5. 31–4:

> ἅδιον ᾀσῇ
> τεῖδ᾽ ὑπὸ τὰν κότινον καὶ τἄλσεα ταῦτα καθίξας.
> ψυχρὸν ὕδωρ τουτεὶ καταλείβεται· ὧδε πεφύκει
> ποία, χἀ στιβὰς ἅδε, καὶ ἀκρίδες ὧδε λαλεῦντι.

---

* Again, of carpets, *idem*, 15. 125. The phrase may have been a cliché in Greek.

You'll sing more sweetly if you sit here beneath the wild olive and these trees. Here cool water is trickling down; here is grass for us to lie on, and here the grasshoppers are chirping.

Theocritus is obviously concerned to conjure up a picture, conventional though it may be. Virgil seems less interested, almost perfunctory. Nor does he trouble to be consistent within a poem: in *Eclogue* 2 the oxen draw the ploughs home at line 66 oblivious of the fact that at line 10 Thestylis was making a salad for reapers. *Eclogue* 9. 40–2 is likewise conventional (despite the doubt about the meaning of the first phrase):

> hic ver purpureum, varios hic flumina circum
> fundit humus flores, hic candida populus antro
> imminet et lentae texunt umbracula vites.

Here is gorgeous spring, here the ground lavishes varied flowers around the streams, here a pale poplar overhangs the cave, and pliant vines weave shades.

It is not of such commonplaces that the *Georgics* are made.

Let us turn to Lucretius and see what he may have suggested. His epithets are for the most part ordinary enough, either stock ones in the epic tradition, such as *navigerum* of the sea, *frugiferentes* of lands, or appropriate ('propria'), as *suaves* of flowers. But then Latin poets rarely attempted to use epithets to make their ideas vivid in the manner of a Keats or a Hopkins. Do we find him going out of his way at all to make his descriptions more picturesque than is needed for demonstration? Yes, sometimes. Take the lines (5. 948–52):

> denique nota vagi silvestria templa tenebant
> Nympharum, quibus e scibant umori' fluenta
> lubrica proluvie larga lavere umida saxa,
> *umida saxa, super viridi stillantia musco,*
> et partim plano scatere atque erumpere campo.

Then as they wandered they came to know the woodland shrines of the nymphs and frequented them, where they knew that waters flowed abundantly and drenched with their flood the wet rocks, *wet rocks, over whose green moss they streamed*, and broke out in places to wash over the level plain.

Here again the epithets are *propria* or commonplace, but the line italicised is put in purely for the delight of dwelling (by repetition) on the image and enhancing it. In the same way Virgil sometimes conjures up a picture purely for its own sake, as at G. 2. 199:

> et qualem infelix amisit Mantua campum
> *pascentem niveos herboso flumine cycnos*;

or land such as unhappy Mantua lost, *that feeds snow-white swans on its reedy river.*

But it is not touches of this kind, nor even the set pieces, that mainly give the *De Rerum Natura* the vividness it has. Rather it is the effect of a poet ranging freely over all nature and choosing his illustrations from a great variety of observed phenomena so as to give his argument universal validity.

> Principio maria ac terras caelumque tuere,

First observe the seas and lands and the sky.

His vision is all-embracing. The main body of his argument, being concerned with the behaviour of atoms which we cannot see, is of necessity non-pictorial; but let us note what a recent writer has said in comment on Eduard Norden's passing remark that 'in Cicero and Lucretius, in keeping with the character of the didactic poem, pictorial intention takes a back place'.[7]

Book 1 offers the pictorial sequence of the delight of young animals in the lush grass and flowing milk of springtime; the windstorm like a torrent in flood; the illustration of the gradual wearing away of ring, ploughshare, stone and statue; the proof of the existence of void by water percolating through rock, by growth of living bodies, and by penetration of sound through walls, and of cold through warm flesh; the glimpse of fishes swimming and bellows blowing, and the hunting dogs tracking their quarry. Book 2 is, if anything, more colourful. The torch race is succeeded by the motes in a sunbeam, a disastrous conflagration, chariots racing, grazing sheep, legions at exercise, the cow looking for its lost calf, shells on the seashore, the theatre with its scented stage, the squeal of bronze hinges, the fluid heap of poppyseed, the peacock's display, the sea whipped to storm, the play of light on a dove's feathers, dung crawling with maggots, ploughman and vine-grower lamenting the poor harvest and declining fertility of the land.

I. INTRODUCTION

Lucretius' normal aim was, no doubt, simply to reinforce his scientific doctrine by adducing a wealth of concrete instances. Even the recital at 4. 387–452 of fifteen examples of sensory illusion might be so motivated, or the eleven examples at 4. 962–1036 of men or animals dreaming about their normal avocations. But when we are given, at 3. 381–90, eight instances of things too light to feel, or at 3. 642–56 five varieties of limbs being lopped off by scythed chariots without their owners being conscious of it, we begin to sense that the poet enjoyed detailing things for their own sake; and the impression is increased when, at 5. 24–36, he enumerates all the labours of Hercules. This predilection becomes explicit at the end of Book 5, where he bursts out in enthusiasm for the variety in landscape and life that has been produced by civilisation.[8]

I believe that Virgil came to realise through reading Lucretius that an accumulation of detailed observations, however commonplace in themselves, may compose a great panoramic picture, and that the framework for this could be a didactic treatise. It is not the imperative verb but the object that is significant; and the total impression transcends the sum of the contributors. The *Georgics* is, in fact, the first poem in all literature in which description may be said to be the chief *raison d'être* and source of pleasure. Take a passage like the following (3. 322–38), which is particularly instructive because it can be compared with a plain prose basis in Varro (2. 2. 10–11), which I will give first:

Aestate cum prima luce exeunt pastum, propterea quod tunc herba roscida meridianam, quae est aridior, iucunditate praestat. Sole exorto potum propellunt, ut redintegrantes rursus ad pastum alacriores faciant. Circiter meridianos aestus, dum defervescant, sub umbriferas rupes et arbores patulas subigunt, quoad refrigeratur. Aëre vespertino rursus pascunt ad solis occasum.

In summer they go out to pasture at daybreak, because then the grass, being dewy, is sweeter than that of mid-day, when it is drier. When the sun is up they drive them to water, refresh them and so make them keener to feed. About the time of the mid-day heat they drive them under shady rocks and spreading trees to cool down till the day gets milder. In the evening air they feed them again till sunset.

I. INTRODUCTION

at vero Zephyris cum laeta vocantibus aestas
in saltus utrumque gregem atque in pascua mittet,
Luciferi primo cum sidere frigida rura
carpamus, dum mane novum, dum gramina canent,
et ros in tenera pecori gratissimus herba.
inde ubi quarta sitim caeli collegerit hora
et cantu querulae rumpent arbusta cicadae,
ad puteos aut alta greges ad stagna iubebo
currentem ilignis potare canalibus undam;
aestibus at mediis umbrosam exquirere vallem,
sicubi magna Iovis antiquo robore quercus
ingentis tendat ramos, aut sicubi nigrum
ilicibus crebris sacra nemus accubet umbra;
tum tenuis dare rursus aquas et pascere rursus
solis ad occasum, cum frigidus aëra vesper
temperat, et saltus reficit iam roscida luna,
litoraque alcyonen resonant, acalanthida dumi.

But when the west winds call and the exquisite warm season
Ushers them out, both sheep and goats, to glade and pasture
At the first wink of the Morning Star let us wend away
To the frore fields, while the morning is young, the meadow pearly,
And dew so dear to cattle lies on the tender grass.
Then, when the fourth hour of the sun has created a thirst
And the plantations vibrate with the pizzicato of crickets,
I'll bring the flocks to water by wells and by deep ponds,
I'll bid them drink the water that runs in the troughs of ilex.
But now it's the noonday heat, make for a shady combe
Where some great ancient-hearted oak throws out its huge
Boughs, or the wood is black with
A wealth of holm-oak and broods in its own haunted shadow.
Then give them runnels of water again and let them browse
About sundown, when the cool star of evening assuages
The air, and moonlight falls now with dew to freshen the glades,
And the kingfisher's heard on the shore and the warbler in woody
thickets.*

What is the didactic content of these seventeen lines? 'In summer drive your sheep and goats to pasture at dawn, to drink at forenoon, to shade at noon, to feed and drink again at sunset.'

* Tr. Cecil Day-Lewis.

All the rest is pictorial detail. And, as in Lucretius, it is not only the studied passages of description that create the effect. The *Georgics*, which have so often been delightfully illustrated, are like a superb documentary of Italy painted by the hand of a Brueghel, peasants in a landscape busy with the tasks and religious rites of the four seasons.* One can readily imagine what Brueghel would have made of this passage (1. 343–50): 'Let all your country-people worship Ceres: for her melt honeycombs with milk and mellow wine and thrice let the luck-bringing victim pass round the young crops, while the whole band of your companions escorts it with triumphant song and dance, loudly summoning Ceres into their homes; nor let anyone put sickle to the ripe corn before in Ceres' honour, his brow crowned with a wreath of oak, he treads artless measures and sings her hymns.'

What the Romans felt about landscape at this time can to some extent be deduced from the paintings on the walls of their houses. Vitruvius gave as typical subjects 'havens, capes, shores, rivers, springs, shrines, woods, mountains, herds and shepherds' as well as mythological subjects. He approved of naturalism, and deplored the new Augustan craze for fantasies.[9] The Campanian landscapes, on the whole a just if somewhat broad and conventional reflection of south Italian scenery, nearly always bear traces of human activity.[10] In the first century B.C. Roman wall-paintings broke free from the narrow frames of the previous century: 'Nature now surrounds the merely human as home of something higher, divine, which embraces all human things.'[11] Both house and garden were in some sense a shrine. Statues of divinities and sacrifices are often a feature of these landscapes.[12] And correspond-ingly Virgil, *deos qui novit agrestes*, invests his poetic pictures of the countryside with the presence of *numina* such as he invokes in his proem. The ancient oak in the passage just quoted is 'a mighty oak *of Jupiter*'. '*Divini* gloria ruris' is the reward of the farmer's labour. At 4. 276, a line bracketed by some imperceptive editors,

---

* For a suggestion of Virgilian influence *à propos* 'The Fall of Icarus' see M. P. O. Morford, 'Bruegel and the First *Georgic*', *G.&R.* (1966), pp. 50–3. A winged Icarus may have fallen from the sky: the ploughman goes on ploughing.

Virgil goes out of his way to mention the use of the flower *amellus* for garlanding the altars of the gods.

But while I believe that, viewed as a whole, the pleasure and significance of the *Georgics* is most akin to that which may be derived from descriptive poetry, the literary counterpart of landscape-painting, this alone could not sustain a poem of more than two thousand lines. There is much more to it than that. The symbolic possibilities of the poem have come to be stressed more and more, indeed perhaps exaggerated, in recent years, in the works of German scholars in particular and of Brooks Otis following them. Virgil could have learnt from Hesiod that a technical treatise can be made a vehicle for personal philosophic and religious ideas. But it was probably Lucretius who brought this home to him more impressively, showing how a wide study of nature could be infused with deep personal feeling and social or philosophic purpose.

The poem is descriptive not only of a varied countryside. It describes a way of life, and one which is held up as an ideal to readers jaded by the 'dolce vita' and harassments of urban society. Besides the tasks of the farmer's year and the festivals that are a relief from them, Virgil gives us vignettes of country life. Thus at I. 293, where he describes the farmer on a wintry night sitting by his fire and sharpening torches, he adds:

> interea longum cantu solata laborem
> arguto coniunx percurrit pectine telas,
> aut dulcis musti Volcano decoquit umorem
> et foliis undam trepidi despumat aëni.

Meanwhile his wife, beguiling her tedious task with song, traverses her web with the humming shuttle, or boils down the liquid of sweet wine-must over the fire and skims the surface of the quivering pot with leaves.

This has little to do with agriculture, but very much with country life, its merits and attractions.

There are religious and philosophic considerations that develop naturally out of the description, and no one would deny that these are a most important element in the poem, as we shall see when we come to consider its structure. For the farmer's life is sometimes taken as typical of all human life, and in it man is brought starkly face to face with the facts of nature and the powers that govern the universe.

And finally, the poem acquired an added dimension from the political significance of agriculture in the age in which it was composed, enhanced by the poet's association with the men who were formulating policy and moving into power. The Ciceronian and the Augustan ages have always been recognised as of more than passing significance, standing out in high relief on the frieze of history. We see in them most clearly what happens when there is liberty without discipline, and what when there is discipline without liberty. The *Georgics* is the poem of the transition. As Klingner has said:

The Augustan idea of Rome and Italy, long waiting to emerge, was helped to fulfilment by the victory of Actium. This aspect is what gives to this didactic poem...its incomparable value. Indeed it helps to establish here a new kind of poetic representation, in which in a limited, directly represented subject, a greater, which embraces it, is present at the same time and imparts significance to the lesser.[13]

The *Georgics* has thus a peculiarly rich texture of motifs, descriptive, philosophical and political, with a compositional structure which is an interplay of moods as well as themes—a highly original work for all its 'debts', more Italian than Greek, but most of all Virgilian. Seneca said no more than the obvious when he remarked that Virgil was interested in what could be said *decentissime*, not *verissime*, and that he wrote not to teach farmers, but to delight readers.[14] The *Georgics* is, in fact, a crucial example of Coleridge's famous definition of a poem as 'that species of composition which is opposed to works of science by proposing for its *immediate* object pleasure, not truth; and from all other species (having *this* object in common with it) it is discriminated by proposing to itself such delight from the *whole* as is compatible with a distinct gratification from each component part'.[15]

II · *Early Life of Virgil*

———◆———

Some account of Virgil's early life and poetic development is desirable for the appreciation of the *Georgics*. As to his life, it is largely a matter of removing accretions. His ancient biographers eked out their material with deductions either too literal-minded or too allegorical from his works. Some modern scholars have added further bubbles of speculation, until it has become hard to remember what we have on reliable evidence.*

A word first about the ancient *Vitae*.[1] For the last twenty years of his life at least Virgil was a famous man. In such cases there are more solid foundations than with those whose merits emerge posthumously. Much indeed will be unrevealed or forgotten. If Virgil told people who the child of the Fourth *Eclogue* was, or that it was only symbolic, this did not become generally known; for a generation later a son of Pollio, Asinius Gallus, could think it worth while to claim that it was he.[2] Still, much that is true must have become embodied in tradition. Aulus Gellius cites 'the friends and acquaintances of Virgil in the things they handed down to posterity about his character and ways'.[3] When we are told on the authority of Melissus, a freedman of Maecenas, that in speech he was very slow and almost like an uneducated man, we may believe it; though we must note at the same time that the poet Julius Montanus, according to Seneca, declared that he would purloin some things from Virgil if he could also steal his voice, his expression and his gesture; for verses that sounded well in his mouth were empty and flat in that of others.[4] (One remembers Gladstone's recantation of his criticisms of *Maud* after hearing Tennyson read it himself.[5]) There are plenty of people, after all, who read aloud much better than they talk.

* One of the most reliable accounts is B. Nardi's *La Giovinezza di Virgilio* (1927), translated by B. P. Rand as *The Youth of Virgil* (1930). He goes down to the end of the *Eclogues*. The only matters of importance on which I would disagree are his identification of the child in *Eclogue* 4 as a son of Pollio, and his dating of 1 before 9, with the consequences that follow.

The best of the *Vitae*, that of Servius' master Aelius Donatus, goes back to Suetonius, who not only had at his disposal information dating from Virgil's lifetime such as the above, but as private secretary to the Emperor Hadrian had access to the imperial archives. Yet even here care is needed. This Life not only repeats 'old wives' tales' which are easily discounted: it gives what looks like valuable information and may yet be erroneous conjecture. Thus we are told that Virgil began to write a poem about Roman history (*res Romanas*), but found the subject uncongenial and passed to the *Bucolics*. Other commentators embroidered. Servius opined that the poem concerned was either the *Aeneid* or one about the exploits of the Alban kings, which Virgil began, only to be put off by the subject and the uncouthness of their names. Now the sole authority for all this may well be the apparently explicit lines *Eclogue 6*. 3–5:

> cum canerem reges et proelia, Cynthius aurem
> vellit et admonuit: 'pastorem, Tityre, pinguis
> pascere oportet ovis, deductum dicere carmen.'

When I was singing of kings and battles, Apollo tweaked my ear and warned me: 'A shepherd, Tityrus, should always feed fat sheep but sing a slender song.'

Every educated Roman in Virgil's day would know how to take that: it was a skit on the famous prologue to the second edition of Callimachus' *Aetia* (19–24): 'And seek not from me the birth of a resounding song: thunder belongs not to me, but to Zeus. For when first I set the tablet upon my knees, Lycian Apollo said to me: "Poet, you should always offer me the fattest possible sacrifice, but a slender Muse."' This passage was a godsend to Roman poets under pressure to write in praise of the exploits of patrons —for what are now known as *recusationes*—as to Virgil here, anxious to side-step the task of celebrating Varus' deeds. '*Reges et proelia*' are simply typical epic themes: in Horace's words (*A.P.* 73),

> res gestae regumque ducumque et tristia bella.

Was Propertius really dreaming of singing about the Alban kings when Apollo interrupted him (3. 3)? Was Horace really eager to tell of battles and the conquest of cities had not Apollo intervened (*Odes* 4. 15)? Was Ovid really contemplating a poem on the Battle of the Gods and Giants when his mistress slammed the door in his face (*Am.* 2. 1. 11–22)?* Surely not. All these were variations, amusingly adapted to the *genre* concerned, on a well-known theme. I should not labour the point if scholars of repute had not taken them at their face value. †

A second source of copious but suspect information is what has been known since Scaliger as the 'Appendix Vergiliana'. Virgil, on his deathbed, according to Suetonius (40), left his writings jointly to Varius and Tucca with instructions that they should not publish anything that he would not himself have published. But it was inevitable that apocrypha should accumulate, if only because biographically minded people hankered to fill in the twenty-eight years of his life before he began the *Eclogues*. Suetonius lists these works, remarking that some people doubted the authenticity of the *Aetna* (17–18) and not including the *Moretum* or *Copa*, which occur however in the later and slightly different lists of 'Donatus auctus' and Servius respectively. None of our best manuscripts of Virgil has these poems, nor do we find any mention of them until eighty years after he was dead. Up to the nineteenth century, however, they were accepted as authentic. Then came the Higher Criticism, and scholars such as H. A. J. Munro pointed out the objections. There was indeed a temporary reaction in this century;[6] but it is now generally considered that they are partly fakes, partly works which did not, and in some cases could not, be by Virgil but became accidentally included, and only in the case of a few of the short poems in the *Catalepton* genuine early works.[7] This does not mean that Virgil wrote no

---

* For the Gigantomachy as typical of epic material see Prop. 2. 1. 19 f. and 3. 9. 48. Yet S. G. Owen had a whole speculative chapter on the contents of Ovid's supposed work (? Battle of Actium): edn. of *Tristia* 2, pp. 63–81.

† 'There is indubitable evidence that Virgil began an epic at this time, some fifteen years before he published the *Georgics*. It seems clear also that the epic was an *Aeneid*, with Julius Caesar in the background': Tenney Frank, *Vergil: a Biography* (1922), p. 68 (accepting *Catalepton* 14 as genuine). The story is also credited by E. K. Rand, *The Magical Art of Virgil* (1931), p. 57, and by Otis, p. 35.

poems before the *Eclogues*: he obviously must have done. He may even have written some poem entitled *Culex*. But whatever he wrote, whatever Varius and Tucca found, hardly anything has come down to us except the two major works he had himself published and the *Aeneid*.

EDUCATION

Virgil was born on 15 October 70 B.C. in the rural district (*pagus*) of Andes, near Mantua. It was clearly this countryside that he remembered as 'home', with its reedy, willow-lined river Mincius slowly making its way from Lake Garda through the lagoon outside the city and down into the Po. Our authorities agree that his father was a smallholder. This could, of course, be a mere conjecture based on the *Georgics*, but it need not be considered inconsistent with the tradition that he was a manufacturer of pottery, since ceramics were a common side-line on Italian farms.* The woods and beehives he is credited with could be generous deductions from the *Georgics*, Books 2 and 4; but at any rate he must have been reasonably well off to afford the education he gave to at least one of his sons. He was probably a Roman citizen (perhaps descended from one of the old colonists of that area), and Virgil may even have been or become, as the Vita Bernensis asserts, a Roman knight in status.

At the age of about twelve the boy went for his secondary schooling to Cremona, and his parents may have moved there, at least temporarily, to be with him.† Cremona is apparently the base of Sabinus in *Catalepton* 10, the brilliant parody of Catullus' yacht-poem (4) in which the yacht is replaced by a muleteer. If it is the virtue of a parody to combine the minimum change in form with the maximum contrast in subject, this must rank as one of the

---

* Suet. 1. Frank, *Vergil*, p. 9. My grandfather worked brick kilns on his farm near Stony Stratford. There are still many potteries south-east of Mantua, some of them ancient.

† *Catalepton* 8. The last word, *prius*, is contrasted with *nunc* in the previous line; it does not imply that Virgil's father lived at Cremona before Mantua, but goes with both.

most ingenious ever produced. It could be by Virgil.* After assuming the *toga virilis* he went on for a short time to Mediolanum (Milan), already a centre of higher education for the province. Suetonius tells us that some of the most famous teachers practised in Gallia Togata, the district north of the Po.[8]

From the literary schoolrooms of Milan he proceeded, about the year 52, to Rome to study rhetoric. He can hardly have felt at home in the city of riots and gang warfare in which Milo had recently killed Clodius; and although later, enriched by his friends, he possessed a house near the gardens of Maecenas on the Esquiline, we are not surprised to hear that the shy, rustic-looking, delicate poet rarely came to the capital, and fled into the nearest house if he was recognised and followed by a crowd drawing attention to him. At Naples he went by the nickname of 'Parthenias'† (curious, that Milton likewise should have been known at Cambridge as 'The Lady of Christ's'). But although pleading one case in court was apparently enough for him, his study of rhetoric not only enabled him to compose effective speeches for the *Aeneid*, but taught him the art of the 'period', which he applied to verse with transfiguring effect. For the rest, we are told that he studied medicine and especially 'mathematics', which might include astronomy and astrology.

But at some time (we do not know when within several years) he took a step which altered the course of his early life. He became an Epicurean. That was nothing uncommon in the period— 'Italiam totam occupaverunt', says Cicero of the sect.[9] But whereas some, like Caesar or Cassius, were presumably attracted by its sturdy rationalism without experiencing anything like a desire to retreat into the quiet of a garden, *ignobile otium* was just

---

* We cannot say *a priori* that it is out of keeping with a character who could conceive the double-barrelled fusillade (*Ecl.* 3. 90): 'qui Bavium non odit, amet tua carmina, Maevi'. It is accepted as genuine by the usually sceptical E. Fraenkel, 'Vergil und Cicero', *Atti Mantova* (1926–7), p. 219.

† This may of course be simply a Greek transposition, made on the assumption that 'Virgilius' came from 'virgo': F. Hornstein, 'Vergilius Παρθενίας', *W.S.* (1957), pp. 148–52. For 'Virgilius' as the better attested form of the name see E. Bolisani, 'Vergilius o Virgilius', *Atti Istit. Veneto* (1959), pp. 131–41. For his delicate health see Suet., ch. 8.

what suited Virgil's temperament. And further, there had probably appeared by now the posthumous *De Rerum Natura* of Lucretius, who had died in 54. One can readily imagine its impact on a budding poet. But it was a professional philosopher of the less strict Syrian school to whom he turned. *Catalepton* 5 is a poem which few, if any, deny to Virgil.

> Ite hinc, inanes, ite, rhetorum ampullae,
> inflata rhoezo non Achaico verba;
> et vos, Selique Tarquitique Varroque,
> scholasticorum natio madens pingui,
> ite hinc, inane cymbalon iuventutis.
> Tuque, o mearum cura, Sexte, curarum
> vale, Sabine: iam valete, formosi.
> Nos ad beatos vela mittimus portus
> magni petentes docta dicta Sironis
> vitamque ab omni vindicabimus cura.
> Ite hinc, Camenae: vos quoque ite iam sane,
> dulces Camenae (nam fatebimur verum,
> dulces fuistis):—et tamen meas chartas
> revisitote, sed pudenter et raro.

Away with you, away now, hollow bombast of the rhetoricians, windbag words inflated in no Attic fashion; and you, Selius and Tarquitius and Varro, stodgy tribe of pedants, away with you, tinkling cymbal of youth. And you, Sextus Sabinus, my friend of friends, good-bye; good-bye now, all you beauties. I am setting sail for the havens of the blessed, to seek the wise words of great Siro, and will redeem my life from all care. Leave me, you Muses; yes, you too, I suppose, must leave me now, sweet Muses (for I will confess the truth; you have indeed been sweet):—and yet, revisit my pages, but modestly and rarely.

This poem is a precious document. It confirms our faith, grounded in the *Eclogues* and *Georgics* but shaken sometimes in the *Aeneid*, that Virgil had a sense of humour, a delicate, fanciful sense, such as the Greeks called χάρις.* The writer of this poem might well have written *Catalepton* 10 also.

---

* Here, however, I should dissociate myself from the view that Horace's famous description of Virgil's style, *molle atque facetum* (S. 1. 10. 44), has anything to do with humour. Quintilian thought otherwise, and interpreted the word '*facetum*'

The bombastic rhetoricians are of the Asiatic school, against which the chaste Atticists were now prevailing. The names of the scholars Selius and Tarquitius are conjectural emendations (by Ellis and Scaliger respectively). If 'Tarquitius' is right, it is interesting; for a man of that name wrote at this period a book on Etruscan lore called *Ostentarium Tuscum*, and Virgil seems to have been versed in such studies.* Varro is of course the great polymath. From dismissals we turn to wistful goodbyes. Sextus Sabinus was presumably Virgil's Euryalus of the day, and an Epicurean must not have a *cura*. The 'docta dicta' ascribed to Siro may be a reminiscence of Lucretius' recently published poem (5. 113):

multa tibi expediam doctis solacia dictis.

As for the Muses, they are evidence that Virgil indeed wrote juvenilia, and knew in his heart that he could never really give up poetry. His wavering recalls Catullus' poem in the same metre (No. 8 *Miser Catulle*), in which he lets himself betray his nostalgic interest in the mistress whom he is ostensibly dismissing for ever.

Some biographers have assumed that Siro was teaching at Rome; but all the evidence connects him and his colleague Philodemus with Naples.[10] If Virgil was not literally setting sail, he was certainly changing his abode. From now onwards we must think of him as living primarily in the neighbourhood of the Gulf of Naples, and at least to begin with in an Epicurean society of poets. He sometimes visited Tarentum on the southern Riviera

as follows: *decoris hanc magis et excultae cuiusdam elegantiae appellationem puto* (6. 3. 20). The word *facetus* is connected with *facio* and means 'well-made', or 'neat' (to use a word we too associate with witticisms). *Mollis* means 'smooth-flowing'; and Horace actually uses the phrase in the comparative fourteen lines later—*magis factos et euntes mollius*. *Mollis* and *facetus* were both epithets associated with the plain style, *fortis* and *acer* with the grand. See C. N. Jackson, 'Molle atque facetum', *H.S.Ph.* (1914), pp. 117–37; and now H. Fuchs, 'Zum Wettgesang der Hirten in Vergils siebenter Ekloge', *M.H.* (1966), pp. 222–3.

* In *Eclogue* 4 the ram which is to go now purple, now yellow, and the lambs which are to go scarlet (43–5), if absurd, are not inventions of Virgil's fancy. Macrobius tells us (*Sat.* 3. 7. 2): 'There is a book by Tarquitius, transcribed from the Etruscan book of omens. There you will find that if a sheep or ram is blotched with gold or purple it is the promise of a ruler of great happiness, and of an increase in his power and race which will heap up glory and prosperity.'

of Italy, later one of Horace's favourite resorts; for we have Propertius' word for it that some at least of the *Eclogues* were written near there (2. 34. 67–8). We know who some of the other poets were. Probus' *Vita*, which contains some good information independent of Suetonius, says: 'he lived for a number of years in leisured freedom following the sect of Epicurus, in conspicuous harmony and friendship with Quintilius, Tucca and Varius'. And Servius on *Eclogue* 6. 13 says: 'both Virgil and Varus had learnt Epicureanism with Siro for master'. Plotius Tucca and Varius are well known as Virgil's future executors, and it was they, with Virgil, who joined Maecenas and Horace at Sinuessa in this same Campania when they were journeying to Brundisium in 37.[11] Quintilius Varus was the intimate friend of Virgil mourned by Horace in *Odes* 1. 24. The facts that 'Varus' and 'Varius' could easily be confused by later commentators or scribes, and that Servius was wrong in applying to *Alfenus* Varus, the triumviral land commissioner, information that concerned *Quintilius* Varus, do not matter. For chance has preserved in a Herculanean papyrus a fragment of Philodemus dedicating a work to just these four, if plausible reconstructions fitting the gaps are accepted in two cases, Πλώ]τιε καὶ Οὐάριε καὶ Οὐ[εργίλιε καὶ] Κοϊντίλιε.[12]

The years 52–42 in Virgil's young life are even more shadowy than the obscure decade in Shakespeare's. It seems more likely that he kept quiet in the garden while the tide of civil war rolled past than that he saw service. When he re-emerges, it is as the author of the *Eclogues*, anxious lest his father lose his home to the agents of the Triumvirs charged with settling veterans on the land. *Catalepton* 8, also widely accepted as authentic, dates from this crisis:

> Villula quae Sironis eras, et pauper agelle
>   verum illi domino tu quoque divitiae,
> me tibi et hos una mecum, quos semper amavi,
>   si quid de patria tristius audiero,
> commendo, in primisque patrem. tu nunc eris illi
>   Mantua quod fuerat quodque Cremona prius.

Little house that belonged to Siro and meagre plot of land (though riches even so to such an owner), to you I commend these whom

I have always loved, together with myself, in case any worse news come from home, and especially my father. You will now be to him what Mantua and Cremona were before.

Siro is known to have been still alive in 45,[13] but it looks as if he was now dead and had left Virgil his small property. The *hos* might include Virgil's mother and his surviving brother Flaccus.

No doubt Virgil paid visits to his old home country in the north, but we must not conclude from the scenery of some of the *Eclogues* that he went back to live there. It was still at Naples (Parthenope), as he tells us himself, that he was living when he finished the *Georgics* (4. 563). It was there that he was ultimately buried, and there that he became a legend. Aulus Gellius has a tantalising passage (6. 20. 1) about a dispute between Virgil and the people of Nola over the irrigation of a neighbouring estate (*rus*) belonging to him. There is no reason why he should not have acquired a farm at Nola, which is not many miles from Naples, without however going to live there permanently any more than Horace lived permanently at his Sabine farm. The point has some relevance; for it is our only external evidence that Virgil ever had anything to do with farming after the age of twelve. In fact we may be sure that he was no *colonus*, but primarily a literary man who was, however, since his childhood deeply interested in natural history and husbandry and had an observant eye, the sort of man who would unaffectedly write of country things the line

singula dum capti circumvectamur amore,

while captivated with love we perambulate from this to that (3. 285).

POLITICS

Politically it is probable that Virgil grew up with Caesarian sympathies. Just about the time when he went to school at Cremona, in 58, Julius Caesar became Governor of Cisalpine as well as Transalpine Gaul, and his connections with the province were older than that. Cremona had been founded with 6,000 colonists from central Italy in 218, the first Latin colony in Transpadane

Gaul, and in 190 there had been added a further 6,000 families, to be dispersed through the surrounding territories. In the Social War of 90–89 these communities remained loyal to Rome. A law of Pompey's father in 89 gave the *Ius Latii* to the municipal centres of Transpadane Gaul, and they were gradually admitted to Roman citizenship. Cremona became a *municipium*, and was the centre of Romanisation for the whole area. But there seems to have been some foot-dragging. Agitation was still going on in 66; and when Crassus as censor in 65 proposed their enfranchisement, he was baulked by his colleague Q. Catulus.[14] It may have been in connection with this that Caesar resigned his quaestorship before its expiry and went to the Transpadanes.[15] Be that as it may, it was he who, perhaps while Virgil was still in the province, conferred citizenship on a town even so far north as Como.[16] In 52–51 there were insistent rumours at Rome that he had, on his own initiative, granted to the other cities beyond the Po the rights of suffrage and tenure of office.[17] No wonder he was popular there. * Hirtius tells us that he was acclaimed when he passed through Gallia Togata in 50, and when next year he crossed the Rubicon and marched on Rome there were with him not a few Transpadanes.[18] He now conferred Roman citizenship on all the Transpadanes, though it was not until some time after his death that the whole peninsula up to the Alps was incorporated in Italy.[19]

There was another reason for Virgil to have Caesarian sympathies. The community of Epicureans that centred round Philodemus and Siro was closely connected with L. Piso Caesoninus,[20] whose daughter Calpurnia had married Caesar in 59 and was deeply devoted to him. Other prominent Epicureans such as Hirtius, Pansa and Dolabella were also Caesarians. And of the poets Quintilius Varus at least was also a Transpadane.[21] The shock of Caesar's murder is vividly recalled at *Georgics* 1. 466–8, where the Sun is said to have hidden his face as a portent:

---

* We must not forget however that Catullus of Verona and Bibaculus of Cremona, the former at least a member now of society at Rome, bitterly lampooned Caesar, though Catullus was later reconciled. Suet. *Jul.* 73; Tac. *Ann.* 4. 34. 8.

ille etiam exstincto miseratus Caesare Romam,
cum caput obscura nitidum ferrugine texit
impiaque aeternam timuerunt saecula noctem.

He gave warning likewise in pity for Rome on Caesar's extinction,
when he veiled his shining face in a murky gloom, and an impious
generation feared that everlasting night would prevail.

But to be a Caesarian did not mean that after the murder of the
Dictator one became automatically an adherent of his adoptive
son. His first political heir was Mark Antony, and in fact it was
one of his lieutenants, C. Asinius Pollio, who is the first public
figure with whom we find Virgil definitely associated. This was
natural enough, for Pollio was not only in charge of Transpadane
Gaul, but a poet who from boyhood had been associated with
Catullus and his circle, the so-called 'modernists' (Neoteroi) to
whom, as we shall see, Virgil was attached.[22] One would infer
reasonably, though not inevitably, that the award which inspired
the First Eclogue was the first occasion on which Virgil actually
saw Octavian (discounting the statement of the Vita Bernensis
that they studied rhetoric together—though seven years divided
their ages—under Epidius).

In Eclogue 5 Virgil made his rustics sing of Daphnis, the
legendary shepherd. Mopsus laments his death, on the lines of
Theocritus 1, but with hints from Bion 1 and Moschus 3; and
then Menalcas, whom lines 85-7 expressly identify with Virgil,
tells in radiant poetry of his translation to the stars. This second
part, though it has an occasional reminiscence of Theocritus, seems
an independent invention. Is it conceivable that the poet had in
mind the Adonis festival of death and resurrection, and the song
for the risen man-god that Gorgo and Praxinoe heard at the palace
at the end of Idyll 15? Virgil never minded borrowing traits from
a context entirely different in feeling.* The image of the mother

---

* The most famous example is Aeneas' protestation to Dido (6. 460) 'Invitus,
regina, tuo de litore cessi', taken almost verbatim from the playful Coma
Berenices of Catullus (66. 39), where the severed lock is addressing the queen
('litore' for 'vertice'). Idyll 15 may have been known to Catullus: at least at
64. 96 he couples Golgo and Idalium, as Theocritus does at l. 100. Virgil's
phrase 'somno mollior' (7. 45) is from ὕπνω μαλακώτερα, which occurs at 15.
125 as well as 5. 51.

complexa sui corpus miserabile nati (22) may have helped to inspire the Christian image of the Pietà. Certainly the contrasting diptych Virgil created was destined to be the ideal prototype for epicedia in the Christian era.*

I fully agree with those who, from antiquity onwards, have taken Daphnis here to represent Julius Caesar.† At his funeral a gilded shrine was placed on the rostra, made after the model of the temple of Venus Genetrix which he had founded two years previously (cf. 22–3).[23] It was observed that for the rest of the year the sun was pale and lacking in radiance, and the crops would not ripen.[24] The phenomenon may be referred to in the line G. 1. 467‡,

cum caput obscura nitidum ferrugine texit,

and also in this *Eclogue* at lines 34–9, which describe the consequent languishing of the fields. In July occurred another phenomenon whose effect on public credulity can hardly be overrated. At the time when Octavian was celebrating posthumous Victory Games for Julius in the Campus Martius there appeared for seven evenings on end a comet in the northern sky. People had long been accustomed to the idea that the souls of great men on their death might become stars, and this one was given the name of *Iulium Sidus*.[25] Octavian placed a statue of Julius in the temple of Venus with a gold star on his head and the inscription 'To Caesar

---

* As Milton's *Lycidas*: 'Yet once more, O ye laurels . . . Weep no more, woeful shepherds . . .'; Shelley's *Adonais*: 'I weep for Adonais—he is dead . . . Peace, peace, he is not dead . . .'

† See D. L. Drew, 'Virgil's Fifth Eclogue', *C.Q.* (1922), pp. 57–64. Further arguments in P. Grimal, 'La "Vme Eclogue" et le culte de César', *Mél. C. Picard* (1949), pp. 406–19. The intrusion of sophisticated topicalities is found already in Theocritus. At 4. 31, a rustic refers to Glauce of Chios and Pyrrhus of Erythrae. Glauce was a citharode and composer of songs popular at Alexandria. At 1. 147 a Sicilian goatherd refers to Aegalian figs. Aegalia was an Attic deme. At 5. 105 Comatas claims to have a bowl made by Praxiteles. At 7. 40 Simichidas praises Asclepiades and Philetus, and it seems likely that real poets are concealed behind the rustic characters in this poem.

‡ Keightley *ad loc.* suggests that in this year there may have been eruptions such as those in Calabria in 1783, which caused obscurity in the atmosphere of the whole of Europe for the greater part of the year. Cf. the eruption of Krakatoa (1883), when it went dark as night in Bandung 150 miles away, and remarkable sunrises and sunsets were seen all over the world.

the Demigod'. The idea of a deified ruler had become common in Hellenistic times, as also the idea that the demigods had originally been men who had greatly benefited mankind. On 1 January 42 the Senate and People declared Julius a god, 'not merely as an official form, but in accordance with popular belief'.[26] A temple was to be built to him in the Forum, and provision was made for the cult in the towns of Italy. Daphnis in this Eclogue is to become a divinity with his altars and festivals. He will be invoked as a surety in vows. And in particular, he will restore happiness to the countryside. The poem is a milestone in Virgil's development. He has become serious, *engagé*; and he has broached the idea that was to grow on him of a man who becomes a saviour-god— Σωτήρ.[27]

In *Eclogue* 9 Moeris, recalling the songs of Menalcas-Virgil, professes to remember one that went (46–50),

> Daphni, quid antiquos signorum suspicis ortus?
> ecce Dionaei processit Caesaris astrum,
> astrum quo segetes gauderent frugibus et quo
> duceret apricis in collibus uva colorem.
> insere, Daphni, piros: carpent tua poma nepotes.

Daphnis, why do you look to the risings of the old constellations? See, the star of Caesar, descendant of Dione, has come forth, the star to make the crops rejoice in their grain and the grapes don colour on the sunny slopes. Graft your pears, Daphnis: your grandchildren shall pick the fruit.

The name of Daphnis, though here he is only typical of husbandmen, seems chosen as a reminder of *Eclogue* 5, and of the man-god who was to restore the countryside as the Iulium Sidus does here.

The reminder was pertinent, for the poem containing it was prompted by new troubles such as were bound to arise as soon as the tension of civil war relaxed. Something had to be done about the released ex-servicemen. Endless controversy has been caused by the speculations of ancient commentators and biographers. But an intelligible story emerges if we disregard what they say and interpret *Eclogues* 9 and 1 in the light of pastoral convention and on the basis only of a few pieces of information given by Servius Auctus* which are so specific that no one, centuries later, could have invented them, and which have all the appearance of going back to some authoritative contemporary source such as Pollio's history of the civil wars.[28]

By the agreement made at the end of 42 B.C. after the Battle of Philippi, Antony went east to continue the task of pacifying the frontiers of Asia Minor, while Octavian stayed in Italy to settle their discharged soldiers on land to be confiscated for the purpose. This was an invidious task, and it is not surprising that in the following year a war broke out between the Antonians and Caesarians which is called the Perusine War because it raged most fiercely round Perugia. By the early months of 40 the Antonians had lost, and Antony's lieutenant Pollio, hitherto in charge of Cisalpine Gaul, withdrew to Venetia at the head of the Adriatic. Octavian now entrusted the task of assigning lands in that area to Alfenus Varus, while the duty of taxing such townships beyond the Po as were exempted from confiscations of land was given to the poet-administrator Cornelius Gallus.[29] Cremona was among eighteen Italian centres designated for land-confiscations, and the detailed execution of the operation there was in the hands of one Octavius Musa, who was called *limitator* or boundary commissioner. Now Servius Auctus has a note on *Eclogue* 9. 7–10 which seems too specific to be an invention: 'To this spot Octavius Musa had extended his surveying-poles, that is to say, through fifteen miles of Mantuan territory, since that of Cremona had proved insufficient.' Whether (as he alleges) because Musa had a grudge against her, or (as seems more probable) for administrative convenience, Mantua was losing land next,

Mantua, vae, miserae nimium vicina Cremonae,

Mantua, alas too near to unhappy Cremona,

and it is natural to suppose that this was adjacent to the Cremonan

---

* The enriched Servius commentary, also called 'Servius Danielis', discovered by Franciscus Modius at Fulda in 1584. The question of its relationship to the shorter Servius is still open. See Büchner, cols. 450–1.

border. There was no general reprieve for her: for at *G.* 2. 198, Virgil refers to

> qualem infelix amisit Mantua campum,

land such as unlucky Mantua lost.

Eclogue 9 seems to have this affair for background. What light can it reasonably be thought to throw? Moeris in it represents the *veteres coloni* who are either being ordered to clear out ('*migrate*') or, as in his case, apparently kept on to work the farm and pay produce to its new, absentee owner (1–6). Menalcas, a poet, has tried to intercede for them. He was rumoured to have been largely successful, but, as often happens, instructions from a central authority were disregarded amid local conditions of chaos and violence:[30]

> audieras, et fama fuit; sed carmina tantum
> nostra valent, Lycida, tela inter Martia quantum
> Chaonias dicunt aquila veniente columbas.

So you heard, and so the rumour ran; but poems such as ours, Lycidas, have no more power amid the weapons of war than, as they say, Chaonian doves have when an eagle comes.

And in the new quarrel resulting from the intercession both Moeris and Menalcas were lucky to have escaped with their lives (7–20). It is important to note that we are not told that Menalcas has himself lost any land, nor that he has any connection with Moeris other than that of champion.* The whole passage could refer, as Servius Auctus supposed, to the fifteen-mile enclave in Mantuan territory measured off by Octavius Musa.

At 27–9 we learn of a petition of Menalcas to Alfenus Varus in

---

* W. Kroll realised this ('Randbemerkungen', *Rh. M.* 1909, pp. 50–5), but he has been too little heeded. '*Nostri agelli*' (3) represents land of the *coloni* in general, '*vestrum Menalcan*' (10) is simply 'your friend and champion'. '*Ipse*' (67) is generally taken to refer to Menalcas, in which case, after what has gone before, the obvious meaning is that when he returns he will refresh their patchy memory of his own songs. Some suppose it means 'the master'. If so, it might be a covert reference to Octavian, whose intervention will put all to rights again.

the shape of a poem which is *necdum perfecta* and will (it is hinted) only be finished and published if it succeeds in its object:

'Vare, tuum nomen, superet modo Mantua nobis,...
cantantes sublime ferent ad sidera cycni.'

Varus, your name, if only Mantua is spared to us...the swans of song shall exalt to the stars.

'Mantua' here could naturally mean the city itself and its environs, as distinct from the more distant territory on the Cremonan marches into which Musa advanced his measuring-poles for fifteen miles. In other words, the reference here is to a *further* stage in the confiscations. And here fits in another important piece of external evidence from Servius Auctus. On line 10 he quotes a passage from a speech by 'Cornelius' (presumably Gallus) against Varus which is surely authentic and could come from a source such as Pollio's history:* 'cum iussus tria milia passus a muro in diversa relinquere, vix octingentos passus aquae quae circumdata est admetireris reliquisti'. The text is not quite right but the meaning is clear:† 'when you were assigning land, having been ordered to leave three miles in every direction from the wall, you scarcely left 800 paces of water which lie around it'. This must refer to the swamps which as lagoons still surround Mantua on three sides. The intention had obviously been to leave the city something to live on, not largely water. And Gallus had a good motive besides humanity or partiality for opposing Varus' harsh interpretation: it gave him a smaller area of exempted *municipium* to tax.

So far I have said nothing of how Virgil was himself affected. But there is no doubt that he is represented by Menalcas (as at 5. 85–7). Lines 19–20 contain a distinct reference to 5. 40, and

---

* Büchner, col. 30. Syme appears to overlook the evidence of this passage when he writes of Alfenus Varus: 'Virgil dedicated to him the sixth of his Eclogues; hence, in the Virgilian *Lives* and the scholiasts, the allegation that he was a land-commissioner' (p. 235, n. 8).

† Kroll inserted a *cum* before *admetireris*, but perhaps the latter word should be transferred to follow the initial *cum*. Tenney Frank, disregarding the *vix*, mistranslated 'you included within the district . . .' (*Vergil*, p. 125). *In diversa* is Peerlkamp's correction for *indivisa*.

23–5, 39–43 are translations from Theocritus,* the poet he had made his own. Now if it is true that the Virgil family home was at Pietole, *three Roman miles* to the south-east of Mantua,† then he was now vitally concerned in this dispute, whereas in the earlier stages he had simply tried to use on behalf of his fellow-country-men the influence which, as a poet, he had acquired with the responsible authorities. It seems possible that the question whether the Virgil farm was confiscated or not depended on whether the swamps were reckoned as part of the city: if Gallus prevailed, his land would be saved. This uncertainty could well be the occasion of the anxiety expressed in *Catalepton* 8.

si quid de patria tristius audiero,

if I hear any gloomier news about my home.

The word 'iussus' in Gallus' speech is arresting. There was only one man who could give orders to Varus—Octavian, whose over-riding power is perhaps hinted at in the reference at 9. 47–50 to his adoptive father.[31] There was likewise only one man before whom such a dispute could be heard—Octavian. The hearing would probably take place at Rome. *Hic illum vidi iuvenem.* And Octavian's verdict (transposed into terms of pastoral poetry) was

pascite ut ante boves, pueri, summittite tauros,

feed your cattle as before, men; rear your bulls.[32]

---

* Probably not from completed Eclogues that have not come down to us, but snatches translated *ad hoc*. H. Oppermann ('Vergil und Oktavian', *Hermes*, 1932, pp. 202–3) says justifiably that Lycidas also represents Virgil, to the extent that it is he who at ll. 32–6 adapts Theocritus 7. 37–41, where the speaker, Simichidas, is Theocritus. But to maintain, as he does, that Moeris also represents Virgil, is to force the meaning of 'carmina *nostra*', which is simply 'songs such as we sing'.

† The late fifteenth-century MS of the Vita Probiana says that Andes, Virgil's birthplace, was 'XXX' miles from Mantua. But Roman numerals are easily corrupted, and Egnatius' scarcely later *editio princeps* of 1507 gives 'III', following the *vetustissimus* of Bobbio. The Vita Donatiana says 'abest a Mantua non procul'. If XXX were right, how could Virgil have called himself so emphatically a Mantuan? Pietole is the traditional place. How could it ever have maintained a claim to a man so famous in his lifetime if it had not the support of truth embodied in common knowledge? See further B. Nardi, 'La tradizione virgiliana di Pietole nel medio evo', *Stud. Med.* (1932), pp. 104–38.

In *Eclogue* 1, where we now find ourselves, Tityrus represents the reprieved peasants (in my submission, those whose land was in the three-mile zone round Mantua city), Meliboeus those outside it. I agree with the scholars, probably now the majority, who believe there was only one eviction, or threat of eviction, of Virgil's family; the idea of two arose from the fact that, out of compliment to Octavian, *Eclogue* 1 was placed first in the collection, though 9 came before it chronologically. But it was a compliment with a sting in the tail—indeed not only in the tail. The resultant effect of the poem is at least as much another appeal for the less fortunate as a tribute of gratitude. '*Barbarus has segetes?*' The promise that accompanied the Iulium Sidus at 9. 50,

> insere, Daphni, piros: carpent tua poma nepotes,

graft your pears, Daphnis, and your grandchildren shall gather the crop,

is recalled with a bitter, ironical *nunc* at 73:

> insere nunc, Meliboee, piros, pone ordine vitis.

now graft your pears, Meliboeus, and plant out your rows of vines.

It is a courageous poem.

Virgil's description of the spot to which, according to Servius Auctus, Octavius Musa extended his measuring-poles (9. 7–10) seems less conventional and idealised than is usual in pastoral:

> certe equidem audieram, qua se subducere colles
> incipiunt mollique iugum demittere clivo,
> usque ad aquam et veteres, iam fracta cacumina, fagos,
> omnia carminibus vestrum servasse Menalcan.

Indeed I had heard that from where the hills begin to fall and descend in a gentle slope, as far as the water and the old beech trees with their broken tops—all this your Menalcas had saved with his songs.

If that is a real locality, it is nowhere near the *city* of Mantua; and in any case all those excursions to Valeggio or Calvisano or Carpenedolo or Montaldo should be renamed 'In quest of Moeris' Farm'—they have no bearing on that of Menalcas-Virgil.[33] And what about the *aequor* that *stratum silet* at 57? It is imported, as everyone knows, from Theocritus 2. 38, and is the sea, nowhere near Mantua. And the tomb of Bianor three lines later? It is introduced to remind us of that of Brasilas at Theocritus 7. 10, but the name may have been suggested, as has recently been urged, by a Hellenistic epigram.* Similarly in 1, though the marshy, pebbly patches on Tityrus' land (46–8) would tally with the disputed land near the Mantuan swamps, those shadows that fall from the high hills in the last line were remembered from some other landscape. The poet simply wanted a peaceful evening close such as he favours elsewhere (2, 6, 9, 10). It must be realised that these *Eclogues* are not allegories in a real landscape: they are Theocritean pastorals with outcrops of reality. We must not expect everything to work out neatly: indeed we may have dust intentionally thrown in our eyes.† In his introduction to 7 Conington remarks: 'The scenery is, as usual, confused. Arcadian shepherds are made to sing in the neighbourhood of the Mincius, while neither the ilex, the pine, the chestnut, nor the flock of goats, seem to belong to Mantua.' Quite so, and no matter. There is no reason to suppose, with one scholar, that these shepherds are descendants of Arcadians captured by Mummius; nor, with another, that because Gallus is made to say at 10, 44–5 that he is a soldier on campaign, whereas elsewhere in the poem he appears to be in Arcadia, he must be having a spell of leave from his military commitments.

Let us return to the story of the evictions. Virgil, however relieved, was now in an embarrassing situation. Varus was presumably still in office. Mantua had been reprieved, so in a sense he still owed him the swans' praises; but it had in fact been reprieved through Gallus. *Eclogue* 6 is his solution. He would use that famous prologue to Callimachus' *Aitia* as basis for a witty

---

* *A.P.* 7. 261; S. Tugwell, 'Virgil, Eclogue 9. 59–60', *C.R.* (1963), pp. 132–3. Similarly in *Eclogue* 2 the name of Alexis may be simply borrowed from an epigram of Meleager (*A.P.* 12. 127) about a beautiful boy which comes next before a pastoral one by him about love for Daphnis; in which case what Suetonius and others tell us about a boy Alexander given to Virgil is probably fiction.

† H. J. Rose's objection, 'I dislike calling a favourite poet a gratuitous liar', is singularly inept (*The Eclogues of Virgil*, 1942, p. 64). His whole chapter on 'The Poet on his Home' is strangely literal-minded. Contrast Conington's Introduction, pp. 9–17.

and elegant *recusatio*. He would recommend unspecified epic-style poets who would be more worthy of the task (cf. Horace's *recusatio* to Agrippa, *Odes* 1. 6: *scriberis Vario*). He had in fact been urged to write pastoral (*non iniussa cano*); and in any case, if he put Varus at the top of the page, any applause the poem earned would redound to his credit, so the debt was paid in a sense (9–12). And with a fulsome, empty compliment about Apollo and no further ado he turns to his pastoral: *Pergite, Pierides*. What follows has no discernible connection with Varus; but whatever the significance of the repertoire of songs Silenus chooses to sing, there can be no denying that it gives quite exceptional honour to one man —Cornelius Gallus, the only poet mentioned by name. It was to Gallus that the debt of song was really owed, and it was paid both here and, with interest, in 10: *neget quis carmina Gallo?*

But meanwhile the idea of a man–god as saviour had been transferred by Virgil from the dead Julius to the living Octavian (1. 6–8):

> O Meliboee, deus nobis haec otia fecit;
> namque erit ille mihi semper deus, illius aram
> saepe tener nostris ab ovilibus imbuet agnus.

O Meliboeus, it is a god who has given us this peace; for a god he will always be to me; on his altar shall a tender lamb from our folds often shed its blood.

This is a milestone.

The fourth *Eclogue* is another milestone. Its significance in its literary and historical context was explained in 1912 by D. A. Slater in an article which has been regarded by too few, with the important exception of Sir William Tarn.[34] Slater's great service was to emphasise the significance of Catullus' *Peleus and Thetis* (64) for the interpretation of this poem.[35] Catullus, after telling of the happy marriage of the Argonaut to the goddess which all the gods and goddesses attended, had put into the mouth of the Fates a marriage-song (323–81)—*veridicum oraclum* (326; cf. 306)—in which they celebrate the love of the pair and prophesy (338–70) the birth of their son Achilles, his prowess and the terrible deeds he will do at Troy, returning at the end to the happy pair again.

Then in an epilogue he had lamented (384–408) that whereas in those days gods used to mingle with heroes as at that marriage, now the world had grown degenerate and wicked, justice had been driven out (398), and the gods refused any longer to visit men or be seen by them in clear light.

It should be obvious that Virgil's *Eclogue* prophesying the birth of a prince and the return of the Golden Age alludes to the marriage-song and epilogue of this influential poem, published some fourteen years before, even if he had not gone out of his way to indicate it by echoing the Fates' refrain,

> currite ducentes subtegmina, currite, fusi,

run, spindles, run drawing your woofs,

with his
> 'talia saecla' suis dixerunt 'currite' fusis
> concordes stabili fatorum numine Parcae,   (46–7)

'Let such ages run' said the Fates to their spindles, the Fates that utter in consort the fixed will of destiny.

The point of the instances singled out in lines 34–6 is at once clear:

> alter erit tum Tiphys, et altera quae vehat Argo
> delectos heroas; erunt etiam altera bella
> atque iterum ad Troiam magnus mittetur Achilles,

there will now be another Tiphys, and another Argo to carry chosen heroes; other wars there will be, and a great Achilles shall once more be sent against Troy.

That is, the destiny sung by Catullus' Fates will repeat itself. But there is no dwelling on the terrible deeds Achilles will do; rather on the peace that will gradually supervene when the child has been born.

The burden of Catullus' world-weary epilogue recalls that of Wordsworth's sonnet *The world is too much with us*:

> Great God! I'd rather be
> A pagan suckled in a creed outworn,
> So might I, standing on this pleasant lea,
> Have glimpses that would make me less forlorn,

Have sight of Proteus rising from the sea
Or hear old Triton blow his wreathèd horn.

Now the occasion of Virgil's poem, as most would agree, is the signature in October 40 of the Treaty of Brundisium, at which Antony and Octavian were reconciled and embraced before their cheering armies. The treaty was sealed by the marriage of Antony to Octavian's sister Octavia. The echoes of Catullus' poem make it more than likely that the Eclogue is in effect a marriage-song for these two. Virgil had reason to be enthusiastic. Not only did the nightmare of the civil wars seem ended at last, but he was also freed from an agony of divided loyalty. Octavian had become his benefactor by the recent reversal of the evictions, but his patron and friend had been the Antonian Pollio, who now returned to the limelight as negotiator for Antony and, for the rest of the year, as holder of the suspended consulship for which the Triumvirs had designated him two years before. 'This glorious age' (*decus hoc aevi**) was to begin in his consulship. The poem is thus appropriately dedicated to him, as a friend restored. And he could not be anything but pleased at a reference to Catullus, who had singled him out when he was a boy of about sixteen for the most gratifying praise,

leporum
disertus puer et facetiarum.

But the child was not his.

The child was (by this interpretation) the hoped-for offspring of the marriage. It corresponds to Achilles in Catullus 64, to the 'Torquatus parvulus' of that other marriage-song of his, 61.† It is *magnum Iovis incrementum*, 'great scion of Jupiter', because both Antony, through Hercules,[36] and Octavia, through Venus, claimed descent from the father of the gods. *Patriis virtutibus* refers to ancestral virtues, perhaps echoing the 'magnis virtutibus' of the Catullan Fates' salute to Peleus (323). What Virgil is saying

---

* The genitive means 'consisting in'.
† Cf. also Statius' Epithalamium, *Silv.* 1. 2. 266 ff. It was not Virgil's fault that the child turned out to be a girl, Antonia, who was at least to become the grandmother of an emperor, Nero. To go into all the other interpretations that have been suggested would be far beyond the scope of this book.

is: 'Catullus' pessimism is no longer justified. The Sibyl's prophecy is coming true. The tenth age of the Cycle is now here —Apollo's. Already the Virgin-Star of Justice has reappeared. And now we may hope for a child who shall see, as he grows, the Golden Age gradually return. After great deeds he shall live the life of a demi-god, ruling a world at peace by the virtues of his forebears. And in your consulship, my exalted friend Pollio, this regeneration shall begin. It will be a gradual purging. There will be heroic voyages and wars again, till ships and arms vanish as the Golden Age returns. Such is the Fates' marriage-song for Antony and Octavia. Come quickly, child! Now is the time. The universe is expectant. May I live to praise your deeds! Come, child, be born, and begin to recognise your mother by her smile. She must smile on you at your birth, else you will never be a demi-god like Peleus, whose table was shared by the gods and his bed by a goddess.'

Virgil's temperament, always sanguine, and his tendency to hero-worship made it easy for him to be carried away, even without the personal reasons he had for relief and enthusiasm. Slater compares (though it is much less apocalyptic) what Richmond, the future Henry VII, says in Shakespeare of his own marriage that sealed the treaty ending the civil war between the Houses of York and Lancaster:

> O now let Richmond and Elizabeth,
> The true successors of each royal house,
> By God's fair ordinance conjoin together!
> And let their heirs (God, if Thy will be so)
> Enrich the time to come with smooth-faced peace,
> With smiling plenty and fair prosperous days.[37]

In sober fact hindsight makes it seem obvious that the world could not hold Antony and Octavian; the civil wars could only end with the elimination of one or the other. But intense longing for peace can overcome any such realistic doubts. One remembers Dio's description of the hysterical scenes at Misenum barely a year later when Antony and Octavian went aboard Sextus Pompeius' flagship to dine and their armies fell upon each others' necks[38] (or, indeed, Chamberlain greeted by delirious crowds on his return from Munich as he waved a piece of paper signed by Hitler and proclaimed, 'I believe it is peace for our time').

The negotiator of the treaty for Octavian was C. Maecenas, 'ever a reconciler of estranged friends', as Horace was to call him.[39] We do not know which of his influential friends introduced Virgil to Octavian or to Maecenas—the ancient biographers were probably guessing; but by 39/38 both he and Varius had become part of his circle, for it was then that they introduced Horace to him. From now on we must think of Virgil in the context of that circle, though he remained particularly devoted, as *Eclogue* 10 shows, to Cornelius Gallus, who was a Caesarian but independent of it, and no doubt also to Pollio, who after triumphing over Dalmatia became neutral in politics, occupying himself with writing tragedies and the history of the civil wars. What we think of as the Augustan Age was already beginning. It is important nevertheless to remember that, although Octavian was 'Divi filius', Antony was still at this stage the dominant Triumvir;* and Dio in his history[40] only mentions Maecenas once before Actium —Γάιός τις Μαικήνας, ἀνὴρ ἱππεύς (as undertaking administrative functions in Rome and Italy)—though he is more prominent in Appian.

POETRY

We have already recalled Pollio as a boy being praised by Catullus for his good manners and social gifts. At *Eclogue* 3. 84-7, the rustics proclaim that he loves the pastoral Muse and himself writes 'nova carmina', a phrase in which the epithet is otiose unless it means that he wrote 'modernist' poetry. Cinna had written a 'propempticon' (send-off poem) for Pollio some fifteen years before; and at 9. 32-6 Lycidas is made to say that he would not venture to set himself up as a rival to Varius and Cinna. Gallus also, enthusiast for Euphorion and one of the second-generation

---

* Otis is misleading when he refers to 'the peace of the Julian dispensation described in *Eclogue* 4. 21 f.': *Virgil*, p. 134. Antony was the bridegroom. See Syme, pp. 219–21.

Neoteroi, became a close friend of Virgil's, but how early we do not know. So Virgil's affiliation to the Neoteric movement is clear, and the movement was still exciting. It was his nature to enter into the spirit of the present fashion and influence things from the inside rather than to initiate an independent line. Moreover, most of the poets in the movement were Transpadanes, an extraordinary fact when one remembers that their homeland was not yet reckoned politically as part of Italy. From Cremona came Quintilius Varus and Furius Bibaculus. Virgil could possibly have known the former even in his school-days. From Milan came Valerius Cato, the teacher and inspirer of the movement, 'the Latin Siren', 'unicus magister, summus grammaticus, optimus poeta'. Catullus was from Verona (as was Cornelius Nepos, the historian to whom he dedicated a volume of his poems), Cinna from Brescia and Caecilius from Como. Two came from even further afield, Gallus from Forum Julii (Fréjus) and Varro of Atax from Narbonnese Gaul.* It may be that just because they originated far from Rome they were less under the spell of the Roman literary tradition, more open to the rediscovery of what third-century Alexandria and Asia Minor had to contribute. And then there was the chance that an influential literary figure with a Hellenistic background, Parthenius of Nicaea, came into the household of Cinna as a captive from the Mithridatic Wars. He provided Gallus with the extant prose collection of love-stories from mythology for use in his poems, and according to Macrobius helped Virgil with his Greek studies.[41] Lucian bracketed him with Euphorion and Callimachus.[42] Like the Alexandrians, he wrote elegies and poems in various metres. We hear of three books of elegies, one called 'Aphrodite' and two containing respectively laments for, and praises of, his wife Arete; also of an epithalamion and a propempticon.[43]

The Neoteroi, though sufficiently interconnected to be called a school,[44] were not committed to uniformity in poetic practice.

---

* Calvus however came from Rome. We do not know the provenance of Tucca, nor on what evidence Tenney Frank (*Vergil*, p. 14) said that Varius came from Cremona.

We may take it that Virgil would be on the Callimachean side in the controversy revived after 200 years, that is, on the Catullan side against the purveyors of grand epic. He would be in favour of short poems highly wrought, with subtly contrived effects and allusions, and occasional wit or irony. If the *Catalepton* is any guide, he would use various metres—the Alexandrians favoured polymetry. He would not be broadly patriotic in the tradition of Ennius, nor an impassioned preacher like Lucretius: his interest would be in personal matters and in poetry for poetry's sake.

Several attractions could draw Virgil to Theocritus. Though a collection of the Greek Bucolic Poets had been made in the first half of the century by Artemidorus, it is not known whether it included Theocritus (his son Theon produced a commentary on Theocritus—ὑπομνήματα—but the date is unknown). There is little evidence of familiarity with him before Virgil: his epigrams were apparently unknown to Meleager, who collected his Garland about 100 B.C.* Whatever the reason, none of the Neoteroi would appear to have attempted to win for Latin what we at least consider to be the best Alexandrian poetry that has come down to us, the merits of which could hardly escape a born poet like Virgil. More than most poets also Virgil had his roots in the land. The description of Tityrus' farm, for instance (I. 51–8), is obviously written *con amore*. And then there was the attraction of the countryside, *haec otia*, for the Epicurean quietist. 'The wise man will love the country' (ὁ σοφὸς φιλαγρήσει) was one of the maxims of the Master.[45] The first line of the *Eclogues* (even if it was not written to be such) strikes the keynote, *patulae recubans sub tegmine fagi*. There is also, far more than in Theocritus, the longing to escape. The pastoral landscape in the Sicilian is the narrow strip of coast between Etna and the sea, quite close to the walls of the great city of Syracuse where he was born and bred; or, at the furthest, Calabria; or, as seen later from Alexandria, the island of Cos. The escape is only to the country. In Virgil it is an escape not so much from city life as from the horrors and chaos of

---

* The problem is discussed by A. S. F. Gow, *Theocritus*, I (1950), lix–lxii. He is sceptical about the theories of Wilamowitz.

contemporary Italy to an idealised retreat. Magna Graecia and Sicily were too near, too familiar:* Tarentum was to Virgil what Cos was to Theocritus. Hence the change to Arcadia, the inland mountain refuge. We do not know whether any predecessor had so idealised Arcadia. It is much more likely that Virgil chose it because it was the country of Pan, the great god of pastoral poetry, than that he did so because he had read Polybius 4. 20.[46]

The abstruse learning which characterised some Alexandrian poetry is no more a feature of the *Eclogues* in general than it is of Theocritus' *Idylls*. The incongruity sticks out when the rustic at 3. 40 says that his pair of beechwood cups is embossed with portraits of Conon (Astronomer Royal at Alexandria in the third century) and another who partitioned the whole heavens with his measuring-rod, whose name (as some concession to reality) Virgil allows him to have forgotten. There may be esoteric literary significance in the catalogue of songs Silenus sang in 6 and in Gallus' complaint in 10; and in 4 there are certainly allusions to Sibylline, Etruscan and probably Neo-Pythagorean lore. But far more characteristic is the ingenuity with which Virgil works into one coherent poem motifs, phrases and even rhythms taken from several in his model. The two earliest, 2 and 3, are of such virtuosity in this respect that we may conclude that when he began he had little more in mind than to delight his Neoteric audience with literary *jeux d'esprit*. And yet already there was a new and different quality.

Friedrich Klingner, in his admirable study entitled *The Unity of Virgil's Lifework*,[47] has traced his development through the *Eclogues*. Even in what purport to be mimes he is not, like Theocritus, a detached observer of the quaint behaviour, comic or touching, of simple people. He enters into their world, takes them seriously, and uses them to express what are his own

---

* Similarly at *Aen.* 7. 563 ff. the Fury Allecto disappears into the underworld by the *Ampsancti Valles* in remote southern Italy instead of by the chasms of the Nar, used by her prototype, Ennius' Discordia. The Nar chasms were now too familiar, with the busy Via Flaminia running nearby. In defiance of geography Virgil transferred their features to the new locality. (E. Norden, *Ennius und Vergilius*, 1915, p. 39.)

feelings.* And so it is that in the Daphnis (5) he passes quite naturally into voicing his deepest anxieties and hopes, whereas in Theocritus the rustic pieties and superstitions are part of the mime. Virgil is here giving voice to the wave of messianic hope that meets us everywhere in the history of his distracted age. We also have for the first time the theme of agricultural ruin and revival. Ostensibly we are still however in the timeless age of pastoral: any modern application is only implicit. But in *Eclogue* 9 the agricultural topicalities have become unmistakable, and the reference to Julius Caesar explicit; while in 1 these themes are developed, with the man-god now incarnate in the saving 'iuvenis'. In the Pollio (4), with an apology, the Muses of Sicily are left behind. Only a dragged-in reference to Pan (58-9) pays lip-service to pastoral; and the child is destined to rule the whole world (17). By such stages has Virgil's scope almost insensibly extended until the Hellenistic 'idle singer of an empty day' is ready to become the *vates* of Augustanism.

In verse-style the Virgil of the *Eclogues* represents a remarkable advance on the two great hexameter poets who had died a dozen years before, Lucretius with his straggling sentences and Catullus with his monotonous end-stopping. He displays an admirable variety, the rhythm being dictated by the nature of the poem. In the two earliest, 2 and 3, he is interested in reproducing the very cadences of Theocritus. O *crudelis Alexi* echoes ὦ χαρίεσσ' 'Αμαρυλλί, and *mori me denique coges* ἀπάγξασθαί με ποιήσεις. And the line (2. 24)

Amphion Dircaeus in Actaeo Aracyntho

looks like a transliteration, almost letter for letter, of some lost Greek original. *Eclogue* 3. 56-7 exhibits the device of tetracolon with anaphora (here of *nunc*) fitted into two lines (cf. Theocritus 8. 79-80), which occurs in four other places[48] and must have caught Virgil's fancy. Even in the poem which is last both in

* It is this quality of empathy that Brooks Otis, following up ideas of Klingner and Snell, is concerned to emphasise in ch. IV of his *Virgil*; and it is a quality that animates the whole of the *Georgics*.

date and position, the *Gallus*, he is still exploiting such echoes: compare

τῆνον μὰν θῶες, | τῆνον λύκοι ὠρύσαντο, |
τῆνον χὠκ δρυμοῖο λέων ἔκλαυσε θανόντα.

πολλαί οἱ πὰρ ποσσὶ βόες, | πολλοὶ δέ τε ταῦροι, |
πολλαὶ δ᾽ αὖ δαμάλαι καὶ πόρτιες ὠδύραντο,

and

illum etiam lauri, etiam flevere myricae,
pinifer illum etiam sola sub rupe iacentem
Maenalus...

venit et upilio, tardi venere subulci,
uvidus hiberna venit de glande Menalcas.

Only Virgil's anaphora is less mechanical; and once at least, more subtly, he echoes a rhythm not from the corresponding line—

nam neque Parnasi vobis iuga, nam neque Pindi

from one that comes two lines earlier in Theocritus,

πῇ ποκ᾽ ἄρ᾽ ἦσθ᾽ ὅκα Δάφνις ἐτάκετο, πῇ ποκα Νύμφαι; *

No. 2 has 61 sentences in its 73 lines: Corydon is distracted, like the rustic in Theocritus 3, and in no mood to construct periods even if he could. No 3, largely in amoebic couplets, and No. 7, largely in amoebic quatrains, have perforce a simple formalism; while in No. 8 the frequent incidence of refrains precludes any attempt at subtle rhythmic development. Likewise the cosmogonic passage in 6 (31–40) is suitably in Lucretian style, though

---

* See L. P. Wilkinson, *Golden Latin Artistry* (1963), p. 195. A good parallel from the *Georgics* is noted by L. A. S. Jermyn, 'Weather-signs in Virgil', *G.&R.* (1951), p. 32. The metrical form of Cicero's line (fr. 4) describing the flight of a coot,

cana fulix itidem fugiens a gurgite ponti,

is exactly echoed by Virgil in the same context (1. 361), but for the seagull (not for the coot, which appears two lines later):

cum medio celeres revolant ex aequore mergi.

The lines 3. 79,

et longum 'formose, vale, vale,' inquit, 'Iolla',

and 6. 44

clamassent, ut litus 'Hyla, Hyla' omne sonare,

similar in build and subject, may both be reflections of some Greek line.

it displays a trait of the mature Virgil in having a 'Golden Line' to round it off,

> rara per ignaros errent animalia montis.*

The *Pollio* (4) reflects the style of Catullus' *Peleus and Thetis*, which, as we saw, it is concerned to recall. Not only is it largely end-stopped, but it has three successive lines (28–30) built round a molossic word, as are 12 of the first 21 in Catullus' epyllion:

> molli paulatim *flavescet* campus arista,
> incultisque rubens *pendebit* sentibus uva,
> et durae quercus *sudabunt* roscida mella.

Virgil would not have allowed such monotony without some purpose. But this poem also has signs of periodic symmetry. The prophecy begins (4–17) with lines grouped 2+2+3, 2+2+3 (*tricolon abundans*), and this pattern recurs at 46–52.[49] In the *Daphnis* (5) on the other hand the ecstasy of the apotheosis is matched by a headlong, enjambé style with variety of pauses in the most mature Virgilian manner adapted from the 'periodic' style of oratory (60–6):

> nec lupus insidias pecori nec retia cervis
> ulla dolum meditantur; | amat bonus otia Daphnis. |
> ipsi laetitia voces ad sidera iactant
> intonsi montes, | ipsae iam carmina rupes,
> ipsa sonant arbusta: | deus, deus ille, Menalca! |
> sis bonus o felixque tuis! | en quattuor aras; |
> ecce duas tibi, Daphni, duas altaria Phoebo.[50]

But that manner is so completely displayed in *Eclogue* 1 that it is worth analysing it in some detail.

> Tityre, tu patulae recubans sub tegmine fagi
> silvestrem tenui musam meditaris avena:
> nos patriae fines et dulcia linquimus arva,
> nos patriam fugimus: tu, Tityre, lentus in umbra
> formosam resonare doces Amaryllida silvas.

The first two lines, each balanced as between epithets and nouns, are remarkable for their alliterative pattern of 't's and 'm's, while

* Cf. 2. 50: 'mollia luteola pingit vaccinia calta'.

the 'f' of 'fagi' is repeated in 'fines', 'fugimus' and 'formosam' to knit the period together in sound.* This knitting is accomplished still more by the assonance of *pat*ulae, *pat*riae, *pat*riam, *silvestrem, silvas*, and by the reflection of 'Tityre tu' as 'tu Tityre' in 4. Line 3 has a graceful 'homodyne' cadence (compare the haunting, decorative description of Silvanus in 10. 25,

> florentes ferulas et grandia lilia quassans).

Lines 3–4½, besides carrying on the pattern of assonance by anaphora (*nos...nos*), exemplify the Virgilian artifice of making a statement in a line and then repeating the sense in more concentrated form, to which Henry drew attention;[51] cf. 70–1:

> impius haec tam culta novalia miles habebit,
> barbarus has segetes?

The fluent fifth line with its weak caesura rounds off the rhythm, as in the case of line 35.

Tityrus replies in five lines to balance, also knit together by repetitions (*deus – ille – deus – illius – ille*). Meliboeus' next three lines are broken into five sentences: he can hardly speak for misery. Lines 22–3 have *tricolon abundans* with anaphora of *sic*, 38–9 with *polyptoton* of *ipsae – ipsi – ipsa*. In line 55,

> saepe levi somnum suadebit inire susurro

the sibilants are hushing and the rocking rhythm lulling, as in *Aen.* 2. 9,

> suadentque cadentia sidera somnos;

and 'turtur ab ulmo' in 58 gives us the sound of the dove's cooing. Chiastic balance appears in 62,

> aut Ararim Parthus bibet aut Germania Tigrim

(compare the elegant line 5. 70,

> ante focum, si frigus erit, si messis, in umbra).

---

* R. G. G. Coleman, 'Tityrus and Meliboeus', *G.&R.* (1966), p. 79, suggests that we are meant to hear the actual notes of the rustic pipe in the opening syllables, *ti ty tu tu*. This could be supported by reference to the Greek word τιτύρινος (αὐλός) for a shepherd's pipe.

Finally, we may note throughout how often the fifth foot is responsive to the first, either by anaphora or at least by alliteration:

1. Tityre...tegmine
38. Tityrus...Tityre
51. Fortunate...flumina
74. Ite...ite
81. Castaneae...copia
83. Maioresque...montibus

Virgil's artistic medium for the *Georgics* was already fully developed.

In diction too the *Eclogues* are literary. The only suggestions of mimic realism in the shepherds' talk come in the early No. 3, including the old-fashioned colloquialism '*cuium* pecus' derided by Virgil's detractor Numitorius; and even in that poem (60) Damoetas begins the competition with a line that recalls the exordium of the Stoic Aratus, played on an organ, not a Pan-pipe:

> Ab Iove principium, Musae: Iovis omnia plena.

The fact is that, as we saw, these are not real rustics, but rustics like Housman's Shropshire lads, through whom the poet expresses his own feelings. As Snell remarks, 'Virgil has ceased to see anything but what is important to him: tenderness and warmth and delicacy of feeling'.[52] Alphesiboeus at 8. 85-8 (tender in one sense at least) prays that Daphnis may suffer in love,

> ...qualis cum fessa iuvencum
> per nemora atque altos quaerendo bucula lucos
> propter aquae rivum viridi procumbit in ulva
> perdita, nec serae meminit decedere nocti...,

as when a heifer, tired out with seeking her mate through groves and upland woods throws herself down in the green sedge by a river-bank, quite lost, and does not think to return home as night draws on.

That is Virgil speaking, the Virgil we shall find in the *Georgics*.*

---

* Even though the idea may have been suggested by Lucretius' description of a cow looking for her lost calf (2. 355 ff.), or by Varius, whose description of a hound chasing a stag is said to have contributed the last line here (Macr. *Sat.* 6. 2).

Snell tends, I think, to exaggerate the novelty of the Virgilian Eclogue:[53] 'Its perfect form, its grace and its sound make it what it is. Thus, for the first time in Western literature, the poem becomes "a thing of beauty", existing only for itself and in itself.' It is probably true, however, that not even in Theocritus is sheer beauty so much sought for its own sake, though it is hard to see how, for instance, *Eclogue* 8 surpasses *Idyll* 2 (*Simaetha*) in this respect. Also we have already seen that 1, 4 and 9, probably 5 and possibly 6 do not exist 'only for themselves': they have an ulterior political purpose. The formal beauty carries over into the *Georgics*, but so do the political tendency and the love of the countryside. Any neoteric idea of a poem as 'existing for itself and in itself', of art for art's sake, is already receding into the background.

III · *The Conception of the 'Georgics'*

POLITICS

'To-morrow to fresh woods and pastures new.' The *Eclogues* were composed in 42–39 B.C., with the *Gallus* (10) as an afterthought a year or so later. By the time they were finished Virgil was a member of Maecenas' circle. To what poetry should he turn next? Two lines from the proem to Book 3 have naturally been cited as meaning that Maecenas ordered the *Georgics* (40–1):

> interea Dryadum silvas saltusque sequamur
> intactos, tua, Maecenas, haud mollia iussa;

meanwhile let me pursue the woods and virgin glades of the Dryads, your bidding, Maecenas, and no easy one.

'*Iussa*' need not denote a 'command': it can be something milder than that. The poets' *recusationes* are evidence enough that Maecenas did not give them commands.* But in any case this passage, in which Virgil looks forward to the epic he means to write in honour of Octavian, was written in 29 B.C., more than seven years later. In this context the words need mean no more than that Maecenas was holding him to finishing off the *Georgics*, as Horace in *Epode* 14 intimates that he is holding him to completing the book of iambics—*occidis saepe rogando*. And we must take these two lines in conjunction with 3. 284–5:

> sed fugit interea, fugit irreparabile tempus,
> singula dum capti circumvectamur amore.

But time meanwhile is flying, flying irreparably, while entranced by love we linger around each detail.

There can be no doubt that the *Georgics* were a labour of love; and already in *Eclogues* 5, 9 and 1 Virgil had shown his deep

---

* See P. van de Woestijne, 'Haud mollia iussa', *R.B.Ph.* (1929), pp. 523–30. W. E. Heitland, in what is otherwise the most valuable account of the socio-agricultural background to the *Georgics* (*Agricola*, 1921, pp. 174–221), says, 'Maecenas . . . had put pressure on Virgil to write it. At the back of Maecenas was the new Emperor' (p. 224). 'Emperor' is also a misleading anachronism, into which T. E. Page likewise falls: introduction to edn., p. xxii.

concern at the state of the Italian countryside and his longing for its revival.

What the agricultural state of Italy was in the late Republic can be gathered from the technical dialogue *De Re Rustica* published in 37/6 B.C. by the octogenarian Varro, who besides being an encyclopaedic writer was a practical man of affairs.* The attempt of the Gracchi to break up the *latifundia* and revive the old class of yeomen who were also soldiers—*rusticorum mascula militum proles*—had failed. The geography of Italy was against it, for it consisted largely of upland pastures and forest-lands, suitable only for large flocks and herds which could migrate at suitable times of the year. The success of Roman arms overseas was also against it. Not only did it encourage ranching by securing the importation of cereals, but individuals acquired the wealth to buy large estates and the slaves to work them. Scientific knowledge derived from Greece and Carthage favoured the industrial aim of raising large crops of vines and olives, even more than cereals, for the urban market, though prestige and political influence were at least as powerful motives for acquisition of wide acres.[1] Sallust refers to agriculture as slaves' work.[2] Varro assumes that an estate is worked by slaves, and that even the bailiff (*vilicus*) will be one. He is no sentimentalist, though an improvement on Cato in not recommending that old and outworn slaves should be sold off. He regards the slaves as capital equipment to be conserved, recommending, for instance, that for cultivating malarial land poor peasants be hired.[3]

There were, of course, exceptions. We hear of a bee-farm of a single *iugerum* only about thirty miles north of Rome successfully worked by two brothers.[4] There were tenant-farmers, sometimes freedmen set up as such by their former masters—indeed in Augustus' time the word *colonus* usually referred to a tenant.[5] It might pay the owner of a large estate to let an out-of-the-way farm to a tenant at a money-rent or on a sharing system, perhaps

---

* The *dramatic* date of Book 1 is uncertain; of Book 2, ? 67 B.C.; of Book 3, 54 B.C. (Heitland, *Agricola*, p. 178). How much allowance Varro made for historical difference from the time of writing we cannot tell.

with some condition of service attached. Even Horace on his modest Sabine estate, while keeping the home farm in hand under a bailiff and the dwelling-house for his visits, let off outlying farms to *quinque boni patres*.[6] There were also still independent *coloni*, notably in the wide plains of the Po valley, in the mountains where only small plots might be cultivable, and on the southern coast, where Greek traditions persisted.[7] Varro refers to free peasants and their families, *pauperculi cum progenie sua*, as a source of hired labour.[8] He admired these old-fashioned yeomen, but recognised that they had almost vanished from most of the main arable areas. There was always hanging over them the fear of summary eviction. One recalls the vivid description in Horace of the landlord enlarging his palace and pleasure-grounds (*Odes*, 2. 18. 23–8):

> quid quod usque proximos
> revellis agri terminos et ultra
> limites clientium
> salis avarus? pellitur paternos
> in sinu ferens deos
> et uxor et vir sordidosque natos.

What that you are for ever tearing up the next boundary-marks and greedily encroaching on your dependants? Forth they are driven, husband and wife, carrying in their arms their fathers' gods and their ragged children.

And the end of each phase of civil war brought fresh misery and chaos through evictions in favour of released veterans. Freeholding peasants as well as prescribed landlords were dispossessed. Horace lost his father's hard-earned plot. If the new owner did not want to farm (and if he were a professional soldier he might not know how to*), he could leave his predecessor to cultivate it and pay him in kind or in money, like Moeris in the *Eclogue* or like Ofellus in Horace's *Satire* 2. 2. But that was the most that could be hoped.

---

* Sometimes, however, he knew. Syme cites the case of the retired centurion C. Castricius, who caused precepts on agriculture and the good life to be engraved on his tombstone. (*C.I.L.* xi, 600; Syme, p. 450 n.)

The ill-effect of the civil wars on agriculture could not fail to be appreciable.* It was not so much that crops and property were damaged, as in modern warfare; rather that weeds and decay got the upper hand—*squalent abductis arva colonis*. It seems that tenant *coloni* might even be taken overseas to fight in feudal fashion with their landlords: Caesar speaks of a squadron of seven ships holding Massilia for Pompey in 49 with crews raised by Domitius from his slaves, freedmen and tenants.[9] And in general the unavailability of the normal source of hired labour at busy times such as harvest would be sufficient to disrupt agriculture. The precariousness of the food supply in Italy was further brought home when Sextus Pompeius, obtaining command of the sea, cut off normal corn-imports from abroad and serious famine resulted.[10]

Appian lists among the reasons for rejoicing in Italy at the (short-lived) accommodation reached by Octavian and Antony with Sextus, that they would be delivered from the pillage of fields, the ruin of agriculture, and above all the famine that had pressed upon them most severely.[11] Such was the situation at the time when Virgil was drawn into Maecenas' circle.

Before discussing the *Georgics* in relation to Caesarian policy it is necessary to examine two questions (they are only superficially one and the same): for whom was it written, and what kind of farmer did it have in mind?

At the end of his exordium Virgil appeals to Octavian to aid him in his task:

> ignarosque viae mecum miseratus agrestes
> ingredere.

This is simply a Lucretian flourish:[12] if Virgil pitied rustics for their ignorance, it was not by the poem he wrote that they could be enlightened. Even Hesiod in the *Works and Days* is highly selective, and omits much that the complete farmer would have to know. Thus he has only five lines on trees, nothing on beasts

---

* Varro's celebration of the agricultural wealth of Italy (1. 2. 1–7) must not be taken *au pied de la lettre* any more than Virgil's (*G*. 2. 136–76). It may take account of the dramatic date; and in any case it savours of the rhetorical encomium (cf. Strabo 6. 4. 1; Dion. Hal. *Ant. Rom.* 1. 36–7).

or bees, no description of sowing, harvesting or threshing.
Virgil's

> non ego cuncta meis amplecti versibus opto,

I do not desire to embrace everything in my verses,

is, to put it mildly, an understatement. In any case only a highly
sophisticated reader could have appreciated the *Georgics*, and he
would generally be an absentee landlord, if a landlord at all. A
Horace might do a little manual labour up at his farm, to the
surprised amusement of his neighbours:

> rident vicini glaebas et saxa moventem,[13]

but they laughed presumably not because he was doing it badly
or because he was fat, but because he was doing it at all.

Horace assumes that landlords rely on slaves: he had eight on
his own farm.[14] He reminds us of the hard lot of the *fossor* who
dug where the plough would not go, describing him with wry
humour as delighting, in his holiday dance, to stamp on the earth
he hates:*

> gaudet invisam pepulisse fossor
> ter pede terram.

The astonishing thing about the *Georgics* is that in the whole poem
there is no reference to slavery, which was casually assumed by
Hesiod and was the *sine qua non* of Varro's treatise.[15] The nearest
approaches are the word *tibi* in the line about holiday-makers,
1. 343,

> cuncta tibi Cererem pubes agrestis adoret,

let all your farm hands worship Ceres;

and the scene on another holiday at 2. 527–31, where *ipse* (suggesting αὐτός, the master) institutes shooting-matches for *pecoris
magistri*. And both these instances come from set-pieces which are
not typical, while either could refer to free workers.

This omission must be intentional. Though sometimes he refers
to activities that seem to presuppose quite a large farm,[16] the kind
of farmer Virgil seems generally to envisage is the *colonus*, without
distinction between freeholder and tenant. He is more than a

---

* 3. 18. 15–16. I remember a college waiter who annually, after the staff supper
in the hall, used to dance with evident satisfaction on the High Table.

pauperculus, but he still works with his own hands. Now it might be said in explanation that this happened to be the class of farmer with which he was most familiar. For not only was it still prevalent in his native Po valley: at the time when he wrote the *Georgics* he was living at Naples in the fertile *Ager Campanus*, which was peculiar in consisting of smallholdings let by the state to *coloni*. And round Tarentum in Magna Graecia, where he stayed, he would find plenty of smallholders of the traditional Greek type. But he must have been aware that conditions over most of Italy were very different. So this explanation can only be partial, and still does not account for silence about slavery, since even quite a modest *colonus* would have some slaves.*

Heitland suggested that Virgil shirked the whole topic because any reference to the labour question or to land tenure bristled with difficulties and would provoke controversy, which Maecenas and 'the Emperor' were anxious to avoid; or even that Maecenas gave him a hint that, with the wholesale discharge of soldiers imminent, he should stick to generalities, a hint not unconnected with the fact that the patron was himself a speculator in land.[17] All this seems to imply a degree of political pressure in the interests of expediency to which the poets of the circle do not seem, on other evidence, to have been subjected. They were not a 'propaganda bureau'. It is also too negative an explanation for one of the mainsprings of enthusiasm in the poem, the sense of immediacy in its exhortations: *ipse—ipse manu*. Hesiod's *Works* would suggest such an approach; but it seems more likely that Virgil's farmer is presented as his own ideal, the old-fashioned yeoman—*vetus colonus*—revived. He must work himself: the whole moral fabric of the poem is based on this.† The ideal is realised in the Corycian old man whose few acres of reclaimed land he had seen outside

---

* The many thousands of veterans settled on the land may more correctly be regarded as small capitalists. See Syme, p. 450.

† For prevailing views at the time see Cic. *de Fin.* 1. 1. 3 (digging and farm-work are 'illiberalis labor'); 3. 2. 4 ('agri cultura, quae abhorret ab omni politiore elegantia'). Catullus opposes to the 'urbanus' the 'caprimulgus aut fossor' (22. 10). Cf. Col. 1 praef. 20 ('communis opinio rem rusticam sordidum opus esse').

Tarentum (G. 4. 125-46), and whose redemptive labour was rewarded by pride in, and enjoyment of, the results. Whatever the motive, Virgil's choice contributed greatly to his poem's vitality in the long run; for since the breakdown of slavery or serfdom a farm has been envisaged as a smallholding by the majority of his European readers; and indeed it was not until that development had occurred that the *Georgics* came into their own in popularity and repute. The very vagueness made for universality.

A sturdy yeoman class, typified by the Sabines, had supplied the sinews of Roman Italy in the great days of the past. Horace represents the financier Alfius as conventionally idealising the man who works his ancestral fields with his own oxen.[18] He never tires of urging the superior merit of a farm that is small, or inveighing against the encroachments of millionaires. *Iam pauca aratro iugera*...[19] But his argument depends less often on morals or politics than on enlightened hedonism. Was it then Caesarian policy to increase the class of small independent farmers? I think we may gather that it was from Horace's alleging among the achievements of Augustus in *Odes* 4. 5

condit quisque diem collibus in suis.

The subject was certainly in the air, and on social and moral grounds there was all to be said for such a movement. But economically it would have been a deleterious reversal of the natural trend. *Latifundia* still occupied, and were to go on occupying, most of the peninsula. The kind of treatise on agriculture that was immediately relevant was not the *Georgics* but the *De Re Rustica*. In the words of Rostovtzeff, 'Public opinion voiced by patriotic and loyal Romans appealed to Augustus to save the peasants. But in fact we hear nothing of any interference on his part with the conditions of land-tenure in Italy...An agrarian law had been too marked a feature of the period of the civil wars to permit of recourse to it, even if it were urgent.'[20] We may surmise, then, that the mainspring of the *Georgics* was not political; and this being so, that Virgil's own enthusiasms were more operative in generating the poem than any promptings from Maecenas.

Hesiod

It seems more likely that the impulse came from literature: having succeeded in becoming the Roman Theocritus, Virgil aspired to be the Roman Hesiod, partly because he was interested in rustic life, partly because Lucretius had shown how great a didactic poem could be as poetry, and partly because Hesiod, so much admired by the Alexandrians of the third century, interested the neo-Callimachean poets of the neoteric movement and yet had not been appropriated.[21]

Servius and Donatus tell us that the *Georgics* was completed in seven years, and we can confirm from historical allusions that it was not completed before 29.[22] What then was he doing in the two years 39/38 to 37/36? Did he rest on his laurels and write no poetry except the Eclogue for Gallus? In a well-known article published in 1930[23] Jean Bayet put forward the theory that the *Georgics* was originally a poem restricted to the compass of Hesiod's *Works and Days* and represented for us by Book 1 (minus the proem, 1–42), which was composed in those two years.* He makes out a strong case for thinking that the historical references in the lament that ends the First Book fit 39–37 and not later years.[24] He is also able to show that some of the alleged debts in this section to Varro's *De Re Rustica*, published in 37/36, could be either commonplaces or derived from a common source.[25] But there remain some which do seem to owe something to Varro.[26] We may doubt therefore whether the book as we have it was completed without knowledge of Varro's work (or at least of his First Book).

It remains true that the specific allusions to Hesiod occur mainly in this book, apart from the famous line 2. 176,

Ascraeumque cano Romana per oppida carmen,

which patently does not fit the subject-matter of Books 2–4 and must mean simply that, now established as the Roman Hesiod,

---

* Phocas' *Vita*, for what it is worth, gives *nine* years, not seven, for the composition of the *Georgics*.

Virgil is singing a didactic poem which retains throughout something of the Hesiodic spirit. There are indications in the *Eclogues* that Virgil was already interested in Hesiod. Mopsus, the name of the shepherd in 5 who sings of the death of Daphnis and of a shepherd in 8, may be taken from that of a seer, son of Apollo and Manto, who was prominent in a work of Hesiod called *Melampodia*. (Ocnus, another son, founded Mantua and named it after his mother.[27]) The meeting of Gallus with the Muses at 6. 64 ff. is a reflection of Hesiod's experience recounted at *Theogony* 22 ff., and the passage credits the 'Ascraeus senex' with having, like Orpheus, drawn trees down from the mountains to listen to his song. Also the Golden Age mythology in 4 went back ultimately to the *Works and Days*, and has reminiscences of it.[28]

'*Quo sidere* terram vertere' begins the *Georgics*, sending us back at once to the world of Hesiod, whose section on agriculture opens (383) with the rising of the Pleiads. It might be thought that this was wholly anachronistic, since the Italian farmer could now use the Julian calendar. But it is noteworthy that Varro devotes a chapter (1. 28), in which he actually refers to that calendar, to relating the various divisions of the year to the constellations, and that elsewhere he frequently indicates times by reference to these, especially the Pleiads. The farmer might no longer observe the stars directly, but he would consult a calendar that still referred to them.[29] Pliny also devoted a large section to astronomy in relation to agriculture and weather.[30]

At a superficial level Virgil exercised his wit in Latinising the odd phrase from the *Works and Days* that might have stuck in the memory of his audience. Thus *nudus ara, sere nudus* reflects γυμνὸν σπείρειν γυμνὸν δὲ βοωτεῖν in reverse.[31] The recognition would gratify the cultured hearer, as with Milton's mannered Grecisms and Latinisms. Or he would adapt a phrase. Thus a remark Cato was said to have made to his son[32] is conflated with Hesiod's oracular advice on shipping (643),

νῆ' ὀλίγην αἰνεῖν, μεγάλη δ' ἐνὶ φορτία θέσθαι,

to produce (2. 412),

> laudato ingentia rura,
> exiguum colito.

This is just the sort of thing he had done with Theocritus in the *Eclogues*.

Hesiod's lines on making a plough (427–31) are not didactic, in the sense that they do not tell you *how* to do it. No more are Virgil's (1. 169–75). Even in Hesiod's day you *could* probably buy one: specialist craftsmen (δημιοεργοί) were already being distinguished from 'do-it-yourself' people (αὐτόγυοι). In Virgil's day you almost certainly *did* buy one: Cato had long ago been able to tell you what were the best firms in Italy for purchasing various farm-implements (135), and a plough is not one of the things listed by Varro (1. 22. 1) as capable of being made by the staff even of a large farm. But from the literary point of view the Roman Hesiod was concerned to work in enough Hesiodic matter to recall the original. Hesiod may really have believed that some days were lucky or unlucky for this operation or that (though Wilamowitz and some other scholars, partly from unwillingness to admit that anyone so sensible could also be so naïve, have denied the authenticity of the *Days*). Virgil included a corresponding passage (276–86); but although he apparently thought it worth while to switch to a later source, some Hellenistic moon-calendar,* his treatment is so perfunctory (and half of the eleven lines are devoted to a grandiose description of Hesiodic Titans and their attempt to pile Ossa on Pelion and Olympus on both), that it is clear that he attached no importance to the subject except as a reminder of Hesiod.† The final words, *nona fugae melior, contraria*

---

* F. Cumont, 'Les présages lunaires de Virgile et les selénodromia', *A.C.* (1933), pp. 259 ff. In the same way he attributes to the rustics in the *Eclogues* superstitions analogous to, but different from, those in Theocritus.

† We must not forget, however, that even Augustus was superstitious about days of the month (Suet. 92). Varro has a passage (1. 37) in which Scrofa says that for some operations you must take into account whether the moon is waxing or waning; whereupon Agrasius says he learnt such a rule from his father about sheep-shearing, and himself observes it also as to the cutting of his own hair, for fear of going bald.

furtis, are a pay-off: on the ninth a slave may abscond successfully, but at least you won't be burgled successfully.

But the main significance of Hesiod for Virgil is of a more general kind. The idea of addressing an independent small farmer who works for himself and of commending honest toil went back to him; and this, as we have seen, was fundamental to the poem.* Belief in the moral value of hard work, a conception alien to Homer, was impressed upon Hesiod by observation of his brother. The gods, he says, have put sweat in the path of ἀρετή (289–92). Idleness is a positive vice, hated by gods and men (303–11). The word ἔργον occurs in some form thirteen times within eighteen lines. Work brings property, and property brings self-respect and respect from others. Here we have the first attempt at formulating a social philosophy which consists in promoting the peasant ideal of justice and hard work to be one for all mankind. This puritan ideal became deeply ingrained in Roman, and so in much of Western, mentality (it is well illustrated in Longfellow's *The Village Blacksmith*). Virgil, like Hesiod, connects justice with hard work, as with traditional pieties and manners: in the country, he says, are

> ...patiens operum exiguoque adsueta iuventus,
> sacra deum, sanctique patres: extrema per illos
> Iustitia excedens terris vestigia fecit.

young men that can stand hard work and are used to having little, religion observed, and elders revered: Justice when she departed the earth left her last footprints among these folk.†

The rustic piety was one of the traits in Hesiod that appealed to Virgil. Unlike Lucretius, he had a sympathy with naïveté and with quaint things *antiquae laudis et artis*. But in treating of the motive for work, and the dispensation that ordained it, he went beyond him, as we shall see.

---

* E. Burck has well observed that the singular imperatives frequently used by Virgil do not occur in the other *scriptores rei rusticae*; they are a continuing reminiscence of Hesiod and his personal *rapport* with his addressee. *De Vergilii Georgicon partibus iussivis* (1926; dissertation), pp. 82 ff.

† 2. 472–4. In Hesiod it is Αἰδώς and Νέμεσις that leave the earth when the Iron Age sets in. But elsewhere he emphasises Δίκη.

The *Works and Days* is far from being a Georgic. In genus it cannot be more compactly described than as 'a didactic and admonitory medley' (Sinclair), and the most comprehensive formulation of its main theme is 'Justice and Work' (Mazon). Out of 828 lines only 235 deal with agriculture, and those almost exclusively with cereals (383–617). What it could teach Virgil was that a didactic treatise could be a vehicle for moral, religious and philosophic ideas, and at least intermittently for poetry. After Book I it is only in this general way that Hesiod influenced the *Georgics*. In emphasising this Bayet is right, whatever view we take of his theory about the composition of the poem. Even if he began with the idea of following Hesiod, Virgil soon came to realise that he was engaged on something larger and warmer, a panorama of rural life in Italy, with all its social and philosophical implications.

Aratus

The link between Hesiod and Virgil is Aratus, whose didactic poem *Phaenomena*, on the stars, with its supplement the *Diosemeiai* on weather-signs, had a remarkable history. Aratus was not an astronomer. He was what was called a 'metaphrast', a versifier of treatises; and his poem was a literary reflection of the great advances made by the Academy of Plato, whose pupil Eudoxus wrote the treatise and constructed the hemispherical *Enoptron* from which he worked. So famous did it become, that the greatest of Alexandrian astronomers, Hipparchus of the second century B.C., had to write a critical commentary on it (ironically, his only work to survive). Avienus wrote another in the fourth century A.D. Indeed innumerable commentaries were made on it, some with illustrations whose descendants are the woodcuts in sixteenth-century editions. It was studied continuously, in fact, as a scientific work until the discoveries of Copernicus and Galileo consigned it to the obscurity of classical scholars' bookshelves.

As a poem, it would probably receive from most modern readers a not much more charitable verdict than that of Quintilian (10. 1. 55): 'Aratus' subject-matter is static: it has no variety, no emotion, no human character, no speeches. But he is adequate to

the task to which he believed himself equal.' This, however, by
no means represents the general verdict of antiquity. His very
restraint, dryness and economy as well as his elegant versification
won the admiration of the Callimacheans. In a well-known epigram Callimachus himself welcomed the poem as in the manner
of Hesiod, 'Ησιόδου τό τ' ἄεισμα καὶ ὁ τρόπος,

and praised its λεπταὶ ῥήσιες.[33] The Roman Callimacheans were no
less enthusiastic. Cinna wrote an epigram for a presentation copy
written on mallow-leaves which had been brought in a small
ship from Bithynia, conceivably no other than the 'phaselus' of
Catullus 4.[34] It was presumably not as a work of science that
Cicero and Germanicus, not to mention Varro of Atax and Ovid,
were attracted to translating it; and in fact Cicero makes his
spokesman Crassus in the *De Oratore* say that the *docti* are agreed
that Aratus had written *ornatissimis et optimis versibus*.[35] Lucretius
and Manilius as well as Virgil were indebted to the poem.

Aratus was severely handicapped by trying to be both compendious and exhaustive. His set-pieces are very few, little more than
the eighteen-line Hymn to Zeus which, following Hesiod, he
composed as prelude, and the account of the three races of Gold,
Silver and Bronze (96–136). The latter is much tidier than
Hesiod's version, and a fine, eloquent stretch of poetry which
makes us regret his lost works and wish he had had his talent put
to less confining use. Occasionally he will sketch a myth, such as
that of the bears that nurtured the infant Zeus on Cretan Ida
(28–37), or of Pegasus and Hippocrene (216–24). Occasionally he
recaptures the imaginative vision of the men who first named the
constellations. Beneath Andromeda is Perseus: 'Her two feet will
guide you to her bridegroom Perseus, over whose shoulder they
are for ever carried. He, taller than the rest, moves in the North.
His right hand stretches towards the throne of his bride's mother;
and as if pursuing what lies before his feet he strides amid star-dust
in the heaven of Zeus' (248–53). There is also a fine description of
December, perhaps inspired by Hesiod (287–99).

But for the most part the poem is a catalogue. Only here and there can we detect the sort of touch that may have hinted to Virgil how he could bring the *Georgics* alive. The *Diosemeiai* is particularly sparing of ornament, but one notes among the signs of rain a passage (1104–12) that has the true Virgilian picturesqueness:

sheep warn the shepherd of storms coming when they hurry to pasture more swiftly than usual, while away from the flock now rams, now lambs, butt each other in sport by the way; or when, some here some there, they gambol, the horned ones on their hind legs, the light ones on all four feet; or when the shepherds find their flocks unwilling to be moved though it is evening when they drive them in, cropping the grass on all sides though urged on by volleys of stones.

This kind of picturesqueness, and this sympathetic interest in animals, is however more Roman than Greek. Another passage may illustrate this. Aratus remarks (946–7) that one sign of rain is 'the unfortunate race, that treat for watersnakes, the fathers of tadpoles croaking from the lake'. Cicero's version reads

> vos quoque signa videtis, aquai dulcis alumnae,
> cum clamore paratis inanes fundere voces
> absurdoque sono fontes et stagna cietis,

you too observe signs, nurselings of fresh water, when you prepare to utter hollow sounds clamorously and wake the streams and ponds with discordant noise.[36]

To this quality in Cicero Virgil may have owed hints of the kind he was adept at exploiting. Other hints seem to have come from the verse translation of Aratus by Varro of Atax quoted by Servius in his commentary.[37] But the most important thing he shared with Aratus was the concept of a divine father who had providentially ordered the universe for the benefit of mankind (see Chapter VI).

There was no poet so pedestrian that Virgil could not find something in him to borrow or transfigure. We know only too well from the extant *Theriaca* and *Alexipharmaca* what the metaphrast Nicander was like; yet Virgil imitates a passage from the former at 3. 425, and borrows a legend from him at 3. 391.[38] Further, we are told by Quintilian that his *Georgica* were 'followed' by Virgil,[39] and though we may be sceptical about the closeness we may guess that the debt extended to things beyond the mere title. Nor is it conceivable that for Book 4 he failed to draw on Nicander's poem on bee-keeping, the *Melissurgica* (possibly part of the *Georgica*). But the fact remains that the little we know of these *Georgica*—recipes, instructions for pigeon-breeding etc.— recalls Virgil neither in manner nor matter.

Lucretius

'The influence, direct and indirect, exercised by Lucretius on the thought, the composition, and the style of the *Georgics* was perhaps stronger than that ever exercised, before or since, by one great poet on the work of another.' So Sellar began his masterly chapter on this subject. It has been reckoned that one line in twelve of Virgil as a whole consciously or unconsciously echoes his great predecessor.[40] It was not his custom to name his sources directly; but his way of beginning a paragraph with 'Principio' or 'Idcirco' or 'Praeterea' is a sort of acknowledgement by imitation. Here we are only concerned with the conception of the poem. Other kinds of influence will be dealt with later.

Lucretius was in a very different tradition from the metaphrasts. Instead of undertaking any subject, however unpromising and however remote from the poet's own interests, and treating it as material for a display of artistic virtuosity, he chose one to which he was passionately committed, deriving his poetic inspiration from Empedocles rather than Hesiod. We have already considered the impact that must have been made on Virgil by the appearance of the *De Rerum Natura* when he was at his most impressionable age, and how its incidental qualities may have encouraged him in his belief that an ostensibly didactic poem could be made essentially descriptive and also charged with moral and philosophic fervour. Having relegated the gods to

the lucid interspace 'twixt world and world,

Lucretius could not resist personifying, at least in word, *rerum*

Natura creatrix, which corresponds to Venus in the exordium. She is free from divine control,

> libera continuo dominis privata superbis.[41]

In Virgil she is something more than a personification because of his Aratean belief in divine providence, of which she is vaguely conceived as either the agent or the equivalent. The *Georgics*, if not a whole *De Rerum Natura*, has at least a far wider scope than a treatise on agriculture.

Both poets detested war, 'fera moenera militiai'. Both also reacted against the hectic life of the age, and of Rome in particular. Virgil, by using the same formula, indicates that he has Lucretius in mind: his

> si non ingentem foribus domus alta superbis...

is obviously meant to recall

> si non aurea sunt iuvenum simulacra per aedes...[42]

and when Lucretius speaks by contrast of true pleasure, it is in terms of *latis otia campis*:

> cum tamen inter se prostrati in gramine molli
> propter aquae rivum sub ramis arboris altae
> non magnis opibus iucunde corpora curant,
> praesertim cum tempestas arridet, et anni
> tempora conspergunt viridantis floribus herbas.

Yet when men lie at full length together on the soft turf near a stream and under a high tree's branches, they need no great wealth to refresh themselves delightfully, especially when the weather is benign and the season scatters flowers all over the green grass.[43]

Both poets were also loud in their denunciation of civil war.

To some extent it was an attraction of opposites. Virgil's early phase of Epicureanism seems so much out of character when we look back on his life as a whole that it is natural to guess that it was only the overwhelming genius of Lucretius acting on a peculiarly receptive poetical nature that induced it. The famous antithesis,

> felix qui potuit rerum cognoscere causas...
> fortunatus et ille deos qui novit agrestes,

runs right through the *Georgics*.* The very uncompromisingness of Lucretius' intellect may have acted as a provocation to Virgil. It was good to be freed from fear of death and Orcus; but still—'there are more things in heaven and earth...' The shy provincial, conscious of his own genius, would not be overborne by the supreme self-confidence of the Roman aristocrat, however much he admired him. It has been said that 'to Aristotle to philosophise was to Platonise'. In the same way it could be said that to Virgil to write didactic poetry was to Lucretise, even if, as with Aristotle, the resultant ideas amounted to a deviation.

Varro

Something must also be said here of the impact of Varro of Reate, though as a technical influence he will be dealt with along with the other scientific authorities, where it is more appropriate.

The *De Re Rustica* has pretensions to being literature. It is a dialogue in the Ciceronian manner. And in several passages of a literary kind it would seem to have influenced Virgil. The invocation to the twelve gods at 1. 1. 5–6 no doubt suggested Virgil's invocation to his different twelve gods in his exordium, which was probably written last as exordia generally were. The eulogy of Italy at 2. 136–76 may also have been suggested by *R.R.* 1. 2. 3–8: 'Vos, qui multas perambulastis terras, ecquam cultiorem Italia vidistis?...' That the Virgilian passage is the later, by as much as seven years, is shown by lines 170–2; and it broadens into praises of much more than fertility. The introduction to *R.R.* 2 (1–3) and other passages might have suggested the Praise of Country Life at 2. 458–540. At 3. 1. 5 we read, 'Our ancestors believed that those who tilled the soil lived a pious and useful life, and that they were the only survivors of the stock of King Saturnus.'[44] One thinks immediately of

> sacra deum sanctique patres; extrema per illos
> Iustitia excedens terris vestigia fecit

---

* E. Paratore has pressed to the extreme the idea that Virgil was reacting against Lucretius, e.g. in seeing Orpheus' visit to the underworld as polemic against Lucretius' contemptuous dismissal of any belief in it (3. 978–1023): 'Spunti lucreziani nelle *Georgiche*', *A.&R.* (1939), pp. 186–93.

and of

aureus hanc vitam in terris Saturnus agebat.

A more interesting possibility is raised by the conclusion to Book 1. Stolo is talking about storage of farm-produce when he is suddenly interrupted.

While he was saying this, the sacristan's freedman came to us in tears, asking us to forgive him for keeping us and begging us to attend the funeral next day. We all sprang up and enquired with one voice, 'What? the funeral? What funeral? What has happened?' He told us through his tears that the sacristan had been knifed by someone and fallen down. He could not see in the crowd who had done it, but had only heard someone saying that a mistake had been made. He himself had picked up his old master, taken him home and sent off his slaves to get a doctor as soon as possible. It was only fair that we should forgive him for seeing to that rather than coming to us. And even though he had not been able to prevent his breathing his last not long after, he was sure he had done right. We found no fault with him, and as we came down from the temple were more grieved at the misfortunes of human life than surprised that such a thing should happen at Rome.* And so we went our ways.

This melodramatic incident can only have been introduced to point the contrast between the violence and turmoil of life in the city and the peaceful pursuits of agriculture.† Did it suggest to Virgil the great finale to his Book 1, where a similar contrast is so strikingly made by the vision of the farmer centuries later ploughing up the weapons, helmets and bones of those who fell at Philippi? One can hardly imagine that the influence was the other way round, that confronted with Virgil's apocalyptic climax Varro thought of inserting this little passage.

Other passages in Varro may have suggested descriptive flourishes in Virgil—that on the terrestrial zones of Eratosthenes (1. 233–9), briefly mentioned at *R.R.* 1. 2. 3–4; or that on the festivities connected with the sacrifice of a goat to Bacchus, both

---

* Varro was one of the fortunate ones who, though prescribed in 43, survived. His friends competed for the honour of concealing him. Calenus won; and neither his slaves nor Varro's betrayed him. (App. 4. 47.)

† Compare the odd little interlude about the arrest of a man for tampering with ballot-boxes (3. 5. 18).

in Attica and Italy (2. 380–96), which recalls one in Varro about goats being driven on to the Acropolis at Athens once a year for a sacrifice but is otherwise quite differently developed (*R.R.* 1. 2. 19–20). It may have been from reading him that Virgil perceived the effectiveness of ranging widely over the earth in examples (*G.* 1. 56–9; 2. 114–30). In a single sentence (1. 57. 2) he would find mention of Cappadocia, Thrace and Hither Spain. At 1. 7. 5–6 Scrofa tells of an evergreen plane near Gortyn in Crete and another in Cyprus reported by Theophrastus, of an evergreen oak outside Sybaris, and the figs and vines of Elephantine in Egypt that do not shed their leaves; of vines near Smyrna and apple-trees round Consentia that bear two crops a year; of alders in Epirus that grow in streams; and of methods of cultivation he had observed when commanding an army near the Rhine.

Bayet believed that it was the appearance of Varro's treatise that persuaded Virgil to enlarge his poem from a Works and Days in which, as in Hesiod, the growing of cereals was practically the only form of agriculture treated, into a full-scale Georgics; and that the orderliness of Books 2–4 after the (alleged) Hesiodic disorder of Book 1 was also due to Varro's example (see p. 56). This is all problematical. But those books at least contain sufficient evidence in technical detail to show that Virgil had studied the venerable scholar's treatise with care, selecting material, regrouping it and enhancing it to suit his artistic purpose.*

But what strikes one particularly on comparison with Varro, or still more with Columella, is what Virgil selects to treat, and how much he decides to omit.† In Book 1 he deals mainly with

---

* For a detailed study of how he did this see P. van de Woestijne, 'Varron de Réate et Virgile', *R.B.Ph.* (1931), pp. 909–29.

† It has been suggested that the unique quadripartite division stems from a eulogy of country life in Cicero, *De Sen.* 15. 54, put into the mouth of Cato (E. de Saint-Denis, 'Une source de Virgile dans les *Géorgiques*', *R.E.L.* 1938, pp. 299–317). But the words used hardly make such a division obvious: 'nec vero segetibus solum et pratis (Book 1), et vineis et arbustis res rusticae laetae sunt, sed hortis etiam et pomariis (Book 2), tum pecudum pastu (Book 3), apium examinibus, florum omnium varietate (Book 4)'. '*Prata*' are not treated in Book 1, '*horti*' can only be included in Book 2 if they are exemplified by '*pomaria*', and '*sed etiam*' cuts right across the content of Book 2. I should prefer to believe that Virgil thought of it himself.

cereals. Book 2 is nearly all devoted to the vine: there are only a few lines on the equally important olive, and other trees receive the most cursory treatment. Cattle and horses, sheep and goats are dealt with in Book 3, but there is nothing on pigs for instance, or donkeys; while of what was known as *pastio villatica*, including poultry, only bees find a place in Book 4.

> Non ego cuncta meis amplecti versibus opto.

He professes that he would have liked, had *spatia iniqua* allowed (he presumably means that he is pressed by the call to epic), to deal with gardens; but he confines himself to describing that of the old Corycian in twenty lines.[45] No doubt he did not wish his poem to be dissipated in interest through a conscientious attempt to be complete; and pigs and hens are not the most poetical of subjects. But what he dealt with must have been a matter of positive choice: these were the subjects that could be made to contribute easily and sufficiently to his grand design. More will be said of this later.

There are many other literary works that Virgil uses casually in the course of the poem, but which cannot be said to have contributed to the original conception. (Chief among them is Homer.) Far from wishing to conceal his '*furta*', he clearly wished recognition of their provenance to be a pleasure to the reader. This comes out most clearly at 1. 370 ff., where Servius tells us that he is closely following the other Varro, Atacinus, and demonstrates it by quoting seven lines (fr. 21 Morel), including the striking one borrowed entire at 377,

> aut arguta lacus circumvolitavit hirundo.

Varro of Atax was, like himself, a second-generation Neoteric, and the borrowing was no doubt intended as a compliment.*

The technical sources, among which I include Cato, will be dealt with in a later chapter.

---

* Servius also tells us that 2. 404,

> frigidus et silvis aquilo decussit honorem

was taken from his *Argonautica*. For the phrase *decussit honorem* cf. Horace, *Epode* 11. 6: *silvis honorem decutit.*

IV · *Composition and Structure*

'When Augustus was returning after his victory at Actium and was staying at Atella (in Campania) to get over a relaxed throat, Virgil read the *Georgics* to him for four days on end, Maecenas taking over whenever he had to give up through failure of his voice.' There is no reason to doubt this circumstantial information retailed by Donatus from Suetonius. It implies that the *Georgics* was finished by the summer of 29, but we could also presume as much from the epilogue, where Virgil says that at the time of writing Caesar was campaigning on the Euphrates.[1] As for Servius' and Donatus' statements that the poem was completed in seven years, we may concede to Bayet that some of Book 1 at least may have been composed earlier than 36, rather than suppose that Virgil lay fallow for two or three years after finishing the *Eclogues*.[2]

Even if we accept seven years as a maximum, this works out at an average of less than a line a day—2,188 lines in roughly 2,600 days. We are therefore justified in expecting to find in this work of a disciple of the Neoteroi any amount of subtlety and refinement. And in fact Suetonius records a tradition that he used to dictate each day a large number of lines he had composed in the morning and then spend the rest of the day in reducing them to a very small number, aptly remarking that he was like a she-bear gradually licking her offspring into shape.[3] We can hardly imagine that he composed a continuous passage which he then boiled down. The morning drafts were probably 'vers donnés' and experiments from which he selected some to shape and weld together. But we must not forget that he would also spend a considerable time in studying and comparing technical sources.

The poem is diversified by integral set-pieces. These Jackson Knight well compared with the choric odes of Greek Tragedy, 'partly giving relief and escape, and partly showing the realities of the wider world in which the action is set'.[4] We may assume that the general proem was written last: Octavian is clearly now supreme alone. The proem to Book 3 refers to the Triple Triumph of August, 29 B.C., and the Epilogue, as we have seen, is from the same year. The Praise of Italy in Book 2 dates itself from the same period (170–2). In the Praise of Country Life at the end of the same book lines 495–6,

> illum non populi fasces, non purpura regum
> flexit et infidos agitans discordia fratres,

he is not swayed by the people's fasces, nor the purple of kings and discord that harries treacherous brothers,

have been plausibly taken to refer to the quarrel between the Arsacids Tiridates and Phraates IV, which was hot news at Rome in 30, when Horace could give *quid Tiridaten terreat* as an instance of present worries;* and the next line,

> aut coniurato descendens Dacus ab Histro,

or the Dacian descending in conspiracy from the Danube,

could well refer to the accession of that people to Antony's side in 31, while *perituraque regna* could be prompted by the imminent downfall of Cleopatra's Egypt. The description of the Corycian's garden (4. 116–48) also proclaims itself as late. It does look as if, by and large, Virgil dealt with the didactic portions first and completed the set-pieces later. But that does not mean that the latter are inorganic: the ingenuity and complexity of the structure have come to be recognised more and more in recent years. For the rest, there are certain indications of development in Virgil's thought and treatment which confirm the natural supposition that in general the remaining books were composed in order.†
But that is not to say that Virgil did not have a preconceived plan, perhaps even a prose draft such as we are told he used for the *Aeneid*.[5]

The vexed question of the Aristaeus episode will be dealt with in a special chapter.

---

* *Odes* 1, 26, 5. For dating it to this time see L. P. Wilkinson, 'The Earliest Odes of Horace', *Hermes* (1956), pp. 495–9.

† On his thought, see p. 123; on his treatment, see Burck, *De Verg. Georg. partibus iussivis*, pp. 77–8.

STRUCTURE

It used to be thought that the *Georgics* consisted simply of didactic matter treated as 'poetically' as possible and relieved by set-pieces, mythological examples, similes and so forth.* Even Sellar hardly goes beyond this.[6] Conington was a step in advance in recognising the importance of *variety* in Virgil's art: 'he passes from writer to writer, the extent of his subject suggesting that variety which his poetic feeling would lead him joyfully to embrace, and he selects and abridges, instead of simply reproducing, always with a view to poetical effect'.[7]

Modern study of the question began in 1924. In that year Wilhelm Kroll devoted a few pages to deprecating the attempts of scholars to introduce logic and system on a technical level by presuming dislocations and interpolations in the text and trying to reconstitute it. He insisted that 'the poet's art showed itself not in reducing practical rules to a poetic form comprehensible to farmers, but in decking the plain framework of the technical parts with as rich a poetic architecture as possible'. And he concluded, after Conington, that the chief artistic principle at work was variety, that contrived ποικιλία which is found, for instance, in Callimachus, and which appealed to poets in the Hellenistic tradition.[8] This principle was indeed recognised by ancient critics. Thus Servius comments on *Georgics* 2. 195: 'Why does he speak of herds here, when Book 3 is allotted to animals? The answer is: for the sake of variety, to prevent his account from becoming monotonous.' It was to find notable embodiment at Rome in the *Metamorphoses* of Ovid.

But in the same year, 1924, appeared a short article by G. Ramain which contained the seeds of further development. He suggested that in his treatment of snakes as pests at 3. 414–39 Virgil was interested in the contrast between the shadow-seeking *vipera* and *coluber* and the dazzling Calabrian *anguis*, 'arduus ad solem'; at 1. 374–89, between the *aeriae grues* and the *bucula suspiciens caelum*, the flitting swallow and the frogs in the mud, the ant

* For recent history of the question of structure in the *Georgics* see Appendix I.

wearing its tiny path and the huge rainbow—the eye alternating between small and great, the ground and the sky.* He further suggested, rather fancifully, that in the Aristaeus episode the friendly, romantic world of Cyrene under the waters of Peneüs was meant to balance and contrast with the unfriendly underworld, visited by Orpheus, both only penetrable by permission of the gods; and that these represented two spiritual worlds forbidden to men.

It will be seen that what is involved here is more than variation. It is artistic principles of balance and contrast, interplay of great and small, *chiaroscuro* of light and shade, striking juxtapositions which we shall find of gaiety and grimness, humour and pathos, mythology and modernity, Italian and foreign. Such relationships have also recently been detected in the arrangement of wall-paintings of this period.[9]

Ramain's remarks on the Aristaeus episode were in sympathy with modern trends in poetry and criticism. This approach led to the finding of much more interconnection of symbolic meaning between different parts of the work, to seeing it more as an organic whole. Erich Burck, no doubt independently, was working on similar lines, and in 1929 he produced a full-scale reinterpretation, most of which can still be read with assent.† Klingner, Büchner and Otis have developed his method, and it has certainly illuminated the poem. The difficulty is to know where to stop, having regard for the small encouragement we get from classical criticism to pursue such lines, but also for the evident fact that Virgil in the *Aeneid* went far beyond any previous writer in investing his work with such qualities. Is not Klingner perhaps going *too* far when he says: 'Virgil's composition is almost in-

---

* 'Un contraste évident, et calculé: celui de la petitesse extrême et de l'extrême grandeur' (cf. S. P. Bovie, 'The imagery of ascent–descent in Vergil's *Georgics*', *A.J.Ph.* (1956), pp. 337–58). I am less impressed by Ramain's discovery of a contrast between the black rooks and the white sea- and marsh-birds, because Virgil describes the behaviour of the latter in five lines without indicating that they are in fact white.

† Except for his disregard of the Aristaeus episode, as substituted after Gallus' death. On this he has now changed his view: *Gnomon* (1959), p. 230, reviewing Richter's edition.

exhaustible, both in great and small. Every word, every sentence, every verse-group, every larger part stands in functional relationship and reciprocity, and together they compose a moving harmony which anyone must feel who has sensibility for such things'?* *Every*? Brooks Otis puts the dilemma thus:

The present problem of Virgilian critics is to preserve a safe *via media* between what can be called the obtuseness and crude literalism of most older commentary on the poem and a more recent tendency to find all manner of mystical meanings and numerical correspondences in it. Basically it makes little difference what the poet consciously intended —we cannot hope to read his mind—if we can in fact reveal what constitutes the 'true' character and meaning of his poetry. In any event, the problem is to find what is there—if symbols, for example, genuine symbols and not will-o'-the-wisps of an infatuated critic—and at all costs to avoid the reading in of purely supposititious and extrinsic meanings.†

The overall effect of the poem has been happily described in terms associated with musical composition. This idea first appeared, to my knowledge, in the number for 18 April 1914 of an American periodical called *The Churchman*, where, in an article on 'Vergil and the Country Pastor', C. P. Parker wrote: 'The work is like a symphony with four movements and various themes plainly set forth and harmoniously interwoven.'[10] (Otis designates the four books as *allegro maestoso, scherzo, adagio* and *allegro vivace*.[11]) Rand, who quotes Parker, says of Book 1: 'Virgil manages his effects with the power of a musician, conducting one and the same theme through harmonies of varying mood with an artful crescendo to a final crash.'[12] Independently (it would seem) the same idea occurred to Klingner, who character-

---

* 'Über das Lob des Landlebens in Virgils *Georgica*', *Hermes* (1931), p. 159.
† P. 147. In practice it may be felt that, though he made valuable contributions, Otis sometimes gave too free rein to his ingenuity. (See L. P. Wilkinson, review of Otis, *C.R.* (1965), pp. 182–5.) Though Virgil sometimes interestingly varies for ulterior reasons the order of the information he derives from his technical sources, he also sometimes follows them so closely that it would be surprising if all his didactic matter could be 'interpreted' or subordinated to a subtler plan. There are also passages whose introduction can still most easily be explained simply as *varietatis causa*.

ised the *Georgics* as a composition in many tones in which a number of themes develop, come to the fore, die away and make place for new ones;[13] while Büchner has called it 'a symphony in words as an image of the cosmos';[14] and Perret has said of the structure of Book 3 : 'One thinks here of one of those fugues for organ in which Bach seems to have made all the great voices of nature roar.'[15] It is significant that the elegies of Tibullus, who began to compose at about the time when Virgil published the *Georgics*, have been compared, quite independently, with symphonies. In 1930 Mauriz Schuster analysed them with this in mind and concluded: 'In Tibullus' poetic technique much reminds us of the art of musical composition, and we should not exclude the possibility that the poet, who by all tokens was naturally musical, was to some extent influenced in his technique by the artistic form built up of motifs which was already being developed at that time.'* The way in which themes are introduced is certainly a striking feature, and I shall give them compendious if sometimes inelegant names. Another feature is the way in which Virgil will casually anticipate a theme in order to bridge over a break between sections and disguise the didactic skeleton beneath.† Horace did the same to disguise as *sermo* the systematic treatise that underlies the *Epistle to the Pisones* (*Ars Poetica*).[16]

The work falls into two pairs of books, as the *De Rerum Natura* falls into three; and, as in Lucretius, each pair has an extensive 'external' proem dealing with matter extraneous to the main didactic body, the Second and Fourth Books having only a short 'internal' proem. The proem to Book 1 introduces the work as a whole, and there is a short epilogue at the end of Book 4. The First and Third Books emphasise hard work, are generally sombre in tone, and end with a catastrophe; whereas the Second and

---

* *Tibull-Studien*, pp. 57–61. He speaks of 'Motivwiederholungen und thematische Verknüpfung', and makes comparisons with Mesomedes' hymns to the Sun and to Nemesis of Hadrian's time, which survive with musical accompaniment; also with the 'Anonymus Bellermanni'.

† Cicero had been similarly at pains to conceal the handbook that was the basis of his dialogue *De Oratore*. W. Kroll, 'Ciceros Schrift *De Oratore*', *Rh.M.* (1903), pp. 552–97.

Fourth deal by contrast with work that is easier, are gay and lively in tone, and end happily. But of course Virgil is too good an artist to make these contrasts absolute; and though Book 4 is rounded off 'happily' in a few lines, what echoes in the memory is 'Eurydicen, a miseram Eurydicen'.

Tabular schemes are useful but unreadable. I shall try to unfold continuously the structure of the poem in such a way as to provide incidentally a reminder of its contents, and shall confine to headings the line-references to what seem identifiable as sections. And as far as is consistent with readability and intelligibility I shall leave comment on philosophic and religious ideas, politics, poetic art, technical sources and rural lore to later chapters, so as not to blur the outline unnecessarily. I am aware that division into compartments, which seems inevitable for exposition, breaks up the panoramic effect; but that can be recaptured by rereading the poem.

BOOK I. FIELD CROPS

1–42. *Proem to the whole work*

Virgil begins with a business-like and neatly economical summary of the contents of the four books, addressed to Maecenas. This takes four and a half lines. Then comes the first of the many surprise contrasts he has in store, something new that starts, with a form of idea-enjambement he cultivates, in the middle of a line: the style changes to the *magnum os* or *os rotundum*, with long vowels that resound the more impressively after the brisk tonelessness of *hinc căněr(e) ǐncǐpǐăm*:

> vos, o clarissima mundi
> lumina, labentem caelo quae ducitis annum...

He has turned from his mortal friend and patron to invoke, first twelve divinities of the countryside, then Caesar Octavian as the thirteenth. The two parts are almost equally balanced ($18\frac{1}{2}$ lines and 19), and they form together probably the longest period in the whole of Latin poetry.[17] This is quite unlike Virgil's normal style: he rarely exceeds the sentence-length of four hexameters

prescribed by the orators as a norm for what could be comfort-
ably managed in one breath and grasped by the hearer.[18] He
wants, in fact, to remind us of the headlong, enthusiastic, anaco-
luthic exordium of Lucretius, whom he also recalls more explicitly
with the line (41),

> ignarosque viae mecum miseratus agrestis,

and pitying with me the rustics that do not know the way.[19]

Two invocatory verbs serve for the whole period, *adsis* at 18 and
ingredere at 42.[20]

43–203. Part I. Field crops: hard work

43–70. Ploughing

This is the most Hesiodic part of the work, though there are
strong echoes of Lucretius in the opening lines.* Hesiod begins
the agricultural part of the *Works and Days* with a line denoting
the opening of the farmer's year (458),

> Πληιάδων ᾽Ατληγενέων ἐπιτελλομενάων,

and Virgil follows suit:

> vere novo, gelidus canis cum montibus umor
> liquitur...

In early spring, when the frozen moisture melts on the white mountains...

Spring will prove to be a specially recurrent theme. *Mihi* in 45
picks up *mecum* in 41: the poet identifies himself with the farmer.
The Hard Work Theme has emerged at once (though here it is
the ox, not *vis humana* as in Lucretius, that is represented, untruly,
as groaning at the plough), the farmer being exhorted to get going
early (*iam tum*) and let his land feel both sun and cold twice.†
Presumably the reference is to land already cultivated, as we
should expect. But at 50 we glide (*ignotum* is the slip-word) into
another theme. If the land is unknown to you, you must study the

---

* 45–6; cf. Lucr. 5. 209 ff.
† For the interpretation of this passage see pp. 227–8.

climate and soil of the locality. The scope has already widened here to contemplate crops other than cereals within your own country, and now it widens again into the Foreign Lands Theme (cf. p. 67), the characteristic products of distant countries (not necessarily even agricultural ones):

> nonne vides, croceos ut Tmolus odores,
> India mittit ebur, molles sua tura Sabaei,
> at Chalybes nudi ferrum, virosaque Pontus
> castorea, Eliadum palmas Epirus equarum?

Look how Tmolus sends us fragrant saffron, India ivory, the soft Sabaeans their incense, while the naked Chalybes send iron, Pontus pungent castor, Epirus mares that win Olympic palms.

(Horses victorious at Olympia are another recurrent theme.) These differences are the result of eternal laws imposed by nature from primeval times, when Deucalion cast stones over the empty earth whence sprang men, a hard race: *ergo age*...With this characteristic use of mythology (a reminiscence of a conceit in Lucretius*) Virgil leads us back to his initial theme: hardy men should start work with toiling oxen right at the beginning of spring. The reservation is now added that this applies only to *pingue solum*: poorer soil should be lightly turned up in autumn, otherwise it may lose such moisture as it has.

In this 28-line section we can observe already much of Virgil's method of composition. A theme is given out, in vivid pictorial terms. A pleasing variation then develops by easy thought-transitions until we find we have come full circle.† Four precepts are here involved: plough rich soil early and deeply, plough it more than once, study climate and soil before deciding how to use new land, and with poor soil turn it up lightly in autumn. What we have really been given, however, is poetry.

71-117. *Improving land*

Mention of poor land leads naturally to ways of increasing yield. Fields can recuperate either by being left fallow or by alternation

---

* 5.926; but it goes back to Pindar (O. 9. 45–6): λίθινον γόνον, λαοὶ δ' ὀνύμασθεν.
† 'Ring-composition', as it is called—a favourite Hellenistic device.

of crops. They can be improved by manuring, by scattering ash, by burning (whatever the chemical reason), by breaking up clods, by reploughing, and also by prayer for dry winters and wet summers, the idea of which leads naturally to irrigation and drainage as correctives. In the course of this passage the Foreign Lands Theme is heard again (102–3):

> nullo tantum se Mysia cultu
> iactat et ipsa suas mirantur Gargara messis,

nothing makes Mysia so proud of its husbandry or Gargara so amazed at its own crops [as a dry winter].

And two other themes have emerged. The first is that of Religion, in the idea that 'god helps them that help themselves' (95–6),

> neque illum
> flava Ceres alto nequiquam spectat Olympo,

nor does yellow Ceres look idly upon him from Olympus on high.

This, already grounded in the invocation to the Twelve Gods, is picked up again in *orate* (100), which serves incidentally to vary the series of practical precepts by introducing a fact of nature that motivates two more. The second is the Military Theme, which appears in 99,

> exercetque frequens tellurem atque imperat arvis,

keeps at his post exercising the earth, and commands his fields.

Frequens is a military term, and the metaphor is picked up again at 104–5,

> iacto qui semine comminus arva
> insequitur,

after throwing the seed grapples with the land.*

118–59. *Struggle against enemies (and Theodicy)*
But however hard you work, however experienced you are, you still have to cope with injurious birds and plants. And here again,

---

* *Frequens: ut miles apud signa:* Cic. *Verr.* 5. 33; cf. Sall. *Cat.* 18. *Terra quae nunquam recusat imperium:* Cic. *De Sen.* 51. *Iacto:* after throwing his spear the legionary ran in and fought hand to hand (Keightley).

at 121, a major topic is introduced in mid-line. The Father himself
has willed that the way of agriculture should not be easy, and sent
all kinds of troubles upon men (by contrast with the idle ease of
the Golden Age), so as to sharpen their wits by cares. The troubles
instanced are not all argicultural, for this is a Theodicy, a justification of the ways of god to men as a whole, which is found in the
spurring of his intelligence and resultant development of the crafts
and arts. At 147 we return to the theme of the Golden Age: upon
its cessation Ceres instituted ploughing, and it was not long before
weeds invaded, leafy shades encroached, and birds had to be
scared away. So in this section too we have come full circle, for
certain weeds and birds, and also shade, were mentioned as banes
at the beginning (119–21). There are also echoes of previous
sections: *subigebant arva* ('subdue') in 125 recalls *imperat arvis* in
99, *insectabere* ('harry') in 155 the *insequitur* in 105; *votisque voca-
veris imbrem* at 157 recalls the injunction at 100 to pray for suitable
weather; while 158

> heu magnum alterius frustra spectabis acervum,

alas you will gaze helplessly at another's great store,

is the observe of 49,

> illius immensae ruperunt horrea messes,

its huge harvests burst his barns.

The last line,

> concussaque famem in silvis solabere quercu,

and shall solace your hunger in the woods by shaking an oak,

picks up the reference to the acorns men proverbially ate in
primitive times at 148, which itself recalls line 8 of the proem—so
carefully and minutely woven is the texture of this poem. But the
heart of this section, arising quite naturally from the agricultural
subject, is the Theodicy, not merely giving relief from didactic
precepts, but providing thus early in the poem a religious-
philosophical mainspring which affects it through and through.
This will be dealt with later (pp. 135–43).

160–203. Arms and devices for the incessant struggle

In his struggle to discipline his land and fight its enemies the hardy farmer needs weapons (tools were ὅπλα to Greeks, but first here *arma* to Romans):

> dicendum et quae sint duris agrestibus arma.

The continued metaphor introduces a section on implements, shorter than the corresponding ones in the handbooks, in which pride of place, first and last, is given to the plough, a reminder of Hesiod. The Religion Theme re-emerges: the homely farm chattels are transfigured into Eleusinian cult-instruments, *Eleusinae matris volventia plaustra, virgea Celei supellex, mystica vannus Iacchi*; and the promise held out to the agricultural initiate is *divini gloria ruris*. As the farmer was to be ready to plough *iam nunc* at the first signs of spring, so he must have his implements ready long before, *multo ante memor*.

How to make a plough leads on to how to make a threshing-floor. (Virgil apologises first for retailing *veterum praecepta* about humble tasks. But these, we recall, are testimony to man's inventive wit, sharpened as Jupiter designed.) Provision must be made for concreting, as protection against the burrowing of small animals; so these pests (before we heard only of birds) are brought in, and extend from crumblers of concrete to predators of great grain-heaps. How do you know if the grain-heap will be great? Watch the first almond-blossom. (We have here the first instance of the Prognostics Theme.) If there is abundance only of leaves on it,

> nequiquam pinguis palea teret area culmos,

the floor will thresh to no purpose ears rich only in chaff.

The thought of disappointing ears leads naturally to that of disappointing seeds. They may have been treated chemically, they may have been carefully selected, yet there will be degeneration unless every year you pick out the largest by hand; for all things have a natural tendency to degenerate. Detailed experience has merged in this philosophic generalisation; and the constant struggle that has been the main theme of this Part is summed up in the famous simile of the man rowing against the stream, unable for a moment to relax. The train of thought-association has been continuous throughout, hardly a line intrusive.

204–350. Part II. The farmer's calendar

204–58. Heavenly bodies given us as signs

Praeterea... With a word used by Lucretius when introducing an *additional argument* Virgil slurs over the transition to his main part, which is still in Hesiodic style, the μηνολόγιον or almanack. Further instructions about jobs concerning crops provide a more genuine carry-over.[21] Constellations must be observed by the farmer as much as by those

> quibus in patriam ventosa per aequora vectis
> Pontus et ostriferi fauces temptantur Abydi,

who, borne homeward over windy seas, brave the Euxine and the narrows of oyster-bearing Abydos.

Here the Foreign Lands Theme blends with one that appears for the first time, Seafaring (a major concern of Aratus). Of course the Italian farmer would in plain fact consult his calendar (see p. 57); but the stars had fired the imagination of man from Homer's Shield of Achilles onwards. Splendid, strongly alliterative, lines relieve what might have been a tedious catalogue:

> candidus auratis aperit cum cornibus annum
> Taurus et adverso cedens Canis occidit astro,

when the bright Bull with his gilded horns opens the year, and the Dog, yielding before his confronting star, goes down.

Like Aratus, Virgil plays with the idea of the creatures whose likeness primitive man saw in the constellations, with a glance (as Keightley pointed out) at the white bulls with gilded horns which led triumphal processions at Rome. We shall glimpse those bulls again, the *maxima taurus victima* in the Praises of Italy (2. 146–7), embodying once more the Religion Theme.

> ante tibi Eoae Atlantides abscondantur
> Cnosiaque ardentis decedat stella Coronae...

let the daughters of Atlas (Pleiads) first fade from your gaze at dawn, and the Cnosian constellation of the fiery Crown set at evening...[22]

> haud obscura cadens mittet tibi signa Bootes,

Bootes as he sets will send clear signs to you.

The idea that the stars signal to individual man, *tibi*, leads into the description (from Eratosthenes) of the five zones of the earth and the twelve signs of the zodiac through which the sun passes in his yearly course. Again a Lucretian link-word is invested with special meaning. It was for this purpose, *idcirco*, that the cosmos was so ordered. The theme of Providence thus emerges. The point is made explicit at 252. It is because of this that we can foretell storms and know when to reap and sow, and when to put to sea, so the Prognostics Theme is kept in view. And with these references to seafaring, reaping and sowing we have come back to the subjects with which the section began at 204 ff.

259–310. *Odd jobs. Waste no time, even in winter*

The last line referred to observing the four seasons. This gives a somewhat artificial lead into the next section, which begins by suggesting how to put wintry nights of rain to good use indoors. The farmer cannot afford to waste any time. Some things can lawfully be done even on religious festivals.* More positively, the moon has ordained various days of the month as lucky or unlucky for various operations. Virgil devotes only eleven lines to the superstitions of Hesiod's *Days* (see p. 58), after which we return to what can be done at night, this time not necessarily indoors.

---

* This section was clearly suggested by Cato 2. 3–4.

    Dies fasti et nefasti played a great part at Rome. There were 109 whole and 11 half holidays in the year, but only public work was forbidden on these, private rest-days being confined to *feriae publicae*. See further Richter's note on 268 ff.

Again the emphasis is on winter (we have heard before about the tasks of the other seasons),* but the times of year are mixed, till the line

> nudus ara, sere nudus: hiems ignava colono,

strip to plough, strip to sow: it is winter that brings the farmer leisure,

introduces, after all this multifarious and incessant work, the relief of the winter convivialities—but not without a further warning, at 305 ff., that there is still plenty to do, some of it, such as hunting, enjoyable enough. This section is more miscellaneous and Hesiodic than anything we have had so far; but its overall effect is to reinforce the message of the Book as a whole: work must be incessant—ἔργον ἐπ' ἔργῳ ἐργάζεσθαι.

311–50. *Transition. A storm*

The set-piece that follows belongs to Part II (*sidera* in 311 harks back to 204) but is essentially transitional. Why tell of the stars that herald the storms of autumn, or the downpours of spring? Even at harvest-time—and then follows the description of an unseasonable and devastating storm, a *tour de force.* Two morals are drawn. The first is, *caeli mensis et sidera serva,* looking back to the almanack but also forward to the weather-signs of the next Part. The second is *in primis venerare deos,* the most explicit expression of the Religion Theme, the description of the serene and sunny festivals of Ceres contrasting with the dark storm that has just cleared away.

351–463. *Part III. The Weather-Signs*

351–92. *Bad weather;* 393–423. *Good weather;* 424–63. *Moon and Sun*

We have already been told that the cosmos was so ordered as to provide an almanack for observant man, and that he must watch the stars if he is not to be caught unawares by the weather. We are now told more explicitly that 'ipse Pater' established weather-signs for the benefit of man (the Providence Theme). So begins

---

* I do not however think that the order of the seasons plays any significant part in the ordering of this Book.

the third main Part, based on the *Diosemeiae* of Aratus. The Sea-faring Theme is soon heard (at 360–4 and again at 372–3, 429, 436–7 and 456–7),* and mythology, in the reference to Nisus and Scylla, at least adds variety. Not that this Part needs relief: Virgil's pictorial skill and expressive use of language is nowhere more in evidence than in his elaboration of the generally un-adorned information given by Aratus. Signs of bad weather (351–92) are followed by signs of good, negative and positive (393–423). Finally, inverting Aratus' order for his own purposes, Virgil comes to the signs given by the Moon and Sun (*Luna...si...si...sin...Sol quoque...signa dabit...* returning at the end to *Sol tibi signa dabit*); and so, in mid-line, to his finale, the portents given by the Sun after Julius Caesar's murder.

463–514. *Finale: portents of Rome's disaster and prayer for redemption*

At 469 begins the recital of portents, other than of the Sun, which followed Caesar's murder, and 489 (*ergo*) identifies the disaster that followed, Philippi. Praying that Octavian may be spared to redeem the state, Virgil enlarges again on its troubles, linking them with his main subject by

> non ullus aratro
> dignus honos, squalent abductis arva colonis,
> et curvae rigidum falces conflantur in ensem,

no due honour is paid to the plough, the fields bereft of cultivators go unkempt, and curved sickles are smelted into the stubborn sword;

and the Book ends with a simile that is parallel to that which ended the first Part, of the man struggling in the boat and always in danger of being swept away:

> ut cum carceribus sese effudere quadrigae
> addunt in spatia, et frustra retinacula tendens
> fertur equis auriga neque audit currus habenas,

as, when chariots have poured out of the starting-boxes, they gather pace from lap to lap, and the driver, tugging in vain at the reins, is carried away by the horses, and the car pays no heed to controls.

---

* Prognostic literature often refers to the sea. It stems originally from the Ναυτικὴ Ἀστρολογία of Thales.

BOOK 2. TREES: THE VINE

1–8. *Proem: invocation to Bacchus*

To turn from the end of Book 1 to the beginning of Book 2 is like waking up from a nightmare on a fine morning. Though the professed subject is to be trees in general, it is Bacchus who is addressed, and rightly. Although all trees were his care, the vine was particularly so; and the vine is to occupy pride of place, partly because this is to be a joyous Book, and partly because it needs much more attention than the olive and other trees. In energetic and lyrical verse Virgil invokes him:

> huc, pater o Lenaee, veni, nudataque musto
> tinge novo mecum dereptis crura coturnis,

come hither, Father, Lord of the wine-press, snatch off your buskins and plunge your bare feet with me into the new wine-must.

39–46. *Invocation to Maecenas*

Having enlisted our enthusiasm, Virgil presses straight to his subject, and is well under way before he turns (39) to address Maecenas, as he does in every Book. (Lucretius had set a precedent for such deferment as regards Memmius, for example at 2.66; and in any case it might have seemed inappropriate to address the patron immediately after the god.) He appeals to him, as to Octavian in the previous proem, for co-operative attention, with an assurance that no attempt will be made at exhaustiveness.

9–258. *Part I. Variety, especially as to trees*

9–82. *Methods of propagation*

> Principio arboribus *varia* est natura creandis.

Burck was surely right in diagnosing enthusiasm for variety as the spirit that pervades and distinguishes the first main Part of this Book.* Nine methods of tree-propagation are first enumerated,

---

* I have divided this Book into two main Parts, 9–258, 259–457 (with a finale 458–542). Richter, with as much validity perhaps, divides it into three: namely 9–176: Variety in the production of trees; 177–345: Nature and testing

three natural and six artificial. There is something numinous, we are made to feel, about wild trees. They are a direct gift of the gods—'*Iovi* quae maxima frondet aesculus', 'habitae Grais *oracula* quercus', '*Parnasia* laurus', and the section issues in 'nemorumque *sacrorum*'. With cultivated trees our eye becomes focused on man —'hic', 'hic', 'putator'; but the planter who has eyes to see is promised spiritual as well as material satisfaction:

> iuvat Ismara Baccho
> conserere atque olea magnum vestire Taburnum,

it is a joy to plant Ismarus over with vines and clothe great Taburnus with olives.

Ismarus is in Thrace, Taburnus in Campania; and we may note here a penchant of Virgil, found also in Horace, for coupling mention of Greek places known to Romans mainly from their reading with Italian ones they might know at first hand. The Greek world was a romantic world of mythology (Ismarus was of old associated with Dionysus). In the later books of Ovid's *Metamorphoses* we can sense the pleasure a Roman reader would feel as that world merges into the world of Italian history and contemporary experience. This we may call the Greece–Italy Theme.

After the interlude of the second proem we are given comments on the aforesaid methods of propagation, with some instructions broadening out into a fourteen-line disquisition on grafting. Echoes of Book I may be heard in the *degenerant* of 59, a warning about the fruit of trees grown from seed, and still more in the hammering rhythm of 61–2,

> scilicet omnibus est labor impendendus, et omnes
> cogendae in sulcum ac multa mercede domandae,

to be sure hard work must be put into all, and all must be forced into the trench and disciplined at great expense of labour.

But the tempo is brisk and enthusiasm predominates.

of soil and planting; 346–457: Work for the growth and protection of the plants. Virgil's divisions are not exclusive: it seems to be an objective of his art that they should not be, at least in the first two Books.

83–108. *Variety of trees, especially vines*

From variety in propagation we pass to variety (*genus haud unum*) of trees, and in particular of vines, and so to a discriminating wine-catalogue in which Italian vintages vie with Greek. But all lands cannot produce everything (as was to happen in the Golden Age of the Eclogue, 4. 39). It depends on the soil and geographical conditions. With *aspice* at 114 we pick up again the Foreign Lands Theme that was introduced by *nonne vides* at 1.56. The horizon widens and the imagination ranges beyond the Greek world to the Arabs and Geloni, India with its ebony, the Sabaei with their incense, the tree-cotton of the Ethiopians and silk of the Chinese, the great trees of further India and the lemons of Media (as yet ungrown in Italy), upon which Virgil dilates, as he likes to do upon the later members of a list that might otherwise pall.

109–76. *Variety of lands; Italy the ideal*

But whatever any individual land may produce, there is no land like Italy. From Media rich in groves, the beautiful Ganges, the Hermus turbid with gold and all the fabled wealth of the Orient we are brought back to the ideal land of perpetual spring, of which those wines were a foretaste. Varro has an almost lyrical passage near the beginning of his *De Re Rustica* (1. 2. 6) in praise of Italy, and there is also one in the contemporary Dionysius of Halicarnassus (*Ant. Rom.* 1. 36–7) and in Strabo (6. 4. 1). What we have here is a splendid rhetorical set-piece, which ranges far beyond the sphere of agriculture, and sometimes beyond the sphere of sober truth. Italy is the *Saturnia tellus*, the embodiment of the blessings of the Golden Age. The driving necessity of Jupiter's régime— *duris urgens in rebus egestas*—and the gloomy landscape of the end of Book 1—*squalent abductis arva colonis*—are now out of mind, partly perhaps because this passage, written in 30 B.C. (169–70), reflects a time when recovery had begun to set in, but more because the spirit of this contrasting Book calls for a crescendo here in a major key. The political aspects of the passage will be discussed later (pp. 159–62).

177–258. Variety of soils and their uses

From the heights Virgil descends abruptly to technical details, as is his way. This is more effective than any gradual descent. We come now to *arvorum ingenia*, the various terrains, a subject to which lines 110–13 have already prepared a bridge. There are opportunities here for miniature landscapes. Some are general; others are particular glimpses of regions that the poet knew especially well, Mantua or Tarentum or Campania. For we are still in Italy, and these are illustrations of the land which has just been praised in general terms. Once also, when vines are concerned, the Religion Theme emerges again, as it did with those sacrificial white bulls (192–4):

> hic laticis, qualem pateris libamus et auro,
> inflavit cum pinguis ebur Tyrrhenus ad aras,
> lancibus et pandis fumantia reddimus exta,

this [*sc.* land] provides the liquor for the libations we pour from golden cups when the stout Etruscan blows his ivory pipe beside the altar and on expansive dishes we offer up the steaming entrails.

Virgil next describes, with admirable clarity and economy, three experiments for testing the nature of soils to see what they are fitted for, adding some further clues that depend on observation.

259–457. Part II. Care of trees, especially vines

259–345. Places, methods and times for planting (and Laus Veris)

The series of detailed instructions to which Virgil felt able to devote himself under the impetus imparted by the Praises of Italy is carried on through the next Part—which is not to say that dullness supervenes, thanks to the way in which he takes his chances. The method of planting vines on a hillside is admirably paralleled in the simile of a legion drawn up for battle (279–83), the fullest development we have had yet of the Military Theme; and the simple statement that trees, unlike vines, should be planted deep prompts a fine description of an oak (291–7). An unusually miscellaneous spate of short precepts issues suddenly in a warning description of a plantation-fire (303–11), which is a counterpart to the stormy disasters of 1. 316–34. The injunction to plant in spring (or else early autumn) prompts the only extended set-piece (322–42) in this 200-line stretch, a glorification of spring, which recalls and amplifies the opening lines 1. 43 ff.—*vere novo...*—and the *ver assiduum* of the *Saturnia tellus* that enjoys the blessings of the Golden Age, not without a backward glance at 340–1 to the *durum genus* of 1. 63, which sprang up when the world was young,

> virumque
> terrea progenies duris caput extulit arvis,

and the earthy race of men raised its head in the hard fields.

All in all, it may be said that even in this section the pictorial element transcends the didactic.

346–419. *Care of vines*

Again Virgil descends from poetic heights abruptly to the plainest realism, in this case beginning with manure (346). We are now to hear of the *care* of trees, in the first place of vines. The Military Theme is heard again at 369:

> tum denique dura
> exerce imperia et ramos compesce fluentis,

then is the time to exercise severe command and discipline the straggling branches.

We hear of animal enemies again, larger ones than those of 1. 119–20 and 181–6; among which the goat, by way of an *aition* for his sacrifice to Bacchus, gives an opportunity for a description of the Compitalia, an extension of the Religion Theme which forms a counterpart to the rites of Ceres at 1. 343–50.

Besides animal pests there are numerous other cares involved in tending the vine, and the next twenty lines continue the Hard Work Theme more emphatically. The labour is inexhaustible, the soil must be ploughed up three and even four times a year, and the clods 'eternally' broken up with the back of a mattock:

> redit agricolis labor actus in orbem,
> atque in se sua per vestigia volvitur annus,

the farmer's toil returns forced in a circle and his year treads round in its own tracks.

Even when the vine-leaves have fallen the keen cultivator will be thinking of next year, giving his vines no rest (*persequitur*, like *insequitur* and *insectabere* in Book I). Like the plougher at I. 64, he must start early, ambitious to be first in the field at every operation, last only in gathering. Twice a year the overshadowing trees must be cut back, twice the weeds cleared: *durus uterque labor*. Even when all is done and the last vinedresser celebrates (*canit*) the finishing of his rows, there is still work to be done on the soil and precautions to be taken against damage to the ripened grapes by storms. *Metuendus Iuppiter*: the naming of the god for the weather is a reminder of his dispensation that man must learn skill in the sweat of his brow.

420–57. *Other trees*

Though most of this Book deals with easy and happy collaboration between man and nature, it would be dishonest, and would belie the initial theodicy, if Virgil had belittled the labour involved in viticulture; and he emphasises it here because he is about to turn to trees that require less care (and correspondingly brief treatment): once trouble to plant and rear them and they repay abundantly,

> et dubitant homines serere atque impendere curam?

and do men still hesitate to plant and spend care?

Again, as with Ismarus and Taburnus, he expresses the pleasure of looking at tree-clad mountain-sides, both in Italy and in foreign lands:

> et iuvat undantem buxo spectare Cytorum
> Naryciaeque picis lucos, iuvat arva videre
> non rastris, hominum non ulli obnoxia curae,

and it is a joy to contemplate Cytorus asurge with box-trees and the firwoods of Narycus, a joy also to see fields indebted to no drag-hoes or human care.

Cytorus is in Bithynia, and from reading Catullus he would picture it as *buxifer*; Narycus is in the toe of Italy. From still further prospects of the forests of Caucasus and the yew-trees of Lebanon we are brought back again to the alders that as dugouts are launched on the Po in his own native region. The poem has recovered its carefree enthusiasm for the variety of useful things that are either supplied by nature's bounty or devised by the ingenuity of man.

458–542. Finale. Praises of country life

The finale is another major set-piece, the Praises of Country Life.[23] I shall treat it more fully in another context (pp. 143–5); here I need only indicate its place in the structure of the poem. It is in a way the kernel, the poet's justification for writing his poem at all. Despite all the hardships which he has honestly and faithfully depicted, the men of the country,

> patiens operum exiguoque adsueta iuventus,

a youth prepared to work and inured to simplicity,

can be supremely happy if only they realise their advantages. What have been no more than casual hints in the poem so far—the favour of *flava Ceres*, the *divini gloria ruris*, *genial* winter with its pursuits, Bacchus at the wine-vats, the rustic festivals of Ceres and Bacchus, the thrill of spring, the joy of contemplating orderly plantation of trees, the vine-dresser singing as he completes his rows—all these hints are now gathered up in a rhapsody on the happiness of rural life, balancing the Praises of Italy in the middle of the Book (the Golden Age life in the Golden Age country), and contrasting with the gloomy finale to Book 1, a connection pointed by the almost complete repetition of a line (1. 494; 2. 513),

> agricola incurvo terram dimovit aratro.

This is the true 'dolce vita', not the hectic mirage pursued by worldly men in cities; and to avoid the ambitious cares of riches or of politics is no less a necessity for individual happiness than to abolish the fear of death and the underworld. The gods of the country, Pan, Silvanus and the Nymphs (494), recall the proem to the whole work, as the bowl filled with wine and libation to Bacchus (528-9) recall the proem to this Book. To relieve its length the finale is presented as a triple contrast: between city luxury (460-6) and country sufficiency (467-74); between scientific philosophy (475-82, 490-2) and knowing the gods of the country (483-9; 493-502); and between worldly ambition (503-12) and innocent country pursuits (513-40).

The first pair of Books is now a rounded and complete whole, in which troubles and rewards are fairly merged in a synthesis that is its own justification.

BOOK 3. ANIMALS

The Third Book is divided into two roughly equal parts. So far from there being any attempt here to conceal the division, the Second Part has a short prologue of its own (284-94). The First deals with horses and cattle, the Second with sheep and goats. Why this selection from the varieties dealt with in Varro's Second Book? Why no mules, pigs, asses or dogs? The first answer may be given in Virgil's own words:

> non ego cuncta meis amplecti versibus opto.

His poem would have become too crowded to be significant if he had tried to be exhaustive. But why these particular animals? The horse was not really a farm animal in Italy. As Varro says, it was used for military service, for hauling, for breeding and for racing (2. 15). And on farms even hauling was largely done by oxen. The further answer must be that Virgil was writing a poem with larger meanings. The horse had a significance for men which the ass could hardly claim. Nor was there much to be said about mules, however important they were, that could not more worthily be conveyed in the treatment of horses. And if it is possible for a Virgil to add *honor* to things so *angustae* as sheep and goats, yet even he might be pardoned for feeling that pigs were peculiarly unpoetic: compare the notorious apostrophe of the English didactic poet Grainger,

'Now, Muse, let's sing of rats.'[24]

But first there is an external proem, corresponding in position and length to that of Book 1, which will likewise concern us most when we come to deal with Caesar.

1–48. *Proem*

Virgil begins with two lines of invocation to the gods of herd and flock, one Italian and two Greek—Pales, Apollo Nomios and Pan. He then suddenly turns aside to proclaim that mythological subjects are outworn: he will rather seek glory in the Ennian tradition by composing an epic in honour of Caesar.* Meanwhile he assures Maecenas that he will complete the *Georgics*, with an enthusiasm for his 'untrodden glades' expressed symbolically in terms of hunting over mountains which have also romantic associations with Bacchic excitement, Cithaeron and Taÿgetus—'symbolically', because hounds have in fact hardly any part in this Book, though the horses of Epidaurus have:

> en age segnis
> rumpe moras; vocat ingenti clamore Cithaeron
> Taygetique canes domitrixque Epidaurus equorum,
> et vox adsensu nemorum ingeminata remugit,

up, then, and break through delays; Cithaeron is calling loudly, and the hounds of Taÿgetus, and Epidaurus trainer of horses, and all the woods conspire to re-echo the sound.

49–283. *Part I. Horses and cattle*

49–122. *Selection of parents*

Seu quis Olympiacae... The opening would be wholly abrupt had not the races of Olympia been part of the symbolism in the proem. Virgil begins by emphasising the importance of selection for breeding horses and cattle; and he proceeds to describe the points to be sought in a brood-cow. Mating should take place in youth

---

* For further discussion of this proem see pp. 165–72 and Appendix III.

(60 ff.), an injunction expressed in terms of human marriage which prompts the reflection in 66–8, the lines that so deeply moved Dr Johnson :[25]

> optima quaeque dies miseris mortalibus aevi
> prima fugit: subeunt morbi tristisque senectus
> et labor, et durae rapit inclementia mortis,

all the best days of life for wretched mortal creatures are the earliest and soon vanish; on come diseases and gloomy age and suffering, till merciless death carries us off.

Man and beast are not distinguished. Love and death are dominant themes in this Book, and between them come disease and age. We return to the mood of Book I. The emphasis on annual screening to maintain the quality of the stock (69–71) harks back to that on selecting the largest seeds every year (I. 197–9), which likewise occurred in the context of the ceaseless struggle against the inherent tendency of nature to degeneration. Hard work is once more the keynote—*ante veni* (71), *iam inde a teneris impende laborem* (74), *instant sub tempus et omnis impendunt curas* (123–4).

Turning to horses, Virgil deals in a section of exactly equal length with the choosing of sires. Where in the previous section there were six concluding lines of reflection, here there are six of mythological parallels. It will be noticed that he has dealt only with dams in the case of cattle, only with sires in the case of horses (despite *praecipue matrum*, 51). Nothing could indicate more clearly his adherence to poetic selectivity. Throughout the first Part of this Book the two animals either alternate or are dealt with together, as the poem requires. The schematisation of the chief source, Varro, is deliberately avoided, and instead we have contrasts such as Virgil delights in, between the mettlesome thoroughbred horse and the shambling serviceable cow—*argutum caput* and *turpe caput*.

Age and health are not the only factors in choosing stallions. Pedigree counts, and also spirit (*animus*), already stressed at 77–85, which is revealed in competition. This gives an opportunity for twofold elaboration. (In this Book Virgil tends to paint with a broader brush: instead of creating an overall impression by a mass of detail, he maintains interest by a varied succession of fuller descriptions.) First we have an energetic account based on Homer (who is often in mind in this Book) of a chariot race (103–12). Then we hear of the legendary equestrian *inventores*, Erichthonius the first to yoke the four-horsed chariot and win with it, the Lapiths who first learnt to ride (113–17). The last three lines of this section pick up, with *ille*, the first two, though the sequence of thought has been so widely interrupted that some have wished to transfer 120–2 to follow immediately on 95–6: 'Even him (the ideal sire just sketched), when he weakens through attack of disease or sluggishness of years, you must shut up indoors, showing no mercy to his age's shame...even though often he has turned enemies to flight, and claims Epirus and strong Mycenae for his provenance, and Neptune for originator of his stock.' But the circular form of section-structure is so characteristic, as we have seen, of Virgil's style that we should be chary of tampering. The themes of Disease and Age, first introduced at 67, are heard more loudly here with the poignancy of the actual case.

123–56. *Care of parents*

After the selection of sires comes their treatment before mating, and also that of the dams, who must be kept thin by exercise, and only pampered later when pregnant. Once more, Virgil gives a series of short directions, elaborating only the last (in this case the havoc caused by the gadfly, from which the herd must be protected).

157–208. *Rearing of young cattle* (157–78), *horses* (179–208)

Birth accomplished, care is diverted to rearing and training the young. Calves are earmarked for various destinies, including sacrifice, and reared accordingly (157–78). Virgil dwells on training for farm use, the *servitium* of the yoke. The foal, by contrast, receives an aristocratic training for war or racing (the Olympic Theme is heard again), the description being heightened by a Homeric simile with the wind (179–208).

209–83. *Sex*

The chief danger to the efficiency of both cattle and horses is sexual preoccupation.* Bulls must therefore be kept apart from cows, whose attraction is spoken of in terms like those of human love-elegy. This leads to the admired description of the defeated bull retiring to train severely until it returns with *collectum robur viresque refectae* to fall on its unwary rival like a great breaker of the sea. Thus, the original point so soon forgotten, love has been shown not as a weakener but a strengthener; and the mad violence of this bull has prepared our minds for the terrific Lucretian-style section that follows.

Varro had recommended (2. 1. 18; 5. 12) that male animals should be kept away from females for two months before mating. This was obviously to husband their potency and desire.† But Virgil is not here concerned with propagation of the herd as arranged by the farmer. He is concerned with dissipation of energy at other times, with waste, with *caeci stimulos amoris*. And he now bursts out into a passionate reminder of the havoc lust can cause. Once again, man and beast are not distinguished: *amor omnibus idem*. In their times of sexual excitement all animals grow wilder than ever: *in furias ignemque ruunt*. They career madly across land, water and air, deterred by no obstacle. *Quid iuvenis?* The reckless intrepidity of Leander (unnamed perhaps because he stands for all young men frenzied with love)[26] provides a tragic instance among humans, involving also the death of his beloved. Mares go wildest of all, and two strange beliefs about them, the latter connected with poisons such as stepmothers mix, bring the section to an eerie and gruesome close. This headlong and horrific passage, broadening the theme from horses and cattle to all living

---

* Otis (p. 174), neglecting *avertere* (210), says that 'the *ostensible* reason for the whole section is the strengthening effect of love on the steer or stallion; no industry of man can stimulate their strength like the power of Venus'. This is exactly the opposite of what the text says. But he rightly continues that the primary concern is with love itself.

† Virgil does not mention separating the sexes at 123–37, where he deals with fattening bulls but stinting cows as a preparation for mating.

creatures, like a discordant transposition of Lucretius' exultant opening—

> *vere* magis, quia *vere* calor redit ossibus (272)—

is the unrelieved climax of the First Part of a Book which has so far been mainly concerned with generation.

284–566. Part II. Sheep and goats. Plague

284–94. Proem

A new proem of eleven lines ushers in the sheep and goats. Recognising the difficulty of investing such humble creatures with poetic dignity, Virgil accepts the challenge with Lucretian enthusiasm, singing loudly to keep his courage up. Pales, Italian deity of flocks, one of the trio at the beginning of the Book, is invoked again:

> nunc, veneranda Pales, magno ore sonandum.

In a similar spirit, bracing himself after the heights of *Aeneid* 6 to deal with the wars in Italy, he was to proclaim (7. 44–5)

> maior rerum mihi nascitur ordo,
> maius opus moveo.

He adopts a tone of authority—issuing edicts (295) like a Roman praetor (Keightley).

295–338. Care of sheep and goats (295–321: in winter; 322–38: in summer)

As before, he takes advantage of the impetus imparted by a stretch of high poetry to continue with precepts on the most mundane matters, in this case precautions against scab and foot-rot. As though a farmer touring his farm (*incipiens...post hinc digressus*), as Keightley again remarks, he gives orders for the care in the winter months now of the sheep, now of the goats. He seems specially concerned to advocate the claims of goats (they, not cows, were the Italians' prime source of milk*): they deserve our care all the more because they are not demanding. By contrast,

---

* Conington, in his note on 394–403, inadvertently speaks of 'cattle', despite the clear reminder given by *haedos* at 398.

when the summer comes both sheep and goats can be turned out into the pastures all day with very little herding to do. This is the idyllic passage of pastoral landscape already quoted (p. 12), another concrete illustration of what was generalised in the Praises of Italy (2. 136–76).

339–83. *Libyan shepherd and Scythian cattlemen*

As Burck pointed out, the contrast in that passage between Italy and the East is matched here by the contrast between this temperate pasturage and the two descriptive passages that follow. The first of these depicts the hard life of nomad shepherds of the Libyan plains, with the Military Theme reappearing in the striking simile of the heavily-laden Roman soldier on forced march. The second is a vivid description (a model for Ovid's of Tomis) of the life of Scythian cattlemen, with their herds confined to steadings or liable to be frozen stiff on the icy steppes (*semper hiems* there, instead of *ver assiduum*). Yet even they find some relief, in hunting made easy, and in their snug gaming and beer-drinking round the great log-fire in the underground dug-out—a counterpart to the rustic jollifications of Book 1 (300–4) and Book 2 (380–96; 526–31). These fine descriptive pieces offset one another, as of heat and cold, while together they offset the temperate life and landscape of Italy that precedes. *Quid...prosequar?* asks Virgil, using the rhetorical figure of *praeteritio* to introduce them. This artistic justification provides the only and sufficient answer.

384–403. *Produce* (384–93 : *sheep's wool;* 394–403 : *goat's milk*)

The last line (383), mentioning the fur pelts with which the Scythians keep out the cold wind, leads back to the fleeces which sheep provide. Ten lines deal with measures to secure whiteness in wool, their gift to men, three being taken up with mythological embroidery, a reference to a story (in Nicander) about Pan seducing the Moon with a fleece of dazzling whiteness.[27] Ten balancing lines are then devoted to the chief gift of goats, milk and cheese.

404–73. *Dangers* (404–13: *watchdogs*); 406–8: *thieves and wolves;* 414–39: *snakes;* 440–73: *diseases*

A further ten lines are all Virgil can spare for dogs, but they provide a subtle transition of thought from uses to dangers. Dogs are bred for hunting, but also for protection against robbers and wolves. These lead on to other dangers, in the first place snakes, culminating in a Calabrian species on whose sinister fascination he enlarges, no longer suggesting any remedy. And so we come to diseases, already briefly mentioned at 299. Virgil prescribes remedies that become more and more drastic. As in Book 1, the struggle against the hostile tendencies in nature is relentless. 'Thick and fast as the squalls that drive a storm across the sea is the onset of animal plagues.' In a single summer you may lose

spemque gregemque simul cunctamque ab origine gentem,

present and future flock, your whole stock, root and branch.

474–566. *The Plague*

What this meant could be appreciated by anyone who had seen the desolation round Trieste and in the Noric hill-towns to the north. So begins a finale which, in its parallelism to the description of the horrors of civil war at the end of Book 1 and its ironic contrast with the blessings of country life at the end of Book 2, emphasises the structure of the whole work, as it also emphasises that of its own Book by its parallelism to the finale of the First Part, the havoc caused by sex. The theme of Death, given out at 66–8, has remained in the background, emerging at the climax of the First Part in the tragic ends of Leander and Glaucus (258–68) and again where the beasts perish in the snows of Scythia (368). Virgil now describes, evidently prompted by the end of the *De Rerum Natura*, the plague that has devastated those Alpine regions. The victorious racehorse and the useful ox of the First Part are now shown in their hour of death (498–503; 515–30).* Only as

---

* Klingner, to whom, with Büchner, I am here particularly indebted, suggests in his book (1963, pp. 159 f.) that it was for this effect that Virgil altered Varro's order and dealt with horses and cattle before sheep and goats. As in the

7-2

the result of wholesale burials did the plague finally subside. But even so, contagion could live on in wool and pelts, now to infect humans also; and with a description of revolting symptoms the Book ends. This unexpected persistence of the danger and the starkness of the breaking off are more effective than any peroration could be.

BOOK 4. BEES

1–7. *Proem*

Turning from Book 3 to Book 4 is again like waking from a nightmare, this time from miasma into the pure upper air—*aërii caelestia* in the first line (the ancients believed that honey was gathered by bees from honey-dew which fell from the skies on to the leaves of trees).[28] As in Book 2, there are only a few lines of proem, asking for the attention of Maecenas. And as with the *angustae res* of sheep and goats, the poet states his claim:

> in tenui labor; at tenuis non gloria, si quem
> numina laeva sinunt auditque vocatus Apollo,

slight is the subject of the work but not slight the poet's glory if adverse deities permit and Apollo answers his prayer.

The interplay of great and small is at once given out as a dominant theme:

> admiranda tibi levium spectacula rerum
> magnanimosque duces totiusque ordine gentis
> mores et studia et populos et proelia dicam.

I will set forth in order for your admiration spectacles of a tiny world, great-hearted leaders and the customs, pursuits, peoples and battles of the whole race.

The bees are in fact to be treated with the same mixture of humour (at first) and allegory as Swift's Lilliputians. But why bees only of all the animals reared on farms and country houses —*pastiones villaticae*—to which Varro devoted his Third Book?

corresponding Book 1, a lighter stretch contrived in the middle of the Book makes the ultimate return to sombreness the more impressive; and this return is signalised by the re-emergence of the horse and ox.

First we may answer as before: to include chickens, pigeons, pea-cocks, ducks and geese, hares, snails and dormice, ornamental fish and what not would have reduced the poem to a miscellaneous insignificance. But bees, as Varro and all antiquity acknowledged, were quite exceptional, not merely for their usefulness (honey being then the only sweetener of food and drink), but for their *mores et studia*. Only they, and they supremely, could provide a significant crown for the work Virgil had conceived. Whereas other animals are moved only by ὁρμαί and πάθη, they share with men in the divine λόγος.[29] Their way of life is by nature exem-plary. For the most part the bee-keeper need only give them a helping hand. The Book is thus descriptive as much as didactic in form: *levium spectacula rerum*.

8–50. *The hive*

We begin with instructions for choosing surroundings for the hive, what to avoid and what to seek; then for building the hive itself, in reverse order, what to seek and what to avoid.

51–115. *Settling* (51–66: *swarming*; 67–87: *fighting*)

This done, bees must be attracted to it and induced to settle. As in Book 1, activity begins in spring, whose liberating advent is here likewise characterised in two vivid pictorial lines. The bees swarm out over the countryside to forage. Like the rooks at 1. 412, they are *nescio qua dulcedine laeti* as they tend their nests and young. The watchful bee-keeper can without difficulty (*ipsae*) entice them to the prepared hive. All here is co-operation, sweetness and light (51–66). On the other hand, there may be two kings (*sc.* 'queens'), and this leads to fighting in the air (67–87). Exploiting the con-trast, Virgil describes a pitched battle in human and indeed epic military terms:

> ingentis animos angusto in pectore versant,

mighty passions seethe in their tiny breasts.

The play of large and small has become openly mock-heroic.

Suddenly, ironically, the two concluding lines reduce all the pother to proportion:

> hi motus animorum atque haec certamina tanta
> pulveris exigui iactu compressa quiescent,

these upheavals of heart and these prodigious contests the throwing of a little handful of dust will reduce to calm.

The effect of suddenly looking at things from a distance, as through the reverse end of a telescope, is a playful counterpart of the effect at 1. 493 ff., when suddenly the civil war is seen through the eyes of a peasant centuries after. True scale has been restored. Virgil does not say so, but the reader could hardly fail to reflect that if men can thus dispose of bees, Jupiter can thus dispose of men. To make his point he has characteristically lifted from Varro (3. 16. 30) the act of dust-throwing, there directed against *swarming* bees, and transferred it to *fighting* bees.

88–102. *Selection;* 103–15: *swarming-fever*

In complete control, the bee-keeper must now kill off the inferior king—visibly inferior he will be, and so will his '*plebs*' (88–102). If the bees incline to swarming-fever and will not settle, you must pull the wings off the kings. The Military Theme, which has reached its most dominant in the battle, is heard again at 107–8:

> non illis quisquam cunctantibus altum
> ire iter aut castris audebit vellere signa,

if they (*sc.* the kings) hold back, no one will dare to venture on journeys aloft or snatch up the standards from the camp.

The bee-keeper must also work hard: *ipse ferens—ipse labore manum duro terat—ipse figat et irriget*—to make the hive and its surroundings attractive to the bees. Honey is not simply gathered by men, as it was from trees in the Golden Age.

116–48. *Interlude: gardens; the Corycian old man*

Virgil now requires a break. So far he has dealt with behaviour of bees which, though sometimes comparable to that of men, is mainly analogous to that of other animals and amenable to easy control. They have been treated with patronising amusement, or with a satirical side-glance at the squabbles and ambitions of men. He now wishes to turn to the unique qualities of bees, which make them suitable to be held up as an example to men, and to contemporary Romans in particular. He achieves the break by a brilliant idea for an interlude. There has naturally been much talk already in this Book of flowers and trees, at first growing wild (20–4, 30–2, 54, 61), and now specially planted—*croceis halantes floribus horti* under the protection of the garden-god Priapus, and planted with toil and loving care (109–15). This gives Virgil his cue. Using again the metaphor from sailing as at 2. 41, he says that were he not hastening now into port (epic was calling him, we may surmise), he would perhaps have sung also of gardens.* In the handbooks bees and gardens were not dealt with together, but in separate Μελισσουργικά and Κηπουργικά.† With great skill Virgil both devises his interlude and uses it to delightful effect. Neatly framing it between two lines of excuse at either end, he first contrives, again exploiting the device called *praeteritio* by the rhetoricians, to mention and characterise some flowers and vegetables. This leads to memories of a garden he had once seen near Tarentum,

> ubi non Hymetto
> mella decedunt,

created out of nothing by an old Corycian (from Cilicia). The idea of such a reminiscence probably came from Varro, whose Merula gives, at *R.R.* 3. 16. 10–11, an account of the brothers Veianus of Falerii: 'They were well off because, although their father had left them only a small house and a piece of land certainly no larger than one *iugerum*, they had made an apiary all round the house, and a garden, and planted all the remaining

---

* He must now, he says, leave that to others. Columella, taking the hint, composed his Book on gardens (10) in hexameter verse instead of prose.

† Two contemporaries of Virgil had written prose '*cepuria*', Sabin(i)us Tiro, who dedicated his work to Maecenas, and Valerius Messalla Potitus, probably to be identified with an elder stepbrother of Messalla Corvinus. (Pliny *N.H.* 1. 19; 19. 177; *RE* s.v. 'Valerius', no. 267.)

ground with thyme, snail-clover and apiastrum.' As Horace, prompted by an account in his source, Lucilius, of a journey to the Sicilian Straits, composed from true recollections (and a few imitations) his Journey to Brundisium (*S.* 1. 5), so Virgil may have been reminded by reading Varro of this delightful garden. A couple of lines about the old man's bees (139 f.) help to justify its place in the Book.

In the structure of the poem as a whole this passage is a counterpart to the Praise of Country Life in Book 2. At the same time it is a justification of Jupiter's dispensation at 1. 121–59, occupying a parallel place in the Book.[30] For the old man is first to do everything in its season, 134 ff.; and he comes home only late at night (132–3). This brings him his reward, the enjoyment of his garden in all its variety and fertility. The *morbi tristisque senectus* that are the lot of ageing man, and the effort of constantly rowing against the stream, are shown to be not without compensations.[31]

149–227. *Unique* mores: *Jupiter's gift to bees*

The new attitude to the bees is signalised by a *nunc age*, and by a mythological allusion that is not this time mere embroidery. Bees had kept alive the infant Jupiter with honey when he was concealed in the Dictean cave from the murderous designs of his father Saturn.[32] The myth is an *aition* for the special favour he granted them as a reward, not any material reward, as in the various traditions, but something of far higher worth substituted by Virgil—*mores* unique in the animal kingdom. These comprise communism even of children, loyalty to their home, its laws and leaders, provision for the future, pooling of gains and division of labour (again the last item only of a list is dwelt on in detail). A simile with the Cyclopes divides the section, which then continues with division of labour, the duties of old and young; and next the activities of morning and evening, followed by uniform silence for rest at night,

> omnibus una quies operum, labor omnibus unus,

united they are in resting from work, united in toil.

They are unique also in not propagating by sexual intercourse, and they are prepared to sacrifice their lives in service to the hive. *Ergo*—although the life of the individual never exceeds seven years, the race is immortal. And there is a further unifying factor, utter devotion to their king (210–18).* (This passage is the obverse of the corresponding one in Book 3 (242–83) on the ubiquitous and destructive power of sexual lust.) The section culminates in a philosophic deduction of a Platonic-Stoic nature, attributed to *quidam*, that bees have a share of divine intelligence, which broadens into pantheism (219–27).

228–38. *Honey-harvest*

We return now to the style and mood of the earlier part (8–115), to bee-keeping without overtones. From swarming in spring we have passed to honey-harvesting, which can be done both at the end of May and in November.

239–50. *Pests and remedies*

Hence, at 239, we come to precautions against pests that may trouble the bees in winter.

251–80. *Diseases and remedies*

Pests lead on, as at 3. 440, to diseases ('here too bees are like men in their fortunes') and precautions and remedies for these (251–80).

---

* There have been proposals to reshuffle lines in this section in the interest of logical order (see Conington on 203–5). The sequence of thought is certainly smoother if we transfer 203–5, with Bentley, to follow 196. The bees' self-sacrifice, with the *epiphonema*

> tantus amor florum et generandi gloria mellis,

makes a good climax to the section. At 197 begins a new section, on reproduction. Again it would be smoother if 210–18, the addition beginning *praeterea*, were transposed to follow 201–2, which mention the king, and the passage ended with

> stat fortuna domus, et avi numerantur avorum.

281–314. Death, and renewal by 'Bugonia'

Finally, a whole hive may be carried off by epidemic, and it is time to set forth the famous method of 'Bugonia', with a reference to which Varro began his account of bees (3. 16. 4; cf. 2. 5. 5). It was freely believed in the ancient world, and often mentioned in Greco-Roman writers, that bees could be produced from the carcase of an ox by spontaneous generation.* Virgil attributes this discovery to Aristeaus, and locates its practice in Egypt, the proverbial land of wonders. He then describes the process.

The Aristeaus epyllion, which occupies the rest of the Book, must be treated in a separate chapter because of the uncertainty of its status in the original text. I hope that it has emerged from our analysis that the *Georgics* can claim to be to a large extent an organic patterned poem—hence the use of the singular number. It displays artistic manipulation of contrasts and correspondences, with subtle transitions, while dealing with such large conceptions as the dignity of labour, the delight of variety in nature and in human activities, the pleasures of simple country life, the interplay of Rome and Italy, the power and dangers of lust in all creatures, and of disease and death over them. But there is much that can fit into such patterns only by forced interpretation. Sometimes the contrasts seem motivated purely by an artistic desire for chiaroscuro, and the mythological and suchlike pieces introduced solely for variety. Further, Virgil started from the metaphrastic tradition; and much of the information he gives comes alive only because of the way in which he presents it to our senses. This cumulative impression of a whole country and a whole way of life cannot be conveyed by any analysis. It can only be apprehended by a reading of the whole poem.

Edmund Wilson wrote in *Axel's Castle*:[33] 'How can the *Georgics*, the *Ars Poetica* and Manilius be dealt with from the point of view of the capacity of their material for being expanded into

---

* Cf. the riddle of Samson (Judges 14. 12–18): 'out of the eater came forth meat; out of the strong came forth sweetness'. Answer: bees with their honey from a dead lion (as illustrated on Tate & Lyle's golden syrup tins).

"pure vision"?* To modern readers the subjects of the *Georgics* —bee-keeping, stock-raising and so forth—seem unsuitable and sometimes annoying in verse; yet for Virgil's contemporaries the poem must have been completely successful—as, indeed, granted the subject, it is.' He does not seem to realise just *how* successful it can be, for modern readers as well.

* T. S. Eliot's phrase *re* Dante in *The Sacred Wood*.

V · The Aristaeus Epyllion

As is well known, Servius (and no other source) refers twice to a change having been made in the latter part of Book 4. On *Eclogues* 10. 1 he says: '(Gallus) was...a friend of Virgil, so much so that the Fourth Book of the *Georgics* from the middle right down to the end contained his praises, which afterwards at the bidding of Augustus he changed to the story of Aristaeus.' And on *Georgics* 4. 1: 'It must of course be realised that, as I said above, the last part of this book was changed. For the praises of Gallus stood in the place which now contains the story of Orpheus, which was inserted after the anger of Augustus led to Gallus being killed.'

We must not lay too much stress on the fact that he specifies in the first passage the story of Aristaeus, in the second only that of Orpheus: 'ut supra diximus' shows that he *means* at least to give the same information in both places. But neither this nor '*occisus est*' enhances our trust in a notoriously unreliable witness.[1] (Gallus, having been made first Prefect of Egypt after the fall of Alexandria in the autumn of 30 B.C., got above himself, was accused of treason, and committed suicide in 27.[2] He suffered a posthumous ban on his memory—*damnatio memoriae*.)

The essentials of the episode in Virgil are as follows. The inventor of 'Bugonia' was Aristaeus.* While a man (he later came

---

* Servius' note on 1. 14 gives some of the necessary background. 'He was the son of Apollo and Cyrene, called Apollo Pastoralis by Hesiod. After his son Actaeon was torn to pieces by hounds he left Thebes (as Sallust also says) and at the inspiration of his mother came to the island of Ceos, hitherto uninhabited. Afterwards, leaving there, he crossed with Daedalus to Sardinia.' Servius Auctus adds: 'Pindar disagrees with this view. He says he migrated from the island of Ceos to Arcadia and settled down there; for among the Arcadians he is worshipped as Jupiter (*pro Iove*); as the poet says about this same Aristaeus,

tempus et Arcadii memoranda inventa magistri / pandere.'

Other versions had it that Cyrene, carried off to Africa by Apollo from Thessaly, bore him there. Apollo took him back to Thessaly and put him under Chiron. The Muses taught him prophecy. Once when the inhabitants of Ceos were suffering from famine and pestilence an oracle of Apollo told them to

to be worshipped as a god) he lost all his bees and came to complain to his mother Cyrene, a nymph who lived beneath the source of the river Peneüs in Thessaly (315–32). His mother allowed him to enter there miraculously—*fas illi limina divom tangere* (his father was Apollo). After a meal, libation, prayers and a favourable omen she gave her reply (333–86): 'Proteus, who lives in the Carpathian Sea and is now visiting his native Pallene, is a prophet who can tell you all, if you can catch and hold him in the manner I will now explain to you.' Aristaeus obeyed successfully, and Proteus, glaring and gnashing his teeth, revealed the truth (387–452).

It is Orpheus who is sending you this punishment, because it was while fleeing from your embraces that his wife Eurydice was bitten by a snake and died, much bewailed by her Dryad companions as well. He went down to Orcus, charmed all with his lyre, and persuaded Prosperina to let Eurydice go, on condition he did not look back until he, with her following behind, was in the upper world again. But when they were nearly there love overcame him and he did look back. Reproaching him, she vanished back into Orcus, and Charon would not let him recross the Styx. For seven months he mourned her, till Thracian Bacchants, piqued by his single-minded devotion, tore him to pieces. His head, swept down the Hebrus, continued to call Eurydice.

So saying, Proteus plunged into the sea (453–527). But Cyrene was still there, and comforted Aristaeus: 'It is the Nymphs who are sending this punishment. I will tell you how to placate them, by sacrificing four bulls. Nine days later you must make offerings also to the *manes* of Orpheus and Eurydice.' He obeyed, and on the ninth day found that bees were born from the bulls' carcases (528–58).

We are concerned at present with the structure of this episode and its place in the structure of the work as a whole. Its poetic

send for him. He came and sacrificed to Zeus Ikmaios and Sirius; whereupon the Etesian winds began to blow, and they were relieved. They then made this a yearly practice. For this service, and because he taught them bee-keeping and olive-growing, men worshipped him as a god, Zeus Aristaios, Apollo Agreus and Apollo Nomios. Various versions took him to various other places. See Klingner (1963), pp. 197–8.

quality will be considered later. Let us begin by supposing that Servius' information is substantially true. The praises of Gallus could hardly have stood alone in the place occupied now by the Orpheus story alone, interrupting the romantic narrative about a legendary hero which is wholly objective. That story is in any case, as we shall see, artistically integral to the Aristaeus epyllion. The first version is more plausible, that the whole second part of the Book was replaced by the whole Aristaeus epyllion. Now the lengths of the other books are 514, 542, and 566 lines respectively. Book 4 might be expected also to contain between 500 and 600 lines (the text we have contains 566). The Aristaeus epyllion begins at 315. If we took *a medio* literally, the *laudes Galli* would thus have occupied some 314 lines; and even if we supposed this Book was no longer than the others, 200 lines would be the minimum length for them.

In modern times until quite recently Servius' information was accepted without question.* It was assumed that Gallus was now being praised as Prefect of Egypt. But recent upholders of the story have realised that he had been in office for too short a time for news of any success he had to reach Rome and be celebrated in verse. Büchner has therefore suggested (cols. 296–7) that he was being praised as the elegiac poet of love, relating this to the large part played by death and love in Books 3 and 4 together. But think away the Aristaeus epyllion, inserted later on this supposition: does love then play any part in Book 4?

About 1930, however, several scholars independently began to impugn the story. Norden delivered a famous lecture in that year dismissing it, and before he published this in 1934 he had read the devastating attack of W. B. Anderson.[3] There is one overriding objection to it. Imagine the scene at Atella in the summer of 29.

---

* For theories about the Aristaeus episode see Appendix IV. Attempts have recently been made to demonstrate, by close comparison, that certain passages in this episode were composed subsequently to similar passages in the *Aeneid*, with the argument that they are more appropriate there and would therefore seem to have been hastily adapted here for a substituted ending after Gallus' disgrace and death. (Büchner, cols. 295–6; Richter, notes on 4. 376 ff., 420 f., 473 ff., 499 ff.) But the arguments are not cogent: see Otis, pp. 408–12; Klingner (1963), pp. 207–10.

Octavian, 'sole sir o' the world', on the eve of celebrating his Triple Triumph, is sitting for the fourth successive day, listening to the *Georgics* being read. After 314 lines of Book 4 Virgil's voice has probably given out and Maecenas, to whom the poem is dedicated, has taken over. With what feelings would the latter read, and Octavian hear, two or three hundred lines in praise of Gallus as climax to the poem? Gallus was much less important than either. True, he was a great friend of Virgil's; but unlike *Eclogues* 6 and 10, this is obviously a public poem.* And in any case, how could the poem retain any kind of organic shape with so completely alien an excrescence at the end? We may further ask whether even a *damnatio memoriae* could have been so effective that two or three hundred lines of a poem by the most famous poet of Rome could have disappeared without trace after circulating freely for two or three years. Richter is so impressed by this difficulty that he supposes the whole poem to have remained unpublished until 26/25, after Gallus' death.[4] But what conceivable reason could Virgil have for withholding from publication his completed poem (and then, after drastically altering half of the last Book, leaving unaltered the epilogue indicating that it was finished in 30/29, not to mention the lines 3. 46–8, which suggest that the coming epic, surely by now known to have taken shape as the *Aeneid*, was to deal with '*pugnas Caesaris*')?

We should therefore accept the Aristaeus epyllion as part of the original poem, but not without considering how Servius' story can have arisen. Anderson quoted from Ammianus Marcellinus (17. 4. 5) the statement that Virgil praised Gallus *in postrema Bucolicorum parte* (i.e. in *Eclogue* 10), in support of the suggestion that Servius or some predecessor came across this or a similar passage and mistook the *Georgics* for the *Bucolics*. From such a slip the story of the revised version would readily be elaborated.[5] This simple explanation is by no means impossible. Otherwise we may guess that a few lines about Gallus occurred *à propos* of

---

* E. Norden, 'Orpheus und Eurydice', *Sitz. Berl. Akad.* (1934), p. 630; W. B. Anderson, 'Gallus and the Fourth Georgic', *C.Q.* (1933), p. 39. The objection does not of course depend on the truth of the Atella story; it is only reinforced.

Egypt at 287–94. There is a muddle in the text at 291–3,* and the lines hereabouts are unusually endstopped for Virgil. Hasty revision could have led to either of these phenomena. (It would be easier to improvise individual hexameters than a period with the varied enjambement usual in Virgil.)

This is not to say that there are no difficulties in our present text, quite apart from the question of the relation of the episode to the rest of the work, and they must be briefly dealt with.

(1) At 283, introducing Bugonia, Virgil says

> tempus et Arcadii memoranda inventa magistri
> pandere,

it is time to unfold the memorable invention of the Arcadian master.

Why does he then ask the Muses at 315 what god hammered out this art for men,

> quis deus hanc, Musae, quis nobis extudit artem?,

giving the answer, 'Pastor Aristaeus'? This awkwardness does not seem very significant. 'Arcadius magister' need not have identified Aristaeus, who was associated mostly with Ceos (1. 14) and rarely, to our knowledge, with Arcadia,[6] so that perhaps a better translation would be '*an* Arcadian master'. Also a request to the Muses for information was a device as old as Homer for introducing a new subject: the fact that the poet immediately gives the answer suggests that the question is to be taken as a formality.

(2) Aristaeus is here a man, not a god, but this hardly matters. He was son of Apollo and had been led 'caelum sperare' (325); and in fact he was to be worshipped in Ceos as Zeus Aristaeus (Serv. Auct. on G. 1. 14); so he could be called 'deus', quite apart from the Euhemeristic sense in which Lucretius says of Epicurus 'deus ille fuit' because of his benefits to mankind.

(3) At 454 Proteus says that it is Orpheus who is sending

---

* These three lines occur in all the MSS, but in three different orders. Heyne supposed that 291 and 292, Wagner that all three, were written by Virgil in the margin of his copy, or put there by some critic. See Keightley, Excursus X and p. xvii.

punishment on Aristaeus, whereas at 532–6 Cyrene says it is the fellow-Dryads of Eurydice. But we were told at the start that on her death the Dryads 'filled the mountain peaks with their wailing' (460–3), and the final instructions of Cyrene are for the propitiation of the *manes* of Orpheus and Eurydice (544–7).

(4) It is Cyrene, not Proteus as we were led to expect (397–8), who tells Aristaeus how to atone. But Proteus' essential rôle was to reveal the cause; she then knows what must be done for propitiation (530–47).

(5) Proteus seems otiose, since Cyrene knows all along what to do to recreate the bees. But there is no indication that she knows the atoning sacrifice will have this after-effect, which Aristaeus discovers to his astonishment only on revisiting the grove nine days later (531–6).[7]

(6) The form of sacrifice prescribed by her (538–43) is simpler than that attributed by Virgil to contemporary Egypt (295–314). But one might expect the form developed after long centuries to be more elaborate.[8]

All in all, I do not feel that these alleged discrepancies add up to much. They are more like oversights or carelessness about inessentials than either evidence of hasty revision or subtleties calling for interpretation.

What was in Virgil's mind when he gave his work this surprising conclusion? Having decided to make bees alone the subject of Book 4, he may well have felt that their care and habits could hardly be strung out to five hundred lines or more. How could he contrive what should be a substantial climax not only to the Book but to the whole poem? There was nothing in ancient bee-lore more dramatic than Bugonia—*mirabile monstrum* (554). Varro mentioned it first in his account (3. 16. 4); Virgil decided to treat it last. And for one of his Neoteric upbringing a most natural form of elaboration would be an *aition*, a story explaining the origin of a custom. The parenthetical '*ut fama*' at 318 *may* indicate that there was a tradition at least that he lost his bees—ἀμάρτυρον οὐδὲν ἀείδω, as the Alexandrian said.[9] But if there was no traditional *aition* for Bugonia, a very little invention would supply one. The patron-deity who instituted bee-keeping was Aristaeus, taught by the nymphs.[10] He was son of the healer-god Apollo, pupil of the wise healer Chiron. It was a personal loss (of his son Actaeon) that had taken him to Ceos, where he had rescued the people from pestilence by new sacrifices.[11] He was thus an obvious candidate.

Faced with the necessity of inventing a narrative, Virgil did what he was to do in the *Aeneid*. He selected motifs from Greek literature, especially Homer, and cunningly welded them together. Aristaeus was the son of a nymph, Cyrene. He could appeal to her, as Achilles appealed to Thetis when he suffered losses (*Il.* 1. 348 ff.; 18. 35 ff.). The idea of making Cyrene receive him beneath the waters of Peneüs may have come from Theseus' visit to his stepmother Amphitrite, as described by Bacchylides 16. 97 ff. and depicted on vases.* The list of nymphs is elaborated from *Iliad* 18. 39 ff., the scene of welcome from *Odyssey* 1. 144 ff. and 4. 39 ff.; the capture and questioning of Proteus is varied from *Odyssey* 4. 351–570.[12] Proteus was presumably introduced to reveal a secret. That was his métier. But why, having done so in his first four lines, does he add more than seventy lines of narrative (457–527), which are only relevant in so far as they disclose that Orpheus is now dead (and therefore has *manes* to be propitiated by offerings)? The answer is aesthetic, not logical. It resides in the nature of the epyllion form, which again would suggest itself to one brought up in Neoteric circles, though to us it may seem strange and artificial.

It was a feature of epyllion to have at least one story inset within the primary one. Callimachus' *Hecale*, probably the prototype, has two legends of primitive Athens told within that of Theseus' visit to the aged Hecale, one about (?) Aegeus, and one about Erichthonius which is told by an old crow to another

---

* Norden, *Sitz. Berl. Akad.* (1934) p. 638. Virgil's friend Horace had been reading Bacchylides about this time; see E. Fraenkel on *Epode* 13 (*Horace*, 1957, p. 66 n.) and Porphyrion on *Odes* 1. 15. For detailed treatment of all this passage see Klingner (1963), *Georgica*, pp. 197 ff.

bird.[13] In Moschus' *Europa* we have a story depicted on the heroine's basket (37–62): Io, turned into a heifer by Zeus and driven oversea by Hera, is clearly a reflection of Europa, about to cross the sea on the back of Zeus, who has turned himself into a bull.[14] But for our purpose the crucial example is the *Peleus and Thetis* (64) of Catullus.[15] There the story of Ariadne, as depicted on their marriage-coverlet, occupies more than half the poem (214 lines out of 381, excluding the epilogue). Both stories are about the love of a divinity for a mortal, but the arrival of Bacchus to rescue Ariadne occupies only fourteen lines or so at the end of the inset. The general effect is of contrast between the bliss of Peleus and Thetis and the misery of Ariadne deserted by Theseus on Naxos.[16]

That Catullus would deliberately contrive such a contrast of emotions is shown by his elegiac letter to Allius (68 B). There the heart of the poem is his brother's death, the greatest sorrow of his life; the outer frame is memories of Lesbia's first coming to him, the greatest joy of his life; and the two are connected by the story of Laodameia, who lost her newly married husband Protesilaus at Troy (where Catullus' brother had also died), but for her great love was allowed to be revisited by his ghost.*

It has been suggested that the mixture of happiness and misery in the *Peleus and Thetis* reflects Catullus' own state of mind,[17] perhaps at the time when he wrote the letter to Allius, at the end of which (95–108) he reveals that he knows that Lesbia is unfaithful, and tries to adapt himself to merely hoping that he still comes first in her affections.

It may be complained that the beautiful story of Orpheus and Eurydice, told with such sympathy and compassion, is incongruous in the mouth of the captured, teeth-gnashing, eye-rolling old man of the sea. But what about the old crow in the *Hecale*? Or, if that was intentionally grotesque, what about Catullus' Ariadne? Was it tactful to have the story of her desertion embroidered on a marriage-coverlet? The fact is that what interests

---

* For an analogy between the chiastic pattern of motifs in G. 4. 457–522 and that of Catullus' Allius elegy (68 B) see Appendix V.

the Neoteric poet is the interplay of moods, not the motivation or machinery that is contrived in order to effect it. Similarly the re-emergence of Cyrene after Proteus' narrative, when he could have been made to give the instructions himself, is dictated by the form. The frame had to be completed, however thinly.

The length of the Aristaeus episode makes it very probable that Virgil had all along the epyllion-form in mind, and we must now inquire why, out of many stories of sadness and loss, he chose that of Orpheus and Eurydice to inset. It had never, to our know-ledge, been connected with Aristaeus before.[18] Eurydice's death by a snake-bite was in the tradition; but Virgil apparently invented her flight from his embraces (*dum te fugeret*, 457) as the reason for her not having perceived the danger lurking in the grass. It was lust on his part that was responsible for her death. Klingner suggests that he was prompted by a tradition, recorded by Conon, that Orpheus after death was an angry daemon until appeased by sacrifice.[19] According to this he was torn to pieces by Thracian or Macedonian women for despising them, and thrown into the sea. A pestilence followed, and an oracle said it would continue until the head of Orpheus was found and buried. At last a fisher-man found it, uncorrupted and still singing. It was buried in a tomb which became a shrine at which sacrifices were made and other divine honours paid. Aristaeus was, like these women, to suffer for a crime and to redeem it by an expiatory sacrifice. The contrast between the tragedy of Orpheus and Eurydice, ending in death after highest hopes, in which the poet participates in the elegiac or lyric manner, and the remote fairy-story epos of Aristaeus' visit to his mother and to Proteus, ending in recovery of life, was in the spirit of Catullus, and incidentally proof enough that we are justified in finding elsewhere in the *Georgics* this Neoteric interplay between contrasting moods and styles.

But had Virgil any other reason for introducing the story of Orpheus? No one before had made him lose Eurydice again through looking back at her because of overpowering love. Was he following some tradition lost to us, or are these significant inventions? We must note first of all that the normal version of the story made Orpheus successful in bringing Eurydice back to earth. Before Virgil's time the only variant is in Plato, and he may have been inventing to suit his book.* There is no hint of one in Diodorus, who was diligently collecting Alexandrian myths between *c.* 60 and 30 B.C.;[20] nor does the story of Orpheus' infatuation, though it would have been eminently suitable, occur in the extant collection of love stories compiled by Parthenius to Gallus for use in his poems. If Virgil had a predecessor, he must have been quite a recent one. And here we are in a difficulty through lack of precise dating for the collection of myths made by a contemporary of his, Conon,† who speaks of Orpheus losing Eurydice again through neglecting the injunctions of Pluto and Proserpina.

Norden assumed that Virgil was following a handbook of mythology, probably that used by Servius Auctus.[21] But there is another possibility, put forward by Sir Maurice Bowra in 1952 in an article about which there seems to be almost a conspiracy of silence.[22] He too assumes that Virgil was not inventing, but he takes the source to be an Alexandrian poem, whose contents he deduces by comparing Virgil's version with Ovid's as told at the beginning of *Metamorphoses* 10, with a little help from the *Culex*.[23] I do not think we should attach great weight to the allusive manner in which Virgil tells the story as evidence that it was already known: this allusiveness is studied art, and tells us all we need to know as we go along. But the distinct possibility that he was using, if not a handbook, a recent poem, perhaps an elegy, as model for the Orpheus passage should make us cautious about seeing special significance in what appear to be variants from the main tradition.

But this does not sufficiently answer the question, why Virgil thought Orpheus particularly suitable to be connected with Aristaeus and the origins of Bugonia. It has been suggested that

---

* At *Symp.* 179D Orpheus is only allowed to see a wraith of his wife in Hades because he has not the courage to go there, like other people, by dying.

† See p. 335 n. 19. Conon's work was dedicated to Archelaus Philopator, king of Cappadocia from 36 B.C. to A.D. 17. Supposing Virgil's passage to have been written in 30/29, the chances are that Conon was writing later. But the question remains, would a Greek mythographer take any notice of a Roman poet?

the Mystery Religions provide a clue. The whole episode has been interpreted as a reflection of them—the succession of λεγόμενα, δρώμενα, σωτήρια. Cyrene would be the hierophantic guide. The defences of Proteus would be the trials of the candidate for initiation—by fire, by wild beasts, by water (442). The descent into Hades would reflect the fictitious death undergone by the candidate. Egypt, the land specially connected with Bugonia, was also the great land of the Mysteries.[24]

This is an attractive theory. There were Orphic poems about descent into Hades called καταβάσεις, and Virgil may have taken ideas from these. It is true also that bees are, very occasionally, mentioned as symbols of rebirth, as Norden recalled in connection with *Aeneid* 6. 706 ff., where the souls waiting to be reborn are likened to bees,[25] though we must bear in mind that bees were symbolic of many other things also in antiquity.[26] It is harder to believe that the whole of the *Georgics* should be interpreted with reference to the Mystery Religions.[27] The inclusion of Triptolemus, inventor of the plough, among the *di agrestes* (1. 19) and the references at 1. 163–6 to *Eleusinae matris volventia plaustra, mystica vannus Iacchi* and *virgea Celei supellex* are hardly significant for such speculations; and as for Bacchus and Ceres, whatever their connection with those Religions, their occurrence in a poem on agriculture need not involve it. The difficulty also remains: Why did Virgil invent or adopt a variant version in which Orpheus loses Eurydice again? Can we look further than a Catullan desire to present a poignant contrast?

So much for the introduction of the Orpheus episode. Without it, indeed, the story would not be satisfactory, as Norden showed.[28] But it still remains to inquire whether the Aristaeus episode, apart from providing an *aition* for 'Bugonia', has any organic connection with the rest of the poem. In 1930, that year of relevant new ideas, Bayet suggested that, whereas the theme of Book 3 was love and death, that of Book 4 was chastity and immortality.[29] If Book 3 ends in the Triumph of Death, Book 4 ends in the Triumph of Life. Interpretation on such lines has recently gone further. Klingner has suggested[30] that, as in Catullus' Peleus epyllion and Allius elegy the contrasting themes together compose a unity at a higher level, summarising the poet's own higher life, so Virgil has integrated two stories, of newly granted and ever renewed life and of life passionately resought, almost regained, and then lost with utter finality, into a unity of opposites that expresses his deepest intuitions. The life of the individual is fraught with pain, tragedy and death; but life is also the all-pervading and joyfully stirring spirit of life, which gives and takes back all individual life, so that, universally speaking, 'there is no room for death'. He is, in fact, connecting the epyllion with the pantheistic views attributed to '*quidam*' at 219–27, interpreted as embodying a consolatory theory of the universe in which all the pain, disease and death for man and beast, which are represented in Book 3 without redemption, are redeemed and absorbed into a higher divine order. These ideas are in turn picked up in *Aeneid* 6, where the description of the underworld existence has echoes of the Orpheus passage and the speech of Anchises adopts and develops the views expressed at 219–27 here.

No summary can do justice to the eloquence with which Klingner develops his interpretation, one which indeed seems particularly bound up with German modes of language and thought. What gives one pause is rereading the poem. If Virgil, consciously at least, intended us to draw such conclusions, would he not have described the rebirth of the bees in lines less perfunctory than 554–8? Would he not have given us some clearer indication that this is to be a symbol of resurrection and life everlasting? And in general, can we believe that his mind moved with such modern freedom in the realm of abstract and metaphysical ideas?

Otis meanwhile was speculating along somewhat similar lines. He sees in 219–27 'a theological idea to be set against the death-dealing nature of the second half of III'. 'Death has now been overcome by renewed life; the bees emerge from a putrifying corpse like one of the corpses described at the end of III.' But 'we cannot understand the poem finally until we have understood the actual conclusion, its conception of the moral *cause* and *origin* of resurrection'. 'Resurrection also requires death as its counterpart, and the relation of the two must be at bottom a *moral* relation.'[31] And so, he suggests, we have the Aristaeus epyllion, to the meaning of which Orpheus is the key. 'Despite the nobility and humanity of Orpheus' attempt to win the victory over death, he lacks the strength of character, the control of passion, which are the indispensable conditions of victory. The problem of resurrection is at bottom a moral problem.' The whole poem is then reinterpreted from a new perspective. For Otis all its antitheses are resolved 'when man, exercising his full moral powers of control, work, self-sacrifice and devotion to his *patria*, finds himself supported by the *logos* and indwelling spirit of the whole cosmos... Man is, so to speak, at the centre of a vast network of cosmic sympathy and moral law. There is both *iustitia* and *humanitas* at the heart of things.'* The moral implied in the Orpheus story, and implicitly in the Aristaeus story, is 'the law of self-control which even the most sympathetic *amor* and the most resplendent art must observe'.[32]

It is true that Anchises' speech at *Aeneid* 6. 735–51 expounds a doctrine of purgation from sin by suffering before rebirth. But to make the end of *Georgics* 4 even approach to that there should be much more emphasis on the crime and punishment of *Aristaeus*, while Orpheus' *furor* is punished by death for Eurydice and ultimately for himself, not by any preparation for rebirth. The doctrine that resurrection is in itself a reward for moral self-discipline in this life seems foreign to ancient thought. I confess that I find Otis' interpretation here inflated and fanciful 'uplift', for all its ingenuity.

To sum up, I believe that Virgil would have thought an *aition* for 'Bugonia' a suitable ending for a book on bees, Aristaeus a suitable hero for this *aition*, and epyllion a suitable form for it. He would have looked for a contrasting story to inset in his epyllion. Why he chose Orpheus for this is more a matter of speculation, and also to what extent either the Orpheus passage or (more plausibly) the Aristaeus epyllion has a symbolic meaning for the interpretation of the *Georgics* as a whole.

---

* What then of 'ignoscenda quidem scirent si ignoscere manes'?

VI · *Philosophical, Moral and Religious Ideas*

The quietism of the Epicurean garden, with which the Golden Age dreams and the idealisation of *otia* in the *Eclogues* were in harmony, persists in the very different atmosphere of the *Georgics* as freedom from worldly ambition: '*flumina amem silvasque inglorius*'. In the Epilogue, in which 'great Caesar' is described as treading the way to immortality by his conquests, the poet is happy to contrast himself as '*studiis florentem ignobilis oti*'—'flourishing in the pursuits of inconspicuous leisure'. There are times also in the *Georgics* when we seem to hear the rationalistic tones of Lucretius. Remedies for ulcers in sheep must not be neglected; otherwise

> alitur vivitque tegendo,
> dum medicas adhibere manus ad vulnera pastor
> abnegat et meliora deos sedet omnia poscens,

the trouble grows and thrives by being covered up, while the shepherd refuses to apply healing hands to the wounds and sits beseeching the gods that everything may get better (3. 454–6).

One recalls the plague in Lucretius, with the medical profession cowed and reduced to mumbling—'*mussabat tacito medicina timore*' (4. 1179). At 1. 410 ff. Virgil takes a weather-sign from Aratus (1003 ff.), the low cawing of rooks when rain has passed. He seizes on a phrase which stops short of anthropomorphism, χαίρειν κέ τις ὠΐσσαιτο—'*one would think* they were glad'—and asserts their gladness in fully human terms; then quite unexpectedly draws back and repudiates any idea that they are divinely gifted with prescience, giving instead a biochemical explanation which seems to have been suggested by Lucretius' remarks in a different context (variations of sound emitted by animals in varying circumstances[1]), though the scientific basis is Peripatetic.*

> tum liquidas corvi presso ter gutture voces
> aut quater ingeminant, et saepe cubilibus altis

---

* *Denset...relaxat:* cf. Arist. *Phys.* 8. 7. 260 b 7 ff.: ἔτι δὲ τῶν παθημάτων ἀρχὴ πύκνωσις καὶ μάνωσις. The psychology is reminiscent of Posidonian Stoicism, but the conclusion is anti-Stoic. See Richter's note.

nescio qua praeter solitum dulcedine laeti
inter se in foliis strepitant: iuvat imbribus actis
progeniem parvam dulcisque revisere nidos:
haud, equidem credo, quia sit divinitus illis
ingenium aut rerum fato prudentia maior;
verum ubi tempestas et caeli mobilis umor
mutavere vices et Iuppiter uvidus Austris
denset erant quae rara modo, et quae densa relaxat,
vertuntur species animorum, et pectora motus
nunc alios, alios dum nubila ventus agebat,
concipiunt: hinc ille avium concentus in agris
et laetae pecudes et ovantes gutture corvi.*

Then rooks with constricted throats three or four times repeat their liquid cry, and often in their high dormitories, gladdened by some strange, unusual delight, chatter together among the leaves: they love, when the rain has blown over, to revisit their little brood and sweet familiar nests:—it is not, I believe, that god has endowed them with special powers or fate with a larger fore-knowledge; but when the weather and the shifting atmosphere of the sky has changed course, and the heaven moist with southerly gales condenses what was rare just now, and rarifies what was dense, their minds undergo a physical change, and their hearts feel impulses other than those they felt while the wind was driving up the clouds. Hence that chorus of birds in the countryside, the gladness of the cattle and the rooks' exultant paean.

This passage has naturally been contrasted with that concerning the divine nature of bees at 4. 219 ff. Whereas here Virgil speaks for himself, there the opinions expressed are attributed to *quidam*, and indeed two separate opinions have been made to merge. The first is that the nature of bees is so 'miraculous' that it must be somehow divine.[2] In the words of the Koran, 'The Lord spake by inspiration to the bee'. The second is that the whole universe is permeated with 'deus', and that all living creatures derive their life from this, returning it on death to the stars of heaven.† This is an excellent example of the way in which Virgil will recast a Lucretian idea to express a different approach. Lucretius had

---

* Note again the 'ring-composition'; *corvi presso gutture* in the first line, *ovantes gutture corvi* in the last.

† Conflation of (?) Pythagorean, Platonic and Stoic ideas. See Richter on 415 ff.

claimed that there was no room for death because dissolved bodies supplied *material* for new bodies (3. 964-71); Virgil applies the same idea to *souls*.

> his quidam signis atque haec exempla secuti
> esse apibus partem divinae mentis et haustus
> aetherios dixere: deum namque ire per omnis
> terrasque tractusque maris caelumque profundum;
> hinc pecudes, armenta, viros, genus omne ferarum,
> quemque sibi tenuis nascentem arcessere vitas:
> scilicet huc reddi deinde ac resoluta referri
> omnia, nec morti esse locum, sed viva volare
> sideris in numerum atque alto succedere caelo.

These signs and evidences have led some to believe that bees have a share in the Divine Logos and draw ethereal draughts; for god (they hold) pervades all lands and expanses of sea and depths of the sky; thence flocks, herds, men and all species of wild beast derive, each one at birth, the subtle essence of life; thither moreover all things at the end are returned, dissolved and reabsorbed, nor is there room for death, but alive they fly up to join the stars and mount to heaven on high.

One might argue that Virgil was here simply expressing, without endorsing, philosophic views of others suggested by the context, were it not that similar views are the basis of Anchises' exposition at *Aeneid* 6. 724 ff., where we must assume that the poet is lending the highest authority to a metaphysic with which he is at least more in sympathy than with any other, something analogous to a Platonic myth perhaps. As it is, we must suppose that this is a signpost of the direction in which his ideas were moving in the years that went to the making of the *Georgics* (see p. 70);* and it is indeed a natural culmination of the profound sympathy he shows with the things he is describing, which became ever more

* The repetition of the line
> terrasque tractusque maris caelumque profundum

from *Eclogue* 4. 51 is a reminder that ideas of nature being moved in sympathy with human events had interested him even earlier. Paratore has argued that 'all the premises for the composition of the *Georgics* can be found in the cultural ambience of contemporary Epicureanism' (*Virgilio*, p. 243); but it seems more plausible to diagnose some influences from other philosophies.

evocative of this feeling from Book to Book—crops, trees, animals, bees.

On the other hand, one might think that all this was derived from Pythagoreanism, for the doctrine of the transmigration of souls encouraged such ideas. There is indeed evidence of a considerable revival of this philosophy in Rome during Virgil's youth, connected with the name of Nigidius Figulus. But although there are ideas in the *Fourth Eclogue* shared if not held exclusively by Pythagoreans,[3] we need not suppose that Virgil, who indicates the Sibyl of Cumae (not far from Siro's Epicurean school) as his primary source, became an adherent of the sect;* and Anchises' doctrines, though they contain Pythagorean elements, seem to have come to Virgil through Varro, who in turn may have owed them either to the Stoic Posidonius or to the Academic Antiochus of Ascalon.[4]

Though Virgil here expresses ideas associated with Neopythagoreanism, he is hardly more likely to have been an out-and-out member of that school than Ovid, who puts into the mouth of Pythagoras a moving plea that animals, the friends of man, should not be slaughtered for food.† Still less Lucretius, whose even more moving description of a cow searching and pining for its calf which has been sacrificed inspired Virgil's of the ploughing ox pining for its dead yoke-mate (3. 515–30), which deserves quotation here as the most explicit and elaborate expression of the sympathy that permeates the whole poem. In Lucretius the cow was moved by natural maternal instinct.[5] In Virgil both ploughman and yokemate are distressed at the loss of a fellow-worker. Their feeling is social.[6] '*Quid labor aut benefacta iuvant?*' as one said in laments of the human dead: 'Ah, what avails...?'

---

* His friend Horace clearly thought its tenets pretentious and rather absurd: *Ep.* 15. 21; *S.* 2. 6. 63; *Odes* 1. 28. 9–16; *Epp.* 2. 1. 50–2. Virgil's sympathy with plants and animals has no real parallel in pagan literature. When it reappears in St Francis of Assisi and his followers Christianity has taken the place of pantheism as the notional basis. Paratore, *Virgilio*, p. 259.

† When Virgil at 2. 537 depicts the happiness of the Golden Age as being 'before an impious generation feasted on slaughtered oxen' he clearly has in mind the Bronze Age of *Aratus*—πρῶτοι δὲ βοῶν ἐπάσαντ' ἀροτήρων (132).

ecce autem duro fumans sub vomere taurus
concidit et mixtum spumis vomit ore cruorem
extremosque ciet gemitus. it tristis arator
maerentem abiungens fraterna morte iuvencum,
atque opere in medio defixa relinquit aratra.
non umbrae altorum nemorum, non mollia possunt
prata movere animum, non qui per saxa volutus
purior electro campum petit amnis; at ima
solvuntur latera, atque oculos stupor urget inertis
ad terramque fluit devexo pondere cervix.
quid labor aut benefacta iuvant? quid vomere terras
invertisse gravis? atqui non Massica Bacchi
munera, non illis epulae nocuere repostae:
frondibus et victu pascuntur simplicis herbae,
pocula sunt fontes liquidi atque exercita cursu
flumina, nec somnos abrumpit cura salubris.

Look at that bull, steaming under the strain of the plough. He has
fallen! and blood mixed with foam is gushing from his mouth as he
utters his last groans. See, the ploughman sadly goes to release his yoke-
mate stricken at his brother's death, and leaves the plough stuck in
mid-furrow. No longer can the tall trees' shade nor soft meadows touch
the beast's spirit nor streams clearer than amber that glide down over
rocks to find the plain. His sides collapse, his eyes are listless and glazed
with stupor, and down the drooping weight of his neck sinks to the
ground. What good has he got from toiling and helping, from turning
up the heavy earth with the plough? Yet such have not sapped their
strength by vintage wines or feasts of many courses. Their diet is leaves
and the simple grass of the field, their drink the limpid springs and
racing streams, nor do cares disturb their healthy sleep.

When speaking of the selection of young horses for breeding,
Virgil tells us that one point to look for is

quis cuique dolor victo, quae gloria palmae,

which minds most if beaten, glories most in the prize (3. 102).

In the description of a chariot-race which follows, however, it is
the *rider's* hopes and efforts that are in mind, till the co-operative
strivings of man and beast merge in the *epiphonema* (112),

tantus amor laudum, tantae est victoria curae,

such is their love of praise, such their desire for victory.

In the whole account of the care and training of calves and foals (138–208) Virgil sees things in terms of sympathetic education and feeling from the animal's point of view. And the description of the cow provoking the bulls to amorous rivalry (215–18) is brilliantly anthropomorphic:

> carpit enim viris paulatim uritque videndo
> femina, nec nemorum patitur meminisse nec herbae
> dulcibus illa quidem inlecebris, et saepe superbos
> cornibus inter se subigit decernere amantis.

for the female gradually saps their strength as they gaze at her, and will not allow them to remember woods or pasture, so sweet are her entice-ments, and often she reduces proud lovers to fighting over her with their horns.[7]

This kind of sympathy extends far beyond the horse and the ox, who as man's fellow-labourer naturally evoked it.* The famous simile at 4. 511 ff. is a case in point. Two passages in the *Odyssey* (19. 518 and 16. 216 ff.) describe the nightingale lamenting for Itys and vultures screaming for the loss of their young. Virgil fuses the two ideas, one mythical, the other realistic, and characteristi-cally heightens the pathos by underlining the wanton cruelty of man:[8]

> qualis populea maerens philomela sub umbra
> amissos queritur fetus, quos durus arator
> observans nido implumis detraxit; at illa
> flet noctem, ramoque sedens miserabile carmen
> integrat, et maestis late loca questibus implet

As a nightingale mourning in a poplar shade laments her lost young, whom a hard ploughman has spied and dragged all unfledged from her nest; she weeps all night and perched on a branch renews her piteous song, filling the countryside afar with her sad complaint.

Here the feeling may be said to have been prompted by literature; but who save Virgil, contemplating the felling of trees to realise timber long idle and release land especially suitable for corn-

---

* 'Partner of men in their agriculture, and servant of Ceres. Hence the ancients willed that hands should be kept off it, so that they prescribed the death penalty for anyone who killed it' (Varro 2. 5. 4).

growing, would have spared a thought for the birds stranded in mid-air with their ancient 'homes' gone (2. 208–10)?—

> et nemora evertit multos ignava per annos,
> antiquasque domos avium cum stirpibus imis
> eruit; illae altum nidis petiere relictis,

and overthrows the woods that have been many years unproductive, and uproots from their foundations the ancient homes of the birds; these leave their nests and soar upwards.

Even the smallest animals are humanised, the ant worried about poverty in old age, the *exiguus mus* that has set up its home and granaries underground. Virgil was always amused by the 'play of great and small'. As at *Aeneid* 4. 404, using ants as a simile for Trojans filing down to reload their ships, he borrows a phrase that Ennius had applied to elephants, '*it nigrum campis agmen*',[9] so the gadfly at *Georgics* 3. 149, '*asper, acerba sonans*', awakes memories of the dragon that guarded the apples of the Hesperides in Lucretius, *asper, acerba tuens* (5. 33). Bees at their several tasks are compared with Cyclopes in Vulcan's forge (4. 170–5):

> ac veluti lentis Cyclopes fulmina massis
> cum properant, alii taurinis follibus auras
> accipiunt redduntque, alii stridentia tingunt
> aera lacu; gemit impositis incudibus Aetna;
> illi inter sese magna vi bracchia tollunt
> in numerum, versantque tenaci forcipe ferrum,

as, when Cyclopes are busily forging thunderbolts from stubborn lumps of ore, some blow in and out with the ox-hide bellows, and others plunge the hissing metal in the trough, while Etna groans beneath the weight of the anvils; in rhythmic succession they heave up their strong arms, and turn the iron with gripping tongs.

This play of great and small is also delightfully implied at 4. 26, where surroundings are being chosen for the hive. In the nearby stream you must put stepping stones for the bees, islands on which they may rest and dry their wings. Varro used the diminutive *lapilli* for these (which are really to help them drink: 3. 16. 27). Virgil calls them '*grandia saxa*'. Why? Because he is seeing them from a bee's-eye view, as also when he calls the surrounding water

'*Neptunus*' (29). On the other hand, the bees themselves are constantly seen in this Book from a man's-eye view. They have their *sedes* and *statio*, their *domus* with *portae, fores, limen, cubile* and *Lares*, their *patria, urbs* and *oppidum*, with *cerea regna, sedes augusta, aula* and *Penates*. Their commonwealth will be considered later (pp. 175–82).

It was natural enough that Virgil should speak in anthropomorphic terms of the larger animals in Book 3, horses and cattle (he does not do so of sheep and goats, which are somehow less 'human'); that the defeated bull should 'go into exile' (225) from his 'ancestral kingdom' (228), and when recovered and ready should 'advance his standards' to battle (235). He did not distinguish animals from men when he spoke of the destiny of all *miseri mortales*—disease, age, suffering and death (66–8), investing with poignant feeling what had been a cliché in Homer and Lucretius. He was to use his description of the defeated bull returning to the fight almost word for word as a simile for Turnus in the *Aeneid*, Turnus who was also involved in a conflict with a rival in love.[10] Nor is it very remarkable that he should use of the larger animals words denoting human relationships—*maritum* (125), *patrum, nati* (128), *patrum, matrum* (138). What is striking is that he should even apply to their 'marriage' words that had a religious connotation for Romans—*Lucinam, hymenaeos* (60).

We saw that the farmer is sometimes represented as struggling with his soil and plants, disciplining them, subduing them. But at other times he is helping them (*iuvat*, 1. 95; *opis nostrae*, 2. 427). They can be taught, or induced to follow (2. 77; 52); and they in turn respond and are grateful (1. 147; 2. 64; 1. 88). You may say that these are metaphors—Aristotle's favourite ἡ κατ᾽ ἐνέργειαν μεταφορά sustained to great lengths—or conventional exploitations of the 'pathetic fallacy'. But the use of anthropomorphic language is so pervasive—I have counted more than fifty instances in the first two Books—that it seems rather to be evidence of the disposition which attracted Virgil to pantheism. It runs like life-blood through these Books. Nature is not 'inanimate'—*animos tollunt sata*, the crops 'lift up their spirits' when the moisture penetrates, a phrase commonly used of men but here for the first time, so far as we know, of plants.[11] By patient cultivation wild trees may be induced to shed their *silvestres animos* and readily be civilised *in quascunque voces artes* (2. 51–2); on the other hand fruits deprived of attention degenerate and 'forget' their former flavour (2. 59). The nut-trees 'dress themselves' with blossom, and the apple-trees with fruit (1. 187; 4. 142). Trees, like animals, are spoken of in terms of human relationships: they have *proles* (2. 3), which recognise their mother (2. 268), and from 'the tender body of their mother' shoots are torn (2. 23). Wines are addressed with something more than the mechanical figure of apostrophe (2. 95–102): 'How can I do justice to you in poetry, Rhaetic?—But I mustn't let you think you can rival Falernian'...'In the presence of Amminean even Tmolian and the regal Chian must rise'... 'I'm not forgetting you, Rhodian, nor you, Bumastian' (2. 95–6, 101–2). Young vines are spoken of as if they were schoolboys, the pruning-knife their cane (2. 362–70):

> ac dum prima novis adolescit frondibus aetas,
> parcendum teneris, et dum se laetus ad auras
> palmes agit laxis per purum immissus habenis,
> ipsa acie nondum falcis temptanda, sed uncis
> carpendae manibus frondes interque legendae.
> inde ubi iam validis amplexae stirpibus ulmos
> exierint, tum stringe comas, tum bracchia tonde
> (ante reformidant ferrum), tum denique dura
> exerce imperia et ramos compesce fluentis.

While they are growing up and putting out their first leaves they are delicate and must be treated gently, and while the shoots are given their head to reach up happily skyward into the fresh air you must not take the knife to themselves yet—just pluck their leaves with your finger nails and thin them out here and there. But later, when they have grown tall and are putting strong arms round the elms, then you must prune the leaves, then you must cut back the branches (before that they shrink from the steel), then it is time to exert stern discipline and curb the wayward limbs.

It might almost be Quintilian speaking.

Virgil's *humanitas*, his sympathy with his fellow-men, pervasive in the *Eclogues* and still more in the *Aeneid*, is naturally less in evidence in the *Georgics* outside the Aristaeus epyllion and apart from the general interest he has in the *colonus* and all he does. But it may be worth drawing attention to a phrase used of the countryman at 2. 498–9:

> neque ille
> aut doluit miserans inopem aut invidit habenti.

Servius, thinking that *doluit* was the operative word, sought to defend him from a charge of heartlessness by interpreting the line to mean that the countryman achieves a philosophic state of mind in which he realises that poverty is not an evil any more than wealth is a good. Surely this is mistaken. The operative word (in the first half) is *miserans*. Virgil characteristically assumes that one of the troubles about living in the town is distress caused by the sight of the poor as well as by envy of the rich. It is also characteristic that he should make the Sun veil his face at Caesar's murder not in hatred but in *pity* for Rome (1. 466).

Turning to Virgil after the sturdy rationalism of Lucretius one is inclined to think of him as a sentimentalist. But in fact he shows a realistic attitude to farming, even where the struggle for existence is not involved. The thoroughbred horse that is diseased or superannuated is not, indeed, to be put to death with Catonian ruthlessness; but the instruction is firm (3. 96):

> abde domo, nec turpi ignosce senectae,

put it away indoors and have no mercy on its mean old age.

The inferior king-bee is dealt with summarily (4. 90): *dede neci*. If the hive shows signs of swarming-fever (4. 106), *tu regibus alas eripe*. The *tu* is emphatic: you've got to tear off their wings yourself. If your sheep have scab (3. 452–6), there is no better chance of success than to cut off the head of the ulcer:

> non tamen ulla magis praesens fortuna laborum est
> quam si quis ferro potuit rescindere summum
> ulceris os.

Why '*potuit*'? Because you have to nerve yourself to do it, instead of just sitting and praying that all will come right. If necessary you must kill a sick sheep to save the rest of the flock from contagion (468). It is not that Virgil is heartless: no one less. When harvest-time comes to your hive you may be tempted, he says, to leave honey for the bees, fearing for their future if the winter proves hard, and pitying the wounded spirits and shattered store that will result—yet you must not hesitate to fumigate the hive with thyme and cut away the empty cells, for often you will find that various pests have eaten into them. The more exhausted they are, the more eager the bees will in fact be to rebuild and replenish (4. 239–50). Having noticed the plight of the birds rendered homeless by tree-clearance (2. 208–10) he adds realistically,

> at rudis enituit impulso vomere campus,

but the virgin land gleams as the plough drives through it.

No tears must be shed.

In one other respect we may be justified in sensing that Virgil's treatment goes beyond what is dictated by the exigencies of his subject and expresses a peculiarity of his own psyche—his treatment of sex. The horrific outburst about lust as destroyer which comes as climax of the first part of Book 3 obliterates all memory of normal breeding. Moreover, the only loves of human beings mentioned prove disastrous—Leander, Aristaeus, Orpheus. Sexual jealousy drives the Thracian women to their horrible crime. Love for Dido, and again for Lavinia, causes havoc in the *Aeneid*:

> improbe amor, quid non mortalia pectora cogis?

This view he shares with Lucretius, for whom *libido* is in itself *dira*, and love in a real sense a wound, a suppurating ulcer.[12] Even normal sexual intercourse he assumes to be debilitating (3. 209–10). From the various theories current about the reproduction of bees Virgil, obviously concerned to idealise them, chooses that which represented them as not indulging in sexual intercourse at all, and adds that this saves them from enervation:

> neque concubitu indulgent, neque corpora segnes
> in Venerem solvunt.[13]

This trait might be rationalised as a Stoical belief in subjecting the passions to reason, or indeed as Epicurean avoidance of involving the emotions; but it seems more like a personal obsession of the shy unmarried poet.*

But the dominant moral idea in the poem is that of the dignity of labour. The image of the Sabine peasant, one whose virtuous wife would heap logs on the fire towards sunset to welcome her tired husband home, was already current at Rome;[14] but in the *Georgics* it clearly owes it prominence to the influence of Hesiod. With labour go hardiness, simple pleasures and freedom from the corruption of city life and luxury (2. 503–12). When Cicero in the *De Senectute* expatiates on gardening as a pleasure for the old (54), he instances a number of famous people from Laertes, the father of Odysseus, to M. Valerius Corvinus, and particularly the younger Cyrus, on whom he makes Cato comment, '*nihil illi tam regale videri quam studium agri colendi*', 'he thought nothing so kingly as enthusiasm for agriculture'. Burck has well observed that Virgil, who doubtless knew the passage, has characteristically chosen for his example an old man of the humblest origin, whose only plot was an unwanted piece of land, but who finally was as happy as any Cyrus in his achievement—'*regum aequabat opes animis*'.[15]

Virgil was more a feeler than a thinker. He could organise his feelings into a coherent poem, but he hardly attempted to organise his thoughts into a coherent system. We are told that he intended, after the *Aeneid* was finished, to devote the rest of his life to philosophy.[16] There are indications throughout his three poetic works that he had a 'cosmic sense', and he sometimes introduces passages reminiscent of the *De Rerum Natura*—Silenus' first song in *Eclogue* 6, Iopas' song in *Aeneid* 1.[17] But if he had ever written a philosophic work, one may guess that it would have been more

---

* Suetonius had good authority, Asconius Pedianus, for the story that Plotia Hiera used to say in later life that Varius had invited Virgil to cohabit with her (? or share her—*ad communionem sui*), but that he had most persistently refused (*Vita Verg.* 10). It is quite possible, of course, that his preferences were homosexual, even if repressed.

reminiscent of Plato's *Timaeus*. Much as he admired Lucretius, he
was clear that his mind was of a different cast, and it may well be
that philosophy would never have been more for him than an
'ambition manquée'. In this he was like his friend Horace who,
at the time when Virgil was pressing on to finish the *Aeneid*, was
also, by his own account, aspiring to be a philosopher but unable
to make up his mind about fundamentals, just as he greatly
admired Pindar but realised that he must be content to reach
poetic excellence by a different path.[18] Virgil's self-knowledge
found expression in a famous contrast (2. 475–502):

> me vero primum dulces ante omnia Musae,
> quarum sacra fero ingenti percussus amore,
> accipiant caelique vias et sidera monstrent,
> defectus solis varios lunaeque labores;
> unde tremor terris, qua vi maria alta tumescant
> obicibus ruptis rursusque in se ipsa residant,
> quid tantum Oceano properent se tingere soles
> hiberni, vel quae tardis mora noctibus obstet.
> sin has ne possim naturae accedere partis
> frigidus obstiterit circum praecordia sanguis,
> rura mihi et rigui placeant in vallibus amnes,
> flumina amem silvasque inglorius...
> felix qui potuit rerum cognoscere causas,
> atque metus omnis et inexorabile fatum
> subiecit pedibus strepitumque Acherontis avari.
> fortunatus et ille deos qui novit agrestis...

As for me, above all else I would that the sweet Muses whose devotee
I am, smitten with a great desire, should accept me and show me the
stars of the sky in their courses, the various eclipses of the sun and the
travails of the moon, whence come earthquakes, what force makes
the seas swell high to break their barriers and subside to their level
again, why winter's suns make such haste to dip beneath the Ocean, or
what it is that delays the lingering nights. But if some sluggishness of
wit denies me access to this sphere of nature, may the countryside and
the streams that water its valleys be my delight, let me love the rivers
and woods, careless of fame...Happy the man who has been able to
discover the causes of things, and has trampled underfoot all fears of
inexorable fate and the clamour of hungry Hell. Happy too the man
who knows the gods of the country...

Both the philosopher and the lover of the country achieve, however, the same end, freedom from the cares and ambitions of political and social life. *Frigidus circum praecordia sanguis* does not imply what 'cold blood around my heart' would to us. It refers to the ancient idea that *thought* was conditioned by the blood there.* Virgil pointedly uses by contrast words of *feeling—placeant, amem.* Nevertheless he did have philosophical intuitions which were original even if suggested by predecessors. His eclecticism could be creative. The most important instance comes early in the work, and is, I believe, intended to affect our response to the whole. It is his Theodicy of Labour (1. 121–46). † There was a passage in Lucretius (5. 206–17) dealing with the troubles of agriculture which seems to have profoundly affected him, so much so that he echoes it half-a-dozen times in different parts of the *Georgics*:

quod superest arvi tamen id natura sua vi
sentibus obducat, ni vis humana resistat
vitai causa valido consueta bidenti
ingemere et terram pressis proscindere aratris.
si non fecundas vertentes vomere glaebas
terraique solum subigentes cimus ad ortus,
sponte sua nequeant liquidas existere in auras.
et tamen interdum magno quaesita labore,
cum iam per terras frondent atque omnia florent,
aut nimiis torret fervoribus aetherius sol
aut subiti perimunt imbres gelidaeque pruinae,
flabraque ventorum violento turbine vexant.

Nature by her own force would spread brambles all over the remaining land if she were not resisted by the force of man, accustomed for his livelihood to groan over the strong drag-hoe and furrow the fields with deep-driven ploughs. If we did not turn over the fertile clods with the

---

* αἷμα γὰρ ἀνθρώποις περικάρδιόν ἐστι νόημα: Empedocles fr. 105. Blood as one possibility: Plato, *Phaed.* 96b. Cf. Lucr. 3. 45. Empedocles, Aratus and Lucretius are probably the poets for whom Virgil here implies envious admiration.

† I here draw freely on my article 'Virgil's Theodicy' in *C.Q.* (1963), pp. 75–84. For background see the Fondation Hardt Entretiens on Hesiod, vol. VII (1962), esp. pp. 215–70 (A. La Penna on Hesiod and his influence); also the valuable dissertation of J. Lünenborg, *Das philosophische Weltbild in Vergils Georgika* (Münster, 1935).

ploughshare and subdue the soil to summon them to birth, the crops could not of their own accord spring up into the clear air. And even so sometimes fruit trees won with great labour, when they are leafy throughout the land and all in flower, are either scorched by excessive heat from the sun above or destroyed by sudden rainstorms or chill frosts, or harried by the blast of violent whirlwinds.

Virgil undoubtedly had this passage in mind when, contemplating the agricultural struggle, he wrote (1. 199)

> sic omnia fatis
> in peius ruere,

thus everything is destined to rapid degeneration.

Lucretius refused to believe that the world was providentially ordained for man's benefit—*tanta stat praedita culpa* (5. 199). On the contrary, he believed that in the process of nature destruction was overtaking creation, until finally 'a single day shall give to destruction' the whole universe (2. 1146; 5. 95).* Virgil's temperament was more optimistic and religious, but he had to face up to the Problem of Evil from the start. Whereas Lucretius pointed to the fact that a large part of the world was unfit for human habitation as evidence that it was not created for man's benefit, Virgil went out of his way (that is, the way of his source Eratosthenes) to acknowledge that man has been allotted two temperate zones 'by the bounty of the gods'.[19] He felt a need, in fact, to 'justify the ways of God to men'. Introducing some of the nuisances that harass the farmer—geese, cranes, chicory, shade—he says,

> Pater ipse colendi
> haud facilem esse viam voluit, primusque per artem

---

* It was a common assumption at Rome that the earth was degenerating in fertility, perhaps due to unconscious analogy with the human individual. Columella felt obliged to begin his treatise by arguing against it. Lucretius subscribed to it (2. 1146 ff.), though elsewhere (5. 937 ff.) he speaks only of the arbute-berries and acorns, the food of 'hard' primitive man, as being larger and more plentiful originally; and elsewhere again (5. 1361–76) he acknowledges agricultural progress. Virgil assumes that the peasant turning up ages later the remains of those killed at Philippi will marvel at their '*grandia ossa*' (1. 497). True, soil-erosion was probably an observable fact in Italy.

> movit agros curis acuens mortalia corda
> nec torpore gravi passus sua regna veterno.

The Father himself did not wish the way of cultivation to be easy, and first caused the fields to be worked with skill, sharpening the wits of mortals by care and not suffering his kingdom to lapse into heavy lethargy.

(His kingdom, we may note, is as much the minds of men as the fields that feed them.)[20] He proceeds to develop this theme, first harking back to what went before in the Hesiodic myth:

> ante Iovem nulli subigebant arva coloni;
> ne signare quidem aut partiri limite campum
> fas erat: in medium quaerebant, ipsaque tellus
> omnia liberius nullo poscente ferebat,

before Jupiter's reign no peasants subdued the fields; it was not lawful even to assign or divide the ground with landmarks: men sought the common gain, and the earth itself bore everything more generously at no one's bidding.

This is the Golden Age, and superficially it sounds perfect. We know from Book 4, the bees' republic (149 ff.), that communistic ideas made a strong appeal to Virgil:* they were a symptom of the exceptional nature with which Jupiter endowed bees as a reward for saving him in his infancy; and self-seeking was a feature of the contemporary age which repelled him. And yet he believes that Jupiter devised 'a more excellent way'.†

> ille malum virus serpentibus addidit atris,
> praedarique lupos iussit pontumque moveri,
> mellaque decussit foliis ignemque removit,
> et passim rivis currentia vina repressit,

---

* Communism in the Golden Age is a Hellenistic, not Hesiodic, trait (Richter). Contrast Lucretius' view of primitive men: *nec commune bonum poterant spectare* (5. 958). Evander at *Aen.* 8. 314–27 makes Saturn's Golden Age of 'soft' primitivism succeed an original period of 'hard' primitivism, to last until the ages deteriorated through strife and greed. For the distinction see A. O. Lovejoy and G. Boas, *Primitivism and Related Ideas in Antiquity* (1935), pp. 10–11; M. E. Taylor, 'Primitivism in Virgil', *A.J.Ph.* (1955), pp. 261–78.

† I cannot agree with H. Altevogt, *Labor Improbus* (1952), p. 10, that 'Virgil's love belongs to the easy existence of the Saturnian Age'. He takes Labor here to be an evil spirit, the daemon who is coupled with Egestas at *Aen.* 6. 276 ff.: *ibid.* pp. 7 ff.

> ut varias usus meditando extunderet artis
> paulatim, et sulcis frumenti quaereret herbam,
> ut silicis venis abstrusum excuderet ignem.
> tunc alnos primum fluvii sensere cavatas;
> navita tum stellis numeros et nomina fecit
> Pleiadas, Hyadas, claramque Lycaonis Arcton;
> tum laqueis captare feras et fallere visco
> inventum et magnos canibus circumdare saltus;
> atque alius latum funda iam verberat amnem
> alta petens, pelagoque alius trahit umida lina;
> tum ferri rigor atque argutae lammina serrae
> (nam primi cuneis scindebant fissile lignum),
> tum variae venere artes. labor omnia vicit
> improbus et duris urgens in rebus egestas.

It was he that gave black snakes their noxious poison, bade the wolves ravin, and the sea swell, shook down the honey from the leaves, removed fire, and stopped the wine that flowed in rivers everywhere, so that experience combined with thought should gradually hammer out various crafts, looking to furrows for the cornstalk and striking from veins of flint the hidden fire. Then did rivers first feel the hollowed alders; the sailor then grouped and named the stars, Pleiades, Hyades and the bright Bear, Lycaon's child; then it was discovered how to snare beasts in nets and birds with lime, and throw cordons of hounds around wide coverts; and one now whips a broad river with a casting-net, searching the depths, another drags a trawl through the sea; then came the hard iron and the shrill blade of the saw (for primitive men used to split their wood with wedges), then all the various arts. Relentless toil has mastered everything, and the pressure of pinching poverty.

Let us see how Virgil may have come to this theodicy. Life in the Golden Age in Hesiod's *Works and Days* (109–26) was a paradise of idleness, of 'soft primitivism'. Sophisticated thinkers like Plato could not fail to realise its hollowness.[21] As Milton's Adam, driven from Eden, reflected philosophically:

> With labour must I earn
> My bread? What harm? Idleness had been worse.

Whatever he may have dreamed of in the *Eclogues*, and however much he approved of communal sharing, the Virgil of the *Georgics* could not dwell on an idea so discordant with the life he was concerned to commend. Hesiod himself had concluded that the gods had made sweat the precondition of ἀρετή.[22] To the Cynics labour was one of the goods,[23] and the Stoics made a special hero of Heracles. Aratus significantly mentions ploughing in the Golden Age; and in Italian myth Saturn himself, taking refuge in Latium from Jupiter, introduced agriculture, so that his host Janus ordered him to be worshipped 'as originator of a better life'.[24]

In Hesiod Zeus, angry at Prometheus' attempt to deceive him over a sacrifice, hid from men the means of livelihood, including fire. Prometheus stole fire and gave it back to men. We have here a crude *aition* for the existence of trouble in the world, and a symbolic *aition* for the partial conquest of it. For later generations at least fire became an explicit symbol of technical progress. As such it occurs in Aeschylus and Plato.[25] Any idea that technical progress was contrary to the will of the gods had faded; the very cults of deities of techniques, Prometheus himself (god of smiths and potters in Attica), Hephaestus, Demeter and Athena Ergane contradicted it. The notion that they fostered progress by making it an educative process of discovery may be discerned in a fragment of Xenophanes.[26] According to Strabo, Onesicratus, sent by Alexander to interview Brahmans, claimed to have heard that Zeus was so disgusted with the *hybris* bred of the luxury of the Golden Age that he wiped it out and made work the condition of livelihood.[27] From the fifth century onwards Greece also showed much interest in the inventors of past improvements.[28] Plato certainly never pretended that the development of the arts had not been a blessing.[29] Nearer home, Virgil would be familiar with a passage in Lucretius full of enthusiasm for both the aesthetic and the practical effects of agricultural progress (5. 1361–78):

at specimen sationis et insitionis origo
ipsa fuit rerum primum natura creatrix,
arboribus quoniam bacae glandesque caducae
tempestiva dabant pullorum examina subter;
unde etiam libitumst stirpis committere ramis
et nova defodere in terram virgulta per agros.
inde aliam atque aliam culturam dulcis agelli

> temptabant fructusque feros mansuescere terra
> cernebant indulgendo blandeque colendo.
> inque dies magis in montem succedere silvas
> cogebant infraque locum concedere cultis,
> prata, lacus, rivos, segetes, vinetaque laeta
> collibus et campis ut haberent, atque olearum
> caerula distinguens inter plaga currere posset
> per tumulos et convallis camposque profusa
> ut nunc esse vides *vario distincta lepore*
> *omnia*, quae pomis intersita dulcibus ornant
> arbustisque tenent felicibus obsita circum.

But nature herself, creatress of things, first set the example for sowing and grafting, since berries and acorns fallen from trees sent up in due course swarms of shoots beneath. From her too they learnt to insert grafts into branches and plant new bushes over the land. Then they tried out ways, one after another, of cultivating their beloved plot, and saw wild fruit-trees become tame in the ground by coaxing and fond care. And day by day they forced the woods to recede up the mountains and give up the land below to cultivation, so that on plains and hillsides they might have meadows, ponds, streams, crops and glad vineyards, and let a belt of grey olive trees run between to make a clear division, stretching over mounds and hollows and level ground, even as now you see the whole clearly patterned with the charm of variety, where men beautify it by planting pleasant fruit-trees here and there, and keep it hedged around with fertile shrubs.

Lucretius attributed past progress to Necessity, working by human observation of nature, experiment and sheer luck. For centuries, however, monotheistic ideas had also been developing. Hesiod's Zeus was already on the way to becoming absolute, but, though guardian of Dike, he was a jealous god.[30] The idea of a supreme deity who was also benign was promoted by Xenophanes and the Pythagoreans.[31] The conception of Zeus as Father and Providence would be especially familiar to Virgil from Aratus' prologue:

> τοῦ γὰρ καὶ γένος εἰμέν· ὁ δ' ἤπιος ἀνθρώποισιν
> δέξια σημαίνει, λαοὺς δ' ἐπὶ ἔργον ἐγείρει,

for we also are his offspring, and he in his kindness to men shows them favourable signs, and arouses the people to work.

He tells when the soil is best for the labour of ox and mattock, and when the seasons are right for planting trees and for all kinds of sowing. For himself it was who set the signs in the sky. *Ipse Pater statuit*, says Virgil at 1. 353, recalling this passage.

Plato conceived a fanciful theodicy of 'Plenitude', by which it was inevitable that the universe should contain all things, evil as well as good.[32] But it was the Stoics who gave most thought to Providence and the Problem of Pain. Some suggested that there might be providential purposes as yet unrevealed to us.[33] Chrysippus took refuge in the idea that this must be the best of all possible worlds, or that without evil good would be inconceivable, or that God cannot attend to all details.[34] He also suggested that lions, bears, leopards and boars (cf. Virgil's wolves) were given as a 'training' for the seeds of manliness in us.[35] Both Epictetus and Seneca have the simile of an athlete being trained by painful exercises, which may be derived ultimately from Cynic ideas of *askesis*, perhaps developed by Posidonius. As Seneca says: 'God has a fatherly spirit (cf. Virgil's "Pater ipse") towards good men and mightily loves them: "Let them be exercised by labours, pains and losses, so that they may gather true strength."'[36] The Stoics always thought of the world as man's domain.[37]

I believe that Virgil came to the idea of Jupiter *curis acuens mortalia corda* through meditating on the three poets who were uppermost in his mind, Hesiod, Aratus and Lucretius, and perhaps another, Aeschylus (*Prometheus*), though he may also have been conversant with such Stoic ideas about Providence.* He does not mention Prometheus or the Fall, but by a masterstroke transfers his rôle to Zeus himself, 'Pater ipse', the god of Aratus, Cleanthes and Chrysippus. For the Necessity of the Epicureans he substitutes Providence. As so often, Lucretian ideas are taken over, but given a different causation. Thus the passage about storms at 1. 311–34 contains no fewer than fourteen reminiscences of Lucretius, but

---

* One Hesiodic motif transformed to fit the new idea is Jupiter's hiding of fire not in heaven but in flint (1. 135), so that man must discover how to strike it out. P. Grimal, in Fondation Hardt Entretiens, VII, 260. Maecenas wrote a work called *Prometheus*, but we know nothing of its content: Sen. *Ep.* 19. 9.

it is 'ipse Pater' who wields the thunderbolt (328). Devastating though storms are, man can do something to mitigate them by *phronesis* and *pronoia*,

> hoc metuens caeli menses et sidera serva,

and also by religious observances,

> in primis venerare deos.

The instances Virgil gives at 133–45 show that he has more than agriculture in mind: this is to be a general theodicy.[38]

Explicitly it may not seem a very satisfying one;* but it seems to me to be greatly strengthened by the implicit significance of the way in which the illustrations are presented. It is true that Virgil sums up, 'labor omnia vicit *improbus*', and that is an epithet which is always pejorative.† But the word represents what the individual toiler would say about his work at the time —it does not belie the overall impression of the value of civilised activity. One can hardly read the passage, from *ut varias usus* (133) to *tum variae venere artes* (145), without feeling that Virgil is excited by the thought of the arts and crafts developing in all their *variety*.[39] Indeed it recalls no passage in previous poetry so much as Prometheus' boast in Aeschylus (442–68) of the arts he has given to man, which Virgil may quite possibly have had in mind. Is not the net effect that of Sophocles' chorus,

> πολλὰ τὰ δεινὰ κοὐδὲν ἀνθρώπου δεινότερον πέλει. . . ?

What a piece of work is a man! how noble in reason! *how infinite in faculty.*[40]

In the *Aeneid*, among those who had earned a place in Elysium, Virgil was not to forget those who had enriched life by the invention of arts (6. 663):

> inventas aut qui vitam excoluere per artes.

---

* La Penna expressed this view in the Fondation Hardt Entretiens already referred to (pp. 238–9, 258–9), and J. H. Waszink agreed: 'the justification of Providence is either lacking or very feeble in Virgil' (p. 258).

† Henry, *Aeneidea* (1873–9), II, 175; cf. Altevogt, *Labor Improbus*, who takes *labor* to mean 'das Prinzip des Unfriedens und der Unmüsse', and *omnia vicit* to mean 'auf allen Punkten siegten' (p. 6).

Joy in the *variety*, ποικιλία, of life and landscape is, as we have seen, a recurrent feature of the *Georgics*, especially Book 2. It is, I think, another of the things Virgil learnt from Lucretius. The passage from the latter quoted above culminates in a paean of delight in the patchwork panorama of a farm,

> ut nunc esse vides *vario distincta lepore*
> omnia.

And the summing up of Book 5 (1448–57), with its teeming torrent of examples taken from life as a whole, makes it abundantly clear that Lucretius feels the great reward of progress in the arts to be inseparable from this variety:

> navigia atque agri culturas, moenia, leges,
> arma, vias, vestis, et cetera de genere horum,
> praemia, delicias quoque vitae funditus omnis,
> carmina, picturas, et daedala signa polire,
> usus et impigrae simul experientia mentis
> paullatim docuit pedetemptim progredientis.
> sic unumquicquid paullatim protrahit aetas
> in medium ratioque in luminis erigit oras.
> namque alid ex alio clarescere corde videbant
> *artibus ad summum donec venere cacumen.*

Ships and farms, walls, laws, weapons, roads, dress and all such things, all the rewards and luxuries of life, every one, songs and pictures and polished sculptures intricately wrought, were gradually evolved by practice and the tireless inventiveness of the human mind as it felt its way forward step by step. So little by little time brings everything into common use and thought raises it into the realms of light. For men saw things one after another become clearer to their mind, until they reached to the height of progress in their arts.

Variety as a keynote of the *Georgics* has been sufficiently emphasised in Chapter IV. One passage may serve as a reminder. It conveys delight in the variety of the farmer's livelihood (dives opum *variarum*) and of his annual round (2. 516–22):

> nec requies, quin aut pomis exuberet annus
> aut fetu pecorum aut Cerealis mergite culmi,
> proventuque oneret sulcos atque horrea vincat.

> venit hiems: teritur Sicyonia baca trapetis,
> glande sues laeti redeunt, dant arbuta silvae;
> et *varios* ponit fetus autumnus, et alte
> mitis in apricis coquitur vindemia saxis.

No respite but the season teams with fruit, or young of herds, or sheaves of Ceres' corn, loading the furrows with produce and over-filling the barns. Winter comes round, and the olives are crushed in the presses, the swine come home sleek with acorns, and the woods yield arbute-berries; and autumn lets fall its varied fruit, and high on the sunny rocks the vintage ripens and mellows.

What Lucretius admired, and what Virgil divined to be the result of a great and paradoxical design of 'Pater ipse', has been expressed for us by Gerard Manley Hopkins in his poem *Glory be to God for dappled things*:

> Landscape plotted and pieced—fold, fallow and plough—
> And all trades, their gear and tackle and trim,
> He fathers forth whose beauty is past change.
>   Praise Him.

St Thomas Aquinas, one of the many who developed Plato's idea of the Plenitude of the Universe, said that, if the world were not constituted of things evil as well as good, creation would lose its *summus decor*, since there would be lacking that order by which things are dissimilar.[41] Theodicies are notoriously unconvincing, but Virgil's is at least one of the more plausible.

It seems to me that this passage (1. 118–46), significantly placed near the beginning, sets the philosophic tone for the *Georgics* as a whole, rather than the Praise of Country Life, which comes in the middle, at the close of Book 2, and is a sort of counterpoise to it.* Virgil wanted, for the symphonic structure of his poem, to have a cheerful passage there. He had a precedent in Hesiod, whose description of taking ease in the Dog Days (*W.D.* 582–96), already

---

* Lünenborg, *Das philosophische Weltbild*, pp. 41, 49. Klingner (1963), p. 125, sees the two passages as complementary: the whole truth emerges only from the putting together of various aspects. This is fair enough; but the terms in which Virgil praises country life are too idyllic to represent truth for this purpose. And *latis otia fundis* smacks of *latifundia*, not small holdings.

quoted on p. 5, is in striking contrast with the grim struggle depicted in the rest of his poem.* But by now the praise of country life was probably a stock theme in literature, if not also in the rhetorical schools.† Lucretius had treated it briefly at 2. 20–36; and the more elaborate treatment in Horace's *Second Epode* (*Beatus ille*...) would have a less pointed *dénouement* if it were not a conventional set-piece that the city usurer Alfius was insincerely declaiming. Virgil is in fact giving us a superb variation on this conventional theme, a townsman's dream of country life—*latis otia fundis*—indeed the dream of a literary townsman, who yearns for the romantic, poetic beauties of Greece, for *frigida Tempe* and *virginibus bacchata Lacaenis Taygeta*.⁴² We are back in the idyllic world of the *Eclogues*, especially the *Pollio*. It is true that, as in Aratus' paradise, his peasants plough (112).‡ It is true that there are elements of 'hard primitivism' here and there. The young men are

> patiens operum exiguoque adsueta iuventus

and their bodies are *praedura* (472, 531). But the passage is coloured with soft primitivism in the Golden Age tradition (459–60, 467, 500–1):

> quibus *ipsa* procul discordibus armis
> *fundit* humo *facilem victum* iustissima tellus,

for them, far from the strife of arms, the earth, ever just, pours on the ground of its own accord an easy livelihood—

> secura quies et nescia fallere vita,

secure peace is his and a livelihood that cannot fail—

> quos rami fructus, quos *ipsa volentia* rura,
> *sponte* tulere *sua*, carpsit,

---

* Virgil adapted a line from it (585) elsewhere, at 1. 341, as the commentators note: τῆμος πιότταταί τ' αἶγες καὶ οἶνος ἄριστος—*tum pingues agni et tum mollissima vina.*

† The first example Quintilian gives of a stock *thesis* is: 'Is town or country life the better?' (2. 4. 24).

‡ Virgil certainly had Aratus in mind. This is indicated not only by lines 536–40 (cf. *Phaen.* 132–4), but by the fact that it is Iustitia (Dike at *Phaen.* 127), rather than Hesiod's Aidos and Nemesis, that leaves the earth after the Golden Age (474). Not only are country people juster than townsmen, but earth is most just because it repays in full the labour put into it; cf. Xen. *Cyr.* 8. 3. 38, *Oec.* 5. 12; Cic. *De Sen.* 51. Klingner, *Hermes* (1931), p. 162.

the fruits that the branches and the fields unbidden of their own accord produce, he plucks.

The passage is thus not really in key with the theodicy of Book 1, for country life here is depicted explicitly in the concluding lines (536–8) as a survival from the Golden Age of Saturn, before the new dispensation of Jupiter; whereas the overall message of the *Georgics* is, that *labor* may be *improbus* but is rewarded by *divini gloria ruris*:

> et dubitant homines serere atque impendere curam?

and do men still hesitate to sow and to take trouble? (433).

The idea that the Golden Age life could be restored in Italy was to be made politically explicit at *Aeneid* 6. 791–3 :

> Augustus Caesar, divi genus, aurea condet
> saecula qui rursus Latio regnata per arva
> Saturno quondam,

Augustus Caesar, sprung from a god, who shall re-establish the Golden Age for Latium over fields ruled by Saturn of old.*

The message of the *Georgics* is repeated in a different sphere in the *Aeneid*: the will of Jupiter has ordained that destiny can only be worked out by great effort and hardship for men; but by recognising and conforming to that will they can attain both a better state of mind and an external reward that is worth all the trouble.

St Augustine in his *Civitas Dei* has reported to us the theological views expressed in Varro's *Antiquitates Divinae*. Here we find the tripartite division of religion, which had already a long history, into the natural (that of philosophers), the mythological (that of the poets), and the civic (that of the statesmen). Though attaching most importance to the philosophers', Varro did not reject the poets', and he thought that the statesman could make use of

---

* For Saturn in Italy see *Aen.* 8. 319–58; cf. 7. 49, 180, 203; for Saturn as early identified with Kronos, Livius Andronicus fr. 2; for Italian peasants as his last descendants, Varro, *R.R.* 3. 1. 5.

both.[43] At the beginning of his *De Re Rustica* he invoked, instead of the Muses, twelve gods; not those twelve urban gods, he adds, whose gilded images stand round the Forum, male and female in pairs, but those who are special patrons of husbandmen.* His pairs are Jupiter and Tellus, Sol and Luna, Ceres and Liber, Robigus and Flora, Minerva and Venus,† Lympha and Bonus Eventus; and it is clear that he is making his own choice, not following any cult-grouping, because he explains why he includes each.[44] (His invocation applies only to Book 1, since there is no deity of animals included.)

Virgil, obviously prompted by Varro, leads off with an invocation to twelve gods, likewise chosen by himself and largely divergent. It is significant that he omits Jupiter, the first of Varro's gods, reserving him for the theodicy that begins at line 121. This is clearly intended to indicate that his Jupiter there is the Zeus of the philosophers. He is in a different category from the gods of the countryside, though they may be introduced as implied ministers of his will, as Ceres is at 147:

> Pater ipse colendi
> haud facilem esse viam voluit primusque per artem
> movit agros...

(*accordingly*)

> prima Ceres ferro mortales vertere terram
> instituit.

As Varro's sky-god, paired with Tellus, he is emphasised only in the Praise of Spring (2. 325), the 'Pater omnipotens' who descends in rain to fertilise the Earth-mother. There he is in a mythological tradition going back to Hesiod and no doubt far beyond—more

---

* 1. 4–6. The 'urban' ones are the twelve *Dei Consentes* established, after Greek example, at the *Lectisternium* of 217 in the crisis of the Second Punic War. The number was canonical, though the identity of the gods could change. G. Wissowa, 'Das Prooemium von Vergils *Georgica*', *Hermes* (1917), pp. 96–7, an article of basic importance to which I am much indebted.

† 'Venus Hortorum', a garden and orchard goddess originally introduced from Ardea. There is no trace of her in Virgil. C. Bailey, *Religion in Virgil* (1935), p. 126.

elemental, less personal, than the supreme intelligence who was the god of the philosophers.

There are surprising omissions from Varro's list, even granted that to make up pairs there were too many males to females. Where are the old Italian deities of agriculture, Saturnus and Consus? Where is Mars, originally a god of agriculture as well as war?* But Virgil's list is more surprising:[45] Sol and Luna ('*mundi lumina*'), Liber and Ceres, Fauns and Dryads, Neptune and Aristaeus ('*cultor nemorum*', 14), Pan and Minerva, Triptolemus ('*monstrator aratri*', 19) and Silvanus. It will be seen that they are not entirely paired according to sex. Further, while the crops and trees of Books 1 and 2 are covered, as in Varro, and the horses, sheep and goats of Book 3 are under Neptune and Pan, Aristaeus is introduced as the lord of cattle, also belonging to Book 3, so that there is no patron for the bees in Book 4;† and Pales, Italian goddess of flocks and herds, invoked at the beginning of both parts of Book 3, is omitted here. Most of these deities are discoverers or inventors, πρῶτοι εὑρεταί—most, but not all. Still more surprisingly, apart from Silvanus no god in this list is genuinely Italian; for Liber and Ceres have become, really, Bacchus and Demeter, the Fauns as paired with Dryads are assimilated to Satyrs, and associated with trees,‡ Neptune is here Poseidon Σεισίχθων and Ἵππιος, and Minerva is Pallas the Greek goddess of the olive. Again there is no Saturnus or Consus or Mars.

No explanation of these peculiarities has been found. Probably there *is* no explanation. Virgil was not systematic, as we have seen. We may surmise that he started from Varro, but wished to make his invocation cover his poem as a whole; then let his imagination, not to say whim, have free rein, keeping only to the framework of six pairs. And however deeply he felt for Italian rural tradition, the gods of *poetic* tradition were Greek. The list has thus symbolic importance: it is a forefront indication that the *Georgics* is to be

---

* Cato, *De Ag.* 141, preserves a prayer offered to him at the lustration of fields.
† Virgil did not make a fetish of completeness. He does not mention the bees in his summary of the contents of the *Georgics* in the envoi, 4. 558–9.
‡ Cf. *Aen.* 12. 766: 'sacer Fauno oleaster'.

a poem, not a treatise, nor a source-book for historians of religious cults.* Thus there is a fleeting recollection at 3. 391–3, like an echo from pastoral,[46] of a strange and haunting myth, of Pan luring the Moon into the woods by the offer of a fleece of dazzling whiteness, suggested perhaps by the brilliance of a patch of moonlight in deep forest:

> munere sic niveo lanae, si credere dignum est,
> Pan deus Arcadiae captam te, Luna, fefellit
> in nemora alta vocans; nec tu aspernata vocantem.

Virgil found the story, we are told, in Nicander.† 'It could only have been a Greek', is Servius' comment.

The twelve gods of this invocation belong to the category of mythology, the religion of the poets. But Virgil produces another surprise: *teque adeo*... He introduces as a thirteenth god-to-be of the countryside one from the third category, that of the statesman —Caesar Octavian. Octavian's deification will be discussed later, in the context of politics (pp. 159–65). But it may be here said that it is in connection with him that we have the only reference in the *Georgics* to the gods of the Roman state (apart from casual references to triumphs, etc.); it is the outburst at the end of Book 1 (498–501):

> Di patrii, Indigetes, et Romule Vestaque mater,
> quae Tuscum Tiberim et Romana Palatia servas,
> hunc saltem everso iuvenem succurrere saeclo
> ne prohibete...

Gods of our fathers, native gods, and Romulus and mother Vesta who preservest the Tuscan Tiber and the Roman Palatine, do not forbid this young man at least to succour an age in ruins.

Who the Indigetes were is still a matter of dispute; but Virgil is here probably following a ritual formula. Romulus deified was the old Roman god Quirinus, his home was on the Palatine, and

---

* If this were a real prayer, the last thing a Roman would have done would be to address a god by a periphrasis, as Aristaeus and Triptolemus are here addressed. There must be no possibility of confusion. Wissowa, *Hermes* (1917), p. 95.

† Macr. *Sat.* 5. 22. 9–10. He may also have found in Nicander the story of Jupiter and the bees (4. 149–52): Richter, *ad loc.* Browning wrote a 'Dramatic Idyl' on *Pan and Luna* inspired (if that is the word) by this passage.

'Tuscan' is also a reminder of the earliest history of the city. Augustus was to establish a special cult of Vesta on the Palatine in 12 B.C.[47] This is the sort of patriotic religion we find in *Aeneid* 8. It is in place here in the context of national ruin and redemption. But it is not the sort of religion we find elsewhere in the *Georgics*.

Elsewhere we have two descriptions of rustic Italian festivals; but they are rather odd, not straightforward like Tibullus' *Ambarvalia* (2. 1) or Ovid's *Fasti*. One is of the rites of Ceres at 1. 338–50. At first we may get the impression of a single occasion, an impression subtly increased by the fourfold repetition of the goddess' name. But when we look closer we see that three different festivals are involved—the Cerealia of April 12–19 (339):

> laetis operatus in herbis
> extremae sub casum hiemis, iam vere sereno ;

the Ambarvalia of late May (341–7):

> terque *novas* circum felix eat hostia *fruges* ;

and the beginning of harvest (347–50):

> neque ante
> falcem *maturis* quisquam supponat *aristis*
> quam Cereri...

Bayet, pointing this out, gives it as an example of Virgil's penchant for synthetic description.*

The companion-piece is the rites of Bacchus at 2. 380–96. Meuli has shown that the Roman festival which Virgil treats as parallel with the Rural Dionysia is the Compitalia,[48] and that in so doing he was following Varro. But what interests us here is that the sacrifice of a goat to Bacchus (393–6) is nowhere else attested for

---

* C. Bailey had already concluded that 'Virgil was more concerned to describe a rustic spring festival than any particular act of worship' (*Religion*, p. 54). J. Bayet, 'Un procédé virgilien : la description synthétique dans les Géorgiques', in *Studi in onore di Gino Funaioli*, pp. 9–18, proposes to emphasise the discontinuity by putting a dash at *sereno* (340) and at *tecta* (347), and to obviate the inconsistency between the summer conditions of 341–2 and the spring of 340 by reading 'cum' for 'tum' at 342. I cannot however follow him in seeing the preceding storm-picture as synthetic. 311–15 is a *praeteritio* of autumn and spring storms. 316–34 are elaborations of a surprise storm, first of wind, then of thundery rain, such as summer harvest-time may bring.

this festival; and we are forced to conclude that Virgil has here introduced Greek features into a Roman cult. Bacchus, the patron-god of Book 2, the protector of the vine and god of wine, is in fact not the Italian Liber (so named only at 1. 7, following Varro), but the Greek 'pater Lenaeus' who strips off his buskins and treads the grapes.[49] Again, this is an idealised, composite festival; what matters is the recognition of Bacchus as diffusing his blessings all over the countryside.

It is difficult for us to conceive what romantic feelings educated Romans, at least from the middle of the second century onwards, had about mingling the familiar life of Rome and Italy with the life they met with in Greek literature. As in religion the rather wooden traditions of Italy were transformed by identifications of deities which permitted the transfusion of a mythology of incomparable richness, so in literature forms were taken over (as Aeolian lyric by Horace) with a whole context of subject and feeling, and individual Greek poets were emulated, with delight in the fusion of personal with literary experience. An excellent example is the first marriage-hymn of Catullus (61):

> Collis O Heliconii
> cultor, Uraniae genus...

It gives itself out as Greek, and has many features of the epithalamion tradition going back to Sappho, particularly in form and technique. Moreover, some of the chief features of a Roman marriage, such as the feast, are omitted, though the *Fescennina iocatio* and other Roman customs occur. Yet it was written in honour of a real marriage, that of Manlius Torquatus to Vinia Aurunculeia.[50] An equally good example in the *Georgics* is the proem to Book 3 (to be considered later, pp. 165-72), with its remarkable fusion of imagery taken from the Greek games and the Roman triumphal procession. Those accounts of the festivals of Ceres and Bacchus are warnings to us to read the *Georgics* not as a source-book for Roman customs but as an imaginative poem.

Hesiod in the *Works and Days* takes religious observances for granted. Only once, at 465 ff., does he enjoin one—sacrifice to Zeus Chthonios and Demeter when ploughing begins. This would have been enough to ensure that Virgil introduced an *in primis venerare deos* passage, as he introduced a passage to recall the *Days* at 1. 276–86. But in fact the *Georgics* is permeated with religious feeling. Wissowa, however, gives us a useful, if perhaps exaggerated, reminder: 'It is important for the true appreciation of the manner of the *Georgics* to realise that the religious background of Virgil's representation of agriculture is throughout that of Greek poetry: the piety of the Italian farmer, still existing in his time as the monuments undeniably testify, finds no reflection in his poem.'* Very different is the case of the *Aeneid*, which is packed with antiquarian lore about Roman religion (surely a passionate personal interest of Virgil's) because the subject, especially of the second half, demanded it.

Cyril Bailey rightly called his book *Religion in Virgil* rather than *The Religion of Virgil*. What Virgil really thought, or rather felt, is very hard to determine. The Augustan poets may be ranged in ascending degrees of engagement—Ovid seems to have been interested and amused by the rites of the calendar, charmed and amused by the legends of the gods of mythology. Horace enjoyed keeping the Fontanalia at the Bandusian spring, celebrating private rituals of his own as on the anniversary of the tree's fall, or encouraging rustic Phidyle to make offerings according to her means, though any of these could be a literary pretext; and he had a genuine appreciation of the beauty of the poets' mythology.[51] Tibullus, one feels, had a deeper sympathy with the old religion of the *pagani*, in the sense appreciated by Walter Pater in the opening pages of *Marius the Epicurean*. But Virgil—what did he feel about the *di agrestes* he 'knew', 'Pan, Silvanus and the sisterhood of Nymphs'? One can only give a subjective impression, based on the totality of his work.

If asked to formulate a *Credo*, Virgil would probably have been reluctant; but, if pressed, he might have complied somewhat as

---

* *Hermes* (1917), pp. 98–9. We may compare R. Heinze's dictum about Ovid: 'The question of how this mythical world of the gods should be represented by him in his poem was not one of belief but of manner, and he answered it differently for the *Metamorphoses* and for the *Fasti*' ('Ovid's elegische Erzählung', *Ber. Sächs. Akad. Leipzic* (1919), p. 11.

follows: 'I believe that there is a power working in the universe. Sometimes I call it simply "natura", but with a more positive feeling than Lucretius, who uses the term rather as a personification of the way in which things work: it is a kind of life-force —*quippe solo natura subest*.[52] More often, especially in human and moral contexts, I call it "Jupiter" or "Pater". This is the Zeus of the philosophers, the Stoic *Pronoia* or Providence, and despite many appearances to the contrary I believe its purposes to be ultimately wise and good; but it cannot work without the co-operation of human effort and prayer, perhaps also propitiation. Sorrow and suffering are an essential part of life, for the rest of nature as well as man, and they grieve me deeply; but in the *Pollio* and the *Daphnis*, in the theodicy of *Georgics* I and in the *Aeneid*, I have tried to express the indefinable trust I have, at least in some moods, that these have spiritual value, that progress is possible, and that the future will be brighter than the terrible period in which I passed the first thirty years of my life. "Jupiter" is perhaps too anthropomorphic a conception for a divine spirit which, I feel, permeates the whole of nature. The gods of mythology, poetry and popular belief are embodiments of intimations men have had, at various levels, of the working of this power in different spheres. They represent the numinous feelings I have about the universe as a whole and about particular localities. I do not, of course, believe in their actual and separate existence as traditionally conceived; but their names have the value of accumulated associations, and any terrors they once had have been dispelled by the progress of scientific thought, as exemplified in Lucretius. In my poems I have introduced the appropriate ones, hallowed by literary tradition: Daphnis, Pan and the Nymphs of Pastoral in the *Bucolics*; Bacchus and Ceres (representing the Greek Dionysus and Demeter), Pan and the Nymphs again, in the *Georgics*; the Olympians of epic and tragedy in the *Aeneid*. Had I tried to dispense with these, I should have felt that an essential element was lacking. I also have numinous feelings about people, notably the Caesars, Julius and Octavian; and if all men have a divine spark, why should not some have a special share?'

VII · *Political and Social Ideas*

THE UNIFICATION OF ITALY

The *Georgics* is dedicated, in a sense, to the 'Saturnian land' of Italy:

> *tibi* res antiquae laudis et artis
> ingredior.

What did 'Italy' signify at that time?[1] In the fifth century it had meant a small region in Calabria. The Greeks of Magna Graecia then adopted the name, and by the third century the Romans, victorious in the Samnite Wars, were applying it to the southern part of the peninsula in general. By the time the First Punic War broke out it had spread to cover all the territory of the allies as far north as Pisa and Ancona, in fact to where the Apennines cross the peninsula. It was only the threat of a Carthaginian invasion by land that led to the idea of the Alps as frontier and bulwark of Italy, and to the planting of outposts in Cisalpine Gaul. Hence Polybius refers to the Gauls of that region as 'the Celts in Italy'. For him Italy reached to the Alps.[2]

So much for geographical extension. But what of sentimental aura? The Punic Wars were of course a great binding influence, but they bound the allies to Rome, not to each other. What these gained was several independence, and the protection and share of booty guaranteed by her military genius. The only suggestion of communal Italian feeling came from a Roman, Cato, who probably began his *Origines* with the words 'Italy was originally inhabited...', and who enjoyed reminding haughty Roman aristocrats that there were cities in Italy far older than Rome. What other historians wrote was the history of Rome. Cato celebrated the places from which the soldiers of the Roman–Italian army came, and the qualities contributed by such peoples as the Sabines, among whom he had been brought up.[3]

What brought matters to a head, however, was the growing preponderance of Rome in the alliance, the inability or unwillingness of the allies to supply as many troops as were demanded, the arbitrary exactions of Roman magistrates, desire for higher status, and a sense of injustice that the right to vote at Rome was denied.[4] This led to the allies demanding, not independence, but Roman citizenship, so that at last they did unite in 91 for the Social War. At one time during the war they even thought of trying to become a nation separate from Rome, if they could not get Roman citizenship, and they renamed Corfinium, their chosen capital, 'Italia'; but in the end they won their way.[5] The settlement, by which all free Italians became Roman citizens, was celebrated by coins showing Italy and Rome joining hands. Italy bears a cornucopia; Rome's supremacy is symbolised by a diadem and the resting of her foot on a globe.[6] Italians had already been distinguished from foreigners by wearing the toga. Now Italy was on the way to becoming a nation, and the ruling nation of the world. National, as distinct from city, patriotism had been a rarity in the ancient world.

But this did not happen in a flash. It takes time for sentiment to develop. Even geographically, the frontier had crept north only a short distance beyond Ancona, to the Rubicon, by the time the civil war broke out in 49. Though the Transpadanes received Latin Rights in 89, at the time when Virgil began the *Georgics* his native region between the Po and the Alps had only just become officially part of Italy. But the championship of Julius Caesar had made the inclusion of all Cisalpine Gaul in Italy a certainty, quite apart from the fact that no one would wish a provincial governor, after his example, to command legions on the near side of the Alps. One unifying factor was the long-established use of Latin as a *lingua franca* for military and diplomatic purposes.[7]

The Temple of Tellus, which Varro made the scene of Book 1 of his treatise, had a map of Italy painted on the wall, and the conversation begins with a question whether any land in the world is better cultivated. It is agreed that there is none.* Dionysius of Halicarnassus, who came to settle in Rome just when Virgil was completing the *Georgics*, also has a panegyric

---

* 1. 2. 1–7. Actually there is some idealisation here. Most of Italy consisted in fact of rough upland pasture.

(probably based on a lost work of Varro) of the 'land of Saturn', for its fertility, and for the self-sufficiency that variety of cultivation gives it.[8] Most of all he praises the temperate climate—*hic ver perpetuum*. The East might be fabulous in its excesses, but Italy was the land of the Golden Mean. To these eulogies of the fertile Italy, symbolised by that cornucopia on the coins, Virgil's at *Georgics* 2. 136–76 adds a new dimension: the association of this land with the greatness of Rome.*

> hinc bellator equus campo sese arduus infert,
> hinc albi, Clitumne, greges et maxima taurus
> victima, saepe tuo perfusi flumine sacro,
> Romanos ad templa deum duxere triumphos,

hence comes the war-horse that charges prancing over the battle-field; hence, Clitumnus, your white flocks and the bull, greatest of victims, which, often bathed in your sacred stream, lead Roman triumphs to the temples of the gods.

(The Clitumnus is a small Umbrian river, at whose source, famous for its placid beauty, there was an ancient cult of Jupiter Clitumnus: hence *flumine sacro*.[9]) Next come the works of man:

> adde tot egregias urbes operumque laborem,
> tot congesta manu praeruptis oppida saxis
> fluminaque antiquos subterlabentia muros,

add all those excellent cities and monuments of toil, all those towns piled up by hand on rocky precipices and rivers gliding along beneath ancient walls.

Manu: one has only to look at the Cyclopean walls that are the foundations of Volterra or Cortona or Segni to marvel at what was done by hand. And Virgil adds the latest achievement of engineering, accomplished before his eyes as he looked out from Naples in 37, Agrippa's Portus Iulius, with its long mole and the new canal that connected Lake Avernus with the Lucrine Lake and the sea. And finally there are the peoples and heroes who have

---

* Vitruvius, speaking of climate, says that 'in Italy the inhabitants are exactly tempered to the mean, both in the structure of their body and in their strength of mind for endurance and courage' (6. 1. 11).

made this land great; Marsians and Sabines,* Ligurians and Volscians, they range up and down the peninsula; but the towns are 'Romana oppida', and the capital is 'rerum pulcherrima Roma'.

The two great lakes mentioned, Larius (Como) and Benacus (Garda), had only just become politically part of Italy. Virgil was ideally suited to be the poet of the unification. Born in the far north, he spent his time either there or (when not in Rome) in the far south. When he comes to speak of land suitable for rearing animals, it is his own old haunts, at either extreme, which he commends (2. 195–202):

> sin armenta magis studium vitulosque tueri,
> aut ovium fetum aut urentis culta capellas,
> saltus et saturi petito longinqua Tarenti,
> et qualem infelix amisit Mantua campum
> pascentem niveos herboso flumine cycnos;
> non liquidi gregibus fontes, non gramina derunt,
> et quantum longis carpent armenta diebus,
> exigua tantum gelidus ros nocte reponet.

But if your preference is for keeping herds and calves, or for breeding sheep or goats the bane of plants, then seek out the distant woodland pastures of rich Tarentum or plain-land such as was lost by unlucky Mantua that feeds snow-white swans on its reedy river. There your flocks will lack neither clear springs nor grass, and whatever your cattle will crop in the long days the cool dew of one short night will restore.

There are surprisingly few Italian geographical names in the Georgics—only about thirty; but they are mostly from the parts Virgil knew best: from the north (Larius, Benacus, Mella, Mincius, Padus or Eridanus, Mantua), or from Campania (Acerrae, Avernus, Capua, Clanius, Falernus, Taburnus, Vesaevus) or from further south (Alburnus, Silanus, Tanager, Paestum, Sila, Galaesus, Tarentum). The rooks that foretell the passing of rain (1. 410) belong to the Po valley and the foothills of the Alps, being very rare in the rest of Italy.[10] Pliny tells us that the sowing of beans in spring (1. 215) was a peculiarity of the Po valley, and the

---

* For the Sabines as especially idealised see Horace, Epod. 2. 41–2; Odes 3. 6. 37–44; Livy 42. 34. Etruria may have been mentioned here as a compliment to Maecenas, though his virtues were of a different kind.

use of ash as a fertiliser (1. 81) a special practice of the Trans-padanes.[11] Virgil also remembered the dug-out boats launched on the Po (2. 452), and the shepherds gathering the medicinal plant Aster Amellus on the banks of the winding Mella, a river that flows west of Brescia and so not far from his original home (4. 271).

The consolidation of Italian sentiment was greatly intensified by events which took place while Virgil was composing the *Georgics*. In 32 the breach between Octavian and Antony became open. Antony finally divorced Octavia, and she left his house accompanied by his children, whom she had nobly brought up with her own. Octavian wrested his will from the custody of the Vestals and read its contents to the Senate, including his legacies to his children by Cleopatra and the instruction that he should be buried beside her in Alexandria. This final item was the last straw: it was taken to confirm his rumoured intention of transferring the capital there. Flames of indignation swept through the peninsula, fanned by blasts of lurid propaganda which have smothered history. Late that autumn the whole of Italy swore allegiance to Octavian, town by town,* in what was represented as a crusade for the pure and manly West against the decadent but dangerous East.[12] Italy had acquired an ideology.

In such an atmosphere, but with anxiety converted into jubilation by the defeat of Antony and Cleopatra, *fatale monstrum*, the *Georgics* was completed. It was the perfect background-poem for the times. Actium was, in one sense, a victory for a party largely recruited from Roman knights of the towns of Italy over the degenerate aristocracy of the capital,[13] for the peoples whom Virgil extolled in the *Georgics* (2. 167-8),

> genus acre virum, Marsos pubemque Sabellam
> adsuetumque malo Ligurem Volscosque verutos.

On the shield of Aeneas depicting 'res Italas Romanorumque triumphos' (*A.* 8. 626 ff.) the Caesarians were pointedly described (678-9):

---

* 'Sponte sua', wrote Augustus years afterwards in his *Res Gestae* (25), but complete spontaneity is hard to imagine.

> hinc Augustus agens *Italos* in proelia Caesar
> cum patribus populoque, penatibus et magnis dis,

on this side Caesar Augustus leading the *Italians* into battle with the senate and people, Penates and Great Gods.

And in the triple triumph that sealed the victories it was for the Italian gods that he was represented as inaugurating a perpetual offering:

> dis *Italis* votum immortale sacrabat.

The ideal of the fusion of the complementary virtues of the Italians and Trojans was to be the main theme of the *Aeneid* in its latter part. The description at 7. 641–817 of the 'gathering of the clans',

> quibus Itala iam tum
> floruerit terra alma viris,

the men to whom even then Italy was a flourishing mother,

gave the Italians the pride of having their local names enshrined in a national epic. Their rugged virtues are characterised at 9. 598–620 by Remulus Numanus not without an echo of the *Georgics* (607–8),

> at patiens operum exiguoque adsueta iuventus
> aut rastris terram domat aut quatit oppida bello—

but one-sidedly, and he is promptly killed by Ascanius for his presumption. The Trojans stand for civilisation with its danger of decadence (for the future Rome, in fact), the Italians for hardiness with its danger of brutality. It is only at the end, after losses on both sides that emphasise how hardly the fusion of the two ideals in a higher synthesis is achieved,* that the reconciliation (fore-shadowing the settlement made after the Social War) can come; when Aeneas himself solemnly vows (12. 189–91),

---

* Dante spoke of four, two on each side, as dying '*for Italy*' (*Inf.* 1. 106–8):

> Di quell'umile Italia fia salute
> Per cui morio la vergine Cammilla
> Eurialo e Turno e Niso di ferute.

The separation of the pair Nisus and Euryalus, not necessitated by versification, may have been due to a desire to make representatives of the two sides alternate: they were interwoven in destiny.

non ego nec Teucris Italos parere iubebo
nec mihi regna peto: paribus se legibus ambae
invictae gentes aeterna in foedera mittant.

I will not now ask the Italians to obey the Trojans, nor do I seek sovereignty for myself: on equal terms let both peoples, unconquered, commit themselves to an eternal covenant;

and Juno herself sums up the ideal in one line,

sit Romana potens Itala virtute propago,

let the stock of Rome be mighty by Italian valour.

To this epic treatment of the subject the *Georgics* was a prelude.

THE FINALE OF BOOK I

The magnificently rhetorical passage that bursts out of the weather signs to form the climax of Book 1, broadening the connection of the cosmos with man to include politics, gives the impression of having been composed while the shock of Julius Caesar's murder was still quite fresh, not at the time of Actium thirteen years later, or after it, when the other great set-pieces seem to have been composed.* It is probable that Virgil had been a Caesarian from the first (see p. 24), and after the Mantuan restoration and his entry into the circle of Maecenas he was obviously a devotee of Octavian rather than Antony. But Antony was at first the dominant Triumvir, remembered as the victor of Philippi, whence Octavian had been absent sick.[14] Moreover Octavian's operations against Sextus Pompeius were unsuccessful, even disastrous, until quite late in 36, when Agrippa rescued him by the crowning victory of Naulochus. Now, however, Antony, far away on the Eastern front, failed against the Parthians, and began a terrible retreat that lasted a month from mid-October. It

---

* Apart from the reference to Philippi at 489–92, there are the references to the present state of the world at 509–11,

hinc movet Euphrates, illinc Germania bellum;
vicinae ruptis inter se legibus urbes
arma ferunt; saevit toto Mars impius orbe,

which Bayet showed to fit 39–37 much better than any later years (*R.Ph.* (1930), pp. 137–44).

was on 13 November of that year that Octavian entered Rome in glory.[15] Lepidus by an act of folly had eliminated himself. Appian catches the moment for us:[16]

This seemed to be the end of the civil dissensions of those times. Octavian was now twenty-eight years of age. Cities joined in placing him among their tutelary gods. At this period Rome itself and Italy had been openly infested with gangs of robbers, whose operations were more like barefaced brigandage than secret theft... Octavian aroused astonishment by the extraordinary speed with which he exterminated this evil. He let the yearly magistrates exercise their functions largely in the traditional way. He burnt all papers that contained evidence on the civil wars, and declared he would restore the constitution completely on Antony's return from the Parthians, being persuaded that he too would be willing to lay down his powers when the civil wars were ended. Whereupon he was chosen by acclamation to be a tribune for life, and urged to accept this perpetual magistracy in exchange for his previous one.

This was the earliest moment at which Virgil could have written the prayer that he inserted in his lament for the evils of civil war (1. 498–504). Never before could Octavian have seemed *thus* supreme.

> Di patrii, Indigetes, et Romule Vestaque mater,
> quae Tuscum Tiberim et Romana Palatia servas,
> hunc saltem everso iuvenem succurrere saeclo
> ne prohibete. satis iam pridem sanguine nostro
> Laomedonteae luimus periuria Troiae;
> iam pridem nobis caeli te regia, Caesar,
> invidet atque hominum queritur curare triumphos.

Gods of our fathers, native gods, and Romulus and Mother Vesta who preservest the Tuscan Tiber and the Roman Palatine, do not forbid this young man at least to succour an age in ruins; enough long since have we paid with our blood for the treachery of Laomedon's Troy; long since the palace of the sky has grudged you to us, Caesar, and complained that you are caring for the triumphs of men.

As the world of agriculture had got out of control for lack of the *agricola* so the world of politics had got out of control for lack of a *moderator*.[17] And as Aidos and Nemesis in Hesiod, Astraea or

Justice in Aratus, had left the earth when men deteriorated, so now the fear was that the world had become too wicked to retain its potential saviour.

Suppose this passage were written at the end of 36 or early in 35. That is just about the time we should presume that Virgil was finishing Book I. The finale follows quite naturally and embodies the emotions of the day. Virgil would not feel called upon to modify it later.[18] I much prefer this conception to the idea that the lines about Caesar were inserted after Actium, even though a man of thirty-four could still be called '*iuvenis*'.[19] There was a feeling abroad about this time that Rome must be under a primal curse which someone had to expiate. Horace expresses it at the end of his *Seventh Epode*:

> sic est: acerba fata Romanos agunt
> scelusque fraternae necis,
> ut immerentis fluxit in terram Remi
> sacer nepotibus cruor.

Thus it is: harsh fates have been driving the Romans and the crime of a brother's death, ever since the blood of innocent Remus flowed to the ground to curse posterity.*

At *Odes* 3. 3. 21 ff., written some years later, Juno refers to Laomedon as the primal sinner; and as her speech seems rooted in Ennius, it may be that the idea came from the *Annals* to both Virgil and Horace. In *Odes* I. 2 Horace follows his account of recent portents with

> cui dabit partes *scelus expiandi*
> Iuppiter?

and his final answer is a hope that it will be Caesar. Here the crime is more specifically the murder of Julius; but the prayer

> serus in caelum redeas...
> hic magnos potius triumphos,
> hic ames dici pater atque princeps,

---

* Cf. *Epode* 16: 'impia...devoti sanguinis aetas', 'inominata cubilia'. Horace also used the simile of the chariot-race (G. I. 512–14), with some identical words, at S. I. I. 114 ff., composed in or before 35 B.C.; but I do not think it is possible to deduce who was prior.

late may you return to heaven...here rather may you love great triumphs, here to be called father and leader,

is a clear deprecation of the envy of heaven as fancied by Virgil at *Georgics* I. 503–4. By that time Antony was dead, and Octavian had celebrated, or was about to celebrate, his triple triumph; and Horace would know the *Georgics* as a completed work.

OCTAVIAN IN THE PROEM

On I January 42, the Senate and People, instigated by the Triumvirs, recognised the dead Julius as a god. Thus for the first time at Rome a man became officially so recognised, and Octavian as his adoptive son became 'Divi filius'. Antony consented, after the Treaty of Brundisium, to be one of Julius' priests. A fortnight after the triple triumph of 29 came the dedication of the temple of Divus Julius. How should the deliverer himself be honoured? We have seen that the Italian cities had enrolled him six years before among their tutelary deities. In 30 an adulatory Senate, as yet unpurged of freedmen and provincials, had decreed a quin-quennial festival in his name, and services of thanksgiving on every anniversary of his birthday and of the day on which the news of his final victory arrived. Priests were to pray for him along with the Senate and Roman people. Libations were to be poured in his honour. In 29, when his despatch about Phraates was received, the Senate decreed that whenever poems were recited in honour of the gods his name should be associated with theirs; and when he finally entered the city, his consular colleague offered sacrifices for his safe arrival, an unprecedented honour.

The idea of divine honours for rulers had long been familiar in Asiatic, Greek and Punic lands.[20] There had recently been a wave of claims and expectations. Sextus Pompeius had given out that he was son of Neptune. Antony had been hailed as Dionysus at Athens, Ephesus and Alexandria. These ideas had once been regarded at Rome as foreign, but there were native customs that could ease their acceptance. The cult of the *manes* and the sacrifices of *parentatio* could lead to the worship of a dead ruler, as could philosophic ideas of deification for services to men such as we find in Cicero's *Somnium Scipionis*. Worship of a living man was more difficult, but helped by the notion of worshipping the *genius* of the *paterfamilias* and by Stoic ideas of the divine nature of the human soul.[21]

It is against this background of a wave of popular enthusiasm, heightened to hysteria by relief at the final ending, after twenty years, of the civil wars, that we must read the proem to the *Georgics*. In the cult of Philip and Alexander the ruler had first been represented as additional to the twelve canonical gods,[22] and there is evidence that Octavian, especially after his eastern campaign, was seen as a new Alexander.[23] Virgil had the idea of making him an additional, thirteenth god of agriculture for purposes of his invocation, and giving him as many lines as all the rest together. In general his divinity is still represented as being in the future—*mox* (24), *quicquid eris* (36). Romulus in Ennius had been received only after death into the *concilia deorum*, and another idea then abroad was that Octavian was a new Romulus, there being actually talk of giving him the title of Quirinus *quasi et ipsum conditorem urbis*.* Yet at the end he is bidden to become accustomed *iam nunc* to be called upon with prayers. He is invoked to help not only the farmers, but also the poet—*da facilem cursum*—replacing the Muses normally invoked in proems. This is the first literary document to support the idea of the divinity of a living ruler at Rome. By adoption he was not only *divi filius* but a descendant of Venus Genetrix, ancestress of the Julian *gens*, with whose 'maternal myrtle' (a symbol at Rome of bloodless victory)[24] the poet indicates that this *auctor frugum* can claim to be crowned by a grateful world.

But we must read this passage with historical imagination not only of the momentary situation in which it was written, but also of the long Alexandrian tradition of baroque fantasy and exag-

---

* Suet. *Aug.* 7; Dio, 53. 16; Flor. 2. 34. It may have been the awkward legend of the fratricide, recently used by Horace as a symbol in *Epode* 7, that led to 'Augustus' being preferred. That part of the legend was ignored by Virgil (G. 2. 533), indeed implicitly denied (*Remo cum fratre Quirinus*: *A.* 1. 292); so was another inconvenient tradition, that he was murdered by senators.

geration in panegyric that lay behind it. We must remember the terms in which Theocritus spoke of Ptolemy Philadelphus in *Idyll* 17. We must remember the extravagances of Callimachus' fine *Apotheosis of Arsinoe* in serious vein, and his *Lock of Berenice* in lighter.* Who would have applied standards of strict veracity in appreciating, for instance, Rubens' great series of paintings of the life of Marie de Medicis? And yet we can hardly think without discomfort of Virgil's uttering such adulation to Octavian's face at Atella. The recipient himself was worried about the lengths to which things were going at Rome. Even in the provinces he would not allow temples to be dedicated to himself save jointly in his name and Rome's. He 'most pertinaciously' forbade his worship in the city.[25] It was the *Genius Augusti* that came to be venerated. Horace, after the excesses of *Odes* I. 2, in which he suggested that Octavian was an incarnation of Mercury, drew back: Augustus would be held to be '*praesens divus*' in the future, when he had added the Britons and Parthians to the Empire; he would be deified after death like Romulus and the other demigods who as men had rendered signal service to mankind.[26] And in the *Aeneid* (6. 791 ff.) he is no more than '*vir*' who is also '*divi genus*', though a member of the Julian house which was destined for the skies—'*magnum caeli ventura sub axem*'.

Octavian was prudent, if nothing more, in damping down the excesses. At any time there could be a reaction at Rome. Divine honours paid to Julius in his lifetime were among the things that had outraged good Romans like Cicero, when his statue was carried in procession with those of the gods and placed in the temple of Romulus. Even the mob, we gather, had been hostile, 'not even applauding Victory because of her unpopular neighbour'.[27] There were still probably senators who felt it was a breath of fresh air when Tiberius (if the speech attributed to him

* Frr. 228 and 110 Pf.; cf. Catullus 66. *Novum sidus* (32) here may be a reminiscence of *sidus novum* at Cat. 66. 64, and *Erigonen* (33) of *virginis* in the next line, in which case the *Coma Berenices* was actually in Virgil's mind: E. Cesareo, 'Ottaviano nel proemio delle Georgiche', *Athenaeum* (1931), p. 64. He stresses the Hellenistic nature of this passage. The only Roman idea is marriage *per coemptionem* (*emat*, I. 31: *ibid*. p. 60).

by Tacitus is authentic)[28] addressed to them the memorable words, 'Ego me, Patres Conscripti, mortalem esse et hominum officia fungi, satisque habere si locum principem impleam, et vos testor et meminisse posteros volo'—'Members of the Senate, I call you to witness and wish posterity to remember, that I am mortal and perform the functions of men, and am content if I occupy the chief position.'

THE PROEM TO BOOK 3

At the opening of Book 3 Virgil, after abjuring the themes of traditional mythology (Hercules-saga etc.) as outworn, proclaims his ambition to soar aloft by a way of his own and fly, like Ennius in his proud self-epitaph,[29] upon the lips of men in victory. *Victor*: the word leads into a remarkable symbolic vision of the epic he intends to write (10–39):*

> primus ego in patriam mecum, modo vita supersit,
> Aonio rediens deducam vertice Musas;
> primus Idumaeas referam tibi, Mantua, palmas,
> et viridi in campo templum de marmore ponam
> propter aquam, tardis ingens ubi flexibus errat
> Mincius et tenera praetexit harundine ripas.
> in medio mihi Caesar erit templumque tenebit:
> illi victor ego et Tyrio conspectus in ostro
> centum quadriiugos agitabo ad flumina currus.
> cuncta mihi Alpheum linquens lucosque Molorchi
> cursibus et crudo decernet Graecia caestu.
> ipse caput tonsae foliis ornatus olivae
> dona feram. iam nunc sollemnis ducere pompas
> ad delubra iuvat caesosque videre iuvencos,
> vel scaena ut versis discedat frontibus utque
> purpurea intexti tollant aulaea Britanni.
> in foribus pugnam ex auro solidoque elephanto
> Gangaridum faciam victorisque arma Quirini,
> atque hic undantem bello magnumque fluentem
> Nilum ac navali surgentis aere columnas.
> addam urbes Asiae domitas pulsumque Niphaten

---

* For recent controversy concerning this proem see Appendix II.

fidentemque fuga Parthum versisque sagittis;
et duo rapta manu diverso ex hoste tropaea
bisque triumphatas utroque ab litore gentis.
stabunt et Parii lapides, spirantia signa,
Assaraci proles demissaeque ab Iove gentis
nomina, Trosque parens et Troiae Cynthius auctor.
Invidia infelix furias amnemque severum
Cocyti metuet tortosque Ixionis anguis
immanemque rotam et non exsuperabile saxum.

I will be the first, if only I live so long, to return from the Aonian height with the Muses in my train; I will be the first to bring back palms of Edom to you, Mantua; and in a green meadow I will set up a marble temple beside the water where the broad Mincius wanders through lazy windings and fringes his banks with slender reeds. In the midst I will set Caesar, as possessor of the shrine. In his honour, a victor resplendent in crimson robe, I will have a hundred four-horsed chariots driven beside the river. All Greece, deserting for me the Alpheus and the groves of Molorchus, shall contend in racing and in boxing with raw-hide gloves. Myself, my head adorned with trimmed olive-leaves, will bring offerings. Already I feel the joy of leading solemn processions to the shrines of the gods and seeing the bullocks sacrificed, or watching the shifting scenery of the stage and the curtain being raised by the Britons embroidered on it. On the temple-doors I will have engraved in gold and solid ivory the battle with Ganges' sons and the arms of Quirinus victorious; and here the Nile in mighty flood asurge with warfare, and columns rising cast from the bronze of ships. To these I will add the conquered cities of Asia, Niphates routed, and the Parthian that trusts in arrows shot backwards in flight, and trophies seized by force from enemies far apart, two triumphs, over peoples from each of the furthest coasts. Parian marbles shall stand there also, living images, the seed of Assaracus and the great names of the Jove-descended race, Tros our ancestor and the Cynthian founder of Troy. Wretched envy shall dread the Furies and the bleak stream of Cocytus, the writhing snakes and giant wheel of Ixion, and the boulder never mastered.

How can we account for the remarkable form in which Virgil presented his conception of the epic he had in mind? The answer is, it seems to me, that he had been reading Pindar. If so, this is the first evidence of the impact of that poet on Roman literature, though he was soon to influence Horace to a marked degree. At this date Horace was just beginning to compose odes in the manner of the older Greek lyric poetry, and no doubt the friends would read and discuss Pindar together.[30] The description at *Aeneid* 3. 570 ff. of Etna erupting is based on *Pythians* 1. 19 ff.[31]

In the first place Virgil assumes, with complete self-confidence, the Pindaric rôle of master of ceremonies. At the end of the previous Book he had conceived of himself as driving a team of verses:

> sed nos immensum spatiis confecimus aequor,
> et iam tempus equum fumantia solvere colla,

but we have covered vast ground in our laps, and now it is time to unyoke the steaming necks of our horses.

In Book 3 he picks up this highly Pindaric metaphor of the chariot of song, at 17. The hundred four-horsed chariots that he drives are his verses.* He is a victor in the contest of poetry, *primus* because he will be an innovator, the inventor of a new, non-annalistic Latin epic. Like Epicurus in Lucretius, he will win a victory of the mind—*pervicit, victor, nos exaequat victoria caelo* (Lucr. 1. 72–9). And as Ennius in Lucretius brought a crown of glory from Helicon to Italy (1. 117), he will bring back palms, the symbols of victory, to his native Mantua; not to the capital, be it noted, but to an outpost of the new Italy—a proud παρα-προσδοκίαν which encouraged many other poets to claim to have glorified their humble birthplace, whether Venusia, Assisi, Sulmo or Bilbilis (10–12). There he will build a temple in a meadow by the Mincius for Caesar Octavian† (like that of Zeus

---

* Cf. Pindar, *O.* 6. 22 ff., 9. 81; *P.* 10. 65; *N.* 1. 7; *I.* 2. 1 f.; 5. 38; fr. 124 a. Thomas Gray, *The Progress of Poesy*:

> Behold, where Dryden's less presumptuous car
> Wide o'er the fields of glory bear
> Two coursers of ethereal race,
> With necks in thunder clothed, and loud-resounding pace.

The idea that a poet must go a new way ('temptanda via est', etc.) is also Pindaric (*Paean* 7b 11–2 Sn.): Fleischer, p. 296.

† *Tenere* was commonly used of the god to whom a temple belonged, e.g. Ovid, *P.* 2. 2. 83–4; *M.* 7. 587–8; 9. 332; *F.* 6. 74; *A.* 2. 17. 4.

by the Alpheus), and will institute games of running and boxing that will draw all Greece from Olympia and Nemea—all this with Pindar clearly in mind (13–20). The symbolism of the temple and its adornment that follows is remarkable: it was not common in antiquity to visualise poetry in terms of architecture and sculpture. But it was quite common in Pindar: 'Raising upon golden pillars the fair-walled porch of our chamber, we shall construct, as it were, a splendid hall, and to begin our work we must set up a front that will shine afar.' 'There has been built in Apollo's golden valley for the prosperous Emmenidae and for Xenocrates a Pythian victor's treasure-house of song...And the front shall proclaim in pure brightness...a famous victory won with the chariot in the vale of Crisa.' Skilled craftsmen fashion songs like sculptors; and foundations are laid in the names of the gods.[32]

But strangely mingled with this symbolism of the Greek games is that of the Roman Triumph. With astonishing audacity, surely imbibed from Pindar (though Lucretius 4. 1–25 may have helped), the shy son of a Mantuan countryman represents himself as a symbolic *triumphator*, for conquering from the Greeks another province of poetry. The Muses are the captives he will lead in his train.* The palm was deposited by *triumphatores* in the temple of Capitoline Jupiter, and *Tyrio conspectus in ostro* may refer to the *toga picta* they wore. His head bound with a wreath of olive-leaves (as a bearer of offerings) he will lead the solemn procession to the shrines of the gods. The plays he will stage were a feature of Roman (not Greek) games, such as were held at this time at the dedication of the temple of Divus Iulius.[33] Figures of Britons would be woven in the curtain, seeming themselves to be raising it (in a Roman theatre it was let down to the ground when the performance began and raised again at the end). Why the Britons? Presumably because Octavian had contemplated subduing them in 34 B.C. (21–5).†

---

* *Deducam*: cf. *deduci triumpho*, Horace, *Odes* 1. 37. 31.

† As he was to do again in 27 B.C. Dio, 49. 38; 53. 22. Horace, *Epode* 7. 7. Cf. the phrase in the contemporary proem to G. 1 (30): *tibi serviat ultima Thule*, probably referring to the most northerly of the Shetland Isles.

We return now to the marble temple itself of line 16, and come to the carvings on the doors, which will represent the victories of the god to whom it is dedicated (26–36). Octavian is now the *triumphator*, who on August 13, 14 and 15 of 29 B.C. celebrated a triple triumph, for his victories in Illyricum and others won by subordinates, for Actium, and for Egypt. His dedication a fortnight later of the temple of Divus Iulius may have combined with Pindar to suggest to Virgil the symbol of a temple dedicated to him.[34] We pass in review reliefs in gold and ivory of the victories of Quirinus (? Octavian himself: see p. 163) over the 'orientals' (*Gangarides*) at Actium and the Nile, showing the columns of naval bronze,* and of his successes in dealing with the Armenians and Parthians. In addition there are trophies 'snatched *utroque ab litore*'. This probably refers to the Morini on the English Channel and the Bastarnae on the Black Sea.† In the temple itself are marble statues of the progeny of Assaracus (grandfather of Anchises), Tros his father, and finally *Troiae Cynthius auctor*, Apollo, beneath whose temple on the promontory the Battle of Actium had been fought, and who had for some time been recognised as the tutelary god of Octavian's house.[35]

In conceiving his temple Virgil undoubtedly had in mind also the shrine of Palatine Apollo, already under construction, which was to be dedicated on 28 October.[36] Propertius' elegy for the occasion (2. 31), which has unmistakable echoes of Virgil's proem, gives some details. It had a 'golden' portico and ivory doors (cf. 26), on which were carved reliefs of two victories of the god (over the Gauls and Niobe). The temple itself was of marble (cf. 13), and in it were marble statues, of Apollo himself, with his mother and sister on either side (cf. 16; 34–6). In *Aeneid* 8 Virgil

---

* Columns made from the bronze beaks of captured ships. Some were set up in the Capitol, some in the temple of Divus Iulius. Serv. *ad loc.*; Dio, 51. 19.

† Octavian's claims to success in dealing with the Parthians were recognised by special honours (see p. 162: Dio, 51. 20). In this same year, 29, C. Carrinas defeated the Morini ('extremi hominum Morini': *Aen.* 8. 727), and M. Crassus defeated the Bastarnae, one of his objects being to recover standards lost by C. Antonius (Dio, 51. 20; 25–6; cf. 38. 10). Though these were allowed later to celebrate triumphs, in May 28 and July 27 B.C. respectively, Dio emphasises that Octavian, as sole *imperator*, was given the credit for both victories.

fuses the two occasions, the triple triumph and the dedication of Palatine Apollo, more completely in the reliefs on Aeneas' shield. He would certainly have known in 29 what was intended both for the triple triumph and for Apollo's shrine. There is nothing to preclude this proem's being part of the work as read by him to Octavian at Atella. It *may* have been added just after the triple triumph; but there is no need to take it as evidence that the *Georgics* was not published until late in 28 or even in 27.*

Invidia (37-9), cowering in fear of the tortures of the damned in Hell, is not expressly said, like what has gone before, to be part of the plastic display, and is hard to visualise as such.[37] The personification could thus refer to the envy that Virgil's poetic triumph will arouse, in other poets especially, or, as has more generally been supposed, to envy of Octavian's successes and supremacy. I think it is quite general, and able to refer to both.[38] Envy of merit in general is also a Pindaric motif:

$$\pi\alpha\nu\tau\grave{\iota} \; \delta' \; \grave{\epsilon}\pi\grave{\iota} \; \phi\theta\acute{o}\nu o\varsigma \; \grave{\alpha}\nu\delta\rho\grave{\iota} \; \kappa\epsilon\widetilde{\iota}\tau\alpha\iota$$
$$\grave{\alpha}\rho\epsilon\tau\widetilde{\alpha}\varsigma.^{39}$$

Horace some years later, at the beginning of his Epistle to Augustus, speaks of such *invidia* as a liability of the living benefactor. There he makes him the great exception to the rule. But in an earlier passage (*Odes* 3. 24. 30 ff.) we may sense that envy of him was something really to be anticipated:

heu nefas,
virtutem incolumem odimus,
sublatam ex oculis quaerimus, *invidi*.

The word is thus not too weak for such an offence: those who envy the saviour of Rome must go in fear of the tortures of the

---

* As was suggested by D. L. Drew in an interesting article on 'Virgil's Marble Temple' in *C.Q.* (1924), pp. 195–202, and accepted by Richter (note on 26 f.) and by Perret, p. 53. N. Terzaghi, 'Sulla seconda edizione delle Georgiche', *Athenaeum* (1960), pp. 132–40, believes that this proem was composed for a new edition after Gallus' death. But by then the form the epic was taking must have been well known; and would not Virgil have addressed Caesar as Augustus from 27 onwards?

damned.* But that need not imply that Virgil had not also in mind the *invidia* to which poets were liable. He had spoken of it at *Ecl.* 7. 26, as Horace was to speak of it at *Odes* 4. 3. 16. This is the Βασκανίη of Callimachus' *Aitia* Prologue and Epigram 21 Pf., the Φθόνος-Μῶμος of the end of his *Hymn to Apollo*, whose treatment (being kicked out by Apollo) seems hardly less drastic than that envisaged here. But again Virgil may just as well have been thinking of Pindar. And indeed a somewhat similar contrast is drawn at the beginning of *Pythians* I (5–28), between the poet's music, which lulls both the eagle of Zeus and the god of war, and the fear felt for it and for Zeus by the sinners tortured in Tartarus.

Interea (40) he is eager to complete the *Georgics. Mox tamen* (46) he will gird himself to tell of Caesar's fiery battles, and to establish the glory of his name for all the years that stretch from Tithonus' birth down to Caesar:†

> Mox tamen ardentis accingar dicere pugnas
> Caesaris, et nomen fama tot ferre per annos
> Tithoni prima quot abest ab origine Caesar.

These lines are awkward. Though 10–39 clearly promise that some day—*modo vita supersit*—the poet will celebrate Octavian in epic, the symbolical way in which the vision is presented might be held not to commit him as to precise subject-matter; but *dicere pugnas Caesaris* is uncomfortably precise.

What would Octavian be led to expect? He was human enough to want to have his martial exploits celebrated by poets, and their elaborately tactful refusals are in such terms as to suggest that Maecenas at least was apt to propose just that.[40] Of course vague promises were not taken at face value. When Horace exhorted

---

* Norden sees particular reference to Mark Antony, whose abuse of Octavian is retailed by Suetonius, and who is unmistakably included among the great sinners in Hell at *Aeneid* 6. 621 ff. ('Vergils *Aeneis* im Lichte ihrer Zeit', *Neue Jahrbücher für das klassische Altertum*, VII, 1901, p. 320).

† Tithonus was a son of Laomedon, and so only collateral with the Gens Iulia. But he was fabled for longevity, and the date of his birth was thus suggestive of immemorial antiquity. The sentence is rather artificially contrived so as to make Caesar the last word, cf. Horace, *Odes* I. 2.

Valgius to give up unmanly lamenting (*Odes* 2. 9. 18–20) with the suggestion

> et potius nova
> cantemus Augusti tropaea
> Caesaris,

the Emperor will hardly have been fluttered with expectation. But our passage is different. Octavian must have known that Virgil was really contemplating an epic, and its subject must have been of the greatest interest to him.

We can only surmise how it came about that the aspirations of this proem were converted into the plan of the *Aeneid*. As in Naevius and Ennius, the Trojan origins were retained as a starting-point and used as a symbol. Octavian was in a sense *in medio*, with specific references at 6. 791 ff. and at 8. 678 ff., where, on the Shield of Aeneas, the Battle of Actium also figured, and the motif of the damned in Hell also found a place.[41] But it cannot be said that this passage was in any real sense a sketch for the *Aeneid*. Virgil was undoubtedly wise in going back to legend and letting it speak symbolically to his generation. History, as Aristotle said, is 'less philosophic' than poetry, and to write of recent wars would be to walk

> per ignes
> suppositos cineri doloso.

Norden may also have been right in thinking that, while this proem was written under the immediate impression of Octavian the Triumphator, before long the image which both ruler and poet had come to prefer was that of Augustus the Prince of Peace.[42]

The way in which Virgil, after two lines of invocation to rural deities analogous to the invocation of Bacchus at the beginning of Book 2, abruptly begins to talk of his own plans to rival Ennius, is unsatisfactory. It is quite possible that he originally composed or contemplated a purely literary proem, but inserted 10–39 under the overwhelming impact of Octavian's successes in 29.[43]

AUGUSTANISM

In the epilogue to the *Georgics* Virgil states that he had been writing

> Caesar dum magnus ad altum
> fulminat Euphraten bello, victorque volentis
> per populos dat iura viamque adfectat Olympo,

while great Caesar was thundering in war beside the deep Euphrates, and victoriously spreading the rule of law among willing peoples, and treading the path to heaven.

Here for the first time we hear proclaimed the Augustan ideal of empire, *paci imponere morem*. Horace puts more brutal words of prophecy into the mouth of Juno (*Odes* 3. 3. 43–4):

> *triumphatisque* possit
> Roma *ferox* dare iura Medis.

Virgil trusts, characteristically, that the recipients are glad.

Whether the religious, moral and patriotic revival which had begun, at least in Caesarian circles, some years before Actium was a spontaneous movement or an official policy is hard to determine. Octavian himself, though it bears the stamp of his personality,* was fully occupied with campaigns for most of the time: between 38 and the summer of 29 he was only in Rome for a total duration of about two years, and on these visits he would be overwhelmed with business.† Nothing that we know of Maecenas suggests that he would have initiated a campaign for hardiness and simplicity, for the old Sabine virtues already idealized in Horace *Epode* 2. 39–42, and later by Virgil at *Georgics* 2. 167 and 532. In one of his *Satires*, composed before 30 (2. 2. 103), Horace asks the rich man, 'Why, when you are rich...are the ancient temples of the gods

---

* 'His devotion to the ancient ideal of the family and even to the ancient worship of the gods appears to be deep-rooted and genuine'...'Identity in origin and sentiment with a large class in Italy' (Syme, p. 454). In 29 he revived the Augurium Salutis and the Arval Brotherhood, filled up priesthoods and began rebuilding temples.

† L. P. Wilkinson, *Horace and his Lyric Poetry* (1945), p. 18. 1. 500 seems to be the only reference to Octavian in the *Georgics* dating from before 30/29. In Horace he hardly figures before Actium (*Epode* 9). *S.* 2. 1, if composed as an introduction to Book 2, may be even later.

going to ruin?'[44] This was well before the measures of 28 for the repair of temples. It seems probable that the movement was largely spontaneous, and that the poets themselves played a part in its direction.

The current enthusiasm for the old martial worthies whose statues Octavian was to set up around his new forum (Suet. 31. 5) finds expression in the Praises of Italy (2. 169–70):

> ...extulit, haec Decios Marios magnosque Camillos,
> Scipiadas duros bello...*

But more significant perhaps is Virgil's admiration for the common Roman legionary (3. 346–8):

> non secus ac patriis acer Romanus in armis
> iniusto sub fasce viam cum carpit, et hosti
> ante expectatum positis stat in agmine castris

just like the keen Roman, armed as his fathers were, when he makes a forced march under his cruel pack, and before his enemy realises has pitched camp and stands in battle order.

Perhaps he was thinking of the famous forced march that saved Rome in 207, when C. Claudius Nero and his troops were said to have covered 240 miles in six days to join the other consul on the Metaurus, and Hasdrubal only realised he was doomed when the sound of two trumpets revealed that both consuls were present in the camp.

Essentially, however, Virgil was a man of peace. The idyllic description at 4. 125 ff. of a garden created out of nothing on unwanted land near Tarentum acquired additional significance from the fact that the old man was a Corycian (from Cilicia) and so

---

* So the MSS. 'Marios' has been suspected, as chronologically intrusive in this list and not occurring in other such lists. Marius, guilty of 'impia arma', is mentioned nowhere else in Virgil (as neither is Sulla). Richter goes so far as to substitute 'Curios' in his text. If emendation is called for, I should prefer to take *Marios* to have been a misreading of *magnos* (repeated). All the names that follow have an epithet, and a double *magnos* would give additional point to *maxime Caesar*. We should then be left with two neatly balanced lists of four names each—Marsos, pubem Sabellam, Ligurem, Volscos and Decios, Camillos, Scipiadas, Caesar—each introduced by *haec*. But the vulgate text is supported by the MSS of Quintilian, who quotes this passage at *Inst. Or.* 9. 3. 24.

almost certainly a former pirate, one of those settled in that area by Pompey after his successful cleaning-up operation in 67.* At 1. 508 Virgil had lamented the beating of sickles into swords; here at least was a man whose sword had been beaten into a sickle. The chaste family—*casta pudicitiam servat domus*—with children cling-ing to their parents' necks, is part of the idealised country life (2. 523–4). All this was in the spirit of the new movement. So was the respect for tradition—*res antiquae laudis et artis*; still more the piety pervading the poem, though, as we have seen, the religion was rarely that of the Roman State or even of the Italian country-side.

To what extent is the bees' state in *Georgics* 4 intended as an exemplar for the new Rome?[45] Appius in Varro (3. 16. 4–9) noted their gregarious nature (*ut homines*), their co-operation in work and building, their *ratio et ars*. From them men may learn to do work, to build, to store up food. Their combs are ideally con-structed on the best mathematical principles. Their product is most pleasing to gods and men. Their commonwealth is like the states of men—*rex, imperium, societas*. They seek only what is pure. They are not destructive, though brave in resisting anyone who tries to destroy their own work. They are 'the winged ones of the Muses', because the clashing of cymbals attracts them together, and like the Muses they have been assigned flowery, untouched mountains for their habitat. They follow their king wherever he goes, and if he is tired carry him on their backs, so eager are they to save him. Not idle themselves, they hate the lazy, and drive out drones, even if superior to them in numbers. They live as in an army, taking turns to sleep and work; and their leaders get some things done to the sound of the voice, as if in imitation of the trumpet. This they do when they exchange signals of peace and war. Merula adds (*ibid.* 18) that, according to Menecrates, there are two kinds of king, the black and the striped; the latter is so much better that any bee-keeper having both should kill the former, for he is sedi-

* Servius on 4. 127, citing Suetonius. The brothers Veianius in Varro (3. 16. 10), the account of whose apiary and gardens probably gave Virgil the idea for this passage, were likewise two ex-soldiers who had fought, we are told, under Varro himself in Spain.

tious and ruins the hive either by driving out his better or by taking the swarm with him if he is driven out. When the hive becomes over-populated, they send out a colony as the Sabines used to do in similar circumstances. The colonists cluster like grapes, with a hum as of soldiers about to break camp, and then take flight (*ibid.* 29–30).

Virgil had predecessors from Homer onwards in likening bees to men by implication. What does he add to Varro, and how much of this can be seen in terms of the current social and political movement?

His idealisation perhaps goes further than Varro's.

> solae communes natos, communia tecta
> urbis habent...
>   ...et in medium quaesita reponunt

they alone have children in common and share the houses of their city...and they put their gains into a common store.

Following immediately on the myth of the Cretan bees, these traits must be regarded as the first of Jupiter's rewards. Virgil conveniently forgets that ants also have a similar community, and that *in medium quaerebant* was at 1. 127 a feature of Saturn's, not of Jupiter's, dispensation, though *laborem experiuntur* is appropriate to the latter. With the sharing of quarters and even of children as an ideal, Virgil would be familiar from Plato's *Republic*. Indeed Athens may well have been fleetingly in his mind when he dealt with 'Cecropian' bees (177, cf. 270).* But although selfish acquisitiveness was frowned upon by the new movement, so that Horace could praise former generations pointedly with the words

> privatus illis census erat brevis,
> commune magnum,[46]

their private property was limited, their public large,

---

* Romans would also think of Athens when they became at this time specially conscious of themselves as bulwarks against the oriental. The Praises of Italy in *Georgics* 2 have been compared with Sophocles' chorus εὐίππου, ξένε, τᾶσδε χώρας... in the *O.C.* (668 ff.): H. Krappe, 'A source of Virgil, *Georgics* II, 136–76', *C.Q.* (1926), pp. 42–4.

communism of children and habitation was hardly consonant with its emphasis on the family home as the focus of life.*

The emphasis on public work to which everyone enthusiastically contributes, *munere quamque suo*,† was obviously timely, and its relevance to human beings in Virgil's mind is attested by his simile in reminiscent terms of bees for the Carthaginians building their city at *Aeneid* 1. 430 ff. Their one-mindedness was also an agreeable contrast to the confused dissensions of the civil war period (184):

> omnibus una quies operum, labor omnibus unus.‡

The emphasis on the non-existence of sexual intercourse among bees (197–9), while it might be said to harmonise with the movement against sexual irregularities and excesses, was hardly relevant to the movement for encouraging an increase in the citizen birth-rate. On the other hand, the example of self-sacrifice was apposite (203–5):

> saepe etiam duris errando in cotibus alas
> attrivere, ultroque animam sub fasce dedere:
> tantus amor florum et generandi gloria mellis,

often too as they rove they bruise their wings on hard rocks and voluntarily give their lives beneath their burden, such is their love of flowers and glory in generating honey.

As a result of all this, their unexhausting method of gathering young from leaves and their self-sacrifice for the common good, although the individuals live for seven years at most,

> at genus immortale manet, multosque per annos
> stat fortuna domus, et avi numerantur avorum,

yet the stock remains immortal, and for many years the fortune of the house stands firm, and generation is added to generation.

---

* Dahlmann, p. 556, compares 155,

> et patriam solae et certos novere penates

with 2. 514, the peasant's 'patriam parvosque nepotes'. But in the former case the *penates* are the community home, in the latter we have the peasant's cottage.

† Bees do not, in fact, specialise, but the ancients believed they did: Arist. *H.A.* 9. 40, 625 b 18; 627 a 20 ff.

‡ Again, bees do not, in fact, cease building at night (189–90); but see Arist. *H.A.* 627 a 26, Pliny, *N.H.* 11. 26. (Richter.)

So far there is little to show that the bees symbolised for Virgil more than his own feelings about the necessity of working together for the common good, though these, influencing others or shared by them, may have contributed to the moulding of Caesarian policy. But the words (201–2)

> ipsae regem parvosque Quirites
> sufficiunt,

even if 'Quirites' is another example of 'the play of great and small', could not fail to indicate that he had the Roman people in mind, and this being so, 'regem' could not fail to suggest Octavian. The lines that follow are a striking climax to the section on the god-given nature of bees.

> praeterea regem non sic Aegyptus et ingens
> Lydia nec populi Parthorum aut Medus Hydaspes
> observant. rege incolumi mens omnibus una est;
> amisso rupere fidem, constructaque mella
> diripuere ipsae et cratis solvere favorum.
> ille operum custos, illum admirantur et omnes
> circumstant fremitu denso stipantque frequentes,
> et saepe attollunt umeris et corpora bello
> obiectant pulchramque petunt per vulnera mortem.

Moreover they do not pay court to their king like Egypt and wide Lydia or the peoples of the Parthians or Median Hydaspes. While the king is safe they are all of one mind. Lose him and they break faith and themselves tear apart the honey they have constructed and break up the trellised combs. He is the guardian of their works, him they admire and all throng round, thickly buzzing, and press in crowds, and often raise him on their shoulders and expose their bodies to war and seek in wounds a glorious death.

Horace, when he wrote

> dulce et decorum est pro patria mori,

had Simonides in mind, and from Tyrtaeus onwards Greeks had extolled the glory of dying for the city-state; but to die for a king himself, save perhaps for an Alexander, was a rare idea. The contrast was also significant between self-abasement before a monarch and the familiar Roman scene of supporters jubilantly escorting, even carrying shoulder high, from the Forum to his home someone like Cicero who had scored a personal success.* *Non sic Aegyptus*: the mention of the lands through which Octavian was even now making a triumphal progress could not fail to bring him to mind, though '*amisso*' might recall men's thoughts rather to the havoc that had followed the removal of Julius, as portrayed so vividly at the end of Book 1.† *Custos* (215) was a word which was to attach itself to Octavian (Horace, *Odes* 4. 15. 17):

> custode rerum Caesare non furor
> civilis aut vis exiget otium.

If we admit the topical overtone here, what about the earlier passages that lie outside the central one on *natura apium*? The battle between the two kings and their supporters at 67–87 is treated in the ironical spirit of the first part of this Book, the 'play of great and small', but now with deeply serious intent. The prowess of the leaders and the stubborn bellicosity of the armies are quasi-heroic, and the poet's attitude is revealed by the 'pay-off' lines at the end:

> hi motus animorum atque haec certamina tanta
> pulveris exigui iactu compressa quiescent

these upheavals of spirit and all these great contests will be put down and laid to rest by the throwing of a little dust.

This is the poet who was to make Anchises reproach Caesar and Pompey (*Aen.* 6. 832),

> ne, pueri, ne tanta animis assuescite bella;

do not, my children, do not accustom your minds to acceptance of such great wars.

'Pueri' puts the proud leaders in their place *sub specie aeternitatis*. Our present passage is not topical, but parallel to that in Book 1, where the peasant on the field of Philippi ages later ploughs up

---

* Virgil's application is new and significant, since Aristotle had only spoken of a leader's being so carried when he was unable to fly: *H.A.* 9. 40, 624 a *fin.*

† If a queen is lost and irreplaceable, the hive will perish from listlessness; but the picture of dissension and violent destruction here given is an anthropomorphic invention (Royds, pp. 85–6).

crumbling, rotten javelins, and with his substantial mattock knocks helmets that are hollow (494–6). Is it fanciful also to feel in '*pulveris exigui*' an overtone of the fate of 'our proud and angry dust'? It was, after all, just those words that Horace applied (*Odes* I. 28. 3) to the grave of the proud intellectual adventurer Archytas; and three handfuls of dust was what would have been thrown on real soldiers killed in battle.

But what about the comparison of the two kings in the section that follows? Even granted that the description echoes Varro on bees (3. 16. 18 and 20), he, like Aristotle (*H.A.* 5. 22) and Pliny (*N.H.* 11. 51), envisaged several rivals, not two only. What would anyone writing in 32–29 B.C., or reading in 29, understand by the following lines?

> deterior qui visus, eum, ne prodigus obsit,
> dede neci; melior vacua sine regnet in aula.
> alter erit maculis auro squalentibus ardens
> (nam duo sunt genera): hic melior insignis et ore
> et rutulis clarus squamis; ille horridus alter
> desidia latamque trahens inglorius alvom.

The one who seems inferior, lest he prove a wasteful obstruction, put to death; let the better one reign in the vacant palace. One will be ablaze with golden flecks (for there are two kinds); this, the better, is distinguished by his face and bright flashing mail; the other shaggy with sloth and dragging ingloriously a distended paunch.

And their followers are like them:

> namque aliae turpes horrent, ceu pulvere ab alto
> cum venit et sicco terram spuit ore viator
> aridus; elucent aliae et fulgore coruscant
> ardentes auro et paribus lita corpora guttis,

for the one lot are foul and unkempt, as when a parched traveller emerges from thick dust and spits the grime from his dry mouth; the others gleam and glitter, burning with gold and patterned with symmetrical spots.*

---

* These ideas may of course have been suggested to Virgil by Varro's descriptions of the drone, 'lato ventre', and of sick bees, 'pilosae et horridae, ut pulverulentae' (3. 16. 19–20). The comparison is not with the traveller himself, but with his dusty gob on the ground.

This is surely a reflection of the propaganda that accompanied the final breach of the two leaders in 32. Note the words of shining that characterise the superior king and his followers— *auro, ardens, rutulis, clarus, elucent, fulgore coruscant ardentes auro*— and compare the descriptions of Octavian at Actium in *Aeneid* 8. 678 ff.:

geminas cui tempora flammas
laeta vomunt patriumque aperitur vertice sidus...

with twin flames shooting from his joyous brow and his father's star manifested upon his head,

and of Agrippa,

tempora navali *fulgent* rostrata corona,

with the naval crown of the ships' beaks resplendent on his brow.

The better bees are smart with their evenly balanced spots, whereas the worse king and his followers are a dishevelled crew —*horridus, turpes horrent*, and again the idea is repeated:

hinc ope barbarica *variisque* Antonius armis.

It is hard to believe that these images were not connected in Virgil's mind. Horace spoke of Romans in Antony's forces at Actium being commanded by 'wrinkled eunuchs' and of Cleopatra as accompanied

contaminato cum grege turpium
morbo virorum

by a herd of foul disease-infected men.[47]

It was about this time that Antony was forced to defend himself by issuing a pamphlet *De Ebrietate Sua*.[48] The speech which Dio puts into the mouth of Octavian before Actium has passages that probably echo the propaganda of the period, about the degeneracy of Antony and his followers.[49] And Plutarch retails the story of an Egyptian soothsayer who told Antony that it was the nature of his *genius* to be high-spirited on its own, but to be rebuked in the presence of that of Octavian.[50]

Dahlmann[51] refers to the passage in Seneca, *De Clementia* I. 19, in which, addressing the young Nero, he uses the bees as a pattern. Monarchy, says Seneca, is an invention of nature. The king bee has the best and safest *cubile*. Free from work, he super-intends that of others. He is the champion, chosen by contest, superior in size and beauty. The bees only tolerate one ruler. If he dies, the community collapses. Seneca clearly has our passage from his favourite poet in mind, and we are thus encouraged to interpret it in human terms.* (In any case it is hard to see how a bee could be observed by the beekeeper as distinguished for its *face* (92): the ancients had no microscopes.)

But we must beware of going too far. In the section that follows, on swarming-fever (103 ff.), when the bees are disposed to desert the hive, the instruction is to tear off the wings of the kings. In no circumstances could Virgil have wished us to apply this to Octavian. Nor do I think that Aristaeus 'stands in some way for the sinful self-destruction, atonement and revival of the Roman people'; for as Otis,[52] who countenances this suggestion, rightly admits, he is being punished for his own great offence (*magna commissa*), so can hardly be identified with Octavian.[53] That being so, the whole connection becomes too tenuous to be applicable.

---

* Suitably to his subject, Seneca dwells on the 'fact' that the king bee has no sting. Nature wished him to rely on the goodwill of his people, not to be aggressive or vengeful. Dahlmann notes (p. 561) that Virgil omits this characteristic.

VIII · *Poetic Approach and Art*

No long poem can be all poetry, as Coleridge remarked. That is to say, it cannot seek to evoke continuously the intensity of feeling we associate with lyric poetry. The pedestrian may serve to enhance the elevated, as in Wordsworth's *Prelude* or in Eliot, and also contribute in its own right to the total effect. An epic poem can be sustained also by plot and characterisation. Didactic has no such advantage. For plot Lucretius found a substitute in edifice of argument: *alid ex alio clarescere* is the attraction that draws his reader continually onward, and instead of *dénouement* he has completeness of demonstration. Even so his last book, for all the brilliance of some of its passages, is an appendix rather than a climax. Lucretius' task was to expound and illustrate, Virgil's to portray in the guise of instruction. But without an element of personal involvement, of passion, a didactic poem is unlikely to come alive. In Hesiod this was imparted by a sense of injustice, in Lucretius by a belief that he could release men to happiness by banishing fear of death, in Virgil by a belief that a return of Rome's ruling class to the old values symbolised by country life could cure a sick generation. For continuity of argument Virgil's substitute was orchestration, and he relied much more than Lucretius on variety.

One obvious source of colour and variety was mythology. In so far as this provided passing allusions, as when the spider is 'hateful to Minerva' or the swallow has 'the marks of bloody hands on her breast', there is perhaps a mild pleasure of recognition for the reader.[1] But longer references are apt to seem intrusive. Erichthonius as inventor of four-horsed chariots and the Lapiths of riding on horseback seem dragged in at 3. 113–17. So do the horses of gods and heroes at 3. 89–94. These last are obviously intended, as Conington says, to ennoble the subject, and for that purpose those of Pollux, Mars and Achilles might serve; but Saturn turning himself into a stallion to conceal an amour from his wife and whinnying over the slopes of Pelion is a grotesque conception more suitable to Ovid's *Metamorphoses*. Again the brief disparagement of Bacchus' gifts, as having caused, for instance, the riot between the Centaurs and Lapiths (2. 454–7), seems an odd and unsatisfactory conclusion to Book 2 before the finale.* As for the lines on the pursuit of Scylla by Nisus (1. 406–9 = *Ciris* 538–41), the *Ciris* seems to be a later work, and we may give Virgil the benefit of the doubt as to their authenticity here, where they are apposite enough.

Greek names had an aura attractive to the Romans. A line of divinities adapted from Parthenius, friend and mentor of the poet in his youth, rounds off a section euphoniously (1. 437),

> Glauco et Panopeae et Inoo Melicertae;

and there is an appropriate impressiveness about the legendary physicians (3. 550),

> Phillyrides Chiron Amythaoniusque Melampus,

or the constellations as named by the earliest sailors (1. 138),

> Pleïadas, Hyadas, claramque Lycaonis Arcton.

Virgil recaptures something of the imagination of those first astronomers: whereas Varro says simply that honey should be gathered when the Pleiads rise, before Arcturus is above the horizon, and after the Pleiads have set, in Virgil this becomes (with Arcturus omitted: 4. 232–5),

> ...Taÿgete simul os terris ostendit honestum
> Pleas et Oceani spretos pede reppulit amnis,
> aut eadem sidus fugiens ubi Piscis aquosi
> tristior hibernas caelo descendit in undas.

...as soon as the Pleiad Taÿgete has shown her comely face to the world and spurned with scornful foot the streams of Ocean, or when the same star, fleeing from the sign of the watery Fish, sinks more sadly down the sky into the wintry waves.

---

* Otis (p. 168), who finds this a 'splendid conclusion', interprets it as saying, 'When so much has been given, how can man so greatly abuse it?' and thus providing a transition of thought to 'sua si bona norint' in 458. But Virgil has phrased it as a disparagement of *Baccheïa dona*, not of men, unequivocally. This is a good example of how he can be credited with desirable sentiments for which the text gives no warrant.

Why '*tristior*'? Surely not only because bad weather accompanies her, but because the carefree arrogance of youth in its beauty, as suggested by the first two lines, is followed inevitably by such decline. *Optima quaeque dies...* Jupiter's reward to the Cretan bees (4. 149 ff.) has a symbolic significance which makes it integral; and of course the myths of the Golden and Iron Ages are important. But by and large mythology plays no great part in the *Georgics*, outside the Aristaeus epyllion, and such contribution as it does make may generally be classed as 'ornament'.

Virgil had other and betters means of keeping his poem alive. We have seen how he contrived contrasts of light and shade, of gloom and gaiety, of Italy and foreign lands, city and country life, winter and summer, springtime and harvest, rain and sunshine. His vigilance in avoiding *satietas* is constant, and extends to unobtrusive details of style.[2] Take the following passage (1. 259–75), in which advice is given on what to do at odd times, when bad weather or public holidays preclude normal agriculture. There are fourteen suggestions, but only two imperatives, both in the same line (*torrete, frangite*, 267): the result is anything but monotonous. (I have italicised the operative words):

> frigidus agricolam si quando continet imber,
> multa, forent quae post caelo properanda sereno,
> *maturare datur*: durum *procudit arator*
> vomeris obtunsi dentem, *cavat* arbore lintres,
> aut pecori signum aut numeros *impressit* acervis.
> *exacuunt alii* vallos furcasque bicornis,
> atque Amerina *parant* lentae retinacula viti.
> nunc facilis rubea *texatur* fiscina virga,
> nunc *torrete* igni fruges, nunc *frangite* saxo.
> quippe etiam festis quaedam exercere diebus
> *fas et iura sinunt*: rivos deducere *nulla*
> *religio vetuit*, segeti praetendere saepem,
> insidias avibus moliri, incendere vepres,
> balantumque gregem fluvio mersare salubri.
> *saepe* oleo tardi costas agitator aselli
> vilibus aut *onerat* pomis, lapidemque revertens
> incusum aut atrae massam picis urbe *reportat*.

Whenever wintry rain keeps the farmer indoors, he *has a chance to do* at leisure many things he would else have to do in a hurry when the weather clears. *He hammers out* the hard tooth of the blunted plough-share, *scoops* tree-trunks into troughs, *brands* his cattle or *numbers* his corn-sacks. *Some sharpen* stakes or two-pronged forks, and *prepare* Amerinian withies to tie up straggling vines. *Now is the time to* weave pliant baskets of bramble-shoots, *now you should roast* your corn, grind it now with a stone. And then even on holy days *certain tasks are permitted* by the laws of god and man. *There is no religious ban* on irrigation work or fencing your crop with a hedge, setting traps for birds, burning briars, or dipping your bleating flock in the health-giving stream. *Often, too, the driver* of the dawdling ass *loads* its flanks with oil or cheap fruits for market, and comes back from the town bringing a millstone ready-shaped or a lump of pitch.

Monotony is also subtly avoided by the weighting and arrange-ment of the clauses that embody the different suggestions. In the first group the brief '*cavat arbore lintres*' is sandwiched asyndeti-cally between two longer clauses, of which the second, divided in subject (cattle—sacks) but united by a common verb, occupies a complete line. The pair that follows consists of two complete lines. The next three are joined by anaphora of *nunc*, but the verbs are one subjunctive and two imperatives. The group of five things permitted on holy days is again rounded off by a whole-line item, balantumque gregem fluvio mersare salubri;

and the two more spacious cola of the final three lines provide a satisfying conclusion to the movement of the section.

The pictorial quality which contributes so much to the overall effect of the poem emerges here in the sketch of the man going to market. Comparison with Aratus may illustrate it more clearly. Expect a storm, he says (976 ff.) 'if on a misty night snuff gathers on the nozzle of a lamp; or if in winter its flame now rises steadily, now emits sparks like light bubbles in rapid succession'. Virgil turns this into a human picture (1. 390 ff.: '*Even girls plucking their wool by night* do not fail to remark the approach of a storm when they see the oil sputter in the blazing lamp and mouldering snuff gather on the wick.' Note too that he fuses two observations into one, being concerned with vividness rather than conscientious completeness. This can be better illustrated by another comparison with Aratus. The latter concludes a list of signs of coming rain (949–53) with four features of the crow's behaviour. 'By a jutting promontory the chattering crow stalks, or dips its head maybe shoulder-deep in the river, or even dives right in, or hoarsely cawing zigzags beside the water.' Virgil focuses on a single aspect, and the result is a memorable image:

> tum cornix plena pluviam vocat improba voce
> et sola in sicca secum spatiatur arena,

then the raven mercilessly calls at the top of its voice for rain, and stalks alone with herself on the dry sand.

Virgil has followed Cicero in substituting raven for crow. He does not want the dipping and diving, for he has just had that (382–7, where he colours Aratus 942–5 with a reminiscence of *Iliad* 2. 461). But he remembers the solitary rooks, μοῦνοι ἐρημαῖοι, uttering warning cries at Aratus 1003, and also the popular (*dicuntur*) idea of ravens and rooks wilfully calling for rain and wind (*poscere*, *vocare*) mentioned by Lucretius at 5. 1084–6— hence 'vocat improba'. And his alliteration somehow enhances the mock-dignity of the bird's seaside promenade.*

There is indeed no better way of observing Virgil's aims and methods than by comparing him with his original when it is available. Varro's lists of points to be sought in a cow for breeding, or in a foal, are turned by judicious selection and expansion, and by imaginative addition, into a lively, readable paragraph.[3] Here is Varro on the foal (2. 7. 5):

Qualis futurus sit equus, e pullo coniectari potest: si *caput* habet non magnum, nec membris confusis si est, oculis nigris, naribus non angustis, auribus applicatis, *iuba* crebra, fusca, subcrispa subtenuibus saetis, *inplicata in dexteriorem partem cervicis*, pectus latum et plenum, umeris latis, *ventre modico*, lumbis deorsum versus pressis, scapulis latis, *spina maxime duplici*, si minus, non extanti, coda ampla subcrispa, cruribus rectis aequalibus intro versus potius figuratis, genibus rutundis

---

* Similarly Aratus' simple 'when the moon is red expect wind' (803) becomes in Virgil 'wind always makes golden Phoebe flush' (1. 431).

nec magnis, *ungulis duris*; toto corpore ut habeat venas quae animadverti possint, quod qui huiusce modi sit, cum est aeger, ad medendum appositus... Equi boni futuri signa, si cum gregalibus in pabulo contendit in currendo aliave qua re, quo potior sit; si *cum flumen travehendum est gregi, in primis progreditur* ac non respectat alios.

No need to translate this lengthy list: I have italicised in it the features picked up by Virgil (3. 75–88):

> continuo pecoris generosi pullus in arvis
> altius ingreditur et mollia crura reponit;
> primus et ire viam et fluvios temptare minantis
> audet et ignoto sese committere ponti,
> nec vanos horret strepitus. illi ardua cervix
> argutumque caput, brevis alvus obesaque terga,
> luxuriatque toris animosum pectus (honesti
> spadices glaucique, color deterrimus albis
> et gilvo). tum, si qua sonum procul arma dedere,
> stare loco nescit, micat auribus et tremit artus,
> collectumque premens volvit sub naribus ignem.
> densa iuba, et dextro iactata recumbit in armo;
> at duplex agitur per lumbos spina, cavatque
> tellurem et solido graviter sonat ungula cornu.

From the first a well-bred horse in the paddock picks his feet up higher than the herd and brings them down again lightly. He is first on the road, first to venture into menacing rivers and to entrust himself to the unknown bridge, nor is he startled by chance noises. His neck is high, his head well-tapered, barrel short and back full-fleshed, his gallant chest rippling with muscles. As to colour, chestnuts and greys are the finest, whites and duns the worst. Again, if the clash of arms sounds from far off, he cannot keep still, ears pricking, limbs aquiver, and in his nostrils rolls the breath of pent-up fire. His mane is thick, and falls, when tossed, over his right shoulder. A double ridge runs along his spine. He digs into the ground, and his solid hoof thuds heavily.

Virgil has decided to alternate short lists of points with descriptions of behaviour (even so the device of including colours as a parenthesis, though it lends variety, is a little awkward). He begins with gait, not dealt with by Varro. *Mollia crura reponit* is actually a phrase applied by Ennius (*Ann.* 556) to cranes, and the similarity of movement may have struck and amused him. He continues

where Varro ends, with leadership, surprisingly omitting com-
petitiveness (*contendit in currendo*) as a trait to watch for, perhaps
because he was to exploit it in the next paragraph with regard to
race-horses. *Minantis* emphasises the courage of the foal, and its
readiness to venture on to an unknown bridge (which would be
of wood) adds a vivid image. *Argutum* describes the head with a
poetic economy more effective than Varro's details (as '*turpe
caput*' does for the cow at 52). The colours are not from Varro.*
To provide his second description Virgil passes to budding warhorses (only casually mentioned by Varro, in section 15). Then
back to the list of points, from which *duris ungulis* is selected for
expansion into a more vivid image, both visual and auditory, the
latter again a reminiscence of Ennius (*Ann.* 439); just as, in the
case of the cow, Varro's *codam profusam usque ad calces* (2. 5. 8)
becomes a picture, rounding off a sentence in a complete line
(3. 59),

> et gradiens ima verrit vestigia cauda,

and as she walks she sweeps her tracks with the tip of her tail.

Time and again throughout the poem an object or fact is turned
into an image in this way, to its great enhancement. Thus a
planted tree, though slow-growing, will 'give shade to grandsons
long after', a plane-tree 'provide shade for drinkers' (2. 58; 4. 146).
For 'there will be a storm' we have 'the farmers will keep their
herds near their byres', or 'you will be trapped by a clear night'
(1. 355; 426). Fertility of land: 'its huge harvests burst the
granaries'; or 'from no plains will you see more wagons moving
homeward behind lumbering oxen' (1. 49; 2. 205). Keep a
watchdog: 'you will not be nervous of Iberian brigands stealing
up behind you' (3. 408). You can graft oak on to elm becomes
'pigs have munched acorns under elms' (2. 72). A wine called
Lageos is 'destined to trip up the feet and twist the tongue' (2. 94).
Some are brief glimpses of simile: bees warring are thick as hail,
or as acorns raining down when you shake an oak-tree; bees

---

* But the idea of distinguishing four colours and expressing preferences may have
been suggested by Varro on *cows* (2. 5. 8): *colore potissimum nigro, deinde robeo,
tertio helvo, quarto albo.*

emerging from a carcase are as rain from a storm-cloud in summer or as arrows from taut bowstrings with which nimble Parthians start a battle (4. 81; 314). An old stallion covering a mare with frenzied impotence is like a great fire raging ineffectively in a stubble-field (3. 97–100).

On a larger scale there are landscapes, some of them idyllic in the tradition of the *ecphrasis* of the *locus amoenus*. One has already been quoted (p. 12). The account of the ideal habitat for bees (4. 8–32) is reminiscent of the virgin meadow described by Hippolytus at the beginning of Euripides' play (75–8), untrampled by flocks (cf. 10–11), traversed by flowery brooks (cf. 18–19, 30–2) and shaded by trees (cf. 20), through which the bees roamed in spring:

> ἔνθ' οὔτε ποιμὴν ἀξιοῖ φέρβειν βοτὰ
> οὔτ' ἦλθέ πω σίδαρος, ἀλλ' ἀκήρατον
> μέλισσα λειμῶν' ἠρινὴ διέρχεται
> Αἰδὼς δὲ ποταμίοισι κηπεύει δρόσοις.

Hippolytus had gathered flowers there for Artemis, 'fairest of all the maidens in Olympus'. The virgin goddess was especially connected with bees, those symbols of chastity.* They were her emblems on coins of Ephesus, where her priests were called Μελισσονόμοι and Ἐσσῆνες.[4] It is not impossible that Virgil had this passage in mind.

After warnings of what to avoid, the positive advice proceeds (18 ff.):

> at liquidi fontes et stagna virentia musco
> adsint et tenuis fugiens per gramina rivus,
> palmaque vestibulum aut ingens oleaster inumbret,
> ut, cum prima novi ducent examina reges
> vere suo, ludetque favis emissa iuventus,
> vicina invitet decedere ripa calori,
> obviaque hospitiis teneat frondentibus arbos.
> in medium, seu stabit iners seu profluet umor,
> transversas salices et grandia conice saxa,

---

* 'The bee-keeper must be particularly careful, when he has to deal with the combs, to keep clear of sexual intercourse for a day previously' (Col. 9. 14. 3). Many similar references in Robert-Tornow, *De apium*, etc., pp. 13–14.

pontibus ut crebris possint consistere et alas
pandere ad aestivum solem, si forte morantis
sparserit aut praeceps Neptuno immerserit Eurus.
haec circum casiae virides et olentia late
serpylla et graviter spirantis copia thymbrae
floreat, inriguumque bibant violaria fontem.

But let there be nearby clear springs and moss-lined pools and a little
stream gliding through the grass, and let a palm or big wild-olive shade
the porch, so that when the kings shall lead out the early swarms to
greet the spring and the young ones revel in their freedom from the
cells, a neighbouring bank may invite them to shelter from the heat
and a tree be there to welcome them into its foliage. Whether the water
is still or flowing, throw into the middle of it willow boughs crosswise
and huge stones, so that they may have frequent bridges to alight on
and spread their wings to the summer sun in case a shower has wet them
or a gust of the east wind hurtled them into the deep. Round about let
green spurge-laurel grow and wild thyme smelling afar and masses of
heavy-scented savory, and let violets drink the freshening brook.

More self-consciously lyrical is the Praise of Spring, introduced
at 2. 323 with little particular relevance save that this is to be a
happy Book and that there has been a long stretch of didactic
matter since 176 containing only short pieces of relief, the battle-
order simile at 279–84, the description of the oak at 291–7, and the
plantation fire at 303–11.

ver adeo frondi nemorum, ver utile silvis,
vere tument terrae et genitalia semina poscunt.
tum pater omnipotens fecundis imbribus Aether
coniugis in gremium laetae descendit, et omnis
magnus alit magno commixtus corpore fetus.
avia tum resonant avibus virgulta canoris,
et Venerem certis repetunt armenta diebus;
parturit almus ager Zephyrique trementibus auris
laxant arva sinus; superat tener omnibus umor,
inque novos soles audent se gramina tuto
credere, nec metuit surgentis pampinus Austros
aut actum caelo magnis Aquilonibus imbrem,
sed trudit gemmas et frondes explicat omnis.
non alios prima crescentis origine mundi

inluxisse dies aliumve habuisse tenorem
crediderim: ver illud erat, ver magnus agebat
orbis, et hibernis parcebant flatibus Euri,
cum primae lucem pecudes hausere, virumque
terrea⁵ progenies duris caput extulit arvis,
immissaeque ferae silvis et sidera caelo.

Spring it is that favours the woodland leaves, spring the forests; in spring the ground swells and calls for the fertile seeds. Then the almighty Father of heaven descends in fruitful showers into the lap of his joyful spouse and mingling with her great body greatly breeds all kinds of fruit. Then do the pathless copses resound to the singing of birds and the beasts of the herd know that their time to seek a mate is come again, and the bountiful earth bares its bosom to the warm west winds. Everywhere a mild moisture prevails, and the grasses can safely venture up to meet the young suns, nor do the vine-shoots fear gales rising from the south or storms driven down the sky by mighty north winds, but thrust their buds out and unfold all their leaves. Such days shone out, I believe, when the infant world began, and even so they ran. It was springtime then, the great world was keeping spring and the east winds forbore their wintry blasts, when the first cattle drank in the light, and the earthborn race of men reared its head in the hard fields, and the wild beasts were sent forth into the forests and the stars into the sky.

This set-piece is artfully constructed.⁶ It gathers momentum through three sections of five, eight and seven lines. Within those, the first two lines form a tricolon bound together by anaphora of a type favoured by Virgil, in which the third limb is a whole line, *ver*...*ver*...*vere* (see p. 210 n.). They give out the theme emphatically. The first section deals with fertilisation on the cosmic scale, the second with the result on the mundane scale; but they are bound together by the anaphora of *tum*. Other repetitions—*magnus* ...*magno, alios*...*alium, ver*...*ver* again, the assonance of *avia*... *avibus*, the alliterations of *tument terrae, commixtus corpore, virgulta* ...*Venerem, primae*...*pecudes, silvis*...*sidera*, all go to create a hieratic effect⁷ as well as imparting musicality. The last section deals with the dawning of the world, and issues in a fine 'super-flux' which also embodies an idea that caught Virgil's imagination,

immissaeque ferae silvis et sidera caelo,

recalling the crowning line in the same context at *Eclogue* 6. 40,

> incipiant silvae cum primum surgere, cumque
> *rara per ignaros errent animalia montes.*

The inspiration undoubtedly came from two passages in Lucretius. The first, 1. 250–61, deals with the ἱερὸς γάμος, the holy marriage of heaven and earth that produces all fertility, an idea as old at least as Hesiod and probably much older, ubiquitous in folklore.[8] It describes in idyllic terms the resulting fertility and joy in the world. The second is from the famous hymn to Venus in the exordium (1. 10–20), describing the sexual excitement that seizes all animals in spring. But whereas Lucretius gives only a couple of lines to the holy marriage, a mere metaphor to him, Virgil makes more of it, and by calling 'pater Aether' *omnipotens* associates the sky-god more closely with Jupiter.* He also develops the sexual imagery much more intensively. Lucretius, even in the latter passage, concentrates on the wild careering of the animals—*persultant, tranant, sequitur cupide*, and the ubiquity of the spirit of desire: *genitabilis aura favoni* and ten lines later *generatim saecla propagent* are the nearest he comes to the sexual act itself. Virgil's language, even when not specifically about this, is pervadingly suggestive: *tument, genitalia semina poscunt, fecundis imbribus, in gremium coniugis, commixtus corpore, Venerem repetunt, parturit, laxant sinus, audent se credere, surgentis, actum imbrem, trudit gemmas, frondes explicat omnis.*[9] His conception of a sentient universe is never more apparent.

The final section deals with a subject which had already attracted Virgil (*Ecl.* 6. 31–40), and again the suggestion may have come from Lucretius (5. 783–820). But the idea that every spring is in a sense a repetition of the first creation, as every Easter is thought of as being a recurrence of the first Easter, does not come from him. The belief that the world was born in spring— *vere natus orbis est*, as the *Pervigilium Veneris* proclaims—comes from Greco-Egyptian astrology, in which the vernal equinox was 'the birthday of the world', as the Neopythagorean Nigidius

---

* Klingner (1963), pp. 106–10; but I think he exaggerates the religious significance.

Figulus also held.[10] From similar sources came the idea of the stars (or planets) being released into the sky by the Demiurge at the creation, the metaphor being from the release of horses on to a racecourse.[11]

But Virgil is far from being only a 'beauty-poet'. He devotes equal care to describing what is repulsive—the effects of contagious disease, for instance, at 3. 561–6:

> ne tondere quidem morbo inluvieque peresa
> vellera nec telas possunt attingere putris;
> verum etiam invisos si quis temptarat amictus,
> ardentes papulae atque immundus olentia sudor
> membra sequebatur, nec longo deinde moranti
> tempore contactos artus sacer ignis edebat.

They could not even shear the fleeces corroded with poisonous filth, nor touch the rotten web; and indeed if anyone ventured to put on the repulsive clothing, inflamed pustules and foul sweat ran all over his foetid limbs, and before long the burning curse was consuming his infected body.

On the other hand, he does not revel in such 'realism'. It has been suggested that when he is describing the ugly process of Bugonia, instead of merely saying 'this is done in early spring', he went out of his way to provide relief by three pleasant images (4. 305–7):

> hoc geritur Zephyris primum impellentibus undas,
> ante novis rubeant quam prata coloribus, ante
> garrula quam tignis nidum suspendat hirundo.

This is done as soon as the west wind ruffles the water, before the meadows brighten with fresh colours, before the chattering swallow hangs her nest from the rafters.

He may even have altered the appropriate season from the Dog Days (cf. 425–7) to spring for this very purpose.

The pictorial quality is much enhanced by Virgil's genius for expressive rhythms and sounds. I have analysed elsewhere at length one section (1. 43–392) which is particularly rich in this respect because the weather-signs lend themselves to it.[12] Here I

will therefore give only a few examples taken from other parts
of the poem.

There are simple rhythms within the compass of a line—paired
and plodding oxen (3. 169),

> *iunge pares*, et *coge gradum* conferre iuvencos;

and the Cyclopes forging thunderbolts in heavy rhythm (4. 174),

> illi inter sese magna vi bracchia tollunt;

and a very rare rhythm for the mares impregnated by the wind
making off wildly over rugged rocks and corries and the bottoms
of valleys (3. 276),

> saxa per et scopulos et depressas convallis,

perhaps suggested by Lucretius' 'per tumulos et convallis'
(5. 1375). There is metaphor from metrical subtleties, as when the
ram, after being dipped, is sent off downstream in a line (3. 447)
in which there is a 'released' movement (coincidence of pulse and
accent in the last four feet),

> mersatur, missúsque secúndo défluit ámni,

like the line of similar movement where the chariot plunges out of
control, unreined by any caesura at the $4\frac{1}{2}$ position (1. 514),

> fertur equis auríga neque aúdit cúrrus habénas.*

The year treading round in its own footsteps is matched by
involuted word order,

> atque *in se sua per* vestigia volvitur annus,

which may have been suggested by a combination of a phrase
from his friend Varius (*mundi resonat canor in vestigia se sua volven-
tis*) with Lucretius' idea of expressing a man standing on his head
by topsy-turvy word order,

> qui capite ipse sua in statuit vestigia sese.[13]

* Day-Lewis reproduces the effect with the irregular rhythm of
'his horses run away, car out of control, quite helpless'.

At 3. 343–5 the metre is as cumbrous as the nomad Libyan herdsman, and all his trappings are strung round him with -*que*:

> omnia secum
> armentarius Afer agit, tectumque laremque
> armaque Amyclaeumque canem Cressamque pharetram.[14]

The rare rhythm of three successive anapaestic words* vividly
expresses the spasmic acceptance of sperm by the sex-starved cow
or mare (3. 137):

> sed *rapiat sitiens Venerem* interiusque recondat.

At 4. 61 the rare stop after the word-type *contemplator* ($- - - \cup$) at
the beginning of a line emphasises the pause during which the bee-
keeper watches his newly released hive to see where they will
make for. Another rare stop, at the hephthemimeral caesura,
separates the booming break of a huge wave from the seething
backwash that follows (3. 240):

> neque ipso
> monte minor pro*cum*bit; at ima exaestuat unda
> verticibus.

The rhythm and sticky consonants of '*explent collectumque*' go well
with the bees' *gluten* (glue) to which they refer (4. 40). A sudden
descent may be represented by a heavy single monosyllable at the
end of a line. That this is no mere fancy is shown by the fact that
on five occasions, two in the *Georgics*, it is found with the verb
ruere:[15]

> G. 1. 313: *ruit* imbriferum *ver.*
> G. 3. 255: ipse *ruit* dentesque Sabellicus exacuit *sus.*
> *Aen.* 2. 250: *ruit* Oceano *nox.*
> Hor. *Epp.* 2. 2. 75: lutulenta *ruit sus.*
> Juv. 10. 268: et *ruit* ante aram summi Iovis ut vetulus *bos.*

More elaborate is the scene of routing a snake at 3. 420–2. Immediacy is given by the staccato imperatives with short, sharp cola

---

* The line should perhaps be added, despite the elision, to the list in my *Golden
Latin Artistry*, p. 82 n.

and the rattle of broad *a*-sounds: 'pick up stones, sticks, anything to hand'; then a full line allows the snake smoothly to rear its head; then '*deice*', 'down with it', reserved for the beginning of the line as the decisive verb so often is:

> cape saxa manu, cape robora, pastor,
> tollentemque minas et sibila colla tumentem
> *deice*.

For a dactylic verb so held up we may compare

> ecce supercilio clivosi tramitis undam
> *elicit*...(1. 108–9)

> et pluvia ingenti sata laeta boumque labores
> *diluit*...(1. 325–6)

> aut Athon aut Rhodopen aut alta Ceraunia telo
> *deicit*...(1. 332–3)

> antiquasque domos avium cum stirpibus imis
> *eruit*...(2. 209–10)

> ecce autem duro fumans sub vomere taurus
> *concidit*...(3. 515–16).[16]

Such effects were a gift of the flexible word-order of Latin. Milton wrote

> Comes the blind Fury with the abhorrèd shears
> And slits the thin-spun life.

In Latin the images could have been presented to the mind in their true sequence:

> the thin-spun life | the blind Fury | with the abhorrèd shears | coming | slits.

Quite a different effect may be created by a *spondaic* verb running over (before punctuation), as at 3. 316–17, where the goats can be trusted to come home leading their young with udders so full they hardly clear the threshold:

> atque ipsae memores redeunt in tecta, suosque
> *ducunt*, et gravido superant vix ubere limen.

This drew from Conington one of his rare remarks on expressiveness: 'the pause after the first foot expresses the slowness of their approach with their burden of milk'. (He should have added 'spondaic' before 'first'.) *

When the Roman legionary after a forced march takes the enemy by surprise, the creeping spondaic rhythm is suddenly succeeded by staccato, suggesting the brisk drill of the disciplined guardsman (3. 347–8):

> hosti
> ante exspectatum positis stat in agmine castris. †

Here is the Portus Julius, which Agrippa made in 37 by joining lakes Avernus and Lucrinus and building a mole to protect their outlet to the sea (2. 161–4):

> an memorem portus Lucrinoque addita claustra
> atque indignatum magnis stridoribus aequor,
> Iulia qua ponto longe sonat unda refuso
> Tyrrhenusque fretis immittitur aestus Avernis?

Or shall I speak of ports and the barrier built along the Lucrine, and the deep indignant with mighty chafings, where the Julian water sounds afar as the waves are hurled back, and the Tyrrhenean surge rushes into the roadsteads of Avernus?

The heavy movement and the sibilants of the second line express the booming and dashing of the breakers against the mole, echoing afar in the repeated 'on' sounds of the next, while the sibilants in the fourth are for the inrush through the new channels.

Ancient critics' assignment of the *Georgics* to the 'middle style' is sheer pedantic *Systemzwang*. It is true that, so far as we can tell, it

---

* It can also represent effort (4. 164; 196), or solemnity (1. 477), or heaviness (3. 375): S. E. Winbolt, *Latin Hexameter Verse* (1903), p. 17.

† The fact that similar rhythms and sounds are used at 1. 449 for hail dancing on a roof

> in tectis crepitans salit horrida grando,

is no reason for scepticism about the expressive effect: see Wilkinson, *Golden Latin Artistry*, p. 52.

avoids the colloquial. Diminutives are a touchstone in this difficult investigation. Whereas the *Eclogues*, which are more akin to the lyric-elegiac spirit, display twelve different examples (including *capella* thirteen times), the much longer *Georgics* have, apart from *lapillus*, only the three animals *capella* (2), *bucula* (2) and *asellus* (2).* It is true also that the metre differs only in slight tendencies from that of the *Aeneid*; and that however dry the subject-matter may become, the verse is never allowed to degenerate into prosiness. But apart from this Virgil follows the only sound principle, the classical one of τὸ πρέπον, *decorum*, propriety. There are no other generalisations that can be made about the style or diction of the poem. They vary with the subject.[17] A few examples will illustrate this.

A great oak-tree is described (2. 291–7) in such terms that the opening words could be repeated verbatim at *Aeneid* 4. 445–6 as part of a simile for Aeneas immovable by Dido's appeals:

> aesculus in primis, *quae quantum vertice ad auras*
> *aetherias tantum radice in Tartara tendit.*
> ergo non hiemes illam, non flabra neque imbres
> convellunt: immota manet multosque nepotes,
> multa virum volvens durando saecula vincit,
> tum fortis late ramos et bracchia tendens
> huc illuc media ipsa ingentem sustinet umbram.

The oak above all, which raises its head as far towards heaven as its roots strike down towards hell; wherefore no storms nor blasts nor

---

* Animals are a special category. *Capella* is rarely found in prose, *capra* or *caper* rarely in 'high' poetry (B. Axelson, *Unpoetische Wörter* (1945), p. 40). 'Asinus', the ordinary word for ass, never occurs in high poetry (A. E. Housman, 'The Latin for *Ass*', *C.Q.* (1930), pp. 11 f.); cf. our 'donkey'. *Puella* is also generally avoided in high poetry (Axelson, p. 58); but it occurs three times in the *Georgics*: 1. 11; 340; 4. 476, where the 'higher' word *virgines* would not scan. *Pueri innuptaeque puellae* (4. 476) is repeated twice even in epic: *Aen.* 2. 238; 6. 307. Here another element may be present, a touch of tender emotion more characteristic of elegy. Similarly *natus* had a more tender feeling than *filius* (Marouzeau, *Traité*, p. 167). When Dido breaks down from an indignant queen to a pathetic woman (*A.* 4. 328), she uses one of the very few diminutives in the epic, *parvulus*. It is one of the few blemishes in Day-Lewis' translation of the *Georgics*, still more disturbing in his *Aeneid*, that he lapses sometimes into gratuitous and discordant colloquialisms.

rains uproot it; immovable it remains, and triumphantly outlasts many generations of men as time rolls on. Far and wide on all sides it stretches the arms of its boughs, a central trunk sustaining a huge expanse of shade.*

The battle of the bees is of course made pure epic, for mock-heroic purposes (4. 67–85), being indeed wholly anthropomorphic and based on no observed behaviour. Nor is there anything 'middle style' about the proems and finales of Books 1 and 3, or the praises of Italy and of country life in Book 2.

But for contrast let us examine the first purely didactic paragraph we come to (1. 71–93):

> alternis idem *tonsas cessare* novalis
> et *segnem* patiere *situ* durescere campum;
> aut ibi *flava* seres mutato sidere farra,
> unde prius laetum siliqua quassante legumen
> aut tenuis fetus viciae *tristisque* lupini
> sustuleris *fragilis* calamos *silvamque* sonantem.
> urit enim lini campum seges, urit avenae,
> urunt *Lethaeo perfusa papavera somno*:
> sed tamen alternis facilis labor, arida tantum
> ne *saturare* fimo *pingui* pudeat *sola* neve
> *effetos* cinerem immundum iactare per agros.
> sic quoque mutatis *requiescunt* fetibus arva,
> nec nulla interea est *inaratae* gratia terrae.
> saepe etiam sterilis incendere profuit agros
> atque levem stipulam *crepitantibus* urere flammis:
> sive inde occultas viris et pabula terrae
> pinguia concipiunt, sive illis omne per ignem
> excoquitur vitium atque *exsudat* inutilis umor,
> seu pluris calor ille vias et caeca relaxat
> *spiramenta*, novas veniat qua sucus in herbas,

---

* Some of the 'grand' language that occurs occasionally in the *Georgics* is an echo of Lucretius, as the fifth line here from *D.R.N.* 1. 202,

> multaque vivendo vitalia vincere saecla.

But Tartarus as the utmost depth comes from Homer (*Il.* 8. 16; cf. Hesiod, *Th.* 720), as does the oak as symbol of unshakability (*Il.* 12. 131 ff.): see Klingner (1963), p. 100. It is this aspect, of course, not its long life or provision of shade, that Virgil is concerned to develop in the Aeneas simile.

seu durat magis et venas astringit *hiantis*,
ne tenues pluviae *rapidive* potentia solis
acrior aut Boreae *penetrabile* frigus adurat.

There are ninety-five words here of the kind that mainly determine the colour of a passage (nouns, verbs, adjectives and adverbs). Of these at least seventy are neutral, as much at home in verse as prose. *Fimus* (dung) is the sort of word that used to be thought of (in antiquity also) as by nature unpoetic, but to Virgil it was just another fact of the farm. Others are names of plants, naturally more often found in prose but not intrinsically unpoetic. The remainder (italicised) merit scrutiny, whose results must however be taken *cum grano* in view of the patchy nature of our evidence. Are they poetic words, or neutral words used in an unusual way, or unpoetic?

The most obviously poetic phrase here is *Lethaeo perfusa papavera somno*, both for the word *Lethaeus* and the idea of poppies drenched in sleep. Wholly poetic also are *tristis* in the transferred sense of 'bitter', *inaratus*, *penetrabilis* in the active sense and *rapidus* in the sense of 'consuming', while *exsudare* intransitive is a Virgilian innovation.[18] *Sola* looks like a plural for metrical convenience. Some of the words occur in poets and in Pliny and Columella, who were particularly influenced by Virgil—*tondere* of plants, *effetus* and *pinguis* (meaning 'rich') of soil. *Flavus* is a mainly poetic word (Th.L.L.), *cessare* and *requiescere* of inanimate subjects seem mainly poetic usages. Words found solely or mainly in poetry and Silver prose are *silva* in the sense of 'undergrowth', *situs* in the material sense of 'dirt', etc., *spiramentum* and *hiare*. *Fragilis* in the literal sense seems more poetic than in the metaphorical; it was rare in any case before Silver Latin. *Segnis* is peculiar in being uncommon except in the comparative before Silver Latin; as used of things it may be slightly poetic. *Crepitare* is found mainly in poets, but is used by Plautus of the teeth and the bowels—which is a warning of the hazardousness of this kind of investigation. The tricolon in 77–8 with anaphora of *urit* is not merely ornamental but expressive: one *feels* the land being exhausted by these crops. All in all, a contemporary Roman reading this passage would probably have felt that it was in common language but with a certain novelty or unusualness in the use of words that distinguished it from versified prose.*

Nor must we overlook novelties that have become familiar. The line preceding this passage contains what may count as the first of all the examples in extant Latin of that common Grecism the proleptic adjective.[19] *Iacuisse* at 3. 436 is the first example of perfect infinitive used for present.[20] So far as we know, before 3. 110 *nimbus* had never been used of anything dry, such as sand or dust, nor had water been called 'glassy' before 4. 350.[21] Richter (on 1. 165) lists a number of adjectives in *-eus* first found in Virgil, ten being from the *Georgics* (from meaning 'made of...' they came to mean 'used for...' or 'like...').

On the other hand epithets in the *Georgics* are rarely striking or recherché, unless the geographical and mythological can so be called. These seem to be introduced in order *angustis...addere rebus honorem*. Occasionally they are simply 'learned' in the Alexandrian manner, for example, 'Hellespontic' Priapus. More often they refer to places noted for a product, 'Narycian' or 'Idaean' pitch, 'Pelusiac' lentil, 'Idumaean' palms, 'Ituraean' bows, 'Balearic' slings, 'Sicyonian' olives. Commerce under Roman rule had united the world, but one may doubt whether the African herdsman would really have an Amyclaean dog and a Cretan quiver. It was certainly not 'Strymonian' cranes that worried the Italian farmer. Such ornamental epithets are quite likely to be literary allusions to passages unknown to us. Similarly 'oyster-bearing' Abydos (1. 207) might be a translation of some Greek compound.[22]

Tastes change in these matters (contrast Shakespeare with Pope). To our age epithets in Latin poetry seem unadventurous. They tend to be used for purposes of structural symmetry without much thought of semantic enhancement. In the *Georgics* frost is

---

* Of course an ordinary word can *become* poetic by conjunction (*iunctura*). For possible use by Virgil of normal words in a subtly abnormal way (as alleged by Agrippa, Suet. *Virg.* 44) see L. P. Wilkinson, 'The Language of Virgil and Horace', *C.Q.* (1959), pp. 181–92.

'white', grass is 'green', pitch is 'black', and pigs are 'dirty'. It is only occasionally that we notice them because they call up an image, as of the fat Etruscan trumpeter at 2. 193. More often they carry a moral nuance, as with *ferrea iura insanumque Forum* (2. 501–2). Winter is '*genialis*', a word associated with hospitality (1. 302); it is also '*intractabilis*', the time that is hard to cope with, when you cannot work (1. 211). Cold can be '*sceleratus*' (2. 256) —'wicked', as we say; and besides geese (1. 119) and ravens (1. 388) and snakes (3. 431), toil can be '*improbus*'—'*merciless*', 'unconscionable'. The ploughman felling trees at 2. 207 is called '*iratus*' presumably because he is angry that unsold timber should occupy good arable land; but also, I think, because anyone attacking trees with an axe looks as if he were angry.

It was characteristic of Virgil's mind that he liked to blend ingredients taken from different sources, or otherwise previously separate, to form a new picture or conception;[23] and that whatever he did, he had in view, not truth to facts, but the overall purposes and effectiveness of his poem. These two tendencies, the former of which was subservient to the latter, must be borne in mind in any criticism of it. Hesiod had been consistent only over short contexts; Virgil was more broadly so, but consistency was still not paramount with him.*

We have noted what Bayet calls his *description synthétique* of the rites of Ceres and of Bacchus, creating something more like an ideal than anything an Italian would recognise as having seen (pp. 149–50); and how, in the proem to Book 3, he has blended not only features of the Greek games with those of a Roman triumph, but scenes from the Triple Triumph with sculptures of the temple of Apollo—the latter blend to be repeated more obviously on the shield in *Aeneid* 8 (pp. 169–70). Even the ideal

---

* Where is the *secura quies et nescia fallere vita* of the farmer when we come to the Noric plague? It is noteworthy that at *Aen.* 6. 119 Virgil makes Aeneas plead as a precedent for his being allowed to see his father again, '*si potuit manes accersere coniugis Orpheus*', which clearly assumes the old tradition that Eurydice was brought safely back, regardless of the far more significant variant he had developed in the *Georgics*, destined to eclipse it for all time.

foal was a combination between Varro's ideal racehorse and a warhorse, 'a composite portrait'.*

Another passage where this tendency has confused commentators is 1. 240 ff., on the shape of the world. Here Virgil has intruded into a scientific description of the globe the idea of the Styx and the Greek mythology of Hades, with a literary reminiscence from Lucretius (3. 25 ff.), and others from Homer (*Il.* 18. 489; *Od.* 5. 275). He must have known what he was doing. It was simply that he enjoyed such juxtapositions and had no scientific conscience.[24] This attitude of mind, Roman rather than Greek, was encouraged by rhetorical training, which taught how to create a desired effect by artistic means and by appealing to the emotions. In this connection we may consider two of the most powerful passages in the *Georgics*.

Let us take first the portents at the end of Book 1. Most of the items are retailed, independently it would seem,† by the historians, as occurring in the period concerned, between the murder of Julius Caesar and the Battle of Philippi. The first is the one which provides Virgil with his ingenious transition from the weather-signs, the sun as an unimpeachable reflector of political as well as atmospheric events (463–8). It is not impossible that the months following the murder did in fact witness an unusual obscuration of the sun, which could have been caused by volcanic dust from the exceptionally violent eruption of Etna shortly before, adduced by Servius on the authority of Livy. Here the consensus of historians is noteworthy;‡ and the prominence given to the phenomenon by Virgil, and its exact dating, would be strange if he knew his contemporary readers would recollect no such thing. *Obscenae canes* (470) congregated by night and howled in the city, especially near Lepidus' house, we are told,

---

* W. Liebeschuetz, *G.&R.* (1965), p. 66. Varro expressly says that racehorses, warhorses, horses for draught and for breeding must be judged by differing standards (2. 7. 15).

† I would not be sure about Appian 4. 4, though he has details not in Virgil. Ovid, *M.* 15. 783 ff., and Tibullus, 2. 5. 71, are certainly based on the *Georgics* passage.

‡ Plut. *Caes.* 69. 4; Dio, 45. 17. 5; Appian, 4. 4; cf. Pliny, *N.H.* 2. 98. Plutarch says that this also impeded the ripening of crops.

and *importunae volucres* pecked out the names of the consuls Antony and Dolabella from a tablet in the temple of Castor and Pollux.[25] Besides the volcanic eruptions (471–3), clashings of armour in the sky were reported, and a great earthquake (but the impressively remote locations of these, Germany and the Alps, are peculiar to Virgil: it is no merely local catastrophe that is portended (474–5)).[26] The mysterious loud voice and the speaking of a beast (476–8) occur in Appian,[27] the staying of rivers (479) in Dio.[28] The effusion by statues of sweat (480) is also attested, and if not of tears, at least of blood and milk.[29] There was a great flooding of the Po (481–3).[30] Instances of inauspicious sacrifice (484) are also reported, though the flaw was different from that in Virgil.[31] Wolves appearing in towns by night (486) are corroborated,[32] while thunderbolts and comets (487–8) were commonplaces.[33]

What is unaccounted for? Not much:—pallid spectres (477), gaping earth (479) and blood in the wells (485). Virgil's list of portents was composed within a few years of their real or alleged occurrence. We should expect him to include only what was common talk at the time. And (remembering the 'angels of Mons' in 1914) we must recognise that in any age even 'educated' people are capable of believing in such things, especially in a crisis. By all accounts Augustus himself attached great importance to omens, and Livy as well as later historians retailed them conscientiously from their sources. The burden of proof is on those who believe that Virgil used a catalogue of portents, though such things existed at Rome.[34] Nor do I think that there is any significance in the fact that Apollonius Rhodius in a simile anticipates one or two of his.* It would be much more impressive to recall only what had been matters of conversation at this time, a few years before. Some of the items could be genuine occurrences, which only the nervous tension of the time made seem

---

* 4. 1280 ff. Richter calls this 'bemerkenswert', but in fact the sweating of statues (which could be ordinary condensation) is the only exact similarity (1284); the sun inducing night at midday (1286) is hardly equivalent to Virgil's sun dimmed by *ferrugo*. The heroes are *like* 'pale spectres' (1280), but that is not a portent.

abnormally frequent or significant. Some, like the mysterious voice, the spectres and the weeping statues, could be illusions caused by real phenomena. Blood-oozing wells strain credulity, even in slaughterous times; but only the talking beasts are down-right incredible—and the *bos locutus* was at least one of the most time-honoured of all Roman portents. But the point is that we have here a conglomerate argument rather than a composite picture; yet the power of Virgil's rhetoric is such as to induce even in us 'a willing suspension of disbelief'.

The second passage is the Noric plague. Lucretius had devoted nearly 150 lines (6. 1138–286) to a description of the human plague at Athens, based on Thucydides and Theophrastus. He included six lines (1219–24) on the disappearance of birds and wild animals during that period, and the death in the streets of *fida canum vis*. Virgil devotes nearly 100 lines (3. 474–566) to a description of animal plague, of which the last six deal with infection of men by contagion with the wool or pelts of the dead. It is abundantly clear that he got the idea and much of the detail from Lucretius. Perhaps even the death of the faithful ox was suggested by those 'faithful' dogs. There is no other such description in extant ancient literature of an animal plague. But Virgil needed one here for the economy of this Book (see pp. 99–100):

subeunt morbi tristisque senectus
et labor, et durae rapit inclementia mortis.

He wanted something to balance the finale of Book 1.

Richter has a long and painstaking note on 478 ff. in which, after reviewing the symptoms and consulting a modern compendium of veterinary science, he deduces that they tally most closely with haemorrhal septicemia, which can occur concurrently with petechial fever, but that Virgil may have included some of the symptoms of anthrax, which has from time immemorial been much commoner than these in Europe. Even so, some of the symptoms are left unaccounted for; and more important, the involvement of sea-animals, fishes, snakes and birds (541–7) is admitted to have 'hardly a claim to scientific interest' and no possible connection with the Noric plague. And yet Richter concludes that this description must be valued 'not only as a work of art, but as a remarkable piece of evidence for veterinary history'.[35] Is it not rather apparent that Virgil has conceived a plague that never was on land or sea, a piling up of gruesome symptoms culled from any source, or even his imagination, and affecting, like the *amor* of 242 ff.,

> omne adeo genus in terris hominumque ferarumque
> et genus aequoreum, pecudes pictaeque volucres,

though man is only casually introduced because this is a Book of beasts?

He colours his lurid canvas with the ingenuity of an Ovid or Tacitus, and the sensationalism of a Doré. Against the background of the soaring Alps and the Noric hill-towns we are shown the lowlands above Trieste, still desolate years after the catastrophe. At that time air, water and fields were alike polluted, and limbs wasted by the fire of fever were then rotted by excess of liquid. The plague cheated even the gods of their victims.* Pet dogs went mad ('*blandis rabies*'). The victorious racehorse forgot his keenness: he who used to love to have his neck patted (186) was now too tender to bear any touch. Wine seemed to do some good at first, but it proved that the access of strength only aided drunken rending of their own limbs. (The shocking thought prompts the poet to a rhetorical apotropaic intervention, 'God grant a better lot to the good, and such error only to enemies!') The death of the ploughing ox follows. Then the impotence of the Gods is again laid bare: only ill-matched wild oxen can be found for Juno's processional chariots.† Men return to primitive life, scratch the earth with mattocks, plant with their own fingernails, pull creaking wagons themselves up hill and down dale. The wolf ceases to prowl round the fold because he has more pressing things to think about, and timid hinds and elusive stags wander safely

---

* Tacitean irony (cf. 509 ff., 531 ff., 539 ff.). Where is the *pius poeta* now? There is a strong Lucretian strain in this Book, while the Stoic doctrine of Providence is in abeyance. See Liebeschuetz, *G.&R.*, pp. 76–7.
† Normally cows not only well-matched, but specially chosen as unblemished, were used.

among listless hounds at men's doorsteps. Thus by a gruesome travesty the harmony of the Golden Age dream has become a reality; and the conventional ἀδύνατα have come true. Dead sea-beasts are washed up like wrecks, snakes are terrified and find no safety in their holes, and from the infected air birds crash dead to the ground.* All sense of reality is now forgotten in the sweep of Virgil's rhetoric. We accept the anachronistic assertion that the famous healers of legend proved unavailing and the apparition of the Fury Tisiphone, driving Diseases and Terror before her. And the final irony: when men learn at last to bury the corpses, they still find they can be infected themselves if they try to use the wool or pelts. Even after death the menace lives on.

Rhetoric, at least of the periodic kind, had also great influence on a smaller scale. The artistic devices adapted from it and already displayed in perfect maturity in some of the *Eclogues* are impeccably exploited throughout the *Georgics*.[36] The cola are so managed that appropriateness combines with variety of enjambement and sentence-length, and the figures of rhetoric are so employed as to impart vitality without being obtrusive. Rarely, after the headlong Lucretian-style proem, does a sentence exceed four lines, and the structure tends to be simple and paratactic, for this is poetry to be read aloud. Where there are exceptions, the motive can generally be perceived. The eight-line sentence *me vero primum*...(2. 475 ff.) is again Lucretian, to match its subject-matter. If the account of Bugonia ends with one of seven lines, that is to round off the major part of the book before the Aristaeus epyllion (4. 308–14). It also effectively expresses the gradual, if miraculous, process of generation (*primo...mox et...magis magis ...donec...*). The nine-line sentence at 2. 303–11 is expressive of

---

* Dio records (45. 17. 7) among portents of the year 43 that the Po, after a big flood, suddenly receded, stranding a vast number of snakes; and that countless fish were cast up on the shore near the mouth of the Tiber; and that on top of this there was a terrible (human) plague nearly all over Italy. We do not know the date of the Noric plague, but it could have been 43: in which case Virgil or his informants might have seen the dead snakes and fish and erroneously connected them with the animal and human plagues respectively. So there may be some element of fact behind the fantasy.

the uncontrollable conflagration it describes (notice the stealthy spondees in the second line, and the sweeping dactyls of the last):

> nam saepe incautis pastoribus excidit ignis,
> qui furtim pingui primum sub cortice tectus
> robora comprendit, frondesque elapsus in altas
> ingentem caelo sonitum dedit; inde secutus
> per ramos victor perque alta cacumina regnat,
> et totum involvit flammis nemus et ruit atram
> ad caelum picea crassus caligine nubem,
> praesertim si tempestas a vertice silvis
> incubuit, glomeratque ferens incendia ventus.

For often some careless shepherd lets fall a spark which, smouldering stealthily at first under the sappy bark, gets hold of the timber, and leaping up to the leaves aloft roars to heaven; then running along the branches and tree-tops in victorious mastery wraps the whole planta- tion* in flames and shoots a thick cloud, murky as pitch, into the sky; the more so if a downward gale has swooped on the woods and the blast gathers and fans the conflagration.

The repeated '*en*'-sounds in the last line help to suggest the repeated gusts of wind, as in I. 334,

> nunc nemora ingenti vento, nunc litora plangunt.

Numerical balance of lines is sometimes perceptible, especially when it is pointed by repetition; at 3. 89–94, for instance (3 + 3):

> *talis* Amyclaei domitus Pollucis habenis
> Cyllarus et, quorum Grai meminere poetae,
> Martis equi biiuges et magni currus Achilli.
> *talis* et ipse iubam cervice effundit equina
> coniugis adventu pernix Saturnus, et altum
> Pelion hinnitu fugiens implevit acuto.

This can be felt even to the span of 7 + 7 lines if there is repetition to point it, as at I. 104–17:

> *quid dicam*, iacto *qui* semine comminus arva...
> *quid qui*, ne gravidis procumbat culmus aristis...

---

* Although the cue for this set-piece was a warning not to plant olives among the *vines*, what Virgil has in his mind's eye is rather a forest-fire, as *alta cacumina* clearly shows. There is, however, for once no precedent, either in Homer or in other extant poetry.

Whether the *ear* can be conscious of balance on a wider scale than that, though in a vaguer sort of way the *mind* may be, seems to me doubtful. It is modern scholarship, not by listening but by scanning a text (and a text in codex, not roll, form), which has discovered, for instance (what may even be accidental), that the three successive sections 3. 384–93 (wool), 394–403 (milk), 404–13 (dogs) are of exactly ten lines each.*

The rhetorical figures are used freely. Tricolon crescendo may be combined with anaphora, as (contrasting with the original at *Il.* 1. 70)

> *quae* sint, *quae* fuerint, *quae* mox ventura trahantur,

or

> *nocte* leves melius stipulae, *nocte* arida prata
> tondentur, *noctis* lentus non deficit umor,

or

> *non* umbrae altorum nemorum, *non* mollia possunt
> prata movere animum, *non* qui per saxa volutus
> purior electro campum petit amnis.

Within ten lines at 2. 408–17 we have first this feature:

> *primus* humum fodito, *primus* devecta cremato
> sarmenta, et vallos *primus* sub tecta referto;
> *postremus* metito (antithesis);

then anaphora again:

> *bis* vitibus ingruit umbra,
> *bis* segetem densis obducunt sentibus herbae;
> durus uterque labor: laudato ingentia rura,
> exiguum colito (chiastic antithesis);

and three lines later tricolon with anaphora again:

> *iam* vinctae vites, *iam* falcem arbusta reponunt,
> *iam* canit effectos extremus vinitor antes.†

If this concentration were typical, the effect would be cloying indeed. But Virgil was too good an artist to overdo anything. In tetracola he avoids excessive symmetry:

---

* See Appendix II, on numerical schematism.
† For this form, in which the third colon consists of a whole line, cf. 2. 323–4; 3. 248–9. Other examples of tricolon with anaphora: 2. 368–70; 514–15.

tum pingues agni et tum mollissima vina,
tum somni dulces, densaeque in montibus umbrae;

or

aut illae pecori frondem, aut pastoribus umbram
sufficiunt, saepemque satis, et pabula melli.

Or take the Golden Line,[37] overworked by Catullus. I have
noticed only eleven examples in the 2188 lines of the *Georgics*
(even disregarding, as *pace* some scholars I do, prepositions, con-
junctions etc.); and of these all save 1. 222 round off a sentence,
sometimes with superb effect:

$$a \qquad b \qquad c \quad A \quad B$$

magnaque cum magno veniet tritura calore. (1. 190)
impiaque aeternam timuerunt saecula noctem. (1. 468)
grandiaque effossis mirabitur ossa sepulcris. (1. 497)
pinguiaque in veribus torrebimus exta colurnis. (2. 396)
mitis in apricis coquitur vindemia saxis. (2. 522)
purpurea intexti tollant aulaea Britanni. (3. 25)
sed tota in dulcis consument ubera natos. (3. 178)
primaque ferratis praefigunt ora capistris. (3. 399)
dira per incautum serpant contagia vulgus. (3. 469)
tunsa per integram solvuntur viscera pellem. (4. 302)

What I have called the Silver Line is also effective in rounding off:

$$a \quad b \quad c \qquad B \quad A$$
impositos duris crepitare incudibus ensis. (2. 540)

And in general the patterning of epithets and nouns permitted by
the flexibility of Latin word-order, which was to become such a
feature of elegy and of Horace's odes in particular, plays a part in
the *Georgics* also. We do not have to read far before coming to
two consecutive lines exemplifying this,

$$a \qquad b \qquad A \qquad\qquad B$$
Chaoniam pingui glandem mutavit arista

$$C \qquad d \qquad c \qquad\qquad D$$
poculaque inventis Acheloïa miscuit uvis.

Then there is alliteration, sometimes overdone by Lucretius. In
the *Georgics* it is important, but subtle and unobtrusive. It could

easily escape notice that nine of the eleven lines 2. 440–50 contain an alliterative pair of words: *steriles. . .silvae—franguntque feruntque —cedrumque cupressosque—pandas. . .posuere—fecunda frondibus— bona bello—taxi torquentur—tiliae. . .torno—formam. . .ferroque.* We may note what is certainly effective, and perhaps a predilection— correspondence between the first letter after a strong caesura and the first of the fifth foot:

> *p*ercurrit *p*ectine telas;
> *v*estigia *v*olvitur annus;
> *d*escendens *D*acus ab Histro;
> *s*alientem *s*anguine venam;
> *f*lores et *f*lumina libant;
> *g*enerandi *g*loria mellis;

also found in doubly alliterative lines,

> *t*otaque *t*uriferis *P*anchaia *p*inguis harenis;
> *m*agnus alit *m*agno *c*ommixtus *c*orpore fetus.

On the other hand, there is a much smaller proportion of that alliterative correspondence between the beginnings of the first and fifth feet which we found to be a feature of *Eclogue* I (see p. 47), perhaps because the prevailing enjambement of the *Georgics* is liable to weaken the effect. Euphonious patterns of sound are audible also in lines such as

> auctorem frugum tempestatumque potentem;
> obscenaeque* canes importunaeque volucres;
> imbellem avertis Romanis arcibus Indum.

At the beginning of Book 3 Virgil gives, as one reason for wishing to attempt epic poetry, that mythological themes are now played out—*omnia iam vulgata.* The instances he gives point to Hellenistic poetry.† He is thus saying farewell to the Neoteric type of poetry

---

* Feminine for the sake of the chime with *importunaeque*?

† Eurystheus: Ps.-Theocr. 25; Busiris: Callim. frr. 44–7 Pf.; Hylas: Ap. Rh. I. 1207 ff.; Theocr. 13; Callim. 596 Pf.; Nicander, fr. 48 G.&S.; Delos: Callim. *Hymn* 4. Hylas, first heard of in Hellenistic times, was treated by the newest recruit to Maecenas' circle, Propertius (I. 20), either shortly before or shortly after this was written. (The elegies of Book I date from ?*c.* 30 to 28; Butler and Barber, Introduction, pp. xxii–xxvii.)

on which he had been brought up and transferring himself to the camp of Ennius. But before doing so, as though to insist that his early enthusiasm had not been misguided, he produced what must surely have been the finest of all epyllia and is certainly justification enough for the *genre*,* the Aristaeus–Orpheus episode. Poetically this is so different from all we have discussed hitherto that it calls for extensive treatment.

This was, apart from any lost juvenilia, the first time that Virgil had written narrative poetry, though he had contrived that some of the rustics' utterances in the *Eclogues* should imply a story.[38] The Aristaeus portion is told with Homeric objectivity, and takes many ideas from Homer. But there are features that recall Hellenistic poetry rather, and others, including the perfection of the verse-style, which are his own. Shunning *ambages et longa exorsa* (cf. 2. 46), he puts us immediately 'in the picture' (317 ff.):

> pastor Aristaeus fugiens Peneïa Tempe,
> amissis, ut fama, apibus morboque fameque,
> tristis ad extremi sacrum caput astitit amnis.

The shepherd Aristaeus, having lost his bees, so the story goes, by disease and famine, abandoned Tempe through which Peneüs flows and sorrowfully came and stood by the source itself of the sacred river.

He has come to complain to his divine mother, the nymph Cyrene, whom Virgil conceives as living there beneath her father's waters like Thetis in the *Iliad* (1. 358), who was

> ἡμένη ἐν βένθεσσιν ἁλὸς παρὰ πατρὶ γέροντι

when her son Achilles, standing on the shore at Troy, complained to her of Agamemnon's theft of Briseïs. Aristaeus' complaint has Homeric traits, but these are given a different nuance: the Cyclops' appeal to Poseidon (*Od.* 9. 529), 'if you acknowledge me as your son', becomes (323)

> si modo, quem perhibes, pater est Thymbraeus Apollo,

if, as you assert, my father is really Thymbraean Apollo,

---

* Sellar, blaming 'the despotic will of the Emperor', not only calls it 'an undoubted blot on the artistic perfection of the work', but dismisses it as 'a finished piece of metrical execution' (pp. 189–90). One can only be surprised at such a verdict.

which is bordering on insolence. Where Achilles complains of Zeus for not giving him the τιμή which is his due because he has chosen to go to certain death at Troy (*Il.* 1. 353–4), Aristaeus reproaches his own mother ('*te matre*') with allowing his *honor*, his compensation for undertaking a mortal life of beneficence to agriculture, to be wounded by the death of his bees, ending with the petulant and sarcastic suggestion that she should destroy all he has done,

> tanta meae si te ceperunt taedia laudis,

if you have become so tired of hearing my praises.

Curiously enough the precedent for this sarcasm in Homer is uttered by Thetis to Zeus, not by Achilles to her (*Il.* 1. 515–16): 'or refuse me, as you need not fear to do, so that I may know clearly how far I come behind all the other gods in honour'. And yet the manner comes from elsewhere, from Ariadne denouncing Theseus' treachery at Catullus 64. 132 ff., as the echo *sperare iubebas* indicates. It is the manner we call rhetorical, the self-conscious exploitation of modes of expression found in Homer and other writers, which first appears in Euripides and passed into Hellenistic and Roman poetry intensified by the study of formal rhetoric.[39]

The next scene is inspired by *Iliad* 18. 35 ff., the second occasion on which Thetis comes to comfort Achilles, this time for the death of Patroclus. But whereas on both occasions Thetis arises from the waves and goes to her son, Cyrene remains where she is. And unlike Thetis, she does not immediately recognise the *sonitus* that reaches her, or indeed take any notice of it. This enables Virgil to set his scene, a world of unearthly calm, the subterranean cave where she sits amid her nymphs at their wool-work.[40] Here she resembles Thetis in a different part of the *Iliad* (24. 83 ff.), where Iris finds her in a hollow cave beneath the sea, surrounded by other sea-goddesses, weeping for the destiny of her son. The idea of naming the nymphs came also from Homer (*Il.* 18. 39 ff.); but no artist reared among the Neoteroi would have a list of thirty-three names with only a couple of conventional epithets to relieve it, as Homer does.* That is primitive catalogue poetry such as we

---

* Naturally this may be a late insertion into the 'monumental' *Iliad*.

find in the *Theogony* of Hesiod (who gives fifty names of nymphs at 240 ff. and claims to know three thousand at 364). Virgil chooses twelve, with Clymene as an extra thirteenth, six of them being unknown as nymphs, and others known as something else. After a studied reproduction of the rhythm of one of Homer's lines (43),

> Δωτώ τε Πρωτώ τε Φέρουσά τε Δυναμένη τε,
>
> Drymoque Xanthoque Ligeaque Phyllodoceque,

he adds a line of description,

> caesariem effusae nitidam per candida colla,

their shining hair spread out over their white shoulders.

Then (if we disregard a spurious repetition from *Iliad* 18, 39–40), he continues,

> Cydippeque et flava Lycorias, altera virgo,
> altera tum primos Lucinae experta labores,

Cydippe and golden-haired Lycorias, the one a virgin, the other having just experienced for the first time the labours of the Birth-goddess.

This is simply for variety and 'to give an air of verisimilitude to an otherwise bald narrative'—and for heaven's sake don't let someone tell us that the contrast between the two is somehow symbolic. Next come

> Clioque et Beroë soror, Oceanitides ambae,
> ambae auro, pictis incinctae pellibus ambae,

and Clio and her sister Beroë, both Oceanids, both girded with gold, with painted leather both.

Here Virgil is playing with echoes of sound, consciously no doubt from *Eclogue* 7. 4,

> ambo florentes aetatibus, Arcades *ambo*,

probably consciously also from a description of *Oceanids* in Callimachus, who were

> πάσας εἰνετέας, πάσας ἔτι παῖδας ἀμίτρους.[41]

The rhythm of the next line, checked in the middle and then released,

> atque Ephyre | atque Opis | et Asia Deiopea,

paralleled by 463,

> atque Getae | atque Hebrus | et Actias Orithyia,

perhaps reflects that of some Greek line which caught Virgil's fancy; and to round off the list we have a line devoted entirely to one famous nymph who will have a rôle to play later on:

> et tandem positis velox Arethusa sagittis,

and swift Arethusa, her arrows at last laid aside.

To these Clymene was telling a story, of the love-intrigue of Mars (presumably with Venus, but a variant from Demodocus' tale at *Odyssey* 8. 266 ff., for here the lovers succeed, frustrating Vulcan's efforts), and all the mass of divine love-affairs from the beginning of time. They were so absorbed as they listened and unwound their wool, that it was only Aristaeus' second cry that penetrated to them. Arethusa put her head above the water to investigate and told Cyrene what it was. Cyrene, 'smitten with a strange dread', made the river part and received him into the depths. Even here the Homeric train of thought-association leading from Thetis may still be operative; for in another part of the *Iliad*, 6. 135 ff., Dionysus, fleeing from Lycurgus, plunges into the sea, and 'Thetis received him into her bosom'; while the idea of waters gathered up in a mountainous curve to receive a mortal certainly comes from *Odyssey* 11. 243–4, where the receiving deity is the river Enipeus.

Yes, Homer may have provided the framework; but the detailed treatment is in the Hellenistic manner. The ancestor of this kind of poetry is Callimachus, and its chief Latin representative is the Ovid of the *Metamorphoses*. Callimachean is the selection of nymphal names, some of them seeming to convey learned allusions,[42] the reference to a surprising and little-known variant of a famous story, the touch of humour in the *genre* picture of nymphs, like Roman girls, working wool round a matron, and

Milesian wool at that,* and in the reference to the *densos amores* of the gods, which gave Ovid such scope. It is also wholly in the spirit of Callimachus that at 348 this peace should suddenly be broken, and the light tone changed to one of passionate anxiety. No less Hellenistic is the minute care for sounds and rhythms, in which Virgil surpassed all—the open vowels, the mingling of Greek and Latin words, the alternation of hexameters of Greek and Latin form (the former free-flowing, the latter bound by strict rules of caesura and end-word typology).[43]

Aristaeus first moves through his mother's home spellbound, as well he might be (363 ff.). For it is a miraculous palace under the water (352), where the seats are glassy as water (350) and even the wool is of a greenish, watery colour (*hyalo*, 335), and yet there are hollow caves and rustling woods. *Ibat*—that wonderfully expressive word, especially coming first in a line—suggests smooth, silent movement.† He was also bewildered by the sound of rushing water. For the source of the Peneüs now becomes the source of all the rivers in the world, from the Hypanis (? Bug) and Phasis (Rion), and the Lycus and Caïcus of Asia Minor, through Enipeus, a tributary of Peneüs itself, to Virgil's own rivers, 'father' Tiber, the Anio and the Po.‡ Here once more is the Greece–Rome collocation so exciting to the Roman imagination; and once more the echo of a Greek rhythm in different Latin words,[44]

> in mare purpureum violentior effluit amnis

from *Iliad* 16. 391,

> ἐς δ' ἅλα πορφυρέην μεγάλα στενάχουσι ῥέουσαι.

The point of the scene that follows (374–86) has been explained by Klingner.[45] The idea of the welcome provided, the hand-

---

* Cf. Circe's laboratory staff of Nymphs and Nereids for her spell-production at Ovid, *M.* 14. 264–70.

† Cf. 430, of Proteus' slow approach in the noonday heat', 472, of the shades in the underworld; *Aen.* 6. 268, of Aeneas and the Sibyl, 'ibant obscuri sola sub nocte per umbram'.

‡ The Po (Eridanus), with Phasis and Caïcus, occur at Hesiod, *Th.* 338 f.; so again Virgil has been at pains to make clear the source of an idea he develops.

washing, food and drink, is Homeric,[46] but this is not simply a feast; it is a religious ceremony, a preparation for the prayer and taking of omens, whose favourable acceptance Cyrene counted upon to encourage her son to proceed to the adventurous exploit on which she now instructs him.*

Est... This is the usual beginning of a description, an *ecphrasis*, of a place,[47] here Proteus' temporary resort at Pallene. Again Homer is the basis (*Od.* 4. 351 ff.),[48] with Cyrene playing the part of Eidothea; and down to the successful capture (452) Virgil follows him, though with much abbreviation and with variations, as we shall see. Eidothea's 'you will find him in a hollow cave' (403) becomes a four-line description, '*Est specus ingens*...' (418), of a calm, safe haven. That is Hellenistic. So is the *mise-en-scène* for the appearance of Proteus. Virgil omits the naïvely amusing but unromantic trick of Eidothea and her deodorant activities: Homeric magic serves instead. Whereas Homer makes the seals come out of the sea first and then, without ado, Proteus (450),

ἔνδιος δ᾽ ὁ γέρων ἦλθ᾽ ἐξ ἁλός,

and at noon the old man came out of the sea,

Virgil begins by creating an atmosphere, of noontide heat (425):

> iam rapidus torrens sitientis Sirius Indos
> ardebat caelo, et medium sol igneus orbem
> hauserat; arebant herbae, et cava flumina siccis
> faucibus ad limum radii tepefacta coquebant,
> cum Proteus...

now the torrid Dog-star that parches the thirsty Indians was blazing in the sky, and the fiery sun had exhausted half his course;† his rays scorched the grass, and boiled down rivers, dry-jawed and shrunken, to mud, when Proteus...

---

* *Inanes* at 375 causes some difficulty. Is it a stock epithet for tears, Cyrene being still anxious, as at 357 (Conington), or does she realise, having heard Aristaeus' complaint, that his tears are idle because the trouble is easily remedied? I incline to the former view, otherwise the solemn rites and the elaborate and difficult trial become disproportionate, if not otiose. On the other hand, her manner does now seem confident.

† I.e. 'The Solstice had come and gone and the Dog Days had now arrived' (R. J. Getty, *T.A.Ph.A.* (1948), p. 42).

Only then does Virgil bring on the seals: everything has been concentrated on the dramatic moment of Proteus' appearance, the name of the new arrival reserved for the beginning of a line. Where did Virgil learn this dramatic technique? One recalls the noontide scene in Callimachus, where Pallas is bathing with her attendant nymph Chariclo (*Hymn* 5. 70 ff.):

δή ποκα γὰρ πέπλων λυσαμένα περόνας
ἵππω ἐπὶ κράνᾳ 'Ελικωνίδι καλὰ ῥεοίσᾳ
λῶντο· μεσαμβρινὰ δ' εἶχ' ὄρος ἀσυχία·
ἀμφότεραι λώοντο, μεσαμβριναὶ ἔσαν ὧραι,
πολλὰ δ' ἀσυχία τῆνο κατεῖχεν ὄρος.
Τειρεσίας δ'. . .

for once those two, having loosened the buckles of their robes beside the fair-flowing spring of the Horse upon Helicon, were bathing; a noontide stillness held the mountain-side; they two bathed on, and it was the hour of noon, and a deep stillness held that mountain-side. But Teiresias. . .

Suddenly, at the beginning of a new line, the hunter-son of Chariclo bursts into this dead quiet, sees the nakedness of Pallas, and loses his sight. Is there not a considerable similarity?

At 433 we have a short simile for which there is no precedent in the Homeric passage, increasing the sense of calm:

ipse velut stabuli custos in montibus olim
Vesper ubi e pastu vitulos ad tecta reducit
auditisque lupos acuunt balatibus agni,
considit scopulo medius, numerumque recenset.

He himself, like some mountain herdsman in charge of a steading when the evening star brings home the calves from pasture and the lambs with their bleating whet the wolves, sat down on a rock in the middle and counted his herd.

This again is the thought of a Hellenistic (pastoral) poet. Only when Proteus has lain down to sleep does the moment come to spring; and then once more the ideas are skilfully presented to us in climactic sequence, with the operative verb reserved:

vix defessa senem passus componere membra
cum clamore ruit magno, manicisque iacentem
occupat,

scarcely letting the old man compose his tired limbs, with a great shout he rushes forward, and as he lay there seizes and shackles him.

So far we have been detached observers of a world of romance in which, after Aristaeus' first outburst of petulance, human feelings are not in evidence. It is a fairy story, superbly told. But now comes a complete change. Instead of the manifold revelations of the Homeric Proteus, we have a single story, that of Orpheus, the Neoteric contrasting inset realised with a beauty and sympathy that are wholly out of character. It is Virgil himself speaking.* In Neoteric style the facts are related as briefly as possible, or merely implied, only those being elaborated which generate the desired emotional pattern. 'Your loss is a punishment from Orpheus for a great crime, your lust that led to Eurydice's death.' The single participle *moritura*, 'doomed', conveys the tragic event (458):

> at chorus aequalis Dryadum clamore supremos
> implerunt montis; flerunt Rhodopeïae arces
> altaque Pangaea et Rhesi Mavortia tellus
> atque Getae atque Hebrus et Actias Orithyia,

but the Dryad-band, her companions, filled the mountain-heights with their crying; the steeps of Rhodope wailed, and high Pangaea, and the warlike land of Rhesus, and the Getae, and the Hebrus, and Actian Orithyia.

The sounds of wailing, hauntingly expressed by the *a, ae* and *e* sounds, echo from peak to peak over the Balkan mountains. Then suddenly our vision is narrowed to the desolate figure of Orpheus, seeking to console his love-sick heart with the music of his lyre:

> ipse cava solans aegrum testudine amorem,
> te, dulcis coniunx, te solo in litore secum,
> te veniente die, te decedente canebat.

It is not really Proteus but Virgil who thus addresses Eurydice, as Catullus had addressed Ariadne (253). The pathetic repetition of

---

* This is emphasised by Otis at the beginning of his sensitive analysis and discussion, p. 197. (In his first paragraph of analysis omit 'not' and 'rather': '*non*' has been overlooked.) In the first two lines however the sibilants may, as Anderson suggested (p. 43), be expressive of the hissing rage of Proteus.

te suggests the repeated calling of the name of the dead.* Inconsolable by himself, Orpheus now ventures through the portals of Orcus

> et caligantem nigra formidine lucum,

and the grove murky with black dread [inimitable line],

to try to soften the implacable heart of the terrible king. *Ingressus ...cantu commotae*: allusive participles again suffice to convey what happens, till the tremendous description of the gathering of the shades and the respite of the damned. Participles once more suffice to indicate his triumph, and a parenthesis the all-important condition, as in swift and confident dactyls Eurydice returns towards the world of light:

> iamque pedem referens casus evaserat omnes
> redditaque Eurydice superas veniebat ad auras
> pone sequens (namque hanc dederat Proserpina legem),

and now retracing his steps he had avoided every pitfall, and his restored Eurydice was approaching the air of the world above, following behind (for this condition Proserpina had made)...,

when suddenly a mad impulse caught him off his guard:

> immemor, heu, victusque animi respexit: ibi omnis
> effusus labor...,

forgetful, alas, and weakened in will, he looked back; in that moment all his labour was lost...

(How poignantly the adjectives pile up the suspense, the rare pause at '*respexit*' isolates the fatal moment, and then the rhythm, like his achievement, dissolves in the hurried synaloepha of '*ibi omnis*'.)[49] The poet's sympathy becomes unrestrained: Orpheus' impulse is 'pardonable indeed, if the powers of death knew

---

* Cf. *Aen.* 7. 759-60:

> te nemus Angitiae, vitrea te Fucinus unda,
> te liquidi flevere lacus.

Sometimes the narrator repeats the name itself, as Hylas' at *Ecl.* 6. 43-4 and Eurydice's at 525-7. Cf.

> For *Lycidas* is *dead*, *dead* ere his prime,
> Young *Lycidas*, and hath not left his peer.

pardon'. But all along we have been looking through Virgil's eyes; and Otis is right in seeing here the first great exemplar of the style of the *Aeneid*, in which the poet is no longer an objective narrator but deeply involved.[50] The story continues, a marvel of poetic art inspired by imaginative feeling, so carrying us away that we accept the legend of the voice from the severed head as tragic, not grotesque, and the name of Eurydice, given back by the river bank, echoes on in our ears after the narrative has ceased.

IX · *Agricultural Lore*

But—'iamdudum enim circumrodo quod devorandum est'—
there are readers who are attracted to the *Georgics* largely, or even
primarily, by its natural history and agricultural lore; for whom
Virgil ranks as the most readable of the *Scriptores Rei Rusticae*. I
do not think that expertise in these matters is essential for the
appreciation of the poem—otherwise I should never have had
the hardihood to embark on a book about it, being, if not, like
Nicander of Colophon, 'homo ab agro remotissimus', yet
acquainted with the countryside only from holiday visits.* But I
shall try in this chapter to make good what might be felt to be a
deficiency, if only to a limited extent, relying on what seem the
best authorities.

TECHNICAL SOURCES

With the loss of so much agronomic literature, both Hellenistic
and Roman, it is very difficult to assess how much of Virgil's lore
is his own.[1] Most of what he says can be paralleled even in extant
writers, whose accounts are much fuller. No one should hastily
credit Virgil with being either an expert husbandman or a keen
observer of nature without first reading these authorities.†
Occasionally he seems to have misunderstood a source. In
astronomy, for instance, the Romans were perplexed, as Pliny
complains, when they tried to use Greek sources which might be
based on all sorts of observations, Greek, Egyptian or Chaldaean,
made in different latitudes, not to mention discrepant ones made

---

* Nor should I have done so if I had not ascertained that Sir Roger Mynors,
  uniquely qualified by his combination of experience as a landowner with
  eminence as a Latin scholar, was not contemplating the writing of such a book.
  For literature on agricultural lore in the *Georgics* see Appendix VI.
† Notably, among Greeks, Xenophon, Aristotle, Theophrastus, Aratus; among
  Romans Cato (*c.* 160 B.C.), Varro (37/36 B.C.), Columella (*c.* A.D. 60), the
  elder Pliny (*c.* A.D. 77), Palladius (*c.* A.D. 400). There is also in Greek the
  medieval compilation from earlier works called *Geoponica*, believed to have
  been made in the sixth or seventh century by Cassianus Bassus and revised in
  the tenth for Constantine VIII Porphyrogenitus. A massive new edition of Cato
  by P. Thielscher appeared in 1963.

in the same latitude.[2] Astronomical science was in abeyance at Rome (Caesar employed a Greek, Sosigenes, to reform the calendar); and Virgil was no better in this respect than other Roman writers. Consulting the calendar rather than the heavens, he was capable, for instance, of confusing the morning (cosmical) with the evening (heliacal) setting of the Pleiades.[3] Again he may repeat what experience would have disproved, as in the case of grafting (see p. 244). And we have seen in another context that he had a penchant for blending or compromising.

On the other hand it is hard to suppose that one who, to judge from a little external and much internal evidence, was familiar with the country should purvey only book-learning in his precepts. Varro, who clearly relied mainly on books, tells us that, besides profiting from his own travels as an army officer, he talked with practical farmers, for instance with cattle-owners in Epirus.[4] We must also beware of doubting, on grounds of north European experience, what may be possible in Mediterranean lands now, or have been possible then.

Early in his *Res Rusticae* (1. 8–9) Varro names more than fifty Greek writers on agriculture whose works are available for consultation. Of those whom he names, Virgil appears to have used Theophrastus directly for Book 2, Aristotle for Books 3 and 4.[5] There is no reason why he should not have consulted others on occasion. All of them wrote in prose except Hesiod and Menecrates of Ephesus (the omission of Nicander's *Georgica* is most surprising). Varro adds that all were surpassed by Mago the Carthaginian, whose works had been translated into Latin by order of the Senate.[6] There were also numerous Roman writers, of whom Cato was the most renowned, including participants in Varro's dialogue itself.*

---

* Servius alleges (on G. 1. 43) that Virgil borrowed much from the third book of Cicero's lost *Economica*; but his credit is undermined by the fact that Xenophon's *Economicus*, which Cicero was using, is extant, and its influence, also alleged, can be seen to be tenuous. Some references in our authorities to 'Democritus' are now believed to refer to the Ps-Democritus 'Bolus' of Hellenistic times. Hyginus is, for chronological reasons, no longer considered to have been among Virgil's sources, on which see Büchner, cols. 305–7.

Now these writers are sure to have repeated one another, just as Varro can sometimes be seen to have repeated Cato; so that, apart from a few cases, we cannot determine the immediate source of a statement by Virgil. For instance at 1. 160 ff. (on the farmer's 'arma') he may seem to be following Cato (10. 2 f.) rather than Varro (1. 22. 1 f.), since more of the instruments he mentions occur in Cato; yet *tribula*, not in Cato, occur in Varro, both there and at 1. 52. In the former passage however Varro cites Cato through the mouth of an interlocutor, Stolo. Was Stolo perhaps an intermediary source? Or did Virgil make up the list out of his own head? We cannot tell.[7]

There are also passages of a generally Varronian character into which Virgil has introduced details which we find too in the same context in Columella or the *Geoponica*, and this may point to a common source now lost, such as Diophanes' abridgement in Greek of Mago. Even when he seems to be criticising a predecessor, as at 3. 54–5, where he says that cows for breeding should have *omnia magna, pes etiam* (in contradiction to the corresponding passage in Varro, 2. 5. 8: *pedibus non latis*), we cannot be sure that he is not siding with another authority rather than simply attesting a view of his own.

On the other hand Pliny often criticises Virgil for this precept or that; and granted that the prestige of the poet gave undue weight to his utterances (as we can see from Columella), he would hardly have singled him out if he had been simply repeating what was notoriously to be found in his predecessors.[8] We have noted also that the regions best known to Virgil happened to be those where the *colonus* was still the typical farmer (p. 54); and that certain of his precepts were valid solely or particularly for the Po valley (pp. 156–7). But the scales are weighted against attributing independence to him. For whereas such sound precepts as are found in him alone may always be suspected of coming from a lost source, where he recommends the impossible, even if, as in the case of grafting, he is not alone, this is damaging to any idea of him as a practical husbandman.

FIELD CROPS

What kind of land was suitable for field crops? Virgil's organisation of his poem makes us wait for a partial answer till a passage in Book 2 (177–258), where the characteristics and potentialities of various kinds of land are detailed. Dark,* loamy (*pinguis*) soil and friable soil are best for corn, he says (203–6). It could be dark because of high vegetable content, due to mould from fallen leaves and undergrowth, which would account also for the fertility he next ascribes to land recently cleared of trees (207–11). Elsewhere he says it should be thick (*densa* 226, *spissus* 236), with clinging clods and stiff ridges. On no account must it be too wet—this is so important that Virgil allows himself a personal exclamation unparalleled in the *Georgics* (251–3);† for in that case it is *too* fertile, and all the virtue goes into the stalk, not the ears (and the corn is also liable to disease). The ideal land for everything is that of Campania, which absorbs and exhales moisture with equal facility, promotes spontaneous growth, and does not rust iron implements (217–25). The prescription given in the course of the next section for discovering what land is 'pinguis', well known in antiquity as today, is vitiated by Virgil's omission of the vital element in the operation, the progressive adding of small quantities of water. The test is, how much water will make a clay soil stick to fingers and implements.[9]

With this preamble on choice of land we may turn back to Virgil's starting-point. (1. 43) *Vere novo*: in Italy the spring began officially, according to Varro (1. 28), on 7 February. To Virgil, familiar from childhood with the sight of the Alps, and later of the Apennines, the earliest sign is the melting of snow from the mountain-tops. The first task is to break up the surface of the fields (*scindere, proscindere*). The nearest passage in Varro, which also occurs right at the beginning of his account, says: 'for spring plantings the fallow land (*terram rudem*) should be broken up so as to eradicate the weeds that have sprung up in it, before they can

---

* The Campanians called it 'pulla' (Cato 34. 2; Col. 2. 10. 18; Pliny, *N.H.* 17. 25). † Richter, *ad loc.*

shed their seeds;* and at the same time, when the clods have been dried through by the sun, to make them more accessible to absorb the rain and easier to work. And there should be not less than two ploughings, preferably three.'[10] Virgil agrees with this well enough (63–6; 69).† But is he, too, referring to *spring sowing*, of leguminous plants for instance?

Before trying to answer this we must consider a phrase which has been fertile of controversy. What does Virgil mean by saying (48) that the most rewarding land will be that 'bis quae solem, bis frigora sensit'? There was some doubt even in antiquity, as the words used by Pliny (18. 181) in discussing the passage, 'existimatur voluisse', betray. Pliny took him to mean, plough four times, twice in summer and twice in winter, and commented that the rather thick soil in Italy required five ploughings, while in Tuscany the number even reached nine.‡ But Servius took the view that the reference was to sun by day and frost by night, and this has been revived by Beutler, who takes the words to refer to ploughing and cross-ploughing in *early spring* so as to let the clods feel two loosening influences, the night frost still operative and the increasing warmth of the sun in the daytime.§ At 45–6 (*depresso*) and again at 63–4 Virgil is dealing with rich (*pingue*) soil, which is contrasted with poor soil, which should only be turned up with a shallow furrow in mid-September (*sub Arcturum*). Everything suggests that he is not, after all, envisaging sowing

---

* Pliny, differing, says that ploughing in early spring only encourages weeds which will stifle the corn (*N.H.* 18. 242).

† 50–63, on virgin or unknown land (*ignotum aequor*), are a parenthesis, perhaps suggested by Cato 6 and 34–5.

‡ T. E. Page reminds us (on 48) that 'the ancients used the plough to perform the work for which we now have special instruments, such as grubbers, scarifiers, etc.'. In Greece up to Xenophon's time two ploughings were customary, three occasional. Theophrastus recommended four. (Billiard, p. 51.)

§ 'Zur Komposition von Vergils Georgica I, 43–159', *Hermes* (1940), pp. 411–12. Richter, *ad loc*. For frost as breaking up soil, and wind also (*zephyro* 44), cf. 2. 263–4. 'Putre solum' is best, 'namque hoc imitamur arando' (2. 204). But White points out that in Virgil elsewhere 'bis' generally means 'more than once', specifically 'twice' only in two passages (*Aen.* 9. 779 and 11. 629), suggesting that all Virgil means is 'don't think you can get away with a single ploughing' (*Proc. Virg. Soc.* 1967–8; p. 13).

in spring, but later in the year. The second ploughing (*iteratio*, *offringere*) was crosswise at right angles, especially applied to fallow.

As for the poor soil, if we take *tenui sulco* (68) to be strictly singular, Virgil's advice is wrong, as is also his reason given at 70. White comments: 'It is natural but erroneous to suppose that frequent stirring of the surface will deprive such a soil of its moisture (*sterilem exiguus ne deserat umor arenam*). On the contrary, by opening the pores it will arrest capillary action and help to conserve moisture.'[11]

Next comes an important passage (71–84) on the maintenance of fertility. Either the land must be fallow in alternate years, or it may be sown in alternation with a crop of pulse, vetch or lupin. For while some crops—flax, oats and poppies, for instance*—consume too much of some nutritious element in the soil (*urunt*), leguminous plants (we are left to deduce) are beneficial. (In fact they fix, more than others, the atmospheric nitrogen.) Cato recognised them as fertilisers. He does not mention alternate husbandry, but it was known to Varro, as later to Pliny.† It works well enough even with flax, etc., adds Virgil, if you are not afraid to use plenty of manure and to scatter ashes; and you have the double advantage of the recovery of the land and the extra crop itself.

The mention of the use of ashes, a speciality in Virgil's native region for some crops, leads on to the next topic, the burning of stubble (84–93) on land effete (*sterilis*) after production.‡ Four

---

* Poppy seeds were ground for oil, or used unground in cakes. See Sargeaunt, pp. 96–7. Wild poppy boiled in honey was used as a throat-cure, cultivated poppy as a soporific (Pliny, *N.H.* 18. 229).

† Cato, 37. 2; Varro, *R.R.* 1.44.2–3. Pliny, *N.H.* 18.187; 191. In Greece fallowing was the rule; but we find the Dyalians obliged by a rent contract to alternate corn with vegetables (*C.I.A.* II. 600 l. 23); and Theophrastus recommended fallowing in every third year (Billiard, pp. 73–4).

‡ By a false analogy with animals it was assumed that land was exhausted ('effete') after bearing, and that it weakened with age. Columella combats the idea (2. 1). Burning of stubble is also mentioned in a rustic calendar, *Menologium Rusticum Colotianum*, *C.I.L.* VI. 2305 = *I.L.S.* 8745 (printed by J. E. Sandys and S. G. Campbell, *Latin Epigraphy*, 2nd edn. 1927, pp. 174–6). I owe this reference to Prof. K. D. White, who suggests that the reason why the other agronomists do not mention burning was that in Central and Southern Italy,

conjectural reasons are given for the efficacy of this. Either (1) the land conceives from it mysterious power to produce rich new growth of herbage for pasture;* or (2) the fire burns out all the poison excreted from plants and dries out surplus moisture (he could have added that it kills harmful insects); or (3) it opens pores to admit liquid nourishment to the fresh plants; or (4) it constricts the soil to exclude rain, excessive heat, or frost. In the only other reference to stubble-burning in the agronomists Pliny speaks of Virgil as its great champion (*magno Virgilii praeconio*), and then proceeds to give a single and valid reason which Virgil had not mentioned—the killing of the seeds of weeds.[12]

Of Virgil's suggested reasons the third and fourth are obviously contradictory. From Heyne onwards attempts have been made to save his face by supposing that each explanation applies to a different kind of soil. But from what we know of his methods there is more probability in Richter's suggestion that he had before him a Greek source in which conceptions such as the fostering and the cleansing powers of warmth were adduced. It could well be an Epicurean source, since that sect had a penchant for giving alternative explanations which could even be incompatible.[13] White, on the same lines, suggests that he got the idea directly from Lucretius, who shares this penchant, and points out that there are Lucretian echoes hereabouts.[14] We should not deduce from the absence of references in the other agronomists that he inserted the advice to burn stubble from his own experience without a source; still less that he became his own scientist and collected possible explanations from different treatises, or different farmers.

Shorter precepts follow (94-9). It is a great help to break up lifeless clods with a drag-hoe (*rastrum*) or with a bush-harrow.

as contrasted with Transpadane Gaul, it was out of the question because corn was normally cultivated between vines and olives: 'Virgil on Arable Farming', *Proc. Virg. Soc.* (1967-8), p. 17. The Transpadanes were so keen on that they even burnt stable-dung instead of using it directly as manure (Pliny, 17. 49). E. de Saint-Denis has suggested (on 81) that this accounts for the epithet *immundum* (81); but ash from dung would be no *dirtier* than other ash, and it seems better to regard the epithet as purely pictorial.
* This is all the empiricist could say. Soil chemistry would explain that a small contribution of nitrogen, phosphorous and potash would result.

(For one thing it gives the worms a better chance to operate.) Better still, after the first ploughing with share upright (*proscindere*), to turn back in your tracks and go over the furrows again with the share laid at an angle (*verso in obliquum*; note that there is no reference here to 'second ploughing', *iteratio*, cross-ploughing, which was done later, if at all). This was necessary because the ancient plough had no built-in mould board: the operation turned the soil over, killed the weeds,[15] and broke down the balk.

Nonchalantly seeking to enliven his account with an oblique reference to an old rustic proverb,[16] Virgil continues (100):

umida solstitia atque hiemes orate serenas,

pray for wet summers and fine winters.

This got him into trouble with Pliny—he should have prayed instead for long-lying snow.[17] Perhaps he was thinking of southern Italy, where the summers can be scorching, and where in winter, failing snow, clear frosty weather is desirable. But he may have merely wished to make a transition to irrigation. The first ploughing, and any further ploughing, having been accomplished and the seed sown, there follows the final ploughing, with ridge-boards (*tabellae*) attached to turn it under. We now have seven lines (104–10) about the irrigation of dry land after the seed is sown, and a balancing seven lines (111–17) about the draining of wet land. Varro in the corresponding passage (1. 29. 2) speaks of draining *off* rainwater by ditches; but Virgil introduces irrigation, thinking of dry land (on which small farmers will first break up the clods by hand, *occatio*)—eager perhaps to get in his exquisite adaptation of a Homeric simile (104–10; *Il.* 21. 257 ff.). On wet land there is the problem of preventing the stalks from growing so tall that they collapse under the swelling ears. This could be done either by cutting them back with a sickle, in which case the cuttings could be fed to calves (cf. 3. 176), or by letting animals graze them as soon as they reached the height of the furrows, so levelling the surface of the field (*cum primum sulcos aequant sata*, 113).* And

---

* Pliny, *N.H.* 18. 161. Prof. K. D. White has expressed to me doubts whether lines 111–13 do refer to wet soil, because on wet soil the seed was sown on the ridges, the furrows acting as drainage channels.

finally there is the necessity of drainage, especially in regions liable to flooding by a river (114–17). One thinks immediately of the Po, or even the Mincius.* There were primary drains (*elices*), and secondary (*colliquiae*). The covered ones could have porous substances in them, such as fine gravel (*bibula harena*).[18] The sight of the open ones brimming was an alarm of flooding (326; 372). Drainage was so important that runnels could be dug even on holy days (269).

I have dwelt on these seventy-five lines because they contain a number of points which have been disputed, and have attracted as much agricultural discussion, perhaps, as all the rest of the poem. Against them was directed almost the whole onslaught of Jethro Tull (see p. 307).

The next subject, enemies of agriculture, is lightly touched upon (118–59), more as a way of introducing the theodicy than for any recommendation of remedies: 'ply your drag-hoe assiduously against weeds, scare off birds by noise, and pray for rain in season' —that is the sum total of the precepts. Birds were such a pest that, as we hear later, snares could be set for them even on holy days.[19] Virgil claims the same exemption for the planting of hedges to keep out wild animals such as 'silvestres uri' (? wild cattle: Richter), and farm animals, the goat in particular, whose bite was by an understandable vulgar error supposed to be poisonous; but Columella says that the pontiffs denied this—an interesting glimpse of the persistence of sabbatarian scrupulosity.[20] Pests of the threshing-floor, not only weeds but mice and moles,† could be dealt with by concreting with a compound of *amurca*, the dark fluid extracted from olives. This could also be effective against the depredations of weevils and ants in granaries (178–86). Varro asserts that *amurca* is poison to weeds, ants and moles; and its agglutinative qualities made it in demand for all sorts of uses.[21]

* Cf. *Ecl.* I. 48,
  limosoque palus obducat pascua iunco,
  and Conington's note.
† 'Oculis capti': this is the south European 'talpa caeca', which really is blind (D'Arcy Thompson, 'The Mole in Antiquity', *C.R.* 1918, p. 9). The toad (184) attacks the grain, not the floor.

No less selective and impressionistic is the list of agricultural implements that follows the pests of the theodicy (160–75). As often, Virgil elaborates on the final item, and Hesiod's precedent ensured that this would be the plough. The description of this, the only one in any extant Latin author, has aroused much controversy. White shows reason to suppose that it is of the 'sole-ard' type. *Vomis* is the ploughshare in front, which could be beaten sharp again when blunted (261–2). *Buris* is the ploughbeam, which is trained already on the living tree to curve up at the desired angle from what is destined to be the sole or sharebeam (*dentalia*), the whole being hardened, when cut, by hanging in smoke. *Temo* is the shaft for the oxen, eight feet long, attached to the *buris* ('*a stirpe*'). The *aures* may have been pin-ears attached when needed in order to throw up ridges and cover seed (cf. *tabellae*). What is meant by 'double-backed' (*duplici dorso*) applied to the sharebeam is obscure. Was it grooved, or did it spread out at the rear to form two sections? From the hinder end rose a stilt (*stiva*) with a cross-handle. This served for steering, for maintaining even depth, for tilting, and for pressing down the hinder part to raise the share and prevent its getting stuck.[22]

Next comes sowing (Virgil has indeed already anticipated it at 104 ff.—*iacto semine*). First the seeds must be selected and prepared. In the case of leguminous plants ('*siliquis*' shows that he has these in mind) seeds were sometimes treated with *nitrum*, a mineral alkali, perhaps sodium nitrate, and with *amurca*. Otherwise large pods could disappoint (*fallacibus*) with small fruit. These time-honoured measures (Col. 2. 10. 11) could be a protection against insects and noxious germs; but although they might make seeds germinate better, it is doubtful whether in fact they could make the fruit *larger*, or easier to boil (193–6).* The lines that follow probably refer to seeds of all kinds. Not only must the largest be

---

* Palladius (12. 1) and others say that the Greeks believed that beans were easier to cook if their seeds had been steeped in nitrate water. It would make better sense if it were before *planting* that seeds were warmed (Billiard, p. 112, says that French peasants often warm them up to 35° Centigrade before planting); but it would be difficult to get this meaning out of Virgil's words.

hand-picked, but this must be done from a new lot every year, since old seeds soon degenerate (197–9).*

In preparation for sowing, ridging-boards (*tabellae*) were attached to the plough. The ridge covered the seed, while ditches were formed to draw off rainwater.[23] The time to plant barley was from the autumnal equinox until the winter rains began (208–11). Wheat and emmer (*farra*) were sown after the morning setting of the Pleiads, which took place early in November (219–26). If you sowed them too early they might be choked by other growths; if too late, they might be drowned with rains.†

Also sown in autumn were flax, poppies, vetches, the humble *phaselus* bean‡ and lentils, from the end of October till the middle of the frosty season (212–14; 227–30). Field beans too were sown at that time in most of Italy, but in springtime in Virgil's own native district (hence, no doubt, *vere fabis satio* at 215).[24] In late spring were sown lucern and millet, which last had to be grown from new seed every year (*annua cura*).

The work to be done when the corn begins to come up is glanced at only in passing, in the theodicy passage (150 ff.). On harvesting too Virgil, like Hesiod, says surprisingly little. The corn having acquired a ruddy colour (*rubicunda Ceres*: 'tawny' might be nearer) was cut in mid-summer (297). At 1. 316 we catch a glimpse of the farmer leading out his reapers into the field —all his *pubes agrestis*, they would be, with neighbours to help out, and hired labourers too, at least on larger farms.[25] You grasped a handful (*merges*) with your left hand and cut it off with a sickle— how high up on the stalk depended on localities and circumstances.§ If not burnt as stubble, the straw could be cut and used

---

* Sorting for size *could* be done by a kind of sieve (*capisterium*: Col. 2. 9. 11). Degeneration of seed in germinating power becomes marked in the fourth year, almost total in the fifth (Billiard, p. 110).

† *Vanis avenis* refers to an ancient belief that corn which lay too long in the earth came up as wild oats: see Theophr. *H.P.* 8. 7. 1; 8. 8. 3; *C.P.* 4. 4. 5 ff. Virgil, *Ecl.* 5. 37.

‡ The Italian 'fagiolo dall'occhio' (Boissier).

§ Varro, 1. 50. 1; Billiard, p. 128. Pliny (*N.H.* 18. 296) knew of a reaping machine, *vallus*, used on large estates in Gaul, for which see White, *Agric. Impl.* pp. 157 ff.

to make a warm covering for the floor of sheep-stalls as well as for fodder (3. 297). Cutting of both straw and hay was best done at night, when the dew would make it pliant (*lentus*, transferred epithet)—and incidentally less sore for the left hand to hold (289–90).[26] The ears of corn were laid out to dry (*tostas*, 298) and then threshed on the threshing-floor (*area*) whose making is described at 178 (where *creta* is white clay).*

The threshing-floor was situated on elevated ground, and open to the breezes for purposes of winnowing (3. 134). The *tribula* of 1. 164 were heavy sledge-like boards with flints or iron teeth embedded on the underside, designed to release the grain from the straw. *Traheae* in the same line were some other kind of drag, perhaps used after it.[27] These were sometimes drawn by cattle (3. 132–4). *Vannus* was a large osier basket used in winnowing. The corn was stored in barns, *horrea* (1. 49; 2. 518), the heaps being given distinguishing numbers (1. 263). In preparation for domestic use it was lightly roasted, then ground with a stone handmill (1. 267; cf. 274–5).

WEATHER-SIGNS†

The section on weather-signs, heralded by the description of a storm at harvest time (316–34), comes more appropriately in the context of field crops than anywhere else, though we are reminded (355) of the prudent farmer keeping his cattle in certain circumstances within easy reach of their steadings. Extending to more than a hundred lines (351–463), it makes free use of the *Diosemeiai* of Aratus, already translated by Cicero and at least in

---

* Cf. Col. 3. 11. 9; Pall. 1. 34; G. 2. 218. Virgil's description is a blend of Cato (91 and 129) and Varro (1. 51)—see Richter's note. Pliny says it is more laborious to use *creta* than *amurca* (*N.H.* 18. 295).

† The best commentary on this section is L. A. S. Jermyn's article 'Weather-signs in Virgil', *G.&R.* (1951), pp. 26–37, 49–59. He thinks that Virgil may also have used directly a treatise which contains in the same conjunction nearly all Aratus' signs and a number more, the *De Signis Tempestatum*, attributed to Theophrastus and appended by Sir Arthur Hort to vol. II of his Loeb edition of the *Historia Plantarum*. The *Diosemeiai*, supplement to the *Phaenomena*, ed. G. R. Mair, is included in A. W. Mair's Loeb volume containing Callimachus and Lycophron.

part by Varro of Atax. We have seen already (pp. 186–7) how Virgil sometimes improved on Aratus from the poetic point of view. In selecting signs he omitted anything that might be tedious, such as multiplication of instances; and he rearranged them where necessary to suit his compositional purposes. First we have gale-warnings (356–69); then rain-warnings (370–92). Signs that weather is set fair follow (393–423), the first three being simply negatives of rain-warnings, borrowed to make up the balance. Then, to make pleasing variety, we have grouping according to sign-giver instead of interpretation—the Moon (424–39) and the Sun (440–63). Even more than elsewhere the intention in this section is transparently poetic rather than didactic; yet it is of interest to the natural historian; and the fact that its primary sources are extant with less suspicion of lost intermediary ones (though we should also have been glad to have Cicero's *Aratea* in full) makes the study of what Virgil chose to alter particularly worthwhile.

Once again here we may observe his tendency to blend or compromise. Aratus (agreeing with Theophrastus) gives at 913 ff. as signs of a gale blowing up at sea the landward flight of heron, petrel, duck and gull. Cicero (fr. 4) substitutes for the heron 'cana fulix', the coot, presumably referring to its white forehead. He may have known that the heron is a bird of marsh and estuary, not sea; but unfortunately the coot is not a sea-bird either, nor does it make a noise. Virgil (360–4) restores Aratus' heron, rightly however picturing it not as flying in from the sea, but leaving its usual marsh-haunt to soar above the clouds. But he also (no doubt in deference to Cicero) includes the *fulix* (as *fulica*) with the epithet *marina* to explain how its disporting itself on dry land can be a prognostic of bad weather at sea; yet a sea-coot is a non-bird.* We have here then, in all probability, a

---

* Jermyn, *G.&R.* pp. 31–2. G. B. Townend, in his chapter on Cicero's poems in *Cicero*, ed. T. A. Dorey (1965), p. 115, says that Virgil 'recognized the appositeness of Cicero's inclusion of the coot'. But Tennyson was more correct when he described the marshy source of his Brook as 'haunts of coot and hern'. Aristotle said that the heron 'frequents the banks of lakes and rivers' (*H.A.* 8. 3. 593b).

further example not of a natural historian's observation, but of a literary blend.

Jermyn has suggested that another such blend occurs at 398–9, where among three negative signs that the weather is set fair occurs

> non tepidum ad solem pennas in litore pandunt
> dilectae Thetidi alcyones

the halcyons beloved of Thetis do not spread their wings on the shore to the warm sun.

The myth was that during fourteen days of winter the sea was dead calm so that the halcyon could brood on her nest as it floated on the surface. To make a negative picture for halcyon days, as here required, Virgil borrowed the idea that she did *not* then have to be *on shore* and dry her wet wings in the sun from a passage in Aratus (918–19) where wild duck and seagulls beating their wings on shore are a sign that a gale is coming.[28]

For purposes of this chapter grouping by sign-givers is more appropriate than by interpretations. Birds easily claim pride of place here, as we may suspect they did in Virgil's own interests.* The *mergus* of 361 is a gull of some sort, behaving as we observe it to do in England, but the *marina fulica* is suspect of non-existence, as we have seen. *Ardea* (364) is agreed to be the heron. Keightley is sceptical about its flying above the clouds when a gale is coming. He might have dismissed Lucan's assertion at 5. 553 as mere reflection of Virgil; but Jermyn claims to have observed a heron behaving so on the estuary of the Exe, though on that occasion at least what followed was rain, not wind.[29] When rain gathers (374),

> vallibus imis
> aëriae fugere grues.

Vallibus is a locative ablative: 'high-flying cranes take refuge in the bottom of valleys'. (They were pests, and might find a trap set for them there: 120; 307.) The shrill swallow (*arguta hirundo*) of 377 flies low as a sign of rain, as everyone knows; so low,

---

* Anyone interested in these matters should consult Royds, part II. Also W. Warde Fowler, *A Year with the Birds* (3rd edn. 1889), ch. VII, and P. d'Hérouville, *À la campagne avec Virgile* (1930), ch. I.

Aratus observes (944–5), that it skims the ripples on the surface of the water (catching insects, of course, which the increasing moisture has constrained to come down).

Virgil's *alcyon* (399: cf. 3. 338) is probably the kingfisher, though the Mediterranean tern has also been suggested.[30] But it is partly mythical; and so, perhaps, is the unidentified Scylla-Ciris, pursued at 404–9 by Nisus, whose behaviour suggests some kind of falcon. *Liquido in aëre* (404) indicates that the spectacle of this chase is another sign of clear, set-fair weather: if there had been any clouds around, Scylla could have taken refuge in them; as it is, her best chance of escape is to fly straight on as fast as she can (*raptim*), relying on her enemy's dropping behind through missing his stoop (Keightley). The steady onward flight is brilliantly conveyed by an expressive repetition:

> quacumque *illa levem fugiens secat aethera pennis,*
> ecce inimicus atrox magno stridore per auras
> insequitur Nisus;
> > (he stoops and misses)
> > qua se fert Nisus ad auras,
> (he towers again)
> *illa levem fugiens* raptim *secat aethera pennis.*

Noctua, the bird which observes the sunset like an augur as it sits on the housetop and prolongs until late its insistent crying (402–3), is probably the 'little' owl. It was believed to do this particularly in set-fair weather, hence *nequiquam*: for people fancied that, like the raven on the shore, it was calling for rain, but unlike the raven, doomed to querulous disappointment.

The *corvi* of 410 must be rooks. Aratus says (1003–6) that it is a sign that fair weather is re-established when κόρακες, solitary and alone (so emphasised—μοῦνοι ἐρημαῖοι), utter first two separate and then quickly repeated cries, and also when in flocks they take thought for their nests, full of voice. Now rooks are notoriously gregarious (already at G. 1. 381 we have been told that one sign of rain approaching is when an army of rooks abandon their feeding ground in a great column with serried beating of wings). Here Virgil says nothing of their doing anything singly; but he changes Aratus' intial 'twice' to 'three or four', and adds that they caw *presso gutture*, 'with constricted throat'. Both of these details look as though they come from Theophrastus, who says (52), 'and a rook cawing *softly* (ἡσυχαῖον) alone, and if it caws *three* times and after that many times, is a sign of fair weather'. But whatever the literary antecedents, Virgil dwells lovingly on these birds: and a number of authorities have testified that rooks, although uncommon in Italy elsewhere, have in modern times been a familiar sight in the Po valley and the neighbourhood of Mantua.[31] As for the idea of solitariness in μοῦνοι ἐρημαῖοι, Virgil's imagination transferred it, as Jermyn perceived,[32] to the raven (*cornix*) who at 389 struts *sola secum* along the shore calling for rain. Sea and lake birds diving and plunging had been said (with dubious correctness) by Theophrastus and Aratus to be signs of rain, and the picture had been elaborated by Varro of Atax. As at 104, Virgil picks up a hint from predecessors as cue for a vivid variation on a theme by Homer, in this case the simile of the birds in the Caÿster marshes.[33]

Animals other than birds play a smaller part in the prognostics. We have glimpses of pigs tossing straw on their snouts (399) and of a heifer sniffing the air with distended nostrils and upturned head when rain is about (375-6).* This last may be a true sign: at any rate it is widely believed to be so. But what the frogs and ants are doing is an effect, not a prognostic, of rain. Frogs croak *during* rain, as ducks quack, presumably from pleasure. Virgil's line is a masterpiece of expressive and associative sound. Jermyn's comment may be quoted in full:

In Cicero's very free paraphrase [of Aratus] 'the fathers of the tadpoles' becomes *aquai dulcis alumnae*. Now this phrase not only is an almost literal translation of the λιμναῖα κρηνῶν τέκνα of Aristophanes, but contains in *alumnae* a sound-echo of λιμναῖα. Virgil took the hint and improved on it. In his line

et veterem in limo ranae cecinere querelam

* In praising Virgil (p. 35) for adding *patulis naribus* Jermyn overlooks the fact that this, like the admirably expressive line 377 on the flight of swallows, is taken from the version of Varro of Atax quoted by Servius.

the word *veterem* is an obvious pointer to antiquity; *in limo*, both in sound and meaning, echoes λιμναῖα, and *cecinere querelam* reproduces three of the k- sounds of βρεκεκεκέξ.*

As for the ants, it is not eggs that they are seen carrying (an error taken over from Aratus, 966). The narrow path they wear is correctly observed (or guessed), but it is *after* rain that they make it, carrying out larvae and grass-seeds to dry. These seeds are actually stored (cf. 1. 186 *inopi metuens formica senectae*), not by European ants in general, but by two common Mediterranean species whose activities have become proverbial through the Bible.[34]

The behaviour of lamp-wick as a prognostic (390–2) had been recognised by Aristophanes and analysed by Theophrastus and Aratus.[35] Apart from this Virgil's signs from inanimate nature are confined to meteorology. The rainbow (a double one in Aratus)[36] seems odd to us as a *prognostic* of rain (380); we associate it rather with God's promise to Noah, if we are thinking mythologically. Pliny dismissed the idea that it *portended* anything.[37] But it was a vulgar error in antiquity that rainbows sucked up moisture which was then precipitated: *bibit arcus* was a popular expression.[38] Jermyn excellently remarked how in Virgil's series of animal prognostics, when a line beginning with ants ends *et bibit ingens* (380), we expect the contrast to be a bison or some such beast, and are given, παρὰ προσδοκίαν, a rainbow.[39]

Aratus says that when the light of the stars is dimmed not through gathered clouds nor any other kind of intervening obscurity (? fog) nor through moonlight, rain is to be expected (presumably the air has become hazy).[40] Virgil, wishing to reinforce his stock of signs of set-fair weather, simply reverses this one (395):

> nam neque tum stellis acies obtunsa videtur.

He then adds,

> nec fratris radiis obnoxia surgere luna.

---

* *G.&R.* p. 36. The κοάξ κοάξ of Aristophanes is reproduced by Ovid at *Met.* 6. 376:   quamuis sint *sub aqua sub aqua* maledicere tentant.

These correspondences were noted already by Voss.

Commentators take this to mean, 'and the moon rises *seemingly* unbeholden to her brother's light', i.e. so brilliant that she seems to shine with light of her own, not borrowed from the sun;[*] and this agrees well enough with what Aratus says about the full or half moon (802). When Virgil comes to deal with the moon on her own (427 ff.), he has in mind another passage of Aratus (783–7), which concerns the *new* moon: 'The moon, when first she rallies her returning light,

> si nigrum obscuro comprenderit aëra cornu,

is warning farmers and sailors of heavy rain.' This corresponds to Aratus' 'if blurred (παχίων) and with blunted horns she shows only a feeble light on the third and fourth nights, her beams are being dulled by the South wind or imminent rain'. Keightley comments, 'When the air is quite clear from vapour, the whole of the moon may be seen, though very faintly illuminated (by solar rays reflected from the earth), while when there is vapour in the air precursive of rain, only the strongly illuminated portion is visible'. He goes on, however,[41] to compare the lines in the ballad of Sir Patrick Spens,

> I saw the new moon late yestreen
> Wi' the auld moon in her arms.

But there, surely, the phenomenon is taken as a *sinister* portent, whereas in Virgil it is the *absence* of it that heralds bad weather: 'if it embraces *black air* within its blurred horns'—unless of course 'nigrum aëra' can mean 'dark air that is visible', which seems hardly probable.

Aratus says that the signs of the third and fourth day of the moon portend the weather *up to the half moon* (806). Virgil on the other hand says (432 ff.), 'but if at her fourth rising†—for that is the surest indicator—she passes clear and with horns unblunted across the sky, the whole of that day and the succeeding ones *till*

---

[*] Heyne's idea, revived by Jermyn (*G.&R.* pp. 49–50), that it means 'and there is no moon' (to dim the stars) is hardly admissible: this line seems independent from its predecessor.

† 'Egypt pays most attention to the moon's fourth day' (Pliny, *N.H.* 18. 347).

the end of the month ('exactum ad mensem') will be free from rain and winds'. Why does he go beyond Aratus here? I suspect it was through a recollection of another line of Aratus about the third and fourth days (782): 'from them you can learn about the month that is setting in' (or else of Theophrastus) rather than, as Jermyn suggests, from personal observation of the Italian sky.*

The prognostics from the sun are likewise selected out of an abundance in predecessors, and enlivened by vivid touches:

> heu male tum mites defendet pampinus uvas;
> tam multa in tectis crepitans salit horrida grando,

alas, the vine-leaves shall be poor protection then for the ripening grapes,† such precipitant bristling hail tap-dances on the roofs (448–9).

Few lines in Virgil are more expressive than this last, with its heavy spondaic opening bursting out into dactyls staccato with pattering consonants.‡ Again, what is merely a statement in Aratus evokes a shudder of apprehension at 456:

> non illa quisquam me nocte per altum
> ire neque a terra moneat convellere funem,

on such a night let no one advise me to go over the deep or loose my cable from the land.

Making night the setting doubles the fear.

---

* *G.&R.* p. 54. I think he is also mistaken on p. 53 in taking εὖ μάλ᾽ ἐρευθής (784) to refer to the phenomenon of 'the new moon in the old moon's arms'. Theophrastus says that if the moon's outline on the third day is clear, it will be fine for a month (*De Signis*, 51).

† *Pace* Sargeaunt (p. 141), it is clear from such phrases as this, and *pampineae umbrae* (*E.* 7. 58), that *pampinus* could be used of leaves as well as shoots. But he is right in rejecting the interpretation 'tendril'.

‡ On *horrida* Conington comments, 'the radical notion seems to be that of erect points' (the visual image is here of hailstones bristling up from a roof). But he also compares Pindar's φρίσσοντας ὄμβρους (*P.* 4. 81). The comparison is worth pursuing. φρίσσειν has the same radical notion. But there, as in Virgil, the *sound* also is expressive. So it is, as Demetrius observed (*De Eloc.* 82), in the Homeric phrase ἔφριξεν δὲ μάχη. Sir Maurice Bowra (*Pindar*, 1964, p. 244) says that Pindar's phrase catches both the sight and *feel* of rain. W. B. Stanford (*Greek Metaphor*, 1936, p. 142) thinks that Pindar meant 'spiky showers, i.e. Virgil's *horrida grando* which cuts the flesh like a lancet'. There is also the possibility that Homer, Pindar and Virgil all had the thought of *shivering mankind* at the back of their minds as well.

The phrases *claro Aquilone* ('clear Dark-wind'), *serenas nubes* ('serene clouds'), and *umidus Auster* ('wet Dry-wind') are, as Jackson Knight pointed out, oxymora playing on the derivation of winds, selected from two separate passages in Theophrastus, the first two representing fear, and the last hope, belied.[42] The sinister *quid cogitet umidus Auster*, 'what the wet Scirocco is plotting', leads into the *caecos tumultus*, the *fraudem*, the *operta bella* that swelled silently to burst in the murder of Julius Caesar.[43]

TREES

For the ancient husbandman the cultivation of trees, apart from vines and olives, was something of a side-line, though they were needed as supports for vines, for windbreaks and for auxiliary fodder. Enough fruit was grown for home consumption, with an occasional surplus for the local market (G. 1. 273–4); but means of transport were not such as to make large orchards profitable except in the environs of towns. Nor do the ancient Italians seem to have done much forestry, apart from growing small woods for fuel and clearing trees away for the plough.[44] But Virgil does introduce a passage on trees for which particular countries are famous (2. 109–35) as preparation for the Praises of Italy, and another on the variety of trees all over the world, their diverse uses and their beauty (420–53) as preparation for the Praises of Country Life.

At the beginning of Book 2, after the invocation to Bacchus, he treads closely at first in the footsteps of Theophrastus, who began the Second Book of his *Historia Plantarum* with details of the various ways in which trees can be propagated.* He describes three natural ones and six artificial, changing Theophrastus' order in the latter so that our inward eye travels upwards from root to tree-top.[45] The natural ways should really have been two, since

---

* From the copious detail of Theophrastus Virgil selects a few precepts for his poetic purposes, and these are not always correctly remembered or understood (Jermyn, *The Ostrakon*, pp. 3 ff.). On the other hand he does not follow slavishly. He knows, for instance, that silk comes from the Chinese, not the intermediate Bactrians (121; cf. *H.P.* 4. 4. 7–8).

one is based on an ancient misconception, that chemical action can produce plant life spontaneously (cf. I. 22, *non ullo semine*).* Even the καὶ γὰρ οὕτως of Theophrastus, indicating mild surprise, is reproduced by 'mirabile dictu'! (30). The modern reader may echo this exclamation when he comes to pear-trees transformed by grafting to apple-bearers (a possibility which Varro too had countenanced) and big-stoned cornels ripening red on plum-trees.[46]

Virgil is following Theophrastus so closely that we must suppose him to have taken notice of the sentence 'wild things become tame by feeding and other kinds of nurture';† but the wording of the injunction that follows (36),

> fructusque feros mollite colendo,

was probably influenced by Lucretius' description of early man's development of husbandry (5. 1368),

> fructusque feros mansuescere terra
> cernebant indulgendo blandeque colendo,

and through pampering and coaxing cultivation they were able to see wild fruits grow tame in the earth.

The injunction is expanded at 47-52: trees that grow wild are strong and flourishing because of the spontaneous generative power (*natura*) hidden in the earth, but they are no good for fruit. Nevertheless, even these, if you submit them to grafting or transplant them to well-prepared holes, will be found to put off their wild spirit, and through assiduous tendance to follow you readily in learning any lesson you wish to teach them.‡

---

* Diogenes of Smyrna *ap.* Theophr. *H.P.* 3. 1. 4; not to be confused with the idea of Anaxagoras (*ibid.*), adopted by Varro (1. 40. 1), that there are invisible seeds in the air. Theophrastus makes the distinction clear at *H.P.* 3. 1. 6: εἴτε καὶ ἐνυπαρχόντων εἴτε καὶ αὐτῆς πως διατιθεμένης (*sc.* τῆς χώρας). *Posito de semine* (14) must refer to the effect of birds, wind, flooding rivers, etc. in spreading seeds.

† *H.P.* 2. 2. 9; cf. 12 and *C.P.* 3. 24. 4: ὅλα γένη τῶν δένδρων ὥσπερ ἐξ ἀγρίων ἥμερα γιγνόμενα. I borrow the word 'tame' from usage about animals rather than use the clumsy 'domesticated' or tautologous 'cultivated'.

‡ That transplanting could have this effect was generally believed in antiquity; e.g. Pliny, *N.H.* 17. 66: 'transitus mirum in modum mitigat etiam silvestres'. I am indebted to my friend Mr J. S. L. Gilmour, Director of the Cambridge

The surprise occasioned by lines 33–4 is increased at 69 ff., where we hear that arbutus-shoots can be grafted on to nut-trees, apple on to planes, beech on to chestnuts, pear on to ashes and —final flourish—that pigs have munched acorns under elms. Attempts have been made to save Virgil's face by saying that he must have been thinking of epiphytes,[47] or by citing freak cases of reported success in laboratory experiments in grafting.* But Virgil was not alone here either: even Columella in one place asserts that, despite what 'the ancients' have said, the possibilities of grafting are unlimited, though elsewhere he admits that the trees must have similar bark.[48] Pliny, however (17. 103), insists not only on this affinity, but on many others, amounting together to a limitation acceptable to modern science.

Remarks on the variety of methods of grafting (73–82; only a selection from those recognised by ancient authorities) lead into

University Botanic Garden, for the following statement of modern scientific opinion:

'There are really two separate questions here: (1) Can an individual wild fruit tree, if transplanted and well looked after, produce more and better fruit than it would have done in the wild? and (2) What is the method of origin of *permanently* improved cultivated varieties ('cultivars')? The answer to the first question is a limited affirmative—but the improvement would, of course, only last as long as the better growing conditions were maintained. The answer to (2) is, broadly, that new and permanently improved cultivars are produced by selecting the best forms found growing in the wild, and then raising seedlings from these, and again selecting the best forms, and possibly crossing together two forms with desirable qualities. Finally, what is considered a worth-while new cultivar is propagated vegetatively by cuttings, grafting or budding, so that its improved qualities are perpetuated. The production of a new fruit cultivar is a long process, owing to the length of time it takes for a seedling tree to get big enough to bear fruit. The process is shortened, of course, if a big and favourable mutation appears, rather than the more usual phenomenon of *slightly* better forms, which have to be grown again from seed, in the hope that one or more of the seedlings will show a further improvement on its parents.'

* P. d'Hérouville, *Géorgiques I–II, Champs, Vergers, Forêts* (1942), pp. 52–65. He sums up (p. 64): 'En somme, des griefs formulés contre le poète, il reste peu de chose.' I am again indebted to Mr J. S. L. Gilmour for a statement of modern scientific opinion: 'There is no doubt, I think, that Virgil is mistaken in all the cases he cites. I know of no successful grafts between members of different families, and all his pairs are allegedly grafts of this type. There are, indeed, very few cases of successful grafts even between two different genera of the *same* family, far less between genera of *different* families. All the grafts cited by d'Hérouville are between genera of the same family.'

a short passage on differences in methods of propagation required by different trees in different localities (83–8), which in turn issues in the wine-catalogue (89). Many of the ancients were connoisseurs of wine. Julius Caesar established the Mamertine from near Messina as regular for public banquets. Julia Augusta attributed her survival to her eighty-seventh year to having drunk only the wine of Pizzino, grown north of the Adriatic. The taste of Augustus and most of his successors approved that of Sentinum above the previous favourite, dear to Maecenas, Caecuban. This and much else we learn from an extensive critical catalogue of wines in Pliny (14. 20–76), who knew about eighty in the world, two-thirds of them Italian. But there is no known predecessor to Virgil's selective and discriminating list, and it may of course represent his own taste. At any rate he has diverged here from Theophrastus, to whom he returns for ideas at 114–39. There Arabs, Geloni, Indian ebony and Sabaean frankincense all occur in the same order as in him. The Median citron with its sour juice and lingering taste, useful (mixed with wine) as an emetic if you have drunk poison, and as a sweetener of the breath—these points are all elaborated from Theophrastus.[49] Two points seem at first sight to be independent of him, its likeness to the bay—mistakability for it indeed, but for the different scent it diffuses far and wide—and the tenacity of its blossom. But the first proves to be simply due to a false reading in his text of Theophrastus which Athenaeus also found (3. 26: δάφνης for ἀνδράχλης);[50] and the second could conceivably be due to some misunderstanding or corruption of Theophrastus' statement that it bears fruit at all seasons.* So careful must we be in attributing details to Virgil's own observation.

The contrasting praises of all-producing Italy that follow seem to be Virgil's own, but the details belong to panegyric. Though 'bis gravidae pecudes' is a phenomenon not unheard of, and 'bis pomis utilis arbor' is one reported by Varro of Consentia in Bruttium (1. 7. 6), they owe their place here (150) more to legends

---

* H.P. 4. 4. 3: φέρει δὲ τὰ μῆλα πᾶσαν ὥραν· τὰ μὲν γὰρ ἀφήρηται, τὰ δὲ ἀνθεῖ, τὰ δὲ ἐκπέττει.

of the orchards of Alcinous (mentioned at 87) and the Isles of the Blest. The gratifyingly absent lions, poisonous herbs and snakes of 151–4 are precisely the banes whose disappearance was to signalise the Golden Age in *Eclogue* 4:

> nec magnos metuent armenta leones;
> occidet et serpens et fallax herba veneni
> occidet.*

In the passage that follows about the properties of various kinds of soil (already touched on, p. 226), the lines concerning the vine (184 ff.) are not quite clear:

> at quae pinguis humus dulcique uligine laeta,
> quique frequens herbis et fertilis ubere campus
> qualem saepe cava montis convalle solemus
> despicere: huc summis liquuntur rupibus amnes
> felicemque trahunt limum—quique editus Austro
> et filicem curvis invisam pascit aratris:
> hic tibi praevalidas olim multoque fluentes
> sufficiet Baccho vites...

Is this one kind of terrain or two? 'Hic' in 190 might suggest that it is one, but this is hard to conceive. † Can 'a soil which is rich and endowed with sweet moisture and one with thick herbage and generally fertile (like the well-watered alluvial valleys we often look down upon)'—can this be the same as a south-facing slope that encourages bracken? I doubt it. At 112 Virgil has committed himself to saying that 'Bacchus loves open hillsides' (cf. 522), but

---

* 22–5 (minus 23, now transferred to follow 20). *Aconita* has caused trouble because it did in fact grow in Italy (Dioscorides 4. 78). Servius' solution, that it was so familiar it could not deceive, will hardly convince. Sargeaunt suggested it was the pale yellow monks-hood (*Aconitum Anthora*), which deceived by being like a harmless aconite; which seems a little more plausible than Richter's idea that what deceives is not the plant but a snake lurking beneath it (cf. *Ecl.* 3. 92–3), for the snake introduced in the next line seems to be a new and separate item.

† Conington and Page, for instance, assume it to be one; but Keightley is less absolute, while de Saint-Denis translates *quique* by asyndeton in 185 but by *ou bien* in 188.

everything depends on circumstances, as he himself admits later (273):

collibus an plano melius sit ponere vitem
quaere prius.

The drained marsh-land near Forum Appi produced a *grand vin*, the Caecuban. Virgil warns only against a salty or bitter soil (238). Again, although he here recommends a south-facing slope, and at 298 condemns a west-facing one, this may be valid only for Italy, or not even for all of that, or only for certain kinds of soil or of vine, as Pliny insists (17. 19–23).

At line 259 the vine, already emphasised among trees, emerges as the main subject. For it the soil should be either friable by nature or loosened by the agency of frost or cold winds, or by persistent toil with the spade. The good vine-grower will choose out a nursery-plot of similar characteristics to the one which will soon receive the saplings in preparation for their marriage to trees, so that they will not suddenly be homesick for their mothers.* Some even take care to transplant them the same way round, with the same front facing the warm south, and the same back facing the pole, so important is conditioning in the young: 'adeo in teneris consuescere multum est'. It was characteristic of Virgil to single out from Theophrastus (his chief source from 265 to 362) so human a trait, and characteristic of Pliny to sneer that if this had mattered Cato would have mentioned it. Yet Virgil may have been right.† On rich plain-land the vines can be planted close, but on hillsides they should be allowed more generous room,‡ though here too the supporting trees must be so planted that 'ad unguem ...secto via limite quadret' (274–8). What this last phrase means has been much disputed, but the matter should have been settled by an article of F. H. Sandbach, who pointed out that there is no reason to suppose that there is a reference here to a particular army

---

* I take '*similem—et*' to go together, *sc. eum locum*, 'like the place'.
† Pliny, *N.H.* 17. 83. Billiard (p. 185) cites a communication to the Académie des Sciences on 19 December 1921, by Martin Zède, entitled 'Sur l'influence que l'orientation antérieure pouvait avoir sur la reprise des arbres'.
‡ Theophrastus says the opposite, *C.P.* 3. 7. 2.

formation, despite the simile that follows.[51] The *limites* are the broad avenues that divide the vineyard into sections; the *viae* are the narrower paths between vines that should be exactly at right angles to them. All must be equally spaced apart by the regularity of the *viae*. The result will be pleasing to the eye, and ensure that all the trees have equal nourishment and equal room to expand (284-7).

A series of laconic precepts follow which have given ample scope for disagreement:

> neve tibi ad solem vergant vineta cadentem,
> neve inter vites corylum sere; neve flagella
> summa pete aut summa defringe ex arbore plantas
> (tantus amor terrae) neu ferro laede retunso
> semina, neve oleae silvestres insere truncos.

Inter...sere and *insere* both appear to mean 'intermingle' (from *sero, serui, sertum,* not *sero, sevi, satum*). But why does Virgil separate by three such disparate precepts two such cognate ones —'do not mingle hazels with your vines' (presumably because their roots are so large and spreading)...'and do not intermingle wild-olive trunks', since (*nam*) they catch fire easily?* Lines 312-14 give the consequences of the fire:

> hoc ubi, non a stirpe valent caesaeque reverti
> possunt atque ima similes revirescere terra.
> infelix superat foliis oleaster amaris.

Non here covers both *valent* and *possunt reverti atque revirescere,* and the sense will be, 'When this happens, the vines have not the strength to grow again, nor can they, though cut back (to below the burnt part), recover and flourish again as they were before (*similes*) from the earth at their roots.'†

---

* This is not in fact true. There is no oil *pingui sub cortice* in olives, and they do not burn easily like resinous timber (Billiard, p. 225). Virgil may have been misled by Theophrastus, *H.P.* 5. 9. 6.

† The rival view takes *insere* at 320 to mean 'engraft', as it usually does in this Book: 'Do not use wild olives as stock on which to graft tame ones.' It receives some support from Palladius 5. 2. The separated precepts are not then so clearly cognate. Everything from 302 onwards will concern olives, which (not vines) will be the subject of 312-13. When the tame olive grafted on to the wild olive

About the planting, and especially the grafting, of vines Virgil
has little to say. It appears from line 63 that he thought layering
best, but he deals chiefly with the planting out of what he vaguely
calls *semina*—either suckers or slips cut from higher up the tree.
Planting should take place in spring, or else in autumn, when the
ground, hardened neither by sun nor frost, will let in the roots
(315–22). Columella preferred autumn if the climate was dry or
warm, and if the terrain was either poor and arid plain or lean and
steep hillside.[52] Theophrastus reports some arguments for autumn,
though generally favouring spring. Virgil mentions autumn only
to return immediately to spring, whose praises he is poised to sing.
Your slips should not be chosen from the terminals (*flagella*, the
new wood, which is pruned off but is too soft and immature for
this purpose); nor should you break shoots from the highest part
of the supporting tree—*tantus amor terrae*, such is their love of
earth (*sc.* that those nearest to it will prove most likely to take to it
when replanted).*

In planting the sets should be well manured and heaped up with
earth (so that the goodness, ammonia etc., may not evaporate).
Theophrastus recommended manuring vines every four years at
most,† but Virgil is here referring to the establishment of young
saplings. In fact, although manure may produce a higher yield in
vines, the ancients believed it spoiled the taste of the wine, and in
this they have the agreement of modern growers of *crus classés*.[53]

is burnt, the tree reverts to wild olive. This gives more point to *similes*: they
will not be of the same *kind* as before. But *insere* alone can hardly mean 'engraft
wild trunks of olive' (*sc.* with tame olive), as Page wished. It would be necessary to adopt the reading *olea* from M to provide an explicit ablative (with
Wagner, etc.). Moreover not only does the whole of this part of the book
concern vines, but the sentence 298–303, beginning with *vineta, vites*, should
continue to do so throughout.

* 299–301. Virgil is here fancifully embroidering Theophrastus (*C.P.* 3. 5. 3):
'Men prefer layers, for these possess directly the principle of life. If this is
impossible, they take cuttings from the lower part of the tree rather than the
upper, thinking that such cuttings have more life in them'; but he has overlooked the proviso, 'except in the case of the vine' (Jermyn, *The Ostrakon*,
pp. 6–7).

† Theophr. *C.P.* 3. 9. 5. But it is possible that here Virgil is thinking parentheti-
cally of trees in general (*quaecunque—virgulta*, 347), as Theophrastus was in
another passage he had in mind, *C.P.* 3. 6. 1.

The ditches for planting should be quite shallow, according to Virgil (289: actually it depends on latitude—the further south the deeper they should be, so as to retain moisture).[54] Pebbles and rough shells should be dug in, to admit moisture, and also air.* The shells may seem dangerously sharp objects, but their use by modern vine-growers is attested for Trani in Apulia.[55] Some have been known, continues Virgil, 'qui super urgerent' with stones or heavy potsherds, as protection against heavy sun or rain. 'Super urgere' should mean 'press down on', not prop over at an angle, as Conington admits. Again Columella is clearly wrong in supposing the stones or potsherds to be placed *in* the trench. The intention remains obscure—unless Jermyn is right in cutting the Gordian knot by supposing that Virgil was misapplying a precept in Theophrastus that refers to something else.[56]

After planting there was always the labour of breaking up the soil frequently around the roots, with drag-hoe or with plough (for ploughs were driven up and down through vineyards, which was another reason for arranging the trees in regular formation). Then there was the preparation of supports, first smooth canes and rods stripped of bark (which might harbour harmful insects), and ash stakes and forked props, up which the vines would eventually climb to the layers of elm-branches, to which they would be bound by *retinacula* of osier or butchers-broom.[57] Not until the fourth or fifth year will the vine be mature.

Meanwhile it will have to be carefully pruned so as to leave only the healthier-looking shoots, at first with the finger-nails (a knife would cause too much loss of sap). Only when it reaches the elm must it be shaped ruthlessly. The vineyard must also be fenced against the incursions of browsing or destructive animals (362–96).

Even when fully grown, vines demand unceasing labour all the year round. Three or four times a year the soil must be all turned over, and the clods broken up with the back of a drag-hoe; and the vine leaves must be stripped. Twice a year the ground must be weeded, twice the vines trimmed (first to remove the tops of

---

* 348. I put a stop at 347, and take *aut...aut* in 348 to mean 'either...or'; for pebbles and shells can hardly be an *alternative* to manure.

shoots to prevent their developing at the expense of the fruit, and later to enable the grapes to ripen, though enough must be left to protect them from excessive sun and no less from hail).[58] Even after the leaves have fallen in autumn there is still more pruning to do, and the pruned shoots must be carted away and burnt; and finally props have to be brought indoors, or they will rot in winter (397–413). The movement of dust referred to at 418 requires comment. Theophrastus represents the dust as piled round the roots of the trees (ὑποκόνισις); but Columella and Pliny obviously thought of it as stirred up so as to mantle the grapes themselves also, as a protection against sun and fog.[59]

Postremus metito, 'be the last to harvest' (410), is said to be bad advice. By then the sugar is concentrated. The resultant wine will be highly alcoholic, but the freshness will have gone with the verdure, and all sorts of maladies are to be feared.* Various receptacles were used for the grapes—the *lintres* of 1. 262, hollowed out from tree-trunks, and baskets or mats of wicker-work (2. 241–2). The grapes were first trampled (2. 4–8), then pressed (usually in a beam-and-capstan press which derived its name, *prelum*, from the 25-foot beam). Only once (2. 242) does Virgil mention a press. We hear of various kinds of processing. *Passum* (2. 93; cf. 4. 269) was a sweet wine made from grapes dried in the sun. Honey was mixed in to temper generous or sour wines (1. 344; 4. 100–2). Wine boiled and skimmed down produced *defrutum*, a kind of must used either for this same purpose or as a syrup—the Afrikaans 'moskonfyt' (from *mustum confectum*).[60]

At 419 Virgil ends his account of vines. He has been highly selective, as usual, dealing only with those trained over small trees, whereas Pliny recognised five methods (17. 164). Yet he has left himself only thirty-seven lines for other trees. His excuse is that other fruit-trees need little care. Even the olive, so familar a feature of the Italian landscape (*tenent oleae*) and especially of his own Campania, receives here only seven lines (420–6). Elsewhere he has had scattered references to it. Difficult land and niggardly hill-

---

* Billiard, p. 233, but this would not seem to apply to the 'spätlese' wines of the Rhineland, as Prof. K. D. White reminds me.

sides, land with shallow clay, or scrubby and strewn with pebbles, have the merit of encouraging it, and can be recognised by the prevalence already there of wild olives (2. 178–83). We hear nothing about which kind should be planted where, though three varieties are named in an ornamental line, 2. 86. Pliny knew of fifteen. Propagation by truncheons (*truncis*) is recommended at 2. 63. Once they have taken root little care is needed (pruning might have been mentioned). There is the further merit in olives that the fruit can be gathered and pressed in winter-time (1. 306; 2. 519). The spontaneous flourishing of fruit leads into an enthusiastic catalogue of world-wide abundance, which in turn leads into the Praises of Country Life.

CATTLE AND HORSES

Varro's Second Book provides the basis for what Virgil has to say about the animals he chooses to treat in Book 3—cattle, horses, sheep and goats. Indeed van de Woestijne has said: 'There is nothing the poet says that is not found in the prose writer: but what a difference in tone and presentation!'[61]

The nature of the Italian country had led more and more farmers to go over from crops to pasturage. 'Beasts', says Scrofa in Varro (2. 1. 11), 'are the basis of all wealth—*omnis pecuniaepecus fundamentum.*' As for cattle, Virgil envisages them primarily as bred for labour, for ploughing chiefly, but also for draught.[62] Nor does he confine such work to males.[63] Milking of cows is mentioned only at 3. 176–8, where with characteristic sympathy Virgil appeals to the herdsman not to make his beasts, after calving, fill his own pails, like the old-time farmers dedicated to squeezing out the last drop of profit, but to let them spend it on their calves—which he calls 'dulces nati' just like the children who cling to their returning father's neck at 2. 523. Cow's milk was of course drunk by humans, and 'ubera vaccae lactea demittunt' (2. 524) was a sign of prosperity; Augustus particularly liked cheeses made from it.[64] But for some purposes Varro thought both sheep's and goat's milk preferable (2. 11. 1), and in any case sheep were kept in much larger numbers because of the need for wool.[65]

Some calves, chosen for size, good appearance and un-blemished uniformity of colour, were set aside to become *opimi*, fattened for sacrifice. These might be of either sex: the bull is *maxima victima* (for Jupiter) at 2. 147, the cow is for Juno at 3. 532. Virgil says nothing about the breeding of cattle for meat, except by implication at 3. 160. This may be partly from sentiment—he has just deplored, in the finale to Book 2, the original intro-duction of this 'impious' practice. By tradition, primitive peoples had refrained from killing cattle, and an old law to this effect, perhaps of Pythagorean origin, is often mentioned: the ox is the partner of man in 'hominumque boumque labores'. To Virgil he is not, as he was to Varro, just an 'inarticulate (*semivocale*) instrument', as distinguished from a slave, who was an 'articulate instrument' (1. 17. 1).* Although the Romans did eat veal (*vitulina*) and beef (*bubula*), it is remarkable how little we hear of this, apart from the implications of sacrifice. Varro mentions that butchers require a guarantee of soundness when purchasing cattle for the knife, whereas those who purchase them for the altar generally require none (2. 5. 11)—an amusing distinction in view of the pernickety care taken over the exterior appearance of sacrificial animals. Apicius in Book 8 of his cookery-book gives only three recipes for veal or beef as against eleven for lamb or kid, thirteen for hare and seventeen for pig.†

In so far as Virgil departs from Varro (2. 5. 7–8) it is in details and in the pictorial use of images. Appearances mean much to him: he will not disapprove of a cow being brindled (56), just as he obviously admired the white herds of the Clitumnus, while

---

* Addaeus of Macedon (*A.P.* 6. 228) has an epigram consigning an ox, out of gratitude for its labours, to an honourable retirement in pasturage. D'Hérou-ville, *À la campagne avec Virgile*, p. 42.

† Celsus (2. 24) lists beef among a number of foods good for the stomach. The buying of beef and veal is referred to by Plautus, *Aulularia* 374 (cf. *Curculio* 367), but we cannot be sure he is not simply following his Greek original. Useless cattle were disposed of (Col. 6. 22. 1). See further J. André, *L'alimentation et la cuisine à Rome:* Études et Commentaires, xxxix (1961), 138–42.

Varro put white cattle last on his list of preference as being feeblest.[66] Breeding is the aspect on which he concentrates, perhaps because it enables him to describe the ideal, but also because it leads up to the great section on the power of lust which was integral to his design. The ancient confinement of mating to between the ages of four and twelve is noteworthy, and as regards cows may be sound, though modern practice is to begin much earlier; but bulls should be young, and they are liable to get too heavy with age.[67]. The quality of the herd must be continually maintained by selection (69–71). There is no mention however of cross-breeding, which was known to Columella (7. 2. 4–6.). After an intervening passage on sires for horses we return to cows, but in no clear-cut way, for the passage 123–56 is confused in presentation. Here Virgil seems sometimes to be thinking of horses, sometimes of cattle.* We begin by assuming that he is still talking of horses, as 'his animadversis' leads us to suppose. But the prescriptions about diet before mating come from Varro's section on cattle;[68] and 'cursu quatiunt' at 132 ('harass them by making them run') must refer to cattle, since horses were mated in spring, not after threshing-time (133). At 138, where we are told that we are passing from the care of sires to that of dams, we might conclude that we are going over definitely to cattle, and the reference in 140 to drawing waggons would seem to confirm this—did not bounding along the road, fleeing across the meadows and swimming swift rivers in the next two lines conjure up rather a picture of horses. But then again the gadfly of 146–56 is mentioned by Varro in connection with cattle,[69] and 'mugitibus' in 150 makes it clear that these are in mind. The injunctions themselves, to feed up the males and keep the females thin before mating and to allow the females a quiet, sheltered life when they are pregnant, are sound enough, and the danger from the gadfly not exaggerated.

Next we come to the rearing of calves. What is meant by 'notas et nomina gentis inurunt' (158) has been much disputed.

---

* Nor is 'ipsa autem...armenta' at 129 a clear way of indicating that we are turning by contrast from the treatment of males to that of females.

Were the calves somehow marked to indicate the gentile name of
the owner, a practice attested for antiquity,[70] or with some sign
of pedigree, or both? Columella says of the swineherd: 'if he has
not got a good memory, and so cannot recognise the offspring of
each sow, he must put distinguishing marks on each and the same
one on her litter, with liquid pitch, either a letter or some other
sign'.[71] Larger animals were branded. On the whole it seems
likelier that the reference is to pedigree. We should expect
indications (159–61) of ultimate destination to be recorded in a
stock-book; but these would be no use if the calf could not be
identified. The progressive training of calves for the yoke is
described in much the same spirit as the education of children
would be; and Virgil urges the herdsman to pluck corn in blade
for them with his own hand as well as not to deprive them of
milk.

With his account of cattle, mostly female, Virgil has inter-
twined that of male horses (77–88), likewise based on Varro but
coloured also by Xenophon.[72] His interest is in racehorses and
warhorses, and how to breed them, though horses were also
used for riding and (though mules may here have been preferred)
for drawing carriages. No doubt this is simply because he wanted,
for literary purposes, the best contrast with the ox and cow. Once
again he turns the points he selects from Varro into pictorial
images.[73] Sires should be chosen for moral as well as physical
qualities; and in fact the points and the order of preference in
colours—bay, grey, dun and white, it would seem[74]—are awk-
wardly sandwiched between indications of mettle. The prescription that the mane should fall over the right shoulder (86)
has nothing to do with hand-hold for mounting: manes fall
naturally to this side.[75] The 'duplex spina' (87) is really a double
ridge of muscle protecting the spine.*

When the time comes for the 'battles' of mating, the stallion
must be shut up indoors if he is sick or too old (though in fact, as
Aristotle says,[76] he can go on improving at stud from the age of

---

* Keightley. Varro says 'with spine preferably double, or at least not protruding'
(R.R. 2. 7. 5).

three to twenty, and, unlike the bull, does not become burdensome to the female through weight and clumsiness). Exceptional mettle (*animus*) is what is to be sought for in racehorses, apart from youth (95–122).

After the section on breeding of cattle we return again at 179 to horses. The warhorse has to become accustomed to the noises of battle. Virgil has transferred a precept which Varro applies to draught-oxen being trained to go through towns. And indeed it is more important here, a horse being both more timid by nature and destined to have to brave still more alarming noises.[77] Real training does not begin until the fourth year (190). Here again we find the ancients beginning later than is now customary. Page however points out that chariot-racing must have been an even severer strain than modern racing.

Another aspect of training to recruit strength which Virgil advocates is avoidance of sexual intercourse, to be secured by rigorous segregation (209 ff.). This forms an ingenious transition to the subject of sex in general. Here he seems to have in mind passages from Lucretius Book 4 dealing with the checking of human desire; for instance 1063 ff.,

> sed fugitare decet simulacra et pabula amoris
> abstergere sibi atque alio convertere mentem,

but the right thing to do is to shun images and get rid of the food of love and turn your mind elsewhere,

and again (1121 ff.),

> adde quod absumunt vires pereuntque labore—

besides this they squander their strength and wear themselves out with toil.

But the contest of the bulls that follows is a drama created by Virgil's imagination from a passage in Aristotle's *Historia Animalium* (6. 21) which reads simply: 'The bull who is victorious mounts the cows. When he becomes exhausted by his sexual activity he is set upon by his beaten antagonist and often worsted.' In the famous, still more Lucretian, *amor omnibus idem* passage that follows (242–83) there are further indications that Virgil has been browsing thereabouts in Aristotle. The wild boar at 255–7 who toughens his hide for battle by rubbing it against trees comes straight from Chapter 18. So does the statement in 266 that of all animals mares are the most lustful, the myth of their impregnation by the wind in 275, and the reference in 280–3 to the excretion called 'hippomanes' and its use for sorcery.

SHEEP AND GOATS

On sheep and goats Virgil has less to say, scarcely more than a hundred lines (and those partly dedicated to picturesque descriptions), for his plague soon spreads to animals at large.

Sheep were of particular importance in antiquity, since their wool was almost the only raw material for clothing. What the hair of goats was used for in camp and at sea was probably ropes, sacking, etc.—'ad usum nauticum et ad bellica tormenta', says Varro; but Virgil seems to have misunderstood this when he spoke of garments (*velamina*) for wretched sailors.[78] Whiteness was sought in sheep's wool to facilitate dyeing. It is therefore important, says Virgil (388), not to breed from a ram with a black tongue, otherwise the lambs may turn out blotchy.*

Goats have certain advantages. They produce twins more often, and they give more milk. They also fulfil the Golden Age ideal of returning home at sunset of their own accord (*ipsae memores*, 316); but this is an advantage only on open hillsides, for wherever there are cultivated trees or hedges they have to be tethered to prevent destructive nibbling (as we have been warned: 2. 196; 376 ff.). Their milk is the only milk to which Virgil pays atten-

---

* 313. Cf. Arist. *H.A.* 6. 19; Varro 2. 2. 4. Royds (p. 17) calls this a superstition, but I have the following information kindly supplied (February 1968) by Dr M. L. Ryder of the Dryden Field Laboratory, Roslin: 'The statement by Virgil is quite correct. Attention was drawn to this by M. L. Ryder, "Sheep of the ancient civilizations", *Wool Knowledge*, IV (12), 10–14 (1959), who referred to the correlation between a pigmented tongue and a pigmented fleece found in Karakul sheep by R. von Hildprandt, *Animal Breed Abs.* IV (1936), 314. More recently S. Skarman found the same association in Swedish Gotland sheep (*Svenska Faravelsför Tidskr.* XLIII (1963), 127–35).'

tion, though we are left to gather this casually from 'haedos' in 398, sheep having been the subject of the previous section (384–93).* Virgil seems much impressed by the perennial flow of goat's milk (309–10), and he indicates its quantity in a vivid phrase 'grandi superant vix ubere limen'—'their heavy udders scarcely clear the threshold' (317). Yield can be increased by salting fodder to induce drinking (394–7). In marked contrast to his tenderness about allowing calves their mother's milk, Virgil reports without comment that many goatherds put iron-spiked muzzles round the noses of their kids when they are to be weaned from their dams, who will then not let them suck. On the other hand particular emphasis is laid on feeding goats well in winter (320–1; 394–5).

The meaning of the next four lines has been much disputed:

> quod surgente die mulsere horisque diurnis
> nocte premunt; quod iam tenebris et sole cadente
> sub lucem exportant calathis (adit oppida pastor),
> aut parco sale contingunt hiemique reponunt.

It used to be assumed that all this refers to cheese. As Haverfield put it (Conington, 5th edn.): 'Cheesemaking. Virgil only glances at the subject. He presupposes (1) two milkings, morning and evening, (2) two kinds of cheese, one made quickly to be eaten at once and one made to keep by a longer process, and (3) two uses, home and sale.' But de Saint-Denis takes what is sent to town to be milk (Servius says 'cheese or milk'. 'Calathi' can be the bronze

---

* Richter (on 398) asserts categorically that the ancients nowhere bred sheep for their milk. This may be true of primary purpose, but the facts remain that Varro has to advise farmers not to milk sheep, since they then yield more wool and produce more lambs, or at least not for four months after lambing, which suggests that the practice existed (2. 2. 17); that he stated that sheep's milk is the most nourishing drink, above that of goats, though he ranked cheeses made from cow's, sheep's and goat's milk in that order for digestibility (2. 11. 1; 3); that Columella prescribed sheep's milk for the making of 'oxygala' (? cf. curds or yoghourt) (12. 8. 1); and that he asserts that shrub-trefoil (*cytisus*) makes ewes yield a very large quantity of milk (*De Arb.* 28); and finally that he writes: 'the sheep satisfies country people with abundance of cheese and milk...Indeed it provides a livelihood for some tribes who are without corn; hence most of the nomads and Getae are known as "Milk-drinkers"' (*R.R.* 7. 2. 1–2).

or earthenware jars enclosed in wicker still common in Mediterranean lands, cf. *Eclogue* 5. 71, as well as baskets or strainers). Richter agrees. There are two immediate uses: the day's yield is made into 'instant' cheese the same night, as it would not travel through the heat; the evening yield is kept through the cool of night and taken by the shepherd before daybreak to town. Alternatively this is treated with a modicum of salt and stored up for winter use. (Of course there is more to be done to it than that.) Varro distinguishes two types of cheese, 'soft and fresh' and 'dry and old' (2. 11. 3).

The ancient Italians kept sheep and goats within cotes in winter, even longer, it would seem, than our northern farmers.[79] Varro prescribes that these should be in a sheltered position, and open to the south-east, so that the morning sun as it rises may warm them, since the animals feel the cold acutely, particularly the goats. Virgil prefers them to face due south, and is followed in this by Columella.[80] They must be fumigated against snakes by burning cedar-wood or the gum called *galbanum*, a precept found also in Nicander's *Theriaca*. The floor must be strewn with straw and bracken, not only for warmth but for dryness, to prevent scab and foot-rot from developing.[*]

Varro has only a short, quite general, passage on diseases, their causes, symptoms and cures (2. 1. 21–3). Virgil characteristically takes one disease of sheep, scab, and deals with it at some length (440–69). He prescribes two things, dipping in fresh water (*dulcibus fluviis*) or shearing and then smearing the whole body with a mixture (not otherwise attested) of litharge, natural sulphur, pitch, softened wax, squills, hellebore and bitumen. The dipping must surely be intended as a prophylactic rather than as a cure, and the smearing is presented as an alternative to this (*aut*).[†] Cato in the corresponding passage seems to be speaking of prophylactics (96): 'To keep sheep from becoming scabrous:

---

[*] 297–9, 441–3; Nic. 52 Actually scab is caused by an acarian parasite, the *Dermatodectes ovis* (Royds, p. 22).

[†] Nevertheless the ingredients are appropriate to a *cure*, and it was taken as such by Columella, 7. 5. 5 ff. (See Richter's note.) Ointments with a basis of oil, sulphur, tar and hellebore have been used in modern times (Royds, p. 23).

take equal parts of old *amurca* well purified, water in which
lupines have been boiled, and dregs of good wine. Mix well.
First shear the sheep, then smear their whole body with this and
let them sweat for two or three days. Finally wash them in the
sea, or in artificial brine.'* Varro on the other hand prescribes
that sheep with scab should be treated *before* shearing, if need be;
otherwise rub them over afterwards on the same day with wine
and oil mixed with white wax and pig's fat—presumably again
as a prophylactic (2. 11. 6–7). It is possible that Virgil himself was
not clear whether he was prescribing a prophylactic or a cure.
The blood-letting from an artery in the foot (457–60) recalls a
different passage in Varro, in which as a last resort he prescribes
this, generally from the head however, for fever in animals of
whatever species (2. 1. 23).

The other parts of the Book belong to literature rather than
lore, and have already been dealt with as such—the pastoral idyll
of 322–38, the nomad shepherd of Libya and the herdsmen of
the Steppes (339–83), the Calabrian and other snakes (414–39),
and the great pestilence itself (474–566).

BEES

Knowledge of bees in antiquity was much restricted by lack of
the microscope and also of the glass observation-hive, though
opaquely transparent hives made of horn were not unknown—
indeed an Arab tradition credited Aristotle with one;[81] but few
branches of natural history attracted so much attention. Virgil
had at his disposal a number of authorities from Aristotle onwards, including Nicander's *Melissurgica* in verse. † The frequency

---

* Note that Virgil goes out of his way to prescribe *fresh* water.

† The chief extant sources are: Arist. *De Gen.* 3. 10, the conclusion of which is so
admirably scientific that it deserves quotation: 'the facts [*sc.* about bees'
generation] have not yet been sufficiently grasped; if ever they are, then it will
be due to observation rather than theories, and to theories only if what they
affirm agrees with observed facts'. Arist. *H.A.* 5. 21–3 is also important; still
more so the long section 9. 40, which is probably not by Aristotle himself but
by some observant bee-keeper who is however less scientific. There are many
other references scattered throughout the Aristotelian corpus. Varro has a long

(sixteen times) and accuracy of his references to bees in his other works, however, suggest that he had a special interest in them.

Virgil begins at the logical beginning, with seeking a site for the hive (8–32).* It must be sheltered from the wind (for bees can in fact be blown to the ground when heavily laden, and incapacitated from rising again).[82] It must be protected from lizards and birds that prey on bees—bee-eaters, chimney-swallows and the rest—presumably by systematic destruction of any nests established nearby. But the trampling down of flowers by farm-animals seems a hazard hard to avoid, since bees have to forage far afield.† At 113 Virgil suggests wider planting—'tecta serat late circum'; the neighbouring flowers of 30–2 could only supply a fraction of their needs, though they might serve to attract them to the water-supply. This can be either still or flowing, but should be shallow (*tenuis*), and should have willow branches laid athwart and islands of stones. These serve to enable the bees, not to rest or dry their wings, but to drink (here Varro is right and Virgil wrong). The purest water is necessary, both for making honey and for nourishing the young bees, to whom it is transported. We return again a little later (47–50) to the surroundings of the hive. Yew-trees, poisonous at least to horses, had a bad reputation also for bees (cf. *Eclogues* 9. 30), rightly or wrongly. Burnt crabs may seem an oddity, but they were applied to trees as a remedy for some diseases, and they certainly do give off an unpleasant odour, as do stagnant pools and slime (48–9). Can bees smell? Yes, acutely, through the eight terminal segments of their antennae.[83] Can they hear? To Aristotle it was a moot point. The answer appears to be: not in the way that men do: they cannot

section, 3. 16, on bees, also much used by Virgil. Later authorities (who may of course have used sources common to them and Virgil) are Columella, Book 9, Pliny, *N.H.* 11. 11–70, various passages in Aelian, and *Geoponica* 15. 2–9. See H. M. Fraser, *Beekeeping in Antiquity* (1931).

* The first section would be more orderly if 47–50 followed 32 and 45–6 followed 41. It is hard to see any reason why the lines are ordered as they are. There are several places in this Book, as we shall see, where order could be improved without apparent detriment by transposition.

† Pliny thought their range was about 60 paces (*N.H.* 11. 19), but it is really 2–3 kilometres, and can reach 7 in time of famine (Billiard, p. 394).

'hear' by means of vibrations carried through the air, but are very sensitive to vibrations of the ground.[84] Yet again, at 109–15, Virgil will return to the importance of safety and attractiveness in the surroundings, this time as an insurance against swarming-fever.

As for the hives themselves (33–46), they are made of cork-bark sewn together, or of woven osier like an old-fashioned straw 'skep'. The narrowness of the entrance is not, as Virgil says, to prevent extremes of heat and cold, but to keep out unwelcome visitors; yet such extremes are in fact dangerous, especially heat in southern latitudes, and the bees have their own system of thermostatic control based on vibration of wings. For the plastering of holes wax (38) is not used, but propolis is (*fucus*, 39), gathered from the buds of poplars and other trees (not from flowers, as Virgil, misled by Aristotle, alleges).* Bees are good at repairs, but the bee-master can help them by daubing the outside (with cow dung, perhaps mixed with clay) and a thin coat of leaves (45–6). The excavating bees introduced at 42 do not belong. They are wild bees—'solitary', 'mason' and 'carpenter' respectively—for honey bees do not behave so.† But at 2. 453 Virgil speaks of hollowed cork-trees and rotten ilex serving as hives for bees. Such are indeed their natural habitats, but the context suggests that men also appropriated these for agricultural purposes, as is still sometimes done.[85]

The hive established, we begin with spring and swarming (51–66). Actually the first flights are for cleaning, and the longer swarming is delayed the better. Bees do not, in fact, drink on the wing (54–5); indeed when confronted with a river they will go a long way, it is said, to find a bridge.[86] And when they sally out they do not seek water (*aquas dulcis*). But it is true that they seek *frondea tecta*, the branch of a tree, as Aristaeus' new ones do at 557. The medication of hives (62–3) to attract bees was

---

* See Richter on 38 ff. The plastering is to keep the hole narrow. *Oras* stands for εἰσόδους in Ps.-Aristotle (*H.A.* 9. 40. 624a), and it must mean entrances, as again at 188 where the usual form *ora* would not scan. This usage is almost unparalleled, but Richter cites 'carceris oras' from Ennius, *Ann.* 88.
† 'Si vera est fama' reflects a hesitation in Aristotle.

common in antiquity, and is said to have survived into modern times in some places.[87] Its value is doubtful; but more doubt has been thrown on Virgil's other precepts for attracting them,

> tinnitusque cie et Matris quate cymbala circum,

make clanging noises and shake Cybele's cymbals around.

Belief in this was as old as the myth of the Curetes, who thus collected the bees that fed the infant Zeus in the Dictaean cave (cf. 150-2). That bees are in some ways responsive to sound-waves we have seen, but not apparently in this way.* And incidentally Varro, who recommends rhythmic clashing of cymbals or clapping of hands for assembling scattered bees (3. 16. 7), says elsewhere (*ibid.* 30) that you can *frighten* them by clanging brass around.

The battle of the bees that follows (67–87) is a literary flight of fancy, and has already been dealt with as such (pp. 101–2). It is true that bees sometimes rob other hives, which naturally leads to conflicts. Virgil may also have taken some ideas from the behaviour of bees when swarming. The trumpet-calls (71) come from Varro (3. 16. 9); but the queen, who emits them, takes no part in battles save for single combat against a rival. If 'spiculaque exacuunt rostris' (74) has any basis in reality, it could be a misunderstanding of the cleansing of the antennae with the legs.[88] But the fact remains that bees do not fight on the wing. (The corresponding passage in Pliny, 11. 58, may simply have been prompted by Virgil.) The use of a handful of dust to allay the bees (86–7) is recommended by Varro for dealing with *swarming* (3. 16. 30); Haarhoff saw South African farm-boys use it for this.[89] A garden syringe has also sometimes been used. For fighting bees (not represented there as on the wing) Varro recommends a sprinkling of honey-water, or still better, mead, but this

---

* 'Quant au charivari que l'on fait souvent dans les campagnes en frappant sur les instruments de cuisine, il n'est d'aucune utilité' (Layens and Bouvier, cited by D'Hérouville, *À la campagne*, p. 87). 'Most authorities agree that the *tinnitus* and *cymbala*, the door-key and warming pan of today, make no difference at all' (Royds, p. 64).

is as a *distraction* (*ibid.* 35). The passage contrasting the two leaders and their followers, also already dealt with (pp. 179–81), is primarily a development of Varro 3. 16. 18, on different kinds of bee; but the contrast is heightened by hints borrowed from a neighbouring passage, on how to distinguish healthy from unhealthy bees when buying: the former are sleek (*nitidae*), the latter hairy and shaggy (*pilosae et horridae*)—'ut pulverulentae', Varro adds, thus suggesting the odd simile of the traveller's dusty gob (97–8).[90]

I have left aside so far the question of kings and queens, though we have met 'reges' already at 21 and again at 68.[91] The ancients generally referred to the most conspicuous bee in the masculine. Xenophon usually does so, though occasionally he says ἡ ἡγεμών (which may, of course, simply be short for ἡ ἡγουμένη μέλιττα, in which case it is of no significance). The only other exception is a passage in Aristotle (*H.A.* 5. 21), where he says that some people call the rulers 'mothers' from an idea that they bear or generate bees, that bees do copulate, and that the drones are male whereas the others are female. These unnamed authorities were not vindicated until the seventeenth century, when the Dutch naturalist Swammerdam (1637–80) ascertained that the 'queen' is really the mother, and no ruler but a timid prisoner (and his great work was not published until 1752). Virgil's ruthless prescription for coping with 'swarming-fever' (103–8), to pull off the wings of the leaders, comes strangely from him; for although Columella says 'spoliandus est alis,' other ancient authorities require only the clipping of one wing.[92]

The Corycian gardener is only incidentally a bee-master (139–41), though he serves to emphasise that Virgil is envisaging throughout a smallholder's sideline, not a commercial enterprise under a *mellarius* such as Varro depicts; but at 148 we return to the natural history of bees, and come to their social life. 'Solae' (153, 155) overlooks the wasp, and the ant, that proverbial hoarder for the winter; but the life of the beehive is certainly one of the most intricate products of evolution. The division of labour (158 ff.) is a fact, but the same bee specialises successively in different tasks. Virgil's details (158–69, 174–83), partly at least borrowed from predecessors, are not correct, any more than Shakespeare's (*Henry V*, I, ii, 183 ff.). Age is the determining factor.* Provisioning is actually carried out by the older bees (not 'minores', as Virgil says, following Ps.-Aristotle); and the building operations (160–2, 178–9), though not confined to a particular group, are actually more often performed by the young. 'Educunt fetus' (163) is a myth.[93] Since Virgil apparently shared the belief that honey was gathered from plants, 'nectare' in line 164 must be an elegant variation for 'honey', not the liquid gathered by bees which we call 'nectar' and which is not turned into honey until it has been deposited in the cells.† The sentries of line 165 are genuine, their duty being to repel intruders;[94] but Aristotle having said that bees can foretell the weather (and all have this faculty), Virgil decided to assign meteorology to these sentries. Some think he is also allotting them the other non-specialist duties of taking burdens from in-coming bees and driving out the drones (these are actually either expelled or killed within the hive by the workers after the swarming-season); but Nettleship defended by parallels the meaning 'alii . . . alii' for 'aut...aut' (167). Bees do not return late at night (180)—they are seldom out after dark. Whether they sleep or not is doubtful: in large hives at least the work goes on all night, and the hum of ventilation can be heard (*siletur*, 189, could only refer to a small one).[95] The false idea, taken from Ps.-Aristotle (*H.A.* 9. 40. 626B), that bees ballast themselves with stones in high winds (194–6) may have arisen from observation of cleansing processes in which they carry dead larvae or pupae out of the hive, or possibly of mason-bees at work.

It is not surprising that the ancients were ignorant of the way in which bees are reproduced. In the first place they did not realise

---

* Bees are, however, very versatile. They respond to the needs of the hive, their glands developing accordingly; and some are regular maids-of-all-work (Von Frisch, *The Dancing Bees*, ch. 7).

† Varro however says 'foris pascuntur, intus opus faciunt' (3. 16. 5). It was a moot point whether bees gathered honey itself or only the substances for making it.

that what they called the leader was really the mother; and even after Swammerdam the *method* of fertilisation was unknown, being discovered only in 1791 by F. Huber. For anatomical reasons this can only occur in flight. The young queen soars out for its honeymoon pursued by the whole crowd of drones, and is impregnated by the winner (if one doomed to die in the act can so be called) after a chase high in the air. At 197 ff. Virgil chooses to affirm that bees gather their offspring from flowers. This was only one of the hypotheses mentioned by Aristotle (*H.A.* 5. 21. 553A) which happened to suit his book, whereas it was well known to be a moot point whether copulation was not somehow involved.* The life of the individual bee is much shorter than the seven years which Virgil, following Aristotle (*H.A.* 5. 22. 554B), allows as a maximum (207). Dzierzon discovered in 1855 that a worker lives only for about six weeks, unless she is born in the autumn and survives through the winter. Even a queen sees five years at the most.[96] That the hive will perish if the queen dies (212 ff.) is true, unless there is a worker grub under three days old to be reared in her place; but Virgil gives his account anthropomorphic colouring (see p. 179 n.).

After the brief but soaring interlude on the divine nature of bees we return (229) to the harvesting of honey. The text and interpretation of this section are in some doubt. It is not clear what precautions you have to take before driving the bees away with smoke† (229–30):

> prius haustu sparsus aquarum
> *ora fove* fumosque manu praetende sequaces.

Accepting this well-attested reading, I agree with F. R. Dale's interpretation: 'Take some water in your hands and protect your face by sprinkling water over it' (to quench any sparks from the

---

* Col. 9. 2. 4. On all this see Royds, pp. 82 ff. 'Apibus *fetis*' (139) can hardly be reconciled with the view Virgil adopts here. The belief that young bees were gathered from flowers is still found in Moses Rusden, *Further Discovery of Bees* (1689). Virgil says remarkably little about the rôle of the drones.

† That used to be the purpose. Today the object is to frighten the bees into gorging themselves so that they are easier to handle (Royds, p. 88).

'trailing', or perhaps 'searching', smoke).* We should expect to
hear at once of the bees' sharp reaction, and Schrader may well
have been right in transposing 236–8 to follow 230. Then 239 ff.,
referring to provision for winter, will also follow on naturally
from the lines about seasons for harvesting. This is to take place
in May and November.† The best honey is that which can be
extracted without interference, the remainder being squeezed out
artificially in presses (cf. 101, 140–1).

In the next section the ideas are again not in logical order in the
text as we have it. They seem to be as follows. You should not let
your bees grow idle, but keep them busy rebuilding their shattered
homes (248–50). But if you are afraid they may die in winter
from malnutrition (239), or shrink from inflicting the distress
that wholesale destruction will cause them (240),‡ you must at
least fumigate your hive with aromatic herbs and cut out empty
cells, otherwise you will find them harbouring pests such as (?)
star-lizards, (?) woodlice, newts, drones (thought of as intruders),
hornets, woodworms and spiders (241–7).

As in the parallel passages in Book 3 (414 ff., 440 ff.), the

* C.R. (1955), pp. 14–15. He cites *Aen.* 12. 420, 'fovit ea vulnus lympha' for
'fovere' in the sense of 'treat' by application. Interpretation has been prejudiced
by the use of 'ora fovent' at 2. 135 to mean '*rinse* their *mouths*'. 'Sparsus' here
hardly fits in with that, whether you suppose, with Billiard (p. 410) that the
water is to be squirted out again at the entrance to the hive to allay the bees
(he reads '*ore* fove' with some MSS and Servius), or to prevent foulness of the
breath (bees dislike strong odours), which water cannot in fact do. The
solemnity of the preceding paragraph has however led some to prefer the
reading '*ore fave*' (cf. *Aen.* 5. 71), a ritual demand for silence before approaching the sacred hive. They draw attention to the grandiose words 'augustam'
and 'thensauri(s)'. A passage in Columella (9. 14. 3, after Hyginus,) might
seem to support this view; but it also mentions both washing and keeping the
breath pure, and may simply be an attempt to do justice to all the meanings
that might be implicit in this passage of Virgil. It is more like Virgil to
return abruptly to commonplace things (see p. 88); and there is a variant
reading 'angustam' for 'augustam' (oddly not mentioned by Richter in his
apparatus, though it supports his interpretation). It would mean 'close-packed'.
† Ps.-Aristotle also postulates two harvests (*H.A.* 9. 40. 626 b) and modern practice
extends to two in countries where there are enough flowers (Billiard, p. 411);
but Varro (3. 16. 34) and Didymus (*Geop.* 15. 5. 1) speak of an extra one, in
September.
‡ Movable frames, which limit the damage, are a modern invention.

mention of pests leads on naturally to diseases. These are treated
in a straggling paragraph probably intended to recall Lucretius.*
Bees are indeed subject to epidemics. They do carry out their
dead (255–6), or at least throw them out, for some have the duty
of cleaning out all débris. But the malady here described has not
been diagnosed, and may be incapable of diagnosis, like the plague
in Book 3.[97] The 'sonus acrior' of line 260 at any rate seems to be
a dramatic fiction, as of groaning. The remedies are no doubt
selected from the same source or sources as the symptoms,† but
when Virgil dwells on one item, as he often does at the end of a
list, he seems to be drawing on his own experience. His description of the sort of michaelmas daisy the countrymen call 'amellus'
(our *Aster Amellus*) is unique in his work, and he seems even to
be searching for botanical terms to suit his purpose. He associates
it with the river Mella, which flows not very far from Mantua,
and nearer still to Cremona, in his childhood region. He may well
have seen the shepherds he mentions gathering this flower on the
sides of its upper valley after grazing.[98]

And so finally to *Bugonia*. It was attested by all ancient
authorities,[99] with the significant exception of Aristotle, that
bees could be generated from a dead ox properly treated. Virgil's
prescription (295 ff.) may be summarised as follows: 'Choose an
enclosed space, and build in it a narrow chamber having, beneath
a tiled roof, four walls facing the four winds and pierced with
windows admitting light which (for some reason unexplained)
must be slanting. Then find a two-year-old bull-calf, block up its
nostrils and mouth while it is still alive, and beat it to death without breaking the hide. Shut up the carcase in the chamber,
surrounded by branches of fresh thyme and spurge-laurel. Bees
will be generated in due course, through a larval stage, from the
putrefying flesh.' The blocking of the natural orifices would be

---

* Unvirgilian rhythm 'apibus quoque nostris' at end of opening line 251;
Lucretian-sounding line, 253; long parenthesis, 253–63; verbal reminiscence
255, 'luce carentum' (cf. Lucr. 4. 39); triple comparison, 261–3 (cf. Lucr.
6. 142 ff.).

† ? Aristomachus, source of Hyginus, whom Columella has before him at *R.R.*
9. 13.

intended to keep in the life principle of the calf, which could thus pass into the emergent bees.

But bees in fact hate carrion, and the whole idea is chimerical. How did it arise? Two types of explanation have been advanced. The first is that bees were observed rising from dried carcases, in which they have been known to nest in countries where trees are scarce, as in parts of Egypt, where Virgil firmly locates the origin of the artificial process, and in other parts of Africa, whence the idea found its way into Mago.[100] The second is that it arose from the remarkable resemblance to the bee of the drone-fly, *Eristalis tenax.*[101] This does lay its eggs in decomposing carcases, on which its maggots feed. But the mystery remains: how did the elaborate, partly ritualistic, prescription achieve such wide currency, and be freely recommended as late as the seventeenth century, when any experiment would have discredited it?[102] Perhaps, as Olivier de Serres reckoned, it was always cheaper to buy new bees than to sacrifice a calf.[103]

X · The 'Georgics' in After Times*

Some time after the death in 27 B.C. of Cornelius Gallus a freedman of Atticus named Q. Caecilius Epirota, who had been devoted to Gallus, made an innovation in his school at Rome by introducing into the syllabus 'Vergilium et alios poetas novos'. At first sight this might seem to be a response to the publication of the *Georgics*, but the phrase used by Domitius Marsus to describe him, 'tenellorum nutriculam vatum', suggests that 'poetae novi' is to be understood in the restricted sense of 'Neoteroi' and that Virgil would be represented by the *Eclogues*.[1] In Quintilian's time reading began with Homer and Virgil.[2] The needs of schools activated scholar-critics, and from Hyginus, the freedman and librarian of Augustus, to Servius and Philargyrius four centuries later a stream of ever more detailed commentaries issued. From now on 'an educated man was a man who knew his Virgil'.[3]

Meanwhile the *Georgics* came to be reckoned also among the agricultural treatises. To Columella, the Spaniard from Cadiz who had migrated to the region of Rome, there to write in the early sixties of our era the fullest and most systematic of these treatises, he was 'vates optimus', whom he cites thirty or forty times in his twelve books. 'Si verissimo vati sicut oraculo crediderimus', he says reverentially.[4] Sometimes it is clear that he uses him simply to grace his pedestrian subject with literary flavour, as when he quotes five charming lines from *Georgics* 2 (204–8) to adorn the precept that the farmer, like the sailor, must observe the constellations, or as many as ten from the passage about feeding flocks in Book 3 (322 ff.), which must have struck him no less than it strikes us as particularly delightful.[5] When he came

---

* An earlier version of this chapter was delivered as a lecture to the Virgil Society and the London Branch of the Classical Association, on 21 January 1967, and summarised in the *Proceedings of the Virgil Society* for 1966–7, pp. 22–5. For literature on the *Georgics* in after times see Appendix VII.

in Book 10 to the subject of gardens, which Virgil had left 'aliis
post me memoranda', encouraged by his friend Silvinus, to whom
his work was addressed, he blossomed into hexameters. This he
only ventured 'in accordance with the wishes of that greatly to be
revered poet, spurred by his almost divine influence (*quasi
numen*)'.[6]

In this spirit of reverence he will report Virgil's view among
others where authorities disagree, as on the question which
direction it is best for a sloping vineyard to face.[7] In recommending selection of vineshoots to prevent degeneration, he insists that
this principle is an ancestral tradition in all branches of agriculture,
but gives Virgil the credit of being the only written authority for
it.[8] Citing him with others for the practice of *Bugonia*, he side-
steps the duty of making up his mind on its validity by saying
that he agrees with Celsus' most prudent view that, as bees
seldom die in such quantities, there is no need to discuss it;[9] and
similarly he says it is unnecessary for a practical farmer to decide
between Virgil, who affirms that bees pick up the heirs of their
race from flowers, and others who say that they produce them by
copulation like other animals. But he goes out of his way to
defend him for stating that mares can become pregnant by wind,
this being extremely well-known as occurring on the Holy
Mountain in his native Spain.*

Seneca has occasion in his eighty-sixth letter to criticise Virgilian husbandry. 'Not to mention all the other things', he has
detected him in error that very day; for whereas it says at
Georgics I. 215-16,

> vere fabis satio; tum te quoque, medica, putres
> accipiunt sulci, et milio venit annua cura,

spring is the time for sowing beans; then too the crumbling furrows
receive you, Median clover, and the annual care of the millet comes
round,

---

* 6. 27. 5-7. G. 3. 269-75; cf. Varro 2. 1. 19. Columella was rather gullible. He
tells us (10. 357 ff.) that the best way to get rid of caterpillars is to get a men-
struating girl to walk three times round the garden:

> volvitur in terram distorto corpore campe.

he has just seen simultaneously, late in June, men harvesting beans and sowing millet. But he adds the sensible comment that Virgil's aim was to delight readers, not to instruct farmers.*

The elder Pliny, scientific at least in intention, was not so tolerant. He pays lipservice to Virgil as a poet, 'praecelsissimus vates', but goes out of his way to correct him as an agriculturalist, particularly on matters concerning horses (with which the poet does seem to have been less familiar), bees (which he was concerned to use for symbolic purposes), vines and soils.† A few examples with regard to soils, where the criticisms are direct and obvious, will suffice. At G. 2. 217 ff. Virgil, describing a certain type of soil *quae tenuem exhalat nebulam*, etc., says that it is good for vines, olives, pasture and ploughing, and instances the Campanian land round 'dives Capua' and that which lies below Vesuvius (perhaps thinking of his own farm). Pliny (17. 25) denies that the same soil is good for both crops and trees, and continues 'nec pulla, *qualem habet Campania*, ubique optima *vitibus*, aut *quae tenues exhalat nebulas*'. Just previously (215) Virgil has suggested that chalky soil is a mere breeding-ground for snakes, and before that (180 ff.) that clay is good for olives but a rich, lush soil for vines. Pliny, on the contrary, knows of places where chalk and clay are considered best of all for vines (*ibid.*). And so it goes on. Virgil remarks at 248 ff. that wet soil produces the tallest vegetation, and that rich soil sticks to the fingers. Pliny comments (17. 26-7): 'nec semper aquosa est terra cui proceritas herbarum, non, Hercules!, magis quam pinguis, adhaerens digitis, quod in argillis arguitur'.[10]

---

* *Ep.* 86. 16. Even Columella has to admit that (faba) 'seritur pessime vere', 2. 10. 9. But in fact spring sowing of beans was a peculiar feature of the Po valley (Pliny, *N.H.* 18. 120), so Virgil may here be simply reporting what he knew from childhood.

† R. T. Bruère, in a most useful article (*C.Ph.* 1956, pp. 228-46), has collected and commented on all the passages in Pliny's *Natural History* which refer, explicitly or implicitly, to Virgil; and although occasionally his alleged echoes fade out on closer inspection (e.g. on p. 229), and occasionally he goes too far (e.g. *G.* 1. 204-7 is apparently overlooked on p. 242), he does substantiate the existence in Pliny of what P. Lejay had called in the introduction to his edition of the *Georgics* (1914; p. xxxvii) 'une attitude de sourde hostilité à l'égard de Virgile'.

That 'Hercules!' shows an impatience which betrays itself on other occasions. Scornfully recalling the fantastic instances of grafting different species of trees which Virgil cheerfully reports at 2. 69–72, Pliny includes elm on cherry, a false reminiscence of 2. 17–18.[11] Commenting on Virgil's 'Naryciaeque picis' (G. 2. 438), he says with evident sarcasm 'Asia picem Idaeam maxime probat, Graecia Piericam, Vergilius Naryciam'. Actually Virgil was using 'pix' to mean pitch-pine wood, not pitch itself, as Pliny hastily supposed; nor was he saying that Narycian was best, only that those woods were good to look at. And as for 'Narycian', this was a learned epithet referring to Locri in Bruttium (originally a colony of Naryx in Ozolian Locri: Aen. 3. 399), and Pliny has just said himself that the best pitch in Italy comes from Bruttium.[12]

It is clear that the natural historian was irked by the authority with which less critical minds, awed by the greatness of Virgil's poetry, invested his technical precepts, an attitude reflected in the language even of Columella. But there is little to suggest that in schools and among the reading public in general the *Georgics* did not share in the supreme reputation enjoyed by the *Aeneid* and *Eclogues* throughout classical antiquity.* He was still to Macrobius 'one who was never involved in any scientific error'.[13]

THE MIDDLE AGES

There is no need to enlarge here on the general reputation of Virgil over the millennium that stretched from A.D. 400 to 1400. In the words of Comparetti, 'The name of Virgil acquired in Europe a significance well-nigh equivalent to that of civilisation itself'.[14] His peak period was that of which Charlemagne is the

---

* O. Ribbeck lists at the end of the first volume of his edition the passages in the *Georgics* imitated by later classical writers. In Macrobius (c. 400) the totals of references to the three works are roughly proportionate to their lengths. One slight reservation: the scribblings on the walls of Pompeii, Herculaneum and Stabiae (*C.I.L.* vol. IV, suppl., index XII), probably made mostly by schoolboys in the period between the eruptions of A.D. 63 and 79, include ten from the *Aeneid*, two from the *Eclogues* and none from the *Georgics* (Comparetti, p. 26 n. 9); but the sample is perhaps too small to be significant.

centre. After that he had a rival in Horace, and later in Ovid. But he alone was both widely and constantly read, and indeed sometimes referred to simply as 'the poet'. What we have here to consider is, whether the *Georgics* maintained its position relatively to the *Aeneid* and *Eclogues*; for when his reputation is spoken of in the big secondary sources on this period—Manitius, Comparetti, Sandys, Raby, Curtius, Laistner, Bolgar, to name only a few— no distinction is generally made between the three works. In considering the frequency of borrowings one must bear in mind first the kinship of subject matter (undoubtedly, for instance, a poet eulogising an emperor, or writing a verse-biography of a saint or bishop, will find more to his purpose in the *Aeneid* than in the other two works); and second, the proportionate length of the *Eclogues*, *Georgics* and *Aeneid*, which is roughly $1:2\frac{1}{2}:10$.

The medieval passion for schematism evolved out of Donatus' commentary and the idea that the three works represented the three canonical styles a graphic scheme of concentric circles known as the 'Rota Virgilii', thus described by Curtius:

The biographical sequence of Virgil's works was regarded by the Middle Ages as a hierarchy grounded in the nature of things—a hierarchy not only of poetical genres, but also of social ranks (shepherd, farmer, soldier) and of kinds of style (plain, middle, grand). It extended to the corresponding trees (beech, fruit-trees, laurel or oak), locales (pasture, ploughland, castle or town), implements (crook, plough, sword) and animals (sheep, cow, horse).[15]

The three works were also held to symbolise respectively man's developmental stages (pastoral, agricultural, martial), and his modes of life (contemplative, sensual, active).[16] Here the *Georgics* is at least accorded proportionate status, in the twelfth and thirteenth centuries.

It is when one begins to analyse that differences appear, and even when all due allowances are made the *Georgics* does seem to recede to some extent. Take manuscripts. Most libraries contained at least one complete Virgil, but there seem to have been fewer *separate* texts of the *Georgics* than of the *Aeneid*, let alone the *Eclogues*.* From the catalogues covered by Manitius the following totals may be extracted, to give some comparative idea:

Virgil work	12th cent.	13th cent.	14th cent.
Complete(?)	36	7	13
Aeneid	9	11	7
Georgics	9	4	–
Eclogues	15	12	8

One receives a similar impression from the secondary sources. 'To know only the *Aeneid*', says Curtius, 'is not to know Virgil. The influence of his *Eclogues* on later times is hardly less than that of his epic.' And again: 'From the first century of the Empire to the time of Goethe all study of Latin literature began with the *First Eclogue*. It is not too much to say that anyone unfamiliar with that short poem lacks one key to the literary tradition of Europe.'[17] No mention of the *Georgics*. Elsewhere he deals with the rhetorical descriptions of nature in the Middle Ages, the so-called *locus amoenus*. Virgil's contribution is almost entirely through the *Eclogues* and *Aeneid*.† 'The picture of nature in the *Georgics*', he says, 'would require an analysis which we cannot permit ourselves to undertake.'[18] This is tantalising; for if by analysis he meant an examination of its influence in the Middle Ages, one cannot help wondering whether there is much evidence for it.

What about those great farming estates that belonged to the monasteries? Did these evoke no poetry on the lines of the *Georgics* from the numerous monastic poets? To begin with,

---

* M. Manitius, *Handschriften antiker Autoren* etc., ed. K. Manitius (1935), pp. 47–55. R. R. Bolgar, *The Classical Heritage and its Beneficiaries* (1954) extracts the figures (p. 430). 'The popularity of Virgil was universal. As a school author his name appears in every list of such books. The *Eclogues* and *Georgics* are named in the catalogues almost as often as the *Aeneid*, but the large number of citations of Virgil without naming any particular work probably refer to the *Aeneid*' (J. S. Beddie, 'Ancient Classics in the Mediaeval Libraries', *Speculum*, 1930, pp. 3–20). In the fifteenth century even the Jagellonian Library at Cracow had no *Georgics*, only *Aeneid* and *Eclogues*.

† *Roman. Forsch.* (1942), pp. 219–56. The sole exception here is a description of a garden by Baudry of Bourgueil which echoes *G.* 4. 30 ff. as well as *Ecl.* 2. 45, *Copa* 10 and *Culex* 390; *ibid.* p. 233. Text in P. Abrahams' ed. pp. 191–4.

though it is difficult to generalise about conditions over a thousand-year span, which might also vary from Order to Order, it is by no means clear that much farm-work was done by clerical monks. Of the original members of the Benedictine community at Monte Cassino very few were clerics or in orders.[19] Though Cassiodorus recommended his monks to study the ancient Scriptores Rei Rusticae ('in a Christian spirit'), he wished farm-work to be carried out by the humbler brethren unsuitable for copying manuscripts.[20] David Knowles concludes that, while it is clear that on occasions the whole community would go out to the fields, and that individuals had charge of scattered fields and plots, the heavy normal work was done by *coloni*, and the majority of the community probably found its natural employment within the sheds and offices of the monastery buildings.[21] In French and German lands social and economic conditions gave the work of the fields to serfs. There were of course exceptions. Knowles tells us that life in Benedict Biscop's abbeys of Wearmouth (674) and Jarrow (688), including even heavy agricultural labour, is nearer in spirit to the life of Monte Cassino in St Benedict's day than is any continental example of which anything is known. But 'by the time of Charlemagne monks had come to be classed as the lettered, and to be set on a level with all clerics. Even earlier, manual work, and above all, agricultural work, ceased to be universal, or even normal.'[22] By the ninth century monastic customaries prescribed that when work in the fields or garden was to be performed in common, special notice was to be given, and the monks proceeded to it reciting psalmody, which continued during their work.[23] Thus by the time of the first revival of Latin poetry, in the monasteries of the Carolingian age, agriculture is unlikely to have been much in the minds of the poets.

In the post-Carolingian era the early Cistercians did work on the land; but hired labour had been permitted from the beginning, and early in the twelfth century lay brothers were introduced, the choir monks being too much occupied with their devotional duties. As the Order spread, the vocation of lay brother came to be treated as an end in itself. In the thirteenth and fourteenth centuries, when farming became more profitable, though monks still rarely worked themselves, they did superintend with interest the exploitation of their lands,* and they did probably use the prose Scriptores Rei Rusticae.[24] A remarkable translation of the fourteen books of Palladius into Middle English verse survives in a manuscript in Colchester Castle. It was commissioned by Humphrey, Duke of Gloucester, and made in 1420, probably by a local monk.[25]

But whether the monks used the *Georgics* to any appreciable extent is more doubtful. In the twenty-six books *De Animalibus* of Albertus Magnus (1193–1280) there appears to be no mention of Virgil; and there are only two mentions in the seven books of his *De Vegetabilibus*.[26] The thirteenth-century treatise on husbandry of Petrus Crescentius refers to Varro, Columella and Palladius throughout, Virgil (unless I am mistaken) only in the short section on bees, and there without quotation.† There is nothing of him in the English treatises of the same century by Robert Grosseteste and Walter of Henley,[27] the last of which held the field in England until the sixteenth century, whereas on the Continent Crescentius' treatise was translated into Italian, French and German in the second half of the fifteenth.

As for the medieval poets, it is unlikely that in any century the classical versifiers of the monasteries, a Raban or a Baudry or a Froumond, were concerned with agriculture, any more than those of the cathedral or court schools, or a busy bishop like Hildebert of Lavardin.‡

---

* D. Knowles, *The Religious Orders in England*, 1 (1948), p. 32. 'The Abbots of Peterborough and Chertsey would have found, we may think, the company of Turnip Townshend and Coke of Norfolk in other centuries more congenial than that of the mystic or philosopher in their own' (*ibid.* p. 47). See further Slicher van Bath, pp. 153 ff.

† Lived 1230–1320; a lawyer of Bologna who took up farming at the age of seventy. His *Opus Ruralium Commodorum sive de Agricultura* in twelve books was the first printed agricultural book (Augsburg, 1471).

‡ Hildebert did once recall, in a few highly mannered lines, the rich estate he had left to go into exile (? real or symbolic). Migne, *Patrologia. Cursus Completus. Series Latina* (1844–55), CLXXI, col. 1418.

There is one partial exception of particular interest. In the first half of the ninth century Walafrid Strabo, a monk who was to become Abbot of Reichenau on Lake Constance, composed his *De Cultu Hortorum*, commonly known as *Hortulus*.* It is a poem of 444 lines, written in Latin which is nearly that of the first century B.C., and in hexameters which are nearly those of Virgil. It has echoes of Virgilian phrasing; and more remarkable, it shows an appreciation of quite *recherché* devices of Virgilian artistry. Thus Walafrid has sensed that a word occupying the sixth foot, if preceded by punctuation, should be either anaphoric or correlative (51). His first paragraph culminates in a Golden Line (35):

> inlita ferventi creverunt tela veneno.

He realises that it is effective to hold up a drastic verb to fall at the beginning of the next line (46):

> umbricolis habitata cubilia talpis
> diruo.

He uses synaloepha expressively to emphasise the clinging of ivy round an elm (102):

> ac velut ulm(um) heder(a) implicuit cum frondibus altam,

and consonantal *u*-sounds expressively to suggest the hollowing out of a gourd (146):

> uasorum poterit, uasto dum uiscera uentre...

There can be no doubt that the first inspiration for the *Hortulus* came from the *Georgics*,† and the monkish gardener does the dirty work *ipse manu* like a good *colonus*. And yet, apart from artistic details, it is quite different. To begin with, Virgil notoriously decided that he must give gardens a miss, so the

---

* A fine edition, with translation by Raef Payne and commentary by Wilfrid Blunt, both of Eton College, was produced in 1966 by the Hunt Botanical Library of Pittsburgh.

† Walafrid also knew well Columella's Book 10, on gardens, the one which is in hexameter verse. His knowledge of the classics was exceptional for his time.

subject-matter is non-Virgilian.* Again, the *Hortulus* is far from being an organic, symphonic construction, nor has it much variety, nor is it closely descriptive. It consists, apart from the proem, of twenty-seven short poems on the uses of various plants, mainly vegetables. Ulterior meaning comes in only at the end, where the lily and the rose are treated as symbols of faith and martyrdom, leading up to a doxology to the Virgin.

It has been held that this is the only poem from the fourth to the thirteenth century which can be considered as georgic in subject-matter.[28] This is nearly true, especially if what is being looked for is something didactic in form. But there is another claimant to which I should like to draw attention. Our childhood poem of the months,

> January brings the snow,
> Makes our feet and fingers glow...

is a member of a very long line, stretching back to the *Monosticha de Mensibus* and *Disticha de Mensibus* attributed to Ausonius.[29] Descriptions of seasons go back even further, to the *Rhetores Graeci*;[30] and a poetic example is to be found in an excursus in Nonnus' epic *Dionysiaca*, 11. 488–521. Now a poem has survived which deals with the months in greatly extended form. It is by Wandalbert, a monk of Prüm in Lorraine, who was born in 813, and the scene is the Rhineland. It extends to 366 hexameters. The title is *De Mensium XII Nominibus, Signis, Culturis Aerisque Qualitatibus.*† The account of each month begins with the origin of its name and the constellations associated with it. This may have diverted the attention of casual readers from the fact that a much longer section follows in each case detailing the rural

---

* Garden-poems became quite common down the ages in spite of this. Already in the second half of the sixth century Fortunatus had written an elegiac poem on a garden near Paris kept up by the widow of King Childebert I, who had planted apple-trees in it *multo amore*. The only reminiscence of Virgil is 'hic ver perpetuum'. F. J. E. Raby, *A History of Secular Latin Poetry in the Middle Ages* (2nd edn. 1957), I, 134.

† *Monumenta Germaniae Historica: Poetae Latini Aevi Carolini*, II, ed. E. Dümmler, 604–16. No mention in Raby; but see M. Manitius, *Geschichte der lateinischen Literatur des Mittelalters*, I (1911), 557–60 for Wandalbert in general, with a brief reference to this poem.

activities of the month. These sections not only have affinities with the *Georgics* as descriptive poetry: they echo them freely and unmistakably, and more frequently than they echo the *Aeneid* or any other poem, which is exceptional.

Since this poem deserves to be better known I will give a substantial excerpt, the closing lines 336–66: December and Epilogue):

> Hoc etiam (*sc.* mense) hiberno terras urente rigore
> maxima nox modicae causantes munera lucis
> agricolas fovet, oblitos tandemque laboris
> ingratosque sibi blandus sopor inrigat artus.
> nec tamen imbrifero desunt sua munera mensi
> nec gelidis cogit penitus cessare sub auris
> tempus et in faciem tellus contecta nivosam.
> tum quoque cum pluviis campus ventoque madescit,
> vomere glaeba iacens[31] sulcanda est, hordea demum
> qua serere aut laetum cupit exercere legumen
> agricola, immundumque fimum iactare per agros
> tum licet. at cum terra hebeti torpore rigescit
> multa domi tamen et tectis properare sub ipsis
> mox vacat, algentis relevant quae frigora brumae.
> retibus hinc varias pelagi prensare volucres[32]
> aut igni aut sonitu per campos fallere, sive
> lentandis usu pedicas aptare repertum;
> amnibus hinc etiam piscosis ponere crates
> vimineas,[33] densosque ad litora figere fasces
> qua vada demisso tranquillant flumine cursum,
> inventum, facilem capiant ut retia praedam.
> hoc sub mense sues pasta iam glande madentes
> distenti et plenam monstrantes ventre saginam[34]
> caedere et ad tepidum mos est suspendere fumum
> terga, prius salis fuerint cum sparsa madore.
>
> Bis sena hos cultus renovant vertigine menses
> huncque modum et morem sibi Gallica rura retentant:
> quem breviter signans digessi carmine, lector,
> Wandalbertus ego, hortatu compulsus amici,
> dulcia me Hreni quo tempore litora alebant[35]
> maxima Agrippinae veteris quis moenia praesunt.

Now too, when winter's parching cold has gripped
The land and night is longest, farmers seize
The excuse of shorter daylight to enjoy
Rest, and at length forgetful of their toil
Give up the aching burden of their limbs
To sleep's perfusive balm. Yet even so
The month of rain has tasks that are its own,
Nor does the season with its icy blasts
And snows that veil the face of earth compel
Total cessation. Even when the fields
With windy showers are sodden, farmers then
Should furrow with the plough the lumpish clods
Where barley later or luxuriant beans
They hope to sow and rear; and foul manure
Can then be tossed about over the land.
But when the soil lies rigid and inert,
Free to get on with much indoors at home
The numbing cold of winter they relieve.
Hence came experienced skill to catch in nets
The varied sea-birds, or with fire and noise
To cheat birds of the field, or set up snares
To catch them;* hence in rivers full of fish
To lower screens of wicker openwork
They learnt; and to the banks, where gently flows
The stream in shallows, closely fitted lurk
Bundles with nets to catch an easy prey.
Swine in this month now sleek from acorn-feed,
Full-swoll'n with pendulous belly to be seen,
Men slaughter, and hang up the chines in smoke
Well saturated first in salty brine.

Such tasks through twelve revolving months they ply,
Such ways of life the Gallic fields preserve,
Which briefly noting, reader, in my song,
I, Wandalbert, recorded, by a friend
Pressed and encouraged, while I passed my days
Along the pleasant margin of the Rhine
Crowned by the ancient ramparts of Cologne.

Some of this is clearly of literary inspiration. For instance, the
variae pelagi volucres were probably outside Wandalbert's real

* I have not been able to construe 'lentandis'.

experience. The general idea for this December passage could come from *Georgics* 1. 287–310 (compare 305 there,

> sed tamen et quernas glandes tum stringere tempus

and

> nec tamen imbrifero desunt sua munera mensi,

introducing in either case a list of winter occupations after a passage on relaxation). But another passage in mind is 1. 125–59 (the arts and skills that Jupiter's dispensation induced).

> *Multa* domi tamen et tectis *properare* sub ipsis
> tum licet

echoes a further passage (1. 259 ff.) on what can be done in rainy weather:

> *multa* forent quae mox caelo *properanda* sereno
> maturare datur.

It is noteworthy how an echo will be awakened simply by the use of a word in the same position in the line: *fallere* (cf. 1. 139)... *inventum* (cf. *ibid.* 140). The weather-sign (1. 400)

> *immundi* meminere sues *iactare* maniplos

seems to have generated the phrase here

> *immundumque* fimum *iactare* per agros,

which is in quite a different context, though a few lines below we do meet pigs sleek with acorns as at G. 2. 520. This monk knew his *Georgics* backwards. Yet there are features which appear not to be borrowed; and indeed the poem as a whole has been credited with reflecting typical peasant life of mid-Rhineland in the ninth century.[36]

The poem has a further interest, for the history of art. From about the same date we have one written near Salzburg in which one distich is devoted to each month.[37] It is clearly intended that each month should have an illustration, and generally one showing someone engaged in an appropriate activity, not merely a personification such as were to be found in Carolingian copies of the fourth-century illustrated calendar of Filocalus. The earliest illustrated (non-Byzantine) medieval calendar which is actually extant is in a Vatican MS of the early tenth century; and here the verse text is a compressed version of an extant martyrological calendar by our same poet Wandalbert, whose portrait appears at the end. The illustrations of some of the months have no connection with the old Roman ones. They show contemporary life, and suggest how a poem like the one we have been considering could have contributed to the formation of the tradition of medieval illustrated calendars which culminates six centuries later in *Les très riches heures* of the Duc de Berry.*

If the monkish poets treated georgic subjects realistically only in such extremely rare cases, did they use them symbolically for religious purposes? Did the Middle Ages evolve an allegorical interpretation of the *Georgics*, as of the *Aeneid*, on Christian lines? Fulgentius, who was the first to start the business systematically with his *De Continentia Virgiliana* in the fifth or sixth century,† flinches at the prospect. 'The *Bucolics* and *Georgics*', he says, 'contain truths of such profundity that it is impossible fully to fathom them.' He does however lift a corner of the curtain to reveal that *Georgics* 1 concerned Astrology, 2 Physiognomy and Medicine, 3 Augury and 4 Music.[38] To Fulgentius the end of Book 4 was 'apotelesmatic', while Boethius saw the story of Orpheus and Eurydice as allegorical of the soul that looks back from the highest good to Tartarus again.[39]

I know of no attempt, in prose commentary or in verse, to allegorise the poem as a whole on Fulgentian lines.‡ Yet we cannot doubt that in schools symbolic Christian interpretations were freely dispensed. These are reflected in the *De Universo* of Raban Maurus, Abbot of Fulda (b. 784), an encyclopedic work

---

* On all this see A. Riegl, 'Die mittelalterliche Kalenderillustration', *Mitth. d. Inst. f. oesterreichische Geschichtsforschung* (1889), esp. pp. 35–51.

† Augustine, Servius and Macrobius allegorised on occasion, but not at all systematically. For the allegorisation of Orpheus and Eurydice see K. Heitmann, 'Orpheus in Mittelalter', *Archiv für Kulturgeschichte* (1963), pp. 253–94.

‡ According to K. Borinski (*Die Antike in Poetik und Kunsttheorie*, II, 1924, p. 183) the seventeenth-century Jesuit Hardouin, who considered almost all the 'ancients' to be forgeries by thirteenth-century Benedictines, 'nur christlich allegorisierende Unterstellungen (Virgils Georgica, Horaz...) liess paradox für echt passieren'.

leaning heavily on Isidore's *Etymologia*.[40] Raban says surprisingly
little about agriculture, and where he does touch on it he does so
in a thoroughly medieval way. There is a section *De Agris*
(14. 30) which, after a few definitions, continues: 'under the
name of field is expressed the human race, inhabiting this world',
and the rest is allegorical, with an occasional reference to the
Georgics such as

> illa seges demum votis respondet avari
> agricolae.

And near the end (22. 14) there is a section *De Instrumentis
Rusticis*, explaining at some length the symbolic significance of
each—'aratrum enim mystice significat opus praedicationis
evangelicae, in quo cultus agri Domini exercetur', and so forth.

We unfortunately know little of the *Georgica Spiritualia* of the
early thirteenth century formerly attributed to Walter of
Châtillon but now to John of Garland. We possess from it 116
disconnected hexameters of a moralistic nature, excerpts such as
might have been culled for a Florilegium.[41] These may of course
be unrepresentative, but they display no connection with Virgil.
He may have influenced the lay-out, but the basis was the Bible.
This poem may have been a forerunner of one that is extant, the
Agricultura Sacra of Thomas Kirchmayer, a well-known Protes-
tant, composed during his exile in Switzerland and published at
Basel in 1550 under the pseudonym of Naogeorgus. This is a
poem in five books of hexameters, indebted, but not markedly,
to Virgil. It instructs man, the spiritual husbandman, in the care
of the soul, his estate.

In the twelfth and thirteenth centuries spiritual interpretation
of the Bible such as was practised throughout the Middle Ages—
allegorical, tropological, anagogical—became applied to the
classics, especially those used in schools.[42] There may well have
been medieval predecessors of another early sixteenth-century
work, that of Michel Guillaume de Tours, whose translation of
the *Georgics* with pious expositions appeared in 1519 and was
twice reprinted. According to him the four books represent the

four cardinal virtues of prudence, temperance, courage and justice. The soul must be cultivated by the Catholic faith, manured by reading the Scriptures and listening to homilies, watered by thoughts of the paradise to come, sown with virtue, and tended with the implements of the Ten Commandments. In Book 4 the young bullock killed for the regeneration of the stock of bees is Christ, the resultant bees are mankind reborn, and the room with four windows where the act is performed is the cross with its four arms of charity, humility, obedience and patience.*

What I have not found so far is any medieval exposition of the *Georgics* embodying the Gospel of Work, which has been much more congenial to modern Christian minds.† The doctrine expounded early in Book 1, that 'the Father himself' created weeds and other pests in order to sharpen men's wits, though incompatible with the view of Hesiod and Genesis that this was a punishment for sin, could surely have been adapted, and the whole association of labour with righteousness and piety, the Hesiodic and Aratean element in the *Georgics*, could have been exploited.

There were certain odd things in the *Georgics* that arrested the attention of Christians from early times. One was the passage in Book 4, *deum namque ire per omnes...* (parelleled of course in *Aeneid* 6), which seemed to presage the doctrine of divine immanence. More extraordinary is their appropriation of Virgil's idealised bees. These, as peculiarly depicted by him, had the especial merit of perpetuating their species without sexual inter-

---

* Hubelei, p. 32. Christianising could also take the form of excision of what is specifically pagan, as when Vincent of Beauvais in his *Speculum Historiae* quotes the famous passage from the end of *Georgics* 2 with the omission of the lines 493–4,

> fortunatus et ille, deos qui novit agrestes,
> Panaque Silvanumque senem Nymphasque sorores.

See B. L. Ullman, 'Virgil in certain medieval florilegia', in 'Virgilio nel Medio Evo', *Stud. Med.* (1932), p. 60. Vincent transfers 495–502 to follow 526.

† For example, the once famous painting 'The Angelus' of Millet, a keen student of the *Georgics*, or the *Géorgiques Chrétiennes* of Francis Jammes which appeared in 1911–14, a poem in simple, self-contained Alexandrine distichs in which piety forms an accompaniment to the peasant's daily round. The medieval notion of Piers Plowman as a symbol for Christ occurred only in popular art and literature (G. Webb, 'The Christ of the Trades', *The Listener*, 6 July 1967, pp. 12–14).

course.[43] There was a remarkable ceremony which took place on Easter Eve, the Blessing of the Candles. At the appropriate moment in the service the archdeacon went to the umbo and pronounced an oration in praise of candles and the materials that composed them, papyrus wick, virgin oil and beeswax. Augustine in his *Civitas Dei* quotes part of a metrical one composed by himself.[44] There is no doubt about the influence of the *Georgics* on the part of these eulogies that concerned beeswax. One extant version quotes it almost verbatim on the courage of bees, 'ingentes animos angusto versat in pectore' (cf. G. 4. 83). Another, perhaps remembering 'fervet opus', exclaims, 'O admirandus apium fervor!' And indeed Jerome, who deplored the whole affair and could find no mention of beeswax in the Scriptures, alleged sardonically that a whole book of the *Georgics* was apt to be trotted out in such oratorial exhibitions.*

The monumental German edition of the Carolingian Latin poets notes at the foot of the page all the echoes from previous literature that the editors have perceived.† Some are no more than tags—'ultima Thule' or 'felix qui potuit' or 'balantumque greges'. Some are conscientiously varied—'infusum Lethaeo munere somnum' or 'superas praeflabat ad auras'. The disproportionate preponderance of reminiscences from the *Aeneid* could easily be explained by the fact that it was the most cognate in subject-matter to these poems, largely eulogies or biographical narratives. But the *Georgics* were clearly well known. In post-Carolingian times Virgil, though challenged by Horace and Ovid, continued to be quoted freely from all his range by representative writers such as John of Salisbury.[45] I will give only

---

* Migne, *P.L.* 30, col. 182. H. M. Bannister, 'The Vetus Itala. Text of the Exultet' *J. T. S.* XI (1909–11), pp. 43–54. L. Duchesne, *Christian Worship: its origin and evolution*, tr. M. L. McClive (1902), pp. 252 ff. Pope Zosimus in the sixth century forbade the practice in Rome itself, but felt constrained to permit it in the suburban diocese. And indeed it proved so popular that, although the latest known text dates from the end of the eleventh century, we hear of its being still in use at Salerno in 1431.

† Even clichés like 'vidi equidem', 'inque vicem', 'ergo age', 'more patrum' are accorded chapter and verse; but at least little can have been missed. G. Zappert's *Virgils Fortleben im Mittelalter* (1851) is marred by inclusion of the vaguest similarities.

one example of how the poets might use him, because of its intrinsic interest.

There is a song in sequence form with rhyme and rhythm, originating probably in the eleventh century, which begins *Parce continuis deprecor lamentis* and deals with love. It is found in two manuscripts, but it is the fuller version of the early thirteenth-century MS in the Laurentian Library that concerns us.[46] Love is first abused in terms borrowed from *Eclogue* 8:

> duris in cotibus
> Rhodope aut Ismarus
> illum progenuit...

Soon we pass to *exempla*—Nisus and Euryalus, Theseus and Pirithoüs, Tydeus and Polynices, David and Jonathan, Pyramus and Thisbe. The next stanza reads

> Sevus Amor ultima
> urget in discrimina—
> non ignis incendia,
> Bosfori non aspera
> perorrescit equora,
> quas dum sepe salebras
> iuvenis temeritas
> superasset, vincitur
> tandem maris estibus;
> operitur Sestias.
> Sestias in speculis,
> ponto perit iuvenis.

Cruel love drives a man into utmost perils. He does not shrink from fiery conflagrations, or the wild waters of the Bosphorus. After the youth's hardihood had often overcome their roughness, at last he was subdued by the surges of the sea. The girl of Sestos waits. The girl of Sestos perishes in her watch-tower, the youth in the sea.

We have seen (p. 96) that in his outburst against Amor (G. 3. 242–83) Virgil introduces Leander as his human example not by name but simply as

> iuvenis magnum cui versat in ossibus ignem
> saevus amor.

The fact that our poet here, after naming others, introduces him likewise simply as 'iuvenis', and uses the same phrase 'saevus amor', would be evidence enough that he had the *Georgics* in mind, even if his crowning example did not prove to be Orpheus and Eurydice, who occupy five stanzas which closely follow the story as told at the end of Book 4.

Nevertheless there are signs that in the later Middle Ages the *Georgics* became less well known than the *Aeneid*.* Even the *Eclogues* seem to recede. Chaucer shows knowledge only of the *Aeneid*.[47] Dante refers more than a hundred times to the *Aeneid*, which is natural enough since it was the inspiration and basis of his great poem. But it is surprising to find that the only Eclogue he ever refers to is the *Pollio* (four times) and that his direct references to the *Georgics* are even fewer.[48] There are, however, two or three other passages of interest that may have been suggested by ones in the *Georgics*.

At the beginning of the *Inferno* (1. 37 ff.) he thus introduces the day on which he was to meet Virgil:

> Temp' era dal principio del mattino
> E'l Sol montava in su con quelle stelle
> Ch'eran con lui quando l'Amor divino
> Mosse da prima quelle cose belle.

The time was early morning, and the Sun was mounting in the midst of the same stars as were around him when the Divine Love first put in motion all those beautiful things.

The date he is indicating is a very special one, not only Good Friday, but the vernal equinox of the centennial year 1300. The world had come full circle astrologically, and was once more being reborn in spring, in the 'dolce stagione', as on the first day

---

* This can only be a matter of impression; but after having formed such an impression I had it confirmed by that of the late Dr F. J. E. Raby (in a letter dated 4 February 1966). No doubt the *Georgics* continued to be read in schools. In the *Sacerdos ad altare* attributed to Alexander Neckham (Caius College, Cambridge, Library MS 385) there is to be found under 'de educatione scolarum' a list of books probably reflecting what was read in the schools of Paris in the late twelfth century. It includes the sentence 'Bucolica Maronis et georgica multe sunt utilitatis'. C. H. Haskins, *Studies in the History of Medieval Science* (1927), p. 372.

of creation which Virgil had imagined at G. 2. 336–42 (see pp. 191–4),

> cum primae lucem pecudes hausere, virumque
> terrea progenies duris caput extulit arvis
> immissaeque ferae silvis et sidera caelo.

Had Dante that passage at the back of his mind?*

In the great scene on the summit of the Mount of Purgatory when Beatrice draws near and Dante recognises 'i segni dell'antica fiamma', he turns to Virgil and finds he has vanished (30. 49 ff.).

> Ma Virgilio n'avea lasciati scemi
> Di sè, Virgilio dolcissimo padre,
> Virgilio, a cui per mia salute diemi;

but Virgil had left us forlorn of himself, Virgil sweetest of fathers, Virgil to whom for my salvation I surrendered myself.

The triple repetition of the name by one so desolated can hardly be other than an echo of *Georgics* 4. 524 ff.:

> 'Eurydicen' vox ipsa et frigida lingua,
> 'a miseram Eurydicen', anima fugiente vocabat;
> 'Eurydicen' toto referebant flumine ripae.[49]

But of course the echo *could* come through an intermediary such as the sequence cited above.

At the beginning of the twenty-fifth canto of the *Paradiso* he says that if ever the sacred poem (more sublime than the love-poems of his youth, he implies), on which he has been wearing himself to a shadow for years, overcomes the cruelty of the citizens who have exiled him,

> Con altro voce omai, con altro vello
> Ritornero poeta, ed in sul fonte
> Del mio battesmo prenderò 'l capello

With altered voice, with altered fleece, on that day I shall return a poet, and at the font of my baptism shall receive the laurel crown.

---

* See A. Bellessort, *Virgile, son œuvre et son temps* (1920), p. 322. The pagan idea that the world was born at the spring equinox persisted in Christian circles (J. G. Frazer, *The Golden Bough* (1890–1915), V, 307; cf. IV, 108).

Was he thinking of Virgil's proem to *Georgics* 3 where he expresses the hope (10–11) that, likewise by virtue of a new and higher kind of poetry, he will return in triumph to his native Mantua? But that is even more speculative.

And there we may leave the Middle Ages.

THE RENAISSANCE

The rôle of Petrarch as midwife of the Renaissance is strikingly illustrated by the freedom with which, in contrast to Dante and Chaucer, he produces quotations from the *Georgics*. His favourite copy of Virgil, still to be seen in the Ambrosian library, is embellished with a frontispiece by Simone Martini ('il mio Simone') showing Servius presenting Aeneas to Virgil, and below them a vinedresser and shepherd, symbolising the three major works.* His quotations tend however to be simply in the nature of tags or mottoes. Thus in the famous speech he made on being crowned poet laureate on the Capitol he took as motto,

> sed me Parnasi deserta per ardua dulcis
> raptat amor;

and he quoted in it (or rather misquoted, in the generalised form favoured by the *florilegia*[50]) 'labor omnia vincit', as he did again to encourage himself on his ascent of the Mont Ventoux, prototype of all modern mountain-climbs.[51] The remarkable thing, however, is that, while he was the true founder of the humanistic *Bucolic*, this keen and lifelong gardener never sought to emulate the *Georgics* in his poetry.[52]

There is one reference worth mentioning. In 1347 Petrarch became Archdeacon of Parma, and bought a house there with a garden attached. Giving his profession now as 'gardener', he kept a garden-journal which has survived. In November 1348 he tried an experiment. He trimmed his vine-stocks, replanted some

---

* Sir Kenneth Clark, *Landscape into Art* (1949): 'For the first time since antiquity the pursuits of country life are represented in art as a source of happiness and poetry' (p. 6; cf. pl. 4). This picture 'originated the landscape of symbolism' (*ibid.* p. 71).

shoots, and turned the rest under, noting that he was not very hopeful because of the lateness of the season, the north wind, the unfavourable moon, and the warnings of Virgil against late planting.[53] (In the event he was quite successful.) But to observe that you are acting against the advice of someone is insufficient evidence that you normally take him as a guide.*

Most of the humanists were city-bred, though Petrarch himself was equally happy in the country, and Guarino of Verona, who had an intense feeling for nature, believed like Horace that periods of town and country residence should alternate. Maffeo Vegio, constrained by plague to reside for some time in the country about the year 1425, confessed his bitter disappointment with the rustic life commended in the *Georgics*, complaining of bugs, midges and floods in a poem which it is a relief to read after the facile eulogies of that life which were soon to pour from the press. However, threats of invasion from abroad began to make the citizens of the Italian communes lift up their eyes to the countryside, both with hankering for its peacefulness and with hope that its hardy peasants would prove their saviours in war. So gradually, insensibly, in the second half of the fifteenth century, interest in the *Georgics* grew,† fostered also by the increasing interest of the age in botany and gardening.

---

* *Ibid.* p. 54 the assertion 'many a good humanist, from Petrarch onwards, managed his estates on the advice of the *Georgics*'. There may be evidence for this in their voluminous surviving correspondence, but I have not yet found it.

† See the preface of Landino to his commentary (1487). Zabughin, I, 231–4. Zabughin states (p. 246) that the first conscious attempt by a poet to take up again the abandoned tradition of the *Ascraeum Carmen* was by Tito Vespasiano Strozzi, whose *Ecloghe Georgiche*, a rustic idyll, borrowed motifs from all four Books as well as from Columella, Book 10. But it is noteworthy that in the first 200 pages of Minterno's influential *De Poeta* (Venice, 1559) quotations from Virgil total: *Aeneid* 512, *Eclogues* 55, *Georgics* 10. C. S. Baldwin, *Renaissance Literary Theory and Practice*, ed. D. L. Clark (1939), pp. 164–5.

There is an important fact to remember if we seek to use frequency of echoes in Neo-Latin poetry as evidence for influence or its absence: a complete change of attitude took place in the centuries following Petrarch. Petrarch himself in his Latin poems shunned verbal reminiscences, and was horrified when a Virgilian hexameter-ending in one of his poems was pointed out to him (*Ep. Fam.* 22. 2; cf. 23. 19); whereas Vida, in his influential *Art of Poetry* (1520–7), itself full of Virgilian tags, recommended borrowing phrases from the classics.

The first of the humanists fully to appreciate Virgil's whole range was one of the greatest, Politian. He found in him a *concordia discors* of landscapes. His *Rusticus*, in 570 Latin hexameters, was composed in 1483 to be recited publicly as an introduction to his lectures on Hesiod and the *Georgics*, and was dedicated to Lorenzo de' Medici as the Maecenas who had enabled him to write it in peace at Fiesole. After a eulogy of country life as contrasted with town, he describes, season by season, its objects and occupations. Like most literary men, Politian was vicarious in his enjoyment of the works of agriculture, and his poem was descriptive, not didactic; but its success inaugurated the Italian vogue in the sixteenth century for didactic poetry. The finest and most Virgilian example, though Virgilian in its hexameters and in some other features adopted from the *Georgics*, and possibly suggested originally by the description of the Noric plague in Book 3, was not on a Virgilian subject. It was on Syphilis. Julius Caesar Scaliger hailed the author of this 'divine poem' (published in 1530), the Veronese physician Girolamo Fracastoro, as the most distinguished poet since Virgil.*

Meanwhile in the society of Bernardo Rucellai's scientific garden at Florence there grew up two poets. One, his own son Giovanni, produced in 1539 a poem entitled *The Bees* (*Le Api*),

---

* It deals with the battle against the strange disease imported to Barcelona from Hayti by Columbus' sailors in 1493, introduced from there to Naples by troops sent to help Alfonso II against Charles VIII of France, spread over Europe by the latter's victorious mercenaries, who captured the city and were soon after disbanded, and carried to the Far East in the ships of Vasco da Gama. The Church called it 'Flagellum Dei', others the 'Morbus Gallicus'. It was Fracastoro who invented the less prejudiced name which his poem has perpetuated, from a fictional shepherd he called Syphilus, who was struck down by the disease for neglecting the worship of Apollo and healed by a decoction of the sacred tree Guaiacum (a remedy used by the Haytians and recommended to him by Cardinal Bembo). Ed. H. Wynne Finch (1935), with medical introduction by J. Johnston-Abraham and an essay (pp. 172–8) by V. Rendall on *Fracastor and Virgil*. See also Zabughin, II, pp. 143–7.

Another famous didactic poem, often imitated, often reprinted down to the eighteenth century, and often compared with the *Georgics*, was M. G. Vida's *De Bombycum cura et usu*, on silkworms (1527). This and other Italian poems on the same subject were the models for one of the earliest of English georgic poems, Thomas Moffat's *The Silkwormes and their Flies* (1599).

based on the Fourth Georgic; and in the same year the other, Luigi Alamanni, began his *La Coltivazione*. Both poems were in Italian, not Latin. Alamanni's is the first true georgics of the Renaissance. Of the many sources he used Virgil is the chief; but his poem, though it moralises and also dwells on the variety of the months, is unvirgilian in being really intended to instruct farmers —not that they are likely to have used it much.* Accordingly it is arranged not by subjects but by seasons, as a *vade mecum* would more logically be. But there is a fifth book on gardening, which not unnaturally tends to repeat what has been said before; and a sixth, on lucky and unlucky days, is added—a mere gesture to Virgil, whose corresponding section had been a mere gesture to Hesiod—closing with a passage on weather-signs. The work is, in fact, rather clumsily planned; and at five thousand lines it is too long.

Alamanni wrote as an exile at the court of François I, whom he idealises as The Happy Man, and to whom his work was dedicated on its completion in 1546. His enthusiasm is for the lands on the French side of the Alps; and it is to France that our scene now shifts. Here in the sixteenth century the *Georgics* tended to be regarded as a technical didactic poem—indeed Henri Estienne was rather apologetic about its digressions; and although Du Bellay praised Alamanni's work, didactic was not among the genres he recommended to French poets. Montaigne however, on his country estate near Bergerac, was a fervent admirer of the *Georgics*, 'le plus accomply ouvrage de la poésie'; and in his numerous quotations from Virgil there is for once a slight relative preponderance from this part of his work.[54]

Another enthusiast had been Ronsard, who knew all Virgil by heart and rated him highest among Latin poets. There are nearly two hundred echoes of the *Georgics* in his poems, besides specific imitations.[55] But although these come from the whole range of the poem, there are several areas of close concentration. There are three sections, in fact, that contribute far more than the others,

---

* Alamanni's borrowings from Virgil are noted in G. B. da Prato's commentary. He severely denied himself more than a very few set-pieces.

the *Laus Italiae* (2. 136–76), the *Laus ruris* (2. 458–540) and the
Aristaeus episode (4. 315–546). Next come the portents and civil
war (1. 463–97), the proem to Book 1 (1–42), the proem to
Book 3 (1–48), and the passage on *saevus amor* (3. 242–83). These
seven passages, totalling about a quarter of the work, account for
about sixty per cent of the references in Ronsard. And what is
more, the same pattern is repeated in later poets, especially in
England. Indeed if we add a few short passages—the storm in
Book 1, the *Laus veris* in Book 2, the battle of the bulls and
Parnassus passage in Book 3 and the Corycian gardener and the
bees' commonwealth in Book 4, and a few tags such as 'labor
omnia vincit', we cover almost all the knowledge of the *Georgics*
commonly shown by European poets (whereas the *Eclogues* were
far more widely adopted, especially in the sixteenth century).
And what these passages have in common is, that none of them
comes from the ostensibly didactic part of the poem. From which
it emerges that it has rarely been taken in as a whole, and as it
should be. For such readers it might as well have survived only in
the form of an anthology. Its treatment, though partly for
different reasons, was analogous to that of Lucretius, who for two
centuries from the middle of the fourteenth was admired as a
poet but disregarded, indeed outlawed, as a teacher, his technical
portions unread.

The English Renaissance followed in the wake of France and
even of Scotland,* and some two centuries behind Italy. Here
again we find the same tendency for the *Georgics* to recede on
closer inspection. A bachelor at Oxford in 1448 begs to have a
lecture on it, which has been imposed on him, changed to one on
Aristotle's *De Anima*.[56] Sir Thomas Elyot, prescribing an ideal
education in his influential work *The Governour* (15–31), commends it in the following terms: 'In the Georgicks, Lorde, what
pleasant varietie there is; the divers granges, herbs and flowers
that are there described, that reading therein, hit seemeth to a

---

* Gavin Douglas, Bishop of Dunkeld and first translator of the *Aeneid* into
English, shows knowledge of the *Eclogues* and *Georgics* in his Prologues (1513),
and in his *Palice of Honour*. Mustard, pp. 1 ff.; Nitchie, p. 82.

man to be in a delectable gardene or paradise.' Mere lip-service. How could anyone who really knew the poem characterise it in this way? Spenser knew the *Georgics*, but took hardly anything from it compared with the *Eclogues* and *Aeneid*. Shakespeare's example of the bees' commonwealth in Henry V probably comes directly from Book 4 ('tent-royal', cf. 'praetoria'); and Iago's famous lines in *Othello*,

> : not *poppy* nor mandragora
> Nor all the *drowsy* syrups of the world...

may have been suggested by 1. 78:

> Lethaeo perfusa papavera somno.[57]

In the pattern of grammar-school syllabuses in the sixteenth century it was often only an alternative to the *Eclogues*, and if any work of Virgil was omitted, it was probably the *Georgics*.[58] As for the manner of study in school, we can get a good idea from the notebook, preserved in the British Museum, of William Badger, a boy at Winchester under Christopher Johnson. It covers three and a half years from his entry to the fourth form aged twelve at Michaelmas 1563. Towards the end of 1564 they embarked on the *Georgics*. Johnson warns the boys not to despise agriculture, which was more highly esteemed among the Romans than at present.* In the third 'dictate' they have got to line 83. Three dictates later they are seventy lines further on, for the 'infelix lolium' and 'steriles avenae' come up as paradigms for metaphorical weeds in the state. By February they are half-way through Book 2, the barrenness of plants that grow too fast being used to point a moral. The republic of the bees is later duly held up as an example; and when the boys want to have a whole day off in the nutting season, they are reminded of what happened to bees that wanted to leave the hive and play in the sky:

> instabiles animos ludo prohibebis inani;

---

* In the first half of the sixteenth century peasants began to be represented in art as uncouth, with distorted and misshapen faces, engaged in drunken revelling (as in Brueghel); this by contrast with earlier idealisation. Slicher van Bath, p. 194.

the ringleaders even had their wings pulled off. It took the form about a year to get through the poem.[59] A century later we find fifth-form boys reading 10–12 lines of the *Georgics* on two afternoons a week; no more, for they have to learn by heart, construe, parse, scan, pick out and define tropes and figures, note elegancies, etc.[60] Milton, in his tractate *Of Education*, recommending that boys become conversant with agriculture so that they may find the *Georgics* easier, indicated the rural parts, along with Lucretius and Manilius, as 'among those parts which are now reckoned most hard'. (According to Toland, he made his nephews and other pupils read Cato, Varro, Columella and Palladius.) No one translated the poem as a whole into English until 1589, when Abraham Fleming made what was avowedly a mere crib; and it does not seem to have been much admired, though Sir John Harington professed that, while unable to endure to hear his ploughmen talking about twy-fallowing, he adored the elegance of Virgil's

saepe etiam steriles incendere profuit agros.*

'O FORTUNATOS...'

In the seventeenth century the *Georgics* was still in the doldrums, both on the Continent and in Britain, as compared with the *Aeneid*. But there were certain developments that stand out. One was the increasing popularity of poems praising country life as against town. These are not true georgics. They advocate retreat from the busy world, and extol The Happy Man—not the *colonus* but the gentleman with a country seat, though he may be exhorted to take a hand in the work on his estate. The social background is the growing prosperity that followed the Renaissance.† The chief literary springs are the *O fortunatos* passage at

---

* Preface to the translation of *Orlando Furioso* (1591). Bacon asserted that 'Virgil got as much glory of eloquence, wit and learning in the expression and observations of his husbandry as in the heroical acts of Aeneas'. But he was grinding an axe (*Advancement of Learning*, Book II, 20, 3).

† One of the first Renaissance writers to express this feeling had been Petrarch, in his letters and his essay *On the Solitary Life*, happier on his estate at Vaucluse

the end of *Georgics* 2, and Horace's Second Epode, *Beatus ille* (with the ironical *dénouement*, that the speaker is an insincere money-lender, conveniently ignored). This *locus* occurs in a number of works of the seventeenth century, both in Italy* and in France, where besides the French poems of the Pléiade there was a veritable craze for neo-Latin poems in praise of country life, of which eight appeared between 1570 and 1583.[61] Germany too comes into the picture, with the *Lob desz Landlustes* of Johann Fischart (*c.* 1590). From these emerged the distinctive genre of the country-house poem.

A poem on the Villa of Caprarola appeared in the *Poemata* of Laurentius Gambara, published at Antwerp in 1569, at the Plantin Press.[62] Antwerp and Amsterdam were great dissemina-tors, and it was the Netherlands that were to be the chief source of country-house poems in the next century. Beginning in 1613 with Van Borsselen's *Den Binckhorst*, they had produced ninety examples by the end of the eighteenth century.† These poems are descriptive, horticultural, moralistic and religious, with excursuses on national history or peasant life as well as on classical or biblical mythology and history. The houses themselves are not described, but the art collections they contain are praised; and indeed the poems were not without influence on landscape-painting. The owners are represented as making a point of participating in horticultural work, which is described season by season. Town and court life are disparaged by contrast. Since the chief subject is

than at Avignon. Another exposition occurs in Leon Battista Alberti's dialogue *Della Famiglia*, published in 1443, where country life is made to win hands down in this ancient topic of rhetorical debate (as it was to do forty years later in Politian's *Rusticus*) : *I tre libri della famiglia*, III, 296 ff., ed. Pellegrini-Spongano.

* For example Luigi Tansillo (d. 1569), *Il Podere* (first published 1770); Lotichius (1528–60), *Elegy* 8: *De secessu suo et oblectamentis ruris*; *Elegy* 12: *Ad villam Phyllidis prope Nicum.*

† A neo-Latin predecessor had already appeared nearly a century earlier, the Dutch humanist Janus Secundus, with a poem entitled *Ad Marcum Antonium Caimum, Mediolanensem, Epistola* v. For the whole history of country-house poetry, in the Netherlands and elsewhere, see the most valuable work of P. A. F. Van Veen, *De Soeticheydt des Buyten-Levens Vergheselschaft met de Boucken* (1960). German specimens are provided by M. Opitz, *Zlatna* (1624) and *Vielguet* (1629).

gardens, the *Georgics* could be a direct source of material only to a limited extent; but Virgil is the chief inspirer of the genre, and dependence on him is the main connecting link.[63]

There was a parallel tradition, 'thin but clearly defined', in England in the earlier part of the seventeenth century. But here we must beware of ascribing too much influence to Virgil. The earliest example, Ben Jonson's *To Penshurst*, was based on Martial, 3. 58 (*Baiana nostri villa, Basse, Faustini*), with elements from Horace's *Beatus ille*; while his *Sir Robert Wroth* draws on the Epode for its first sixty-six lines, and in the remainder on Juvenal's Tenth Satire as well as Virgil's O *fortunatos* passage.[64] Cowley appended a verse-translation of this last to his essay *Of Agriculture* (1668). In the next century it was the turn of houses to follow poetry. Philip Southcote's Wooburn Farm was specifically designed as a *ferme ornée* to provide a peaceful setting for rural life; and William Shenstone's 'The Leasowes', near Halesowen, had a garden so laid out that the climax was 'Virgil's Grove', with an obelisk dedicated to the poet.[65]

Garden-poems form a subspecies of their own.* By far the most important georgic poem of the few produced in the seventeenth century was René Rapin's *Hortorum Libri IV* (1665). Writing still in Latin hexameters, and ignoring Columella 10 though he knew it, he aspired to treat on a grand scale the topics Virgil had left *aliis post me memoranda* (*G.* 4. 148). The four books deal with flowers, trees, waters and orchards. The whole preface is a glorification of Virgil, 'the most excellent poet in the memory of man'; and in his epilogue Rapin claims proudly that he has been

> magni insistens vestigia sacra Maronis.

But the poem is not merely a literary supplement. It was inspired by personal experience, enthusiasm for the country seat at Bâville of his patron, the president Lamoignon, where he was a

---

* The prominent Italian humanist J. J. Pontanus produced in 1505 a poem on the cultivation of citrus fruits, *De Hortis Hesperidum*; and Eobanus Hessius, who edited Walafrid Strabo's *Hortulus*, wrote of gardens outside Nuremberg in his *Noriberga Illustrata* (1532). Charles Estienne's *De re hortensi* (1536) was a very successful work.

frequent visitor, and admiration for the formal gardens created in France in the early part of the century by the predecessors of Le Nôtre, as at Fontainebleau and now at Versailles, where the *parterre d'eau* is exactly contemporaneous with the poem.

Rapin's poem was widely and lastingly influential, not least in England through John Gardiner's verse translation of 1706.* The middle part of Book 3 of Cowper's *The Task* (1784) is a garden georgic; but by that time the direct influence of Virgil is questionable. Cowper acknowledges it; but it is only occasionally detectable, for instance, in William Mason's poem in four books, *The English Garden* (1772–82), which advocated the new romantic landscape-gardening, the creations of 'Capability' Brown, now superseding the formal gardens such as Rapin had celebrated.

THE EIGHTEENTH-CENTURY VOGUE

In England (with which from now on I shall principally be dealing) the *Georgics* came into fashion for the first time at the end of the seventeenth century, with the publication in 1697 of Dryden's translation of what he called 'the divinest part of Virgil'. To this was prefixed a short essay by the young Addison (written in 1693) complaining of past neglect of the poem and introducing it with understanding and enthusiasm.† He insisted on the distinction, often blurred hitherto, between pastoral and georgic. He was feeling for the idea that the net effect was descriptive rather than didactic (see p. 4). He also had a conception of the organic or symphonic unity of the poem. 'Nor is it sufficient', he says, 'to run out into beautiful and diverting digressions (as is generally thought), unless they are brought in aptly, and are something of a piece with the main design of the *Georgic*; for they ought to have a remote alliance at least to the subject, that so the poem may be more agreeable in all its parts.'

There followed an astonishing vogue for georgic poetry which

---

* John Evelyn's *Silva: a discourse on Forest Trees* incorporated Book 2 from the first English translation, made by his seventeen-year-old son and namesake in 1673.
† Twenty-five of the essays in *The Spectator* have mottoes from the *Georgics*.

lasted for most of the eighteenth century. This was the great age of country-house life and agricultural interest, of the educated class catered for by *The Gentleman's Magazine* (founded 1731), whose editor, Edward Cave, assumed the significant pseudonym of 'Sylvanus Urban'. In his introduction to his version of the *Georgics* (1753) Joseph Warton wrote: 'The coarse and common words I was necessitated to use in the following translation, viz. "*plough* and *sow*, *wheat*, *dung*, *ashes*, *horse* and *cow*" etc. will, I fear, unconquerably disgust many a delicate reader.' To such an age the dignity of Virgil's style was reassuring: *angustis hunc addere rebus honorem*. As Addison had rightly said: 'He delivers the meanest precepts with a kind of grandeur, he breaks the clods and tosses the dung with an air of gracefulness.'

One result of this new impetus was an outburst of genuine didactic poetry. An early example was also perhaps the best, John Philips' *Cyder* of 1706. Philips, a Herefordshire man, knew his subject, and blended that knowledge with love of the west country and personal interests such as glass-blowing.* Virgil is his avowed model, but a new formal influence is present which may partly account for the fact that this huge corpus of eighteenth-century poetry is today largely unreadable—the belief that a medium which was suitable for the 'great argument' of *Paradise Lost* was suitable for anything:

> What soil the apple loves, what care is due
> To orchards, timeliest when to press the fruits,
> Thy gifts, Pomona, in Miltonian verse
> Adventurous I presume to sing, of verse
> Nor skill'd nor studious: but my native soil
> Invites me, and the theme as yet unsung.†

Philips was fortunate in satisfying a contemporary taste and so achieving, both at home and in translation abroad, a popularity beyond what his poem's respectable merits deserved. 'It needed

---

* Unlike the rest, he showed some sense of humour. Otherwise this appears only in Swift's *City Shower* (1710), which uses the prognostics of *Georgics* I in a burlesque spirit, and Gay's *Trivia* (1716), its follower.

† Cf. C. Smart, *The Hop-garden* (*init.*): 'I teach in verse Miltonian.'

not to shun the presence of the original' was Johnson's indulgent verdict. The eighteenth century had indeed a passion for the didactic.* Italy rediscovered the exiled Alamanni's *La Coltivazione*, and no fewer than twenty editions of it were produced between 1716 and 1781. Didactic poems on agriculture were primarily an Italian feature in this century, though England could show the patriotic Dodsley, and France Vanière's Latin *Praedium Rusticum* and de Rosset's *Agriculture* besides two poems that each boasted the sub-title *Les géorgiques françoises*, J. Delille's *L'homme des champs* and F. J. de Bernis' *Les quatre saisons*. Delille's translation of the *Georgics* (1769) became a classic, as Joost van den Vondel's (1646) was already in Holland, and as that of Voss (1799) was to become in Germany.

One of the Virgilian themes that constantly reappears in excursuses is that of *Georgics* 2. 136–76 (*sed neque Medorum...*), praise of the poet's native land. The Praises of Italy were matched by Praises of France in Nicholas Bourbon, Du Bellay and Ronsard.[66] Ronsard echoes the passage twenty or thirty times. Rapin goes into ecstasies over the France of the *Roi Soleil*:

> Salve, o magna parens hortorum, patria tellus,

over Touraine, the Ile de France, and Paris itself, which usurps the place of Virgil's 'rerum pulcherrima Roma'.[67] In England the heyday of georgic poetry coincided with her meteoric rise in world prestige, the period that began with the union with Scotland, Marlborough's victories and the Treaty of Utrecht, and lasted into the reign of George III;† and the part of Virgil's

---

* In England a spate of didactic poems was precipitated by Thomson, a generation later than Philips: Somerville, *The Chase* (1735); Armstrong, *The Art of Preserving Health* (1744); Smart, *The Hop-garden* (1752); Dodsley, *Agriculture* (1754); Dyer, *The Fleece* (1757); Grainger, *The Sugar-Cane* (1763); Mason, *The English Garden* (1772–82). These poems are in varying degrees indebted to the *Georgics*, and make specific allusions to it. The *O fortunatos* theme reappears *ad nauseam*. See Mustard, pp. 1–32. Goldsmith's boyhood village schoolmaster, Paddy Byrne, had composed georgics in Irish. Johnson's opinions on these didactic poets were robustly dismissive: see Boswell, *Life of Johnson*: 21 March 1776.

† 'When George III succeeded his grandfather, the name of Britain was held, perhaps, in higher esteem by the nations of the world than ever before or since'

panegyric of Italy that dealt with the greatness of Rome and her sons inspired many a eulogy of 'noble Albion' and 'Happy Britannia', the best known being that in Thomson's *Seasons*. Dyer, in his didactic poem on sheep and wool, *The Fleece* (1757), matches

> tot congesta manu praeruptis oppida saxis

with

> The increasing walls of busy Manchester,
> Sheffield and Birmingham.[68]

By 1785, indeed, when Cowper produced *The Task*, Wolfe and Chatham were only memories, and a temporary decline had set in. But for us at this distance the more discriminating patriotism of

> England, *with all thy faults* I love thee still[69]

comes as something of a relief after endless panegyrics, just as Crabbe's *The Village* does. Cowper's honesty extends to the climate. Instead of 'hic ver perpetuum' we have

> Though thy clime
> Be fickle, and thy year most part deform'd
> With dripping rains, or wither'd by a frost...

It is hard to distinguish between poems advocating withdrawal from the busy world,* poems proclaiming the happiness of the country gentleman, poems purporting to instruct him in country arts, and poems describing the estate and countryside that make him happy. The long line of topographical poems began in 1642 with Denham's *Cooper's Hill*, which is hardly descriptive at all. Of its many successors one of the most respectable was *Grongar Hill* (1726) by John Dyer, already mentioned as

(G. M. Trevelyan). 'Nature has played a part in England's world position because a temperate climate is virtually free of violent storms and earthquakes and because British commerce is based on the use of winds and scientific aids to navigation' (W. P. Jones, *The Rhetoric of Science*, 1966, p. 30).

* 'There is, indeed, scarce any writer who has not celebrated the happiness of rural privacy' (Johnson, *The Rambler*, 1751, 135). One of the earliest English examples, John Pomfret's *The Choice* (1700), was popular for a century. Of these 'retirement' poets Mark Akenside is the only one reputed to have an especial love of nature. G. C. Williams, 'The Beginnings of Nature Poetry in the XVIII Century', *Stud. Philol.* (1930), p. 601.

author of *The Fleece*, who was painter as well as poet, and like Thomson was influenced by Poussin, Salvator Rosa and Claude Lorrain.[70] Thomas Tickell, in a lecture delivered in 1711, urged English poets to imitate the *Georgics*;[71] and in some cases, such as Mark Akenside's much-read *Pleasures of the Imagination* (1744), the debt is avowed; but in others there is no more than a vague resemblance which could be indirect.

The master of descriptive poetry, and indeed the most influential poet in the whole of Europe in the eighteenth century, was James Thomson. Here the *Georgics* were a major element, but it was still mostly the set-pieces, not the agricultural lore, that were developed. *The Seasons* is a philosophical and moral as well as a descriptive poem, but not really didactic. The interesting thing is that in the successive revisions which took place between 1726 and 1744 more and more of Virgil was incorporated, making it increasingly episodic in the process.

> Such themes as these the *rural* Maro sung
> To wide-imperial Rome, in the full height
> Of elegance and taste, by Greece refined.

Towards the end of *Spring* we have the amorous bull and the quivering horse of *Georgics* 3 (786–817). The storm in *Summer* (1103–68) strives to overtrump Virgil, and the latter part of the book includes the praises of Britannia, with her lovely daughters as well as her famous sons (1437–1600). *Autumn* has a storm more closely modelled on that of *Georgics* 1 (311–59), and the themes of the *O fortunatos* passage occupy, rearranged, lines 1231 to the end. *Winter* has yet another storm (118–201), heralded by prognostics from 'the plumy race' borrowed from *Georgics* 1. And there are many other Virgilian touches throughout the poem, as well as elaborations of the Foreign Countries Theme, and descriptions of Libyan or Lapland life like those in *Georgics* 3, coloured by the tales of travel and exploration that were a feature of the age. The vineyard fire of *Georgics* 2 becomes a tropical forest fire.

It was largely through Thomson that Virgil affected the

eighteenth century. Thomson's influence can be traced even in landscape-painting, such as that of Gainsborough.* It spread to the Continent, particularly France, where Saint-Lambert had a success with his *Les Saisons* (1769). † It not only revived interest in the *Georgics*, but introduced nature-poetry, and incidentally intensified the new mania for English landscape-gardening. And it can claim a share of credit for Haydn's *The Seasons*.

Nature was the goddess of these poets, but in two successive conceptions. At first she represented simply scenery, the superficial aspect of things that pleased the eye:

> rura mihi et rigui placeant in vallibus amnes.

But at the end of the seventeenth century there was much talk of the wonders of the universe, both in its immense and its minute order, as evidence for the wisdom of the Creator. This theme soon invaded poetry:

> The spacious firmament on high...

Sir Richard Blackmore was a pioneer, with his *The Creation* in seven books (1712). So the *Georgics*, with their theme of *ipse Pater statuit*, became relevant in a different way. Insensibly the emphasis changed from natural history to physics, to Lucretius' *natura*, and Newton became a symbol, especially after his death in 1727. As such he appears in *The Seasons*; and it is noteworthy that when Thomson, at the end of *Autumn*, introduces a splendid paraphrase of the end of the Second Georgic, he takes out the Lucretian *me vero primum...* passage, and reserves it for his climax:

> Oh Nature! all-sufficient! over all!
> Inrich me with the knowledge of thy works!
> Snatch me to heaven; thy rolling wonders there,
> World beyond world, in infinite extent,

---

* His 'Musidora' in the Tate Gallery was inspired by a story from *Summer*, ll. 1268–1369. On Thomson and painting see E. W. Manwaring, *Italian Landscape in Eighteenth Century England* (1925), esp. pp. 101–8.

† Saint-Lambert in his introduction credited the Germans as well as the English with inventing descriptive poetry, adding: 'Les anciens aimoient et chantoient la campagne, nous admirons et chantons la nature.' See further D. Mornet, *Les sciences de la nature en France au XVIIIe siècle* (1911).

Profusely scattered o'er the blue immense
Shew me; their motions, periods and their laws
Give me to scan.

So by chance the same passage in the *Georgics* provided the text for two frames of mind, one of which historically supervened on the other.*

AGRICULTURE

Renaissance agricultural literature in England begins with Fitzherbert's *Boke of Hosbondrye* (1523), which ran into about eight editions before the end of the sixteenth century. Virgil contributed little or nothing to this, nor to Thomas Tusser's engaging series of poems entitled (in its final form) *Five Hundredth Good Pointes of Husbandry* (1573). But four years later the Lincolnshire farmer and poet Barnabe Googe, who also translated part of *Georgics* I, brought out an English translation of Conrad Heresbach's *Rei Rusticae libri quattuor*. This work was founded mainly on the prose *Scriptores Rei Rusticae*, as were the French treatises of Charles Estienne, Olivier de Serres and Philippe Hégémon, but in it Virgil is mentioned quite often.

In 1669 there appeared an important book, John Worlidge's *Systema Agriculturae*, which embodied such improvements in technique as had been made in the earlier part of the century. It consists of 300 large pages, and includes as appendixes a Farmer's Calendar, a section on prognostics, and a vocabulary of rustic terms. Virgil is here quoted not infrequently, with the reverence of a Columella, but more for corroboration or in the manner of mottoes than as a fount of doctrine. At this period there was considerable influence on English agriculture from Holland, where Roman traditions had survived in practice; and the literary soil was thus prepared for Dryden's translation of the *Georgics*, to which I have attributed the outburst of interest in the poem in the succeeding century.

---

* Joseph Wait, at the climax of his poem *The Enthusiast*, expressed a longing to hear the music of the spheres; or failing that, of the fairies. On all this see Røstvig, II, 398–408, and Jones, *The Rhetoric of Science*, both excellent books.

Two passages may illustrate Worlidge's position as a 'new man' who yet, like Newton, has not quite shaken off old superstitions. On comets as prognostics, after writing in a not unscientific spirit, he gives as a recent example one visible in England in 1664. This, he says, was succeeded by extreme drought and heat, the Great Plague of 1665, and the pestilential diseases of 1666–7. These could conceivably be due to meteorological disturbances; but he betrays his superstition by adding the Great Fire of London (p. 293).* On procedure when all your bees die he writes (p. 188): 'You may experiment with the invention of the Athenian [sic] beemaster of Virgil, wherewith in effect agrees the experiment of our modern and great husbandman Mr. Carew of Cornwal.' He then describes a procedure which is essentially that of Aristaeus. He does not, however, attempt to explain how the maggots become bees. Perhaps he did not really feel any need; for he adds in a somewhat Herodotean spirit: 'or if you are unwilling either to credit or make trial of this experiment, you may purchase a new stock from your neighbours'.

In 1742 James Hamilton, a schoolmaster of East Calder, near Edinburgh, translated the *Eclogues* and *Georgics* with the dual object of inspiring the sons of gentlemen to improve agriculture and of raising money to buy a farm and introduce a Hertfordshire ploughman as instructor. There seems no doubt that in the early part of this century, before the revolution associated with the names of Jethro Tull, 'Turnip' Townshend and Arthur Young, many thought of themselves as practising 'Virgilian husbandry', hard though it is to imagine the *Georgics* as actually being used as a handbook. This may be another consequence of the popularity of Dryden's translation. At all events, in 1724 William Benson published, under the title of *Virgil's Husbandry*, his own translation of Book 2, with the Latin and Dryden's version, followed in the next year by a similar treatment of Book 1. To these he

* He also adduced, in a later edition, a comet of March 1672, as having portended not only exceptionally bad weather, but also the entry of the French King into Holland.

prefixed rather silly introductions attacking Dryden's as 'the worst translation ever made'. Of the poem as a whole he says: 'I am certain that husbandry in England in general is Virgilian, which is shown by paring and burning the surface, by rastering and cross-ploughing; and that in those parts of England which the Romans principally inhabited, all along the southern coast, Latin words remain to this hour among shepherds and ploughmen... There is more of Virgil's husbandry in England at this instant than in Italy itself.'*

This passage provoked a sharp reaction from Jethro Tull, whose revolutionary work, *The Horse-hoeing Husbandry*, appeared a few years later (1733). In a special chapter (IX) entitled 'Remarks on the bad husbandry that is so finely express'd in Virgil's first georgic', he commented: 'It's my opinion that the Italians, in changing Virgil's field husbandry, have acted more reasonably than those who retain it; because I think it impossible for any scheme in general to be worse.' The gravamen of his criticisms is as follows (pp. 40 ff.):

(1) That Virgil enjoins ploughing rich land early, knowing no reason for tillage and hoeing but the killing of weeds (cf. G. I. 63–6; 69).

(2) That he says 'it will be enough' to plough poor land late, else it may lose its moisture; whereas if it is not ploughed, it cannot recoup the moisture it must lose by evaporation (67–8; 70).

(3) Poor land should be ploughed with deep, not shallow, furrow; with shallow the moisture received from dew will not sink in, but evaporate by day (68).

(4) *Mutatis fetibus* and *inaratae gratia terrae*: the precepts are refuted in Chapters VI and XVI (80; 82).

(5) Virgil must mean the burning of stubble on rich land and turf on poor. Burning stubble is to provide a sort of compost; burning poor land, which removes much of the best part of the surface, is so pernicious that it has generally been abandoned.

* In 1725, at just this time, R. Bradley published *A survey of the ancient husbandry, collected from Cato, Varro, Columella, Virgil and others.*

Virgil's reasons are 'utterly unbecoming the character of a philosopher' for reasons he proceeds to give. Virgil would have done better to stop at line 81 (84–93).

(6) 'That field is ill-tilled that wants harrowing, as even Columella knew' (94–5).

(7) Oblique ploughing is not nearly so good as turning the furrows back into the same places, before ploughing thirdly crosswise (97–8).

(8) Virgil might have advised alleviating drought by frequent hoeing so as to let in the dew, and have protected the corn from wet winters by the methods advocated in Ch. XI (100–1).

(9) The passage on lucky days calls out all the contempt of the scientific farmer in the Age of Reason; and he ends with a withering dismissal of Benson (276–7). His own husbandry could truly be called the *Anti-Virgilian*.

It will be observed that these strictures concern little more than one forty-line section, though admittedly an important one from the didactic point of view.

There were not lacking champions to fly to Virgil's defence, as may be seen from Mr Fussell's bibliography. Stephen Switzer and the Private Society of Husbandmen and Planters appealed to Benson's translation, alleging that Tull, like Dryden, had misrepresented the poet.[72] J. Randall, in *The Semi-Virgilian Husbandry* (written 1756, published 1764), discussed the advantage for various soils of the 'Virgilian or Old Husbandry', the 'New or Drill Husbandry' (Tull's), the 'Mixed' and a 'Semi-Virgilian' compromise of his own, one factor in this being the human limitation of ploughmen's intelligence (see esp. p. 158). And eminent authorities such as John Martyn and Adam Dickson continued to praise the Virgilian precepts.[73]

At G. I. 71–83 Virgil recommends alternation of cereal crops *either* with fallow *or* with pulse, vetch or lupine.* In the Middle Ages land was normally left fallow at least one year in three. Fallowing disappeared only gradually even in the eighteenth

---

* Pliny, *N.H.* 18. 187, citing Virgil's alternatives, gives preference to fallowing provided the estate is large enough to afford it.

century, and indeed it could be profitable, given heavy manuring.* Dickson reported that alternation of crop and fallow was still common in Switzerland and some provinces of France. He himself thought there was a lot to be said for it, 'taking our land and our farmers as they are in fact'.[74] But it is noteworthy that Virgil's alternative method, the basis of all modern practice, was read of for so many centuries without being heeded.

An anonymous life of the Methodist divine Adam Clarke alleges that about 1770, at Maghera in Northern Ireland, his schoolmaster father was cultivating a farm according to the rules laid down in Virgil's *Georgics*. But although, despite the difference in climate from that of Italy, his crops proved not inferior to those of his neighbours, it is clear that his behaviour was by now regarded as an eccentricity.[75] And indeed how far those very eclectic rules can ever have taken any practical farmer must remain extremely dubious. What the *Georgics* could still do was inspire an interest in farming, as in the case of Filippo Re, the most distinguished Italian agricultural scientist of the early nineteenth century.[76]

THE NINETEENTH CENTURY AND AFTER

The Sturm and Drang, the French Revolution, the Industrial Revolution and the Romantic Movement put an end to the only great vogue of the *Georgics*. Germany had turned from French classicism, with its adulation of Virgil, to the discovery of the Greeks. France itself now turned against what Voltaire had called

L'auteur harmonieux des douces Géorgiques.[77]

Victor Hugo, converted in 1789 to social democracy, reacted

---

* In the fourteenth century pulses were grown in the fallow year for human and animal consumption in the Netherlands, England and elsewhere; sometimes other crops were grown. The earliest recorded instance of intensive cultivation of this kind comes from Bourbough in French Flanders in 1328: H. Pirenne, *Soulèvement de la Flandre Maritime de 1323–29* (1900), pp. vi–vii, 208; cited by Slicher van Bath, p. 178. For rotation systems see his pp. 58–62; for the disappearance of fallow, pp. 244–54; for manuring, pp. 58–9.

against him, though he never shook off his influence.* In Britain, though the ploughman-poet Robert Burns naturally found the *Georgics* 'by far the best of Virgil',† the Romantics had other ideas. Hazlitt recorded his memory of his first acquaintance with Coleridge: 'He spoke of Virgil's *Georgics*, but not well. I do not think he had much feeling for the classical or elegant.'[78] There was also a general reaction against science as a subject for poetry, which Blake, Wordsworth and Keats made articulate.‡

In so far as the *Georgics* had any vogue in the nineteenth century, it was probably a narrower one, based on the work of classical scholars. But it may also have been a truer one, as inspired by the poem as a whole rather than mainly by the set-pieces. In England Andrew Lang's admiration, expressed in his *Lectures on Virgil*, is illustrated still by the praises of Italy and of Country Life; but Sellar's just appreciation may have redressed the balance, though enthusiasm was perhaps inhibited at an early age in the landed aristocracy by the institution of copying out a *Georgic* as a standard imposition at Eton.§ In France, though Sainte-Beuve's famous *Étude sur Virgile* deals only with the *Aeneid*,[79] it has been claimed that this was the first century in which the *Georgics* were properly appreciated.[80]

---

* As a boy he liked to translate passages of Virgil into the style of J. Delille. As a young man he revolted against all classicism. Later, exiled to Jersey, his hatred of tyrants and their flatterers extended to Augustus and Virgil, the Proem to the *Georgics* being particularly distasteful to him. But he translated Book I into verse in 1816, and at all periods there are references and echoes. *Mugitusque boum*, a poem written in Jersey, shows how haunted he still was. See A. Guiard, *Virgile et Victor Hugo* (1910); H. Heiss, 'Vergils Fortleben in den Romanischen Literaturen', in *Aus Roms Zeitwende*, 2nd Ser., XX (1937), pp. 112–14.

† The Scot James Grahame's poem *The British Georgics* (1809) is a last straggler from the eighteenth-century fashion.

‡ 'The declaration in the preface to the second edition of *Lyrical Ballads* in 1800 marks the end of the century as a logical terminus to an era when science was freely accepted as a subject for poetry' (W. P. Jones, *The Rhetoric of Science*, p. vii; *ibid.* p. 2 for Blake). The chief objection, of course, was to analytical science, as destroyer of the imagination and of religion.

§ H. W. Garrod wrote: 'In the XIX century, by a malicious paradox, the *Georgics* were proclaimed as Virgil's greatest achievement.' And he added, obtusely, as it seems to me: 'He has taken an impossible subject-matter; and the very perfection, technically, of this work only serves to deepen the sense of failure' (*English Literature and the Classics*, ed. G. S. Gordon, 1912, pp. 149–50).

In our own time there has been the remarkable impulse to translate the *Georgics* already referred to. There has also appeared what is perhaps the best of English georgics, *The Land*, by Victoria Sackville-West (1926), a poem descriptive and contemplative rather than didactic, Wordsworthian rather than Miltonian in verse-style, self-consciously restrained in the manner of the 1920s, and dedicated to giving a true picture of rural life in the Weald of Kent. Virgil is the avowed model. Few poems of this length in this age have achieved such success. *

But no georgic poem has ever come near to rivaling the original, and it would perhaps be appropriate to conclude by enquiring why. What was wrong with those worthy eighteenth-century efforts? It seems that either the contestants were too didactic, in which case they failed to leave the ground, or they were a conglomeration of rhetorical variations on set-pieces, in which case they lost contact with the ground and wandered aimlessly like a bunch of inflated balloons. As we read them our mind keeps visualising, not their subject, but a full-bottomed wig. Virgil could write of humble things without incurring the 'risibility' evoked in Johnson by the didactic poets of his age. His verse is his own, whatever the achievements of predecessors with the Latin hexameter; whereas these English poets with their 'verse Miltonian' stand to Milton somewhat as the Mannerists do to Michelangelo. Again, though they loved peace and retirement, and admired the Creator's works, they do not appear to love Nature intimately as Virgil had done, or as Wordsworth was to do.

James Thomson is so much the best, that a comparison between him and Virgil may highlight the differences. It was fortunate for Virgil that he chose didactic treatise as form to develop rather than rhetorical thesis. *The Seasons* lacks, almost completely, the foundation of technical lore that gives the *Georgics* not only variety but consistency and roots in the earth. Moreover, having

---

* Reprinted twenty times, 75,000 copies sold. The authoress, wife of Sir Harold Nicolson (and, incidentally, heroine of Virginia Woolf's *Orlando*), was well known as a writer on gardening. The poem is in four books, one for each season, in blank verse with lyrical interludes, and extends to about 2500 lines (more than Virgil's 2188).

been constantly enriched by additional episodes, it misses the
symphonic composition of the Latin poem. With 5417 lines it is
more than twice as long, yet Thomson is at pains to maintain
throughout a style which Virgil reserved for his higher set-pieces.
It is too often rhetorical, exaggerated, exclamatory, in the manner
of *O fortunatos...*, *Felix qui potuit...*, *O qui me gelidis convallibus
Haemi...* Though eloquent, it has not the subtle variety of
rhythm and music that we find in Virgil, and it is disfigured by
words such as 'successless' and 'friskful'. Though descriptive, it
has neither the eye for detail nor the ear for expressive sound that
makes the *Georgics* so vivid. All is black and white—ideal rustics
and wicked cities, Golden Age life and *convicium saeculi*. Now it is
self-consciously demure, like the tombs of the period with their
frigid sculptured personifications and bland eulogies, now self-
consciously wild and horrific like Salvator Rosa's landscapes and
the Gothic novel to come. When Virgil borrowed, it was
generally to improve. How could any poet write

> where cowslips hang
The dewy head

when Milton had written

> And cowslips wan that hang the pensive head?

The succinct economy and moral sensitivity of

> aut doluit miserans inopem aut invidit habenti

are both lacking in lines of such banal respectability as

> Base envy withers at another's joy
> And hates that excellence it cannot reach.

I have ventured (p. 184) to criticise Virgil for misplaced disparagement of the gifts of Bacchus; but while it is undeniable
that wine can cause havoc, the following is sheer hypocrisy:

> Give me to drain the cocoa's milky bowl,
> And from the palm to draw its freshening wine!
> More bounteous far than all the frantic juice
> Which Bacchus pours.[81]

The incessant eulogies of Nature's bounty and providence cloy:

> but chiefly thee, gay Green!
> Thou smiling Nature's universal robe!
> United light and shade! where the sight dwells
> With growing strength, and ever-new delight.[82]

One hankers for the irreverence of (?) Wilde: 'Nature is too green, and badly lit.' Thomson had also a sort of anti-serendipity, equalled only by Wordsworth, for choosing words which later usage was to make sound ridiculous—an apostrophe to 'awful Newton' or a description of sea-monsters that 'growl their horrid loves'. A line like

> Ye generous Britons, venerate the plough

sounds pompous to us, whereas rightly or wrongly 'non ullus aratro dignus honos' does not.

Virgil's poem seems a more genuine response even than Thomson's to personal experience and a historic moment of time. He had also the advantage that his moment of time was of ecumenical significance; and his poem was dedicated to a Maecenas, not to a Countess of Hartford. *The Seasons* is worth reading as Ausonius' *Mosella*, for instance, is worth reading. But I hope this book has done something to show why the *Georgics* is in an altogether higher class, or rather, unique and supreme.

Appendix I

RECENT LITERATURE ON THE STRUCTURE OF THE 'GEORGICS'

W. Kroll's contribution, the emphasis on *variatio* as an artistic principle, was made on pp. 188–97 of his *Studien zum Verständnis der Römischen Literatur* (1924). He was followed by the American H. W. Prescott, who devoted a few not very illuminating pages of his *The Development of Virgil's Art* (1927; reprinted 1963) to the *Georgics*, and by G. Czech in a Breslau dissertation of 1936, *Die Komposition der Georgica*. In *Stud. It. fil. class.* (1951) U. Albini had an article (pp. 49–64) on 'Struttura e motivi del primo libro delle Georgiche' in which he tried to show by analysis how kaleidoscopic Book I is, suggesting that this was due to the large number of sources being used in comparison with the other Books.

In 1927 K. Witte (*Die Geschichte der Römischen Dichtung*, Part I, 2: *Vergils Georgica*) set out to find the plan of the *Georgics*, guided by what Horace says in *A.P.* He detected three principles at work: (1) τὸ ἔνια παραλείπειν καὶ ὕστερον φράζειν, 'leaving some things aside to be expressed later' (cf. *A.P.* 42–4, 148 f.); (2) repetition of words or thoughts to bind together individual sections or half-books; (3) the construction of counterpart passages (pp. 157–78). Unfortunately in the analysis preceding this chapter he sought to impose upon the poem an abstract and mathematical system which is not illuminating. (See E. Burck, *Phil. Woch.* 1928, p. 296.) Magdalena Schmidt, in *Die Komposition von Vergils Georgica* (1930), emphasising the subjective nature of the poem, also postulated a plan (pp. 9–15); but in her analysis she too got lost in chimerical schemes involving numbers of lines (see F. H. Sandbach's annihilation of these, *C.R.* 1931, pp. 140–1).

G. Ramain's forward-looking article 'A propos de Virgile, *Géorgiques* III, 416–39' in the *Revue de Philologie* for 1924 occupied only seven pages (117–23). In 1929 E. Burck, developing his 1926 dissertation *De Vergilii Georgicon partibus iussivis*, published in *Hermes* (1929, pp. 279–321) an article on 'Die Komposition von Vergil's *Georgica*' which put the study of the poem on a fresh basis. Presuming (like Witte and Schmidt) that Virgil realised he was composing, under the semblance of didactic, an entirely new kind of poem, he too sought for the guiding artistic principle, and found that the poem was much more organic than had been supposed. In future Virgil's use of sources would be studied in order to show, not his dependence, but the significance of his alterations. It should also be mentioned that in this same year of 1929, independently of Burck, D. L. Drew published a short article on 'The Structure of Vergil's Georgics' in *A.J.Ph.* (pp. 242–54). In this he recognised the relevance of what had been called 'digressions', and correctly divided the work into two parts, in which 1 and 3, 2 and 4, corresponded, as shown by a table of topics. Burck's method was applied in greater detail to a limited section (1. 43–139) by R. Beutler in *Hermes* (1940) pp. 410–21. It also formed the basis of K. Büchner's treatment of this aspect in his *Real-Enzyclopädie* article 'P. Vergilius Maro' (1955). F. Klingner made similar assumptions in several articles later absorbed into his *Virgils Georgica* (1963). Brooks Otis went further in his chapter (v) on the *Georgics* in *Virgil: a Study in Civilized Poetry* (1963). (See note on p. 73.) E. Paratore (*Virgilio*, 1961, p. 249) is sceptical about such analyses.

Appendix II

NUMERICAL SCHEMATISM IN THE 'GEORGICS'

Much attention has recently been paid to the finding of ratios between the number of lines devoted by ancient poets to different topics. Even Hesiod has been credited with such interests, the proem of the *Theogony* being analysed as a 35+45+35 structure (H. Schwabl: adversely criticised by M. L. West, *C.R.* 1968, pp. 27–8). It is well known that the Pythagoreans took a mystical interest in the properties of numbers; also that the Greeks were aware that certain proportions were satisfying to the eye. The vogue for Neopythagoreanism in the time of Julius Caesar (see p. 124) has been held to account for proportions diagnosed in Roman poetry, though R. J. Getty thought it went back to Ennius (*T.A.Ph.A.* 1960, p. 323; and pp. 310–23 ff. for Lucan). O. Skutsch has recently drawn attention to numerical relationships between the lengths of groups of poems in Propertius I, assuming conscious management but not speculating on reasons (*C.Ph.* 1963, pp. 238–9); and B. Otis has added the speculation (*H.S.Ph.* 1965, pp. 1–44). J. Perret (*Horace*, 1959, p. 106) divided *Odes* 3 into three blocks of 336 lines (the 'Roman Odes', 1–6; 7–19; 20–30); though the second seems actually to add up to 332 (328 if 11. 17–20 is spurious).

As to Virgil, P. Maury inaugurated the present hunt in 1944 with his 'Le secret de Virgile et l'architecture des *Bucoliques*' (*Lettres d'Humanité*, pp. 71–147). He saw the *Eclogues* as an elaborately symbolic whole, a 'temple', and added up the lines of the component poems variously to produce the well-known 'Pythagorean' numbers of 333 and 666 (the latter being the Triangle of the Great Tetrachys, sum of all the numbers from 1 to 36—also, incidentally, the number of the Beast in the Apocalypse, xviii. 13). By assigning their numerical values to letters, he identified 333 with Caesar (in the accusative) and 666 with Gallus (approximately). J. Perret accepted these findings in the first edition of his *Virgile* (1952), but eliminated the numerical part in the second edition of 1965. Marouzeau rejected them on *a priori* grounds (*R.E.L.* 1945, pp. 74–6), and Otis called them 'very dubious' (*Virgil*, p. 406).

We must not rule out *a priori* any idea that good poets could attach significance to numbers. Cicero in his mystical *Somnium Scipionis* (*De Rep.* 6. 12) speaks of 7 and 8 as 'pleni numeri'. Most of us have a prejudice in favour of round numbers. The proem of the *Culex* contains

10 lines, that of the *Ciris* 100. It is well known that Augustan poets in making up collections of their poems showed this prejudice (A. Kiessling, *Zu Augusteischen Dichtern* 1881, p. 73). When Dante received a Latin poem in 97 lines from Giovanni del Virgilio, he replied in one of the same number, but expressed regret that Giovanni had not written 3 more to make up a full 100 (*Egloghe* 4. 42 f.).

Virgil displayed a liking for 3, 7, 12 and 30. The years of reigns he made elapse (*Aen.* 1. 261–74) between the Trojan landing in Italy and the birth of Romulus numbered 3 (Aeneas) + 30 (Ascanius) + 300 (the Alban kings). Theocritus credited Ptolemy with reigning over 33,333 cities (17. 82–5), and Kazantzakes' modern sequel to the *Odyssey* has that total of lines. It did not escape medieval minds, prone as they were to cabalism of all kinds, that Jesus had lived for 33 years. The *Divine Comedy* consists of 1 + 33 + 33 + 33 = 100 cantos, and there are 10 heavens in the Paradiso. 'Here number is no longer an outer framework, but a symbol of cosmic *ordo*.'*

Nevertheless some preliminary cautions may be in place. By the laws of probability certain numerical relations will crop up. The impressive schemes and codes alleged to have been found in the Shakespearian corpus (sometimes held to be substantiated by *Bacon's* known interest in cryptography) have all been shown to be illusory by two leading American cryptographic experts (W. F. and E. S. Friedman, *The Shakespearian Ciphers Examined*, 1957). When it comes to intricate proportions between numbers of lines in a poem, we must remember that ancient poetry was meant to be taken in by the *ear*, and that beyond a very limited *Präsenzzeit* the ear cannot operate; also that even the eye could take in these sometimes widely separated correspondences much less easily in an ancient roll-form book, which one hand normally wound up as the other unwound, especially if there were no paragraphing marks, than in a modern codex-form book. If poets did indulge in such schemes, it was for their own delectation, not the reader's. Division into sections by content is in any case often a subjective matter. Enthusiasts for numerical schemes should also realise that the more writers they find to whom their scheme applies, the more suspect it may become. Nevertheless there certainly are some valid correspondences, τὸ γὰρ καλὸν ἐν μεγέθει καὶ τάξει ἐστίν, 'for beauty depends on size and organisation' (Ar. *Poet.* 7). Cicero speaks of 'what almost amounts to the counting and measuring of syllables in periodic

---

* E. Curtius, *European Literature and the Latin Middle Ages*, tr. W. R. Trask (1953), Exc. xv, to which I owe most of the above facts.

prose', but he wisely adds that such things 'fiunt magnificentius quam docentur' (*Or.* 147). It is not at all improbable that a slow-working, careful, sensitive artist like Virgil should have taken pains over proportion, whatever interpretation we may place on Suetonius' assertion that in his youth 'maxime mathematicae operam dedit' (*Vita* 15); but it is unlikely that he donned a strait-jacket, let alone several at once, to the hampering of his Muse. Norden (*Sitz. Berl. Akad.* 1934, p. 635) speaks of 'schwebendes Gleichgewicht', but he adds 'Zahlenmässige Bindung wird nicht angestrebt—das wäre in fortschreitender Erzählung leerer Formalismus'.

So much by way of preamble: now for the *Georgics*. The Jesuit Father G. Le Grelle, unaware as he says (pp. 233–4) of Maury's researches on the *Eclogues*, was analysing the *Georgics*, and his results appeared in 1949 ('Le premier livre des *Géorgiques*, poème pythagoricien'; *Ét. Class.* pp. 139–235). If the proem (1–42), and what he defines as the epilogue (462·5–514), are subtracted from Book 1, we are left with a central core of 420·5 lines. There is, as all agree, a major break at 203. Le Grelle takes it as dividing the core into two parts, which he tendentiously names 'Works' and 'Days'. These parts are of 161 and 259·5 lines respectively, and they prove to be in the ratio called 'Golden section', or (since the Renaissance) 'divine proportion'. In this

$$\frac{\text{whole}}{\text{greater part}} = \frac{\text{greater part}}{\text{lesser part,}}$$

and it was discovered early in the thirteenth century to be based on a series ('Fibonacci Series' from Leonardo Fibonacci) 1, 1, 2, 3, 5, 8, 13, 21, 34, 55, etc., in which each number after 1 is the sum of its two predecessors, and the division of any number into the previous one gives an answer progressively nearer to 0·618...

Le Grelle's result looks striking, but there are basic reservations to be made. An unprejudiced analysis might well divide the core into three, not two parts (43–203, 204–310, 311–462·5), since the weather-signs are distinct from what could conceivably be entitled the 'Days' (as in Richter's scheme, pp. 408–9); and indeed, although I should allow that the Epilogue begins at 462·5, 'solem quis dicere falsum audeat...', not all would (H. Wagenvoort, *M.Ph.* 1952, p. 10).

Le Grelle then proceeds (p. 148) to detach lines 204–58, which he calls the 'foyer astronomique', and the kernel of the poem. (He dignifies it with the name of 'triptych', though it is a very lopsided one—27+21+7=55 lines.) If you now subtract this from the second section of the poem, and disregard the opening summary of the whole

(1–4·5), the whole poem can be analysed as 37·5 + 161 + 55 + 204·5 + 51·5 lines. Adding alternately, we get 37·5 + 55 + 51·5 = 144 (12 × 12), which last figure reveals that Virgil has put clues at 232,

> per *duodena* regit mundi sol aureus astra,

and the break-line

> *sol* tibi signa dabit.

The other alternating figures, 161 and 204·5, add up to 365½, the number of days in the year, ruled by the sun. This too looks striking, if inconceivably complicated for the poet, but the omission of 1–4·5 seems rather like 'cooking'.

Le Grelle goes further, and applies the principle of the Golden ratio to shorter sections of Book 1, which he calls 'chrysodes' (pp. 156 ff., table on p. 184). The isolation of these is sometimes arbitrary; e.g. one is made to end (p. 168) at 306, where nearly all editors print only a comma. He also finds a secret astronomic basis for the Book (pp. 195 ff.). The signs of Taurus and Boötes are emphasised at 204–30 because of their agriculturally significant names. The plough described at 169–75 is eclectic, not a real plough but one modelled on the constellation of that name, hence the plural *dentalia*, from the two stars ζ and η. The 'holy of holies' of the Book is 240–3 : it contains the secret, that the poem itself is a symbol of the cosmos. Moreover, the lines dealing with the temperate zone, when isolated, prove to total 333 = Καῖσαρα (cf. Maury, *Lettres d'Humanité*), the half of 666. Virgil emerges as the thorough-going cryptic Neopythagorean that Carcopino and others had long believed him to be.

In 1962 G. E. Duckworth produced his elaborate *Structural Patterns and Proportions in the Aeneid*, based likewise on the Golden section. His pupil E. L. Brown followed this in 1963 with the similarly based *Numeri Vergiliani: Studies in the 'Eclogues' and 'Georgics'*. Brown even deduces that Virgil emphasised his structural mathematics by patterns of what Jackson Knight called 'homodyne' lines—lines in which ictus and accent coincide in the fourth foot; and he unearths more hidden astrology. Meanwhile J. Schilling has pointed out (*Bull. Ass. Budé*, 1961, pp. 226–7) that if we agree that one line is spurious (4. 338 would be a good candidate), the number of lines in the *Georgics* adds up to 2187, which is 3[7].* So now we know what Virgil was busying himself

---

* Mr A. G. Lee points out to me that Schilling has missed a chance here: 2 + 1 + 8 + 7 = 18, and 1 + 8 = 9 = 3 × 3.

with on those afternoons and evenings when he was 'licking into shape' the many verses he had written in the morning. It is astonishing that he only took seven years over it, still more astonishing that he produced such a good poem in spite of all his mathematical preoccupations.

Some scholars seem to have been impressed by these findings, which are expounded with the utmost ingenuity. Thus Jackson Knight, perhaps predictably, told the Virgil Society, on the basis presumably of Le Grelle and an article by Duckworth, that Virgil 'certainly followed, often exactly but sometimes approximately, the "Golden ratio"' (*Proc. Virg. Soc.* 1961, pp. 5–6). It is therefore necessary to insist that they are vulnerable. On the one hand the divisions in the poems discerned according to subject are sometimes quite arbitrary. Duckworth (p. 41) divides the whole of the *Georgics* in a most disputable way into 1352 lines on agriculture and 835 of description, and then points out that these figures are in Golden ratio. Again (p. 104) he finds evidence of Golden ratios in Lucretius, of all poets. Was *he* then a cryptic Neopythagorean? It is hardly more likely that Ovid (as has been sometimes alleged) was a Neopythagorean, though the *Metamorphoses* can yield its harvest of Golden ratios too, if required (Wagenvoort made the experiment on Book 1: *M.Ph.* 1952, p. 10). Duckworth further finds them in the thirteenth Book of the *Aeneid* composed by the Renaissance humanist Maffeo Vegio (*Structural Patterns*), and has to assume that he had 'a subconscious feeling for Virgil's symmetry'. Every fresh discovery should have led him to the conclusion that the whole thing might be a mare's nest. A. Dalzell, in a devastating review (*Phoenix*, 1963, pp. 314–16), noted that Duckworth's own book contained 104 pages of core, 168 of preface, appendixes, etc., and that these totals display the Golden ratio exactly. M. L. Clarke likewise (*C.R.* 1964, p. 45) found that John Betjeman in his *Summoned by Bells* was just as much addicted to Fibonacci series as Virgil, and had nearly as large a proportion of Golden ratios, which would no doubt surprise him. J. Marouzeau got similar results to Maury's from Théophile Gautier's *Émaux et Camées* (*R.E.L.* 1945, p. 76); and he reported a most remarkable analysis showing the extraordinary structural patterns and apparently significant numbers which can be extracted from our text of Tibullus —all moonshine, however, since there are generally admitted lacunae in that text (*R.E.L.* 1946, pp. 77–8). Though Greek mathematicians such as Euclid knew of the Golden section, the evidence for its application to art and architecture is less secure, and the leap implied in its transference to literature very great; nor is there any evidence that the Fibonacci series was known in antiquity (Clarke, *C.R.* p. 44).

Scholars who have examined these findings have generally proved sceptical (e.g. V. Pöschl on Le Grelle, *Anz. für die Altertumsw.* 1953, cols. 1–4; R. D. Williams, *Virgil: Greece and Rome Survey* 1, 1967, p. 41). Leaving Golden ratios aside, the following points seem worth mentioning in relation to symmetry in the *Georgics*.

The name of Maecenas occurs in line 2 of Books 1 and 4, and in line 41 of Books 2 and 3. If this is intentional, it is hard to see why; but the importance of the positioning of proper names in *Horace's odes* has been confirmed in a recent study by L. A. Moritz (*C.Q.* 1968, pp. 116–31).

Book 3 (566 lines) is divided exactly half-way at 283 as between larger and smaller animals. Book 4 also has 566 lines; here the significant break, before the account of Bugonia, comes at 280 in the text we have (possibly altered to some extent if reference to Gallus was really later eliminated); i.e. three lines short of exact symmetry. In Book 1, of 514 lines, there is a break near the exact middle (257), which editors variously place at 256 and 258. Klingner (p. 48) says that the centrality of this break 'can hardly be chance'; but, *pace* le Grelle, it is not one of the main two breaks, which occur at 203 and 350. Moreover, we have strong evidence that most of Book 1 was composed years before its prologue and epilogue; we should therefore have to suppose either that these were carefully tailored to fit the rest with mathematical precision, or *vice versa*. The same applies to Book 3, where the main break is exactly in the middle; for we know that its proem was one of the last things in the poem to be composed (Triple Triumph). Book 2 (542 lines) has nothing that could be called a break anywhere near the middle (271). Why not, if such things mattered?

Perret (p. 60) has found an approximate symmetry in Book 4 on the following lines (O.C.T. numbering):

1–7	Introduction.	7 lines
8–148	Hive, swarming. Corycian old man.	141
149–280	Bees' polity. Collecting honey. Diseases.	132
281–414	Aristaeus' grief.	134
415–558	Restoration of the hive.	144
559–566	Epilogue.	8

Even granting that it is right to allot the interlude about the Corycian to the second section, it is not clear that the Aristaeus epyllion should be divided at 414. There is a more obvious break at 418; but in any case surely the story of Orpheus and Eurydice should count as a distinct section (453–527).

Perret also (p. 68) asserts that the correlation between the theodicy of hard work in Book 1 and the Corycian's reward for it in Book 4 is emphasised by the fact that each theme occupies exactly the same place in the respective Books, lines 125–46. But even if these two sections can plausibly be detached thus from the paragraphs in which they are normally embedded, surely the theodicy in Book 1 begins in 121, not at 125.

Otis (pp. 190 ff.) analyses the Aristaeus epyllion. He assumes a break at 360; but if we put this rather at 362, with Richter, there is no very striking symmetry (29 lines to 24 or 23). Again Cyrene's speech comprises 28 lines; but a corresponding section of 28 can be obtained only by somewhat arbitrarily making a break at 424 and entitling what follows 'Aristeaus and Proteus in the cave', whereas it is much more natural to make the break at 418·5. The balance thus proves 'obvious' (p. 192) in neither case, when we scrutinise the text. Norden's analysis (*Sitz. Berl. Akad.* 1934, p. 635) had shown rougher correlations, whose inexactitude he was concerned to emphasise.

There certainly are some passages that balance exactly. Book 2 has two proems (1–8, 35–46): each is followed by a 26-line didactic section (Richter). In Book 3 there are three successive sections of 10 lines (384–413). The successive sections on cows for breeding and horses for breeding (3. 49–71, 72–94) are each of 23 lines. But more often, as Klingner has pertinently observed, the symmetry is not exact where Virgil could easily have made it so. In other words, he was not a pedant. The main part of the Praise of Country Life in Book 2 falls into two parts of 18 and 19 lines respectively (495–512, 513–531). In Book 3 17 lines on the dying horse are succeeded by 16 on the dying ox (498–530).

Appendix III

———————◆———————

THE PROEM TO BOOK 3

In his *Real-Enzyklopädie* article 'P. Vergilius Maro' (1955) K. Büchner put forward the idea that lines 3–9 and the triumph-symbolism refer to the *Georgics*, not to a future epic (cols. 270–1. Cf. W. Wimmel, *Kallimachos in Rom*, 1960, p. 178). U. Fleischer in an important article, 'Musentempel und Oktavianehrung des Vergil' (*Hermes*, 1960, pp. 280–331), develops this idea (pp. 293 ff.). He also argues that the temple is, in the first place, for the Muses (pp. 304 ff.). Virgil has combined this notion with that of a thankoffering to a living man who is also a friend of the Muses (p. 321). The proem was conceived as a literary one addressed to Maecenas but promising at the end an epic on Octavian's victories. This was converted after Octavian's successes of 30–29 into a eulogy of him (pp. 328–9). Following Büchner, he argues that 'Invidia' refers to envy of the poet (pp. 311 ff.).

W. Richter in his commentary (1957) takes the orthodox line about this, that the proem concerns the future epic, and Invidia represents envy of Octavian (pp. 261–2). (He presumably went to press too early in any case to take account of Büchner's view.) But Büchner's view is rejected by Klingner (1963), pp. 136 ff.; 252. He points out that *cetera* in 3 can hardly mean all subjects other than those like the *Georgics*. If he had had the *Georgics* in mind, Virgil would have instanced as outworn the subjects of the didactic metaphrasts. *Aonio vertice* (11, = Helicon) cannot refer specifically to the didactic poet Hesiod, as it is clearly a reminiscence of what Lucretius said (1. 118) of the epic poet Ennius. *Modo vita supersit* would be a surprising precautionary statement if it referred to the almost completed *Georgics*. And *interea*, etc. (40) clearly indicates that what precedes refers to activity that will take place after the *Georgics* are finished. Klingner also ignores Fleischer's suggestion, surely impossible, that the temple is for the Muses.

W. Wimmel, in *Kallimachos in Rom*, tries to interpret this proem as a Callimachean *recusatio* softened into a vague promise of future eulogy of Octavian (pp. 177–87). He is concerned with tracing the influence of the *Aetia* prologue in particular through Roman literature. But while Virgil was ready on occasion to use that prologue (see pp. 34–5 on *Eclogue* 6), to suppose that it played much part in this proem seems strained. For although the ultimate epic did not turn out like what this might have led one to expect, the spirit of refusal is hardly present here. The apparent echoes of Callimachus—the way, the chariot-driving, envy—could all come just as easily from Pindar, and seem to do so.*

* The interpretation on p. 180 of *ingens* (of the Mincius, 14) in terms of the Alexandrian literary dispute is very doubtful; J. W. Mackail argued that here and in various other passages it had its root meaning of 'native', which suits this context much better than 'vast': *C.R.* (1912), pp. 251–5.

It is true that the idea of the poet as *triumphator* (riding *with* his own Muse, not leading Muses captive) occurs in a Callimachean elegy of Propertius (3. 1. 10–12): but Propertius could have adapted the idea from Virgil.

Appendix IV

RECENT LITERATURE ON THE ARISTAEUS EPYLLION

Heyne and Voss disbelieved Servius' story of Gallus and the substitution, and Keightley thought that at most a few lines on him *à propos* Bugonia in Egypt had been cut out. But Conington and Nettleship accepted it, and for many years this was the orthodox view. E. Burck, in his pioneering article 'Die Komposition von Vergils *Georgica*' in *Hermes* (1929), excluded the Aristaeus episode from consideration, as he then believed it to be a substitute (pp. 316 ff. He has since changed his mind about the extent of the alteration, *Gnomon*, 1959, p. 230). J. Heurgon (*Mél. d'arch. et d'hist.* 1932, pp. 6–60) argued that Orpheus' losing Eurydice again because he looked back at her through uncontrollable love was an innovation of Virgil's; but C. M. Bowra (*C.Q.* 1952, pp. 113–26) deduces that he was following a Hellenistic poem for the Orpheus story.

In 1930 E. Norden, believing himself alone in his opinion, attacked the whole Servius story of the *laudes Galli* and their replacement by the Aristaeus episode. In fact the story had also been rejected simultaneously in part by Magdalena Schmidt (*Die Komposition von Vergils Georgica*, 1930, pp. 161–4): she thought the praises of Gallus had been a short passage only, following l. 294. By the time Norden published his lecture (*Sitz. Berl. Akad.* 1934, pp. 626–83) he had read the scathing attack on Servius' story made by W. B. Anderson, who also believed himself to be alone, in *C.Q.* 1933, pp. 36–45 and 73. A. Klotz (*Würz. Jahrb.* 1947, pp. 140–7) did not accept Servius fully, but suggested that the *laudes Galli* had occupied some 60 lines at the end of the poem. J. Perret (pp. 49 ff.) is sceptical about the story.

Belief in Servius reappears in Büchner, cols. 294–5. He suggests that in the original version Gallus was praised as the elegiac poet of love, and tries to establish the priority of certain passages in the *Aeneid* to some in the Aristaeus episode, which could thus be plausibly a substitute inserted in 26/25 B.C. The difficulty remains, that so large a space should have been devoted to Gallus. Richter in his edition (1957) also accepts Servius' story; but he supposes that the original ending was never published. The story is also accepted by E. de Saint-Denis in his Budé edition (1956), and by T. J. Haarhoff, who thought that Orpheus was meant to stand for Gallus (*C.Ph.* 1960, pp. 101–8). E. Paratore follows the version that makes only the Orpheus episode a substitute (*Virgilio*, 1961, pp. 265 ff.). He sees its relevance to the *Georgics* in the idea of Orpheus as the enchanter-poet of nature, and also, like P. Scazzoso (*Paideia*, 1956, pp. 5–28), as centre of mystery cults of agrarian origin. The connections seem too vague to apply to the whole poem, but the Mysteries *may* be relevant to the Orpheus episode.

The scepticism of G. E. Duckworth (*A.J.Ph.* 1959, pp. 225–37) evoked a rejoinder from R. G. G. Coleman (*A.J.Ph.* 1962, pp. 55–71), who suggested that the substituted epyllion was in itself a tribute to Gallus, an epyllion such as he wrote, with a central theme of tragic love which would have appealed to him; the themes of Egypt, *pietas* and tragic personal loss had a poignant meaning for Virgil after Gallus' death; the *aition* might have occurred in the original version, but the introduction of Orpheus was new; the *laudes Galli* could only have occupied a few lines. But any theory that Gallus is lamented under cover of Orpheus raises the question whether Virgil would risk offending Augustus by thus getting round a *damnatio memoriae*; and if there were only a few lines on Gallus, they could easily have been simply cut out with a minimum of readaptation.

In 1963, however, both F. Klingner in his *Virgils Georgica* and Brooks Otis in his *Virgil: a Study in Civilized Poetry* came out against Servius, basing their belief in the original status of the Aristaeus epyllion on views of its integral relevance to the interpretation of the poem as a whole. C. Segal pursues this symbolistic kind of interpretation still further in 'Orpheus and the Fourth Georgic', *A.J.Ph.* (1966), pp. 307–25. According to him the episode suggests 'that human life framed between the two figures (Aristaeus and Orpheus) is *essentially* tragic. And here emerges the significance of the first half of the Book, the bees: instead of collectivity selflessly devoted to the *genus immortale* we have in the second part individuals engaged in the personal emotions almost to the exclusion of anything else' (p. 323). I confess that, while I admire the ingenuity of this kind of criticism, I find it hard to believe that Proteus, for instance, represents the primal quietudes of life as contrasted with Aristaeus, the man of work and productivity (p. 317); or that Virgil can be interpreted in such terms as 'the unbridgeable gulf between soul and instinct' (p. 325).

Appendix V

◆

CHIASTIC PATTERN OF MOTIFS IN G. 4. 457-522

G. Norwood, *C.J.* (1940–1), pp. 354–5, found chiastic structure of
motifs in the Orpheus and Eurydice passage in Virgil, on the following
lines:

(1)	457–9	Death beside a stream owing to rejection of love.
(2)	461–3	Impressive Greek geographical names.
(3)	464–6	Persistent singing, utterly indifferent to world around.
(4)	473 ff.	Simile of birds.
(5)	478–80	Infernal streams.
(6)	481–503	Heart of the story.
(7)	506	An infernal stream.
(8)	511–15	Simile of a bird.
(9)	507–20	Persistent singing, utterly indifferent to world around.
(10)	512 f.	Impressive Greek geographical names.
(11)	520–2	Death beside a stream owing to rejection of love.

Some of the correspondences here may seem rather vague. But the
remarkable thing is that Norwood seems to have sensed the chiastic
structure without realising that there is a more striking precedent in
Catullus' Allius elegy (68 A), namely:

(1)	1–11	Desire to thank Allius.
(2)	11–26	Catullus' former troubles in love and Allius as helper.
(3)	27–32	Catullus' memory of his joy at Lesbia's coming once.
(4)	33–4	Laodameia's joy in coming, *flagrans amore*, to Prote- silaus' house.
(5)	35–46	Laodameia's sorrow at loss of Protesilaus, killed at Troy.
(6)	47–52	Troy as grave of the heroes, and of Catullus' brother.
(7)	52–6	Heart of the poem: lament for brother.
(8)	57–64	Troy as grave of brother, and of the heroes.
(9)	65–78	Laodameia's sorrow at loss of Protesilaus.
(10)	79–90	Laodameia's joy at Protesilaus' return from death.
(11)	91–4	Catullus' memory of his joy at Lesbia's coming once.
(12)	95–108	Catullus' present troubles in love.
(13)	109–20	Desire to thank Allius (and bless others).

Mr W. A. Camps draws my attention to chiastic form in *Aeneid* 2:
Greeks–Horse–Laocoon–Sinon–Laocoon–Horse–Greeks. Other such
chiastic patterns, in Catullus 64 and the *Aeneid*, have been discovered
by C. W. Mendell, 'The Influence of the Epyllion on the *Aeneid*',
Y.Cl.S. (1951), pp. 212 ff., 222 ff.; and in Aratus 367–85 by D. A. Kidd,
Antichthon (1967), pp. 12–15. It looks as if these were a feature of
Hellenistic poetry.

Appendix VI

LITERATURE ON AGRICULTURAL LORE IN
THE 'GEORGICS'

T. Keightley's *Notes on the Bucolics and Georgics* (1846) is still valuable, and D. G. Mitchell's *Wet Days at Edgeworth* (1884) well worth reading. Virgil's sources were investigated at the beginning of this century by P. Jahn in a series of articles tiresomely distributed over different periodicals (see his own report in Bursian's *Jahresbericht* of 1906 covering Virgil in 1901–4). His conclusions are not always acceptable. As a starting-point for modern discussion we may take E. Burck's inaugural dissertation *De Vergilii Georgicon partibus iussivis* (1926). Two years later threre appeared the most comprehensive account of Virgil's agricultural lore in R. Billiard's *L'agriculture dans l'antiquité d'après les Géorgiques de Virgile*, a delightfully humane critical survey by one who was an expert particularly on the vine. Also attractive, but somewhat less reliable, was a series of studies by P. d'Hérouville, collected in *À la campagne avec Virgile* (1930); *Géorgiques I et II* (1942).

On field crops it is still worth while to consult Adam Dickson's classic *The Husbandry of the Ancients* (posthumous, 1788); and most recently there is K. D. White's *Roman Agriculture*. The weather-signs in Book 1 were treated by L. A. S. Jermyn in *G.&R.* (1951), pp. 26–37, 49–59.

J. Sargeaunt, *The Trees, Shrubs and Plants of Virgil* (1920), is particularly useful for Book 2. (Elfriede Abbe, *The Plants of Virgil's Georgics*, 1965, is beautifully illustrated if not wholly reliable.) T. F. Royds's companion volume to Sargeaunt, *The Beasts, Birds and Bees of Virgil* (1918), is equally useful, especially for Books 3 and 4; and on Virgil's birds there is chapter vii of W. Warde Fowler's *A Year with the Birds* (3rd edn. 1889).

On bee-lore in antiquity there is the German work of J. Klek and L. Armbruster, *Archiv für Bienenkunde* (1920), pp. 263 ff., and several books by E. Zander. In English there is H. M. Fraser, *Beekeeping in Antiquity* (1931), and B. G. Whitfield, 'Virgil and the Bees', *G.&R.* (1956), pp. 99–117. On bees in general see E. Tickner Edwardes, *The Lore of the Honeybee* (1923); C. R. Ribbands, *The Behaviour and Social Life of Honey Bees* (1954); G. Nixon, *The World of Bees* (1954); and best of all, K. von Frisch's *The Dancing Bees* (new edn. in English, 1967).

Appendix VII

———◆———

LITERATURE ON THE 'GEORGICS' IN
AFTER TIMES

The history of the *Georgics* in after times has not hitherto been written, and the material for Chapter x has been collected from a wide range of sources. For the Middle Ages I found no work that had more than the most casual references; but for later times there are some that deserve particular mention.

M. L. Lilly, *The Georgic* (1919), is a useful compilation which draws attention to a very large number of poems that may be investigated under this category. Its rarity in England may be due to its having appeared in America during the First World War. The two volumes of V. Zabughin, *Virgilio nel Rinascimento* (1921–3), proved most valuable for the Renaissance. For country-house poetry P. A. F. Van Veen, *De Soeticheydt des Buyten-Levens Vergheselschapt met de Boecken* (1960), to which my friend Professor J. H. Waszink kindly drew my attention, is a very full treatment with extensive bibliography. The two volumes of M. S. Røstwig's *The Happy Man* (1954–8) are full of ideas as well as information. For English poetry E. Nitchie, *Virgil and the English Poets* (1919), is very useful, as also an article by W. P. Mustard in *A.J.Ph.* (1908), pp. 1–31, on 'Virgil's Georgics and the British Poets'. An excellent recent work which bears indirectly on the subject is W. P. Jones, *The Rhetoric of Science* (1966).

On agriculture, the old work of Adam Dickson, *The Husbandry of the Ancients*, (1788), reflects later history, and a good historical account for background is provided by B. H. Slicher van Bath in his *Agrarian History of Western Europe, A.D. 500–1850* (Engl. tr. 1963). For bibliography see the Rothamsted Library Catalogue (1926) and G. E. Fussell's two volumes, *Old English Farming Books, from Fitzherbert to Tull* (1947) and *More Old English Farming Books* (1950).

List of abbreviations

Abbreviations for periodicals are in accordance with the recognised list in *L'Année philologique*.

The following abbreviations are used for certain modern works:

Billiard   R. Billiard, *L'agriculture dans l'antiquité d'après les Géorgiques de Virgile* (1928).

Büchner   K. Büchner, 'P. Vergilius Maro', in Pauly–Wissowa–Kroll's *Real-Enzyklopädie* VIIIA (1955); separately issued 1956.

Burck (1929)   E. Burck, 'Die Komposition von Virgils *Georgica*', *Hermes* (1929), pp. 279–321.

Comparetti   D. Comparetti, *Virgil in the Middle Ages*, tr. from Italian by E. F. M. Benecke (1895).

Dahlmann   H. Dahlmann, 'Der Bienenstaat in Vergil's Georgica', *Abh. Akad. Mainz* (1954), pp. 547–62.

Fleischer   U. Fleischer, 'Musentempel und Oktavianehrung', *Hermes* (1960), pp. 280–331.

Hubelei   A. Hubelei, 'Virgile en France au XVIe siècle', *Revue du seizième siècle* (1931), pp. 1–77.

Keightley   T. Keightley, *Notes on the Bucolics and Georgics of Virgil* (1846).

Klingner (1963)   F. Klingner, *Virgils Georgica* (1963).

Mustard   W. P. Mustard, 'Virgil's Georgics and the British Poets', *A.J.Ph.* (1908), pp. 1–31.

Nitchie   E. Nitchie, *Vergil and the English Poets* (1919).

Otis   B. Otis, *Virgil: a Study in Civilized Poetry* (1963).

Perret   J. Perret, *Virgile: l'homme et l'œuvre* (1952).

Røstwig   M. S. Røstwig, *The Happy Man*, vol. I (1954); vol. II (1958).

Royds   T. F. Royds, *The Beasts, Birds and Bees of Virgil* (1914).

Sargeaunt   J. Sargeaunt, *The Trees, Shrubs and Plants of Virgil* (1920).

Slicher van Bath   B. H. Slicher van Bath, *The Agrarian History of Western Europe, A.D. 500–1850*, tr. O. Ordish (1959).

Syme   R. Syme, *The Roman Revolution* (1939).

Zabughin   V. Zabughin, *Virgilio nel Rinascimento Italiano*, vol. I (1921); vol. II (1923).

Index of references

Chapter I. Introduction

1 *Virgil* (1874; 3rd edn. 1897).
2 Since then, in the United States, S. P. Bovie (1956), H. A. Hedges (1959).
3 *The Buried Day* (1960), p. 97.
4 21 Sept. 1819 (*The Letters of John Keats*, ed. M. Buxton Forman, 2nd edn. (1935), p. 384).
5 *Roman Vergil*, p. 165.
6 [Dion. Hal.] *Rhet.* 10. 17.
7 *Aeneis VI* (3rd edn. 1927), p. 420. D. E. W. Wormell, in *Lucretius*, ed. D. R. Dudley (1965), p. 51.
8 1361–78, 1448–57. See pp. 138–42.

9 7. 5. 2–3.
10 K. Woermann, *History of Painting*, tr. and ed. S. Colvin, 1 (1880), pp. 133–5.
11 K. Schefold, *Pompeanische Malerei* (1952), p. 73.
12 *Ibid.* pp. 34–43; J. Perret, *Virgile*, p. 73.
13 F. Klingner, 'Die Einheit des Virgilischen Lebenswerkes', in *Röm. Geisteswelt* (4th edn.), p. 287.
14 *Ep.* 86. 15.
15 *Biographia Litteraria*, ch. XIV.

Chapter II. Early Life of Virgil

1 New Oxford Text by C. Hardie (1955). Edition of the Suetonian *Vita* with commentary in A. Rostagni, *Suetonius De Poetis e Biografi Minori* (1956).
2 Serv. on *Ecl.* 4. 11; Jerome on year 767 A.U.C.; Macr. *Sat.* 3. 7. 1.
3 17. 10. 7.
4 Suet. 16; 29.
5 H. Tennyson, *Tennyson: A Memoir* (1897), I, 398.
6 F. Vollmer, A. Rostagni, E. K. Rand, N. W. de Witt and Tenney Frank.
7 P. J. Enk in *O.C.D. s.v.* 'Appendix Vergiliana'; Büchner, cols. 42–160; E. Fraenkel, *J.R.S.* (1952), pp. 1–9. Recent literature up to 1949 is conveniently surveyed by R. E. H. Westendorp-Boerma, *P. Vergilii Maronis Catalepton*, 1 (1949), xxxi–xlix.
8 *De Gram.* 3.
9 *Tusc.* 4. 7.
10 The evidence is again conveniently set out by Westendorp-Boerma, *Catalepton*, 1, 99–101.
11 *S.* 1. 5. 40.

12 Varius and Quintilius occur twice. *Vol. Herc.* VII, 196, *fr.* 12. A. Körte, *Rh.M.* (1890), p. 172; *G.G.A.* (1907), p. 264; Πλω: F. Leo, *Hermes* (1902), p. 27, n.2; W. Crönert, *Kolotes und Menedemos* (1906), p. 127; T. Frank, *C.Ph.* (1920), pp. 107–10.
13 Cic. *Fam.* 6. 11. 2.
14 Dio, 37. 9. 3. *C.A.H.* IX, p. 481.
15 Cic. *Off.* 3. 88; Suet. *Jul.* 8; Dio, *ibid.* 9.
16 Strabo 5. 1. 6.
17 Cic. *Att.* 5. 2. 3; *Fam.* 8. 1. 2.
18 *B.G.* 5. 51; *B.C.* 3. 87.
19 Dio, 41. 36; cf. Tac. *Ann.* 11. 24. This was decided upon in 42, but apparently not immediately implemented.
20 Cic. *In Pis.* 68–72.
21 Frank, *Vergil*, p. 77.
22 Cat. 12.
23 Suet. *Jul.* 84.
24 Plut. *Caes.* 69.
25 Pliny *N.H.* 2. 93.
26 Suet. *Jul.* 88; Dio, 47. 18. 3; *C.I.L.* IX, 2628.

27 See Klingner, 'Die Einheit', *Röm. Geisteswelt*, (4th edn.), pp. 277–8.
28 Büchner, col. 30. In what follows I have drawn freely on my article 'Virgil and the Evictions' in *Hermes* (1966), pp. 320–4.
29 Serv. Auct. on *Ecl.* 6. 6; 9. 7; 10; 27; 28.
30 Described by Appian *B.C.* 5. 49 ff.; Dio 48. 9. 4 ff. Cf. *Ecl.* 1. 11 : 'undique totis usque adeo turbatur agris'.
31 Klingner, *Röm. Geist.* (4th edn.), pp. 278–9.
32 *Ecl.* 1. 42; 45.
33 A recent one, 'Virgil's Home Revisited', is described by K. Wellesley in the *Proceedings of the Virgil Society* (1963–4), pp. 36–43. See also L. Herrmann, *Latomus* (1960), pp. 532–8.
34 *C.R.* (1912), pp. 114–19. *J.R.S.* (1932), pp. 152–9.
35 He points out elaborate similarities even in symmetrical structure (*C.R.* 1912, pp. 117–18).
36 Plut. *Ant.* 4. 1–2.
37 End of *King Richard III*.
38 48. 37.
39 *S.* 1. 5. 29.
40 49. 16.
41 *Sat.* 5. 17. 18; but text dubious.
42 *De Conscr. Hist.* 57.
43 L. Alfonsi, *Poetae Novi* (1945), pp. 56 ff.
44 Alfonsi, *ibid.* pp. 32–4, against Bione.
45 Diog. L. 10. 120.
46 Büchner, col. 242, as against E. Kapp, in *Philosophy and History: Essays Presented to E. Cassirer* (1936); B. Snell, *Die Entdeckung des Geistes* (1948; Engl. tr. *The Discovery of the Mind*, pp. 281 f.), to which I am otherwise indebted.
47 Reprinted in *Röm. Geisteswelt*, (4th edn.), pp. 274–92.
48 5. 32–3 (*ut*), 76–7 (*dum*); 10. 29–30 (*nec*), 42–3 (*hic*).
49 Wilkinson, *Golden Latin Artistry*, p. 192.
50 *Ibid.* p. 195.
51 *Aeneidea*, see Index; 'Theme and Variation'.
52 *Discovery of the Mind*, p. 288.
53 *Ibid.* p. 290.

Chapter III. The Conception of the 'Georgics'

1 W. E. Heitland, *Agricola* (1921), pp. 203–5. For the agricultural state of Italy in the late Republic see A. J. Toynbee, *Hannibal's Legacy* (1965), vol. II, ch. x.
2 *Cat.* 4. 1.
3 *R.R.* 1. 17. Heitland, *Agricola*, pp. 180–2, 186.
4 Varro. *R.R.* 3. 16, 10–11.
5 Tenney Frank, *An Economic History of Rome* (1927), p. 356.
6 *Ep.* 1. 14.
7 Frank, *Econ. Hist. Rome*, p. 327.
8 *R.R.* 1. 17. Cf. Simylus in the *Moretum*.
9 *B.C.* 1. 34; 56.
10 App. 5. 18; 35; 67–8. Dio, 48. 36.
11 5. 74.
12 Cf. *D.R.N.* 2. 10; 6. 27.
13 *Ep.* 1. 14. 39.
14 *S.* 2. 7. 118.
15 Heitland, *Agricola*, p. 218; E. Paratore, *Virgilio* (1961), p. 261. '*Fugae*' at 1. 286 hardly counts.
16 E.g. 1. 49.
17 *Agricola*, pp. 237–8.
18 *Epode.* 2. 3. Cf. for Horace's own views *Odes* 1. 1. 11; 3. 6. 33 ff.
19 *Odes* 1. 31; 2. 3; 15; 16; 18; 3. 1.
20 *The Social and Economic History of the Roman Empire*, 2nd edn. Vol. I, (1957), p. 63; cf. Syme, pp. 449–53.
21 On Virgil's use of traditions in the *Georgics* see F. Klingner, Fondation Hardt, Entretiens II (1953), pp. 140–50.
22 Serv. *Vita Virg.* p. 2. Suet. *Vita Virg.* 25.

23 *R.Ph.* (1930), pp. 128–50, 227–47.
24 Pp. 137–44.
25 Pp. 131–7, against P. Jahn, *Rh.M.* (1903), pp. 391–426.
26 I. 73 ff., cf. *R.R.* I. 44. 3; 104 ff., cf. *R.R.* I. 29. 2; 178 ff., cf. *R.R.* I. 51.
27 *Aen.* 10. 199 and Servius' note.
28 J. Carcopino, *Virgile et le mystère de la quatrième églogue* (1930), pp. 59–61.
29 *C.I.L.* I², pp. 280 f. Nr XXII A. For text of a rustic calendar see J. E. Sandys and S. G. Campbell, *Latin Epigraphy* (1927), pp. 174–6.
30 *N.H.* 18. 207 ff.
31 I. 299. There are six other such reminiscences in Book I, at 127 f., 158, 167, 276 ff., 284 ff., 341 f.
32 Servius *ad loc.*
33 27. Cf. Leonidas of Tarentum, *A.P.* 9. 25; 'Ptolemy the King' in an epigram in (*Vita I* of Aratus).
34 Fr. 11 M.
35 I. 69.
36 G. B. Townend in *Cicero,* ed. T. A. Dorey (1965), pp. 113 ff.
37 On I. 374–87; cf. *Phaen.* 942–5;

954–7. G. B. Townend, *loc. cit.,* E. Malcovati, *Cicerone e la Poesia,* pp. 248 f. On Virgil and Varro of Atax see the good observations of T. E. V. Pearce, *C.Q.* (1966), pp. 301–3; on Virgil and Aratus, Otis, pp. 386–7.
38 *Ther.* 359 ff. Macr. *Sat.* 5. 22. 9.
39 10. 1. 56.
40 On the basis of W. A. Merrill, *Parallels and Coincidences in Lucretius and Virgil* (1918).
41 I. 629; 2. 1117; 1090–3.
42 G. 2. 461–71; *D.R.N.* 2. 24 ff. Cf. 5. 999–1010; 1113–35.
43 2. 29–33.
44 Cf. Cato, Introduction 4: 'From farmers are bred the bravest men and toughest soldiers, and their form of gain is the most righteous (*pius*) and assured and least subject to envy, and those engaged in this pursuit are least likely to be disaffected.' Cf. the long eulogy of agriculture put into Cato's mouth by Cicero, *De Sen.* 51–60.
45 4. 125–46.

Chapter IV. Composition and Structure

1 *Virg.* 27. G. 4. 559–62.
2 Serv. *Vita,* p. 2. *Suet.* 25.
3 *Virg.* 22.
4 *Roman Vergil,* p. 123.
5 Suet. *Virg.* 23.
6 *Virgil,* pp. 184–5.
7 Introduction, pp. 149–50. 5th edn.
8 *Studien zum Verständnis der römischen Literatur,* pp. 188–97.
9 Schefold, *Pomp. Mal.,* pp. 87–96.
10 Reprinted in *C. Weekly* (1914), pp. 74–7, and cited by Rand, *Magical Art,* p. 345.
11 P. 151.
12 *Magical Art,* p. 225.

13 *Virgil* (1936), p. 128–9; Büchner, col. 244.14 Col. 305
15 *Virgile,* p. 63.
16 Klingner, *Ber. Sächs. Akad. Leipzig* (1936), pp. 3–68. Cf. C. O. Brink, *Horace on Poetry* (1963), pp. 5 f., 27 f., 259, 267.
17 E. Norden, *Die Geburt des Kindes* (1924), p. 71.
18 Demet. *De Eloc.* 16; Cic. *Or.* 221–2.
19 Lucr. 2. 14–16.
20 At ll. 11–12 all the words
ferte simul Faunique pedem Dryadesque puellae:
munera vestra cano
are surely parenthetical, not merely

the first line. In reckoning twelve divinities (the reason for the number will appear later, p. 146) Fauns and Dryads may be counted as one each.

21 Büchner, col. 252; Klingner (1963), pp. 44–5.

22 For the astronomy of this passage see R. J. Getty, *T.A.Ph.A.* (1948), pp. 24–34.

23 Admirably dealt with by Klingner, *Hermes* (1931), pp. 159 ff.; cf. his *Georgica*, pp. 119 ff.

24 See James Boswell, *Life of Johnson*, 21 March 1776, ed. Hill, II, 453–4, 533.

25 Boswell, *Johnson*, ed. Hill, II, 129.

26 For the legend see E. Rohde, *Der griechische Roman und seine Vorläufer* (1876; 4th edn. 1960), pp. 133 ff.

27 Macr. *Sat.* 5. 22. 9 f.

28 Arist. *H.A.* 5. 22.

29 H. Dahlmann, *Abh. Akad. Mainz, Geistesw. Kl.* (1954), p. 549.

30 Perret, p. 70.

31 On all this see E. Burck, in *Navicula Chiloniensis* (1956), pp. 156–72.

32 Callim. *Hymn* 1. 45–53.

33 1953, p. 120.

Chapter V. The Aristaeus Epyllion

1 See Norden, *Sitz. Berl. Akad.* (1934), pp. 627–8.

2 27 rather than 26 B.C. (Syme, pp. 309 f.).

3 *Sitz. Berl. Akad.* (1934), pp. 626–83; *C.Q.* (1933), pp. 36–45, 73. See also G. Ramain, *R.Ph.* (1924), p. 122; M. Schmidt, *Die Komposition von Vergils Georgica* (1930), pp. 161 ff.

4 Introduction, pp. 12–13.

5 *C.Q.* (1933), p. 73. Perret, p. 50, and G. E. Duckworth, *A.J.Ph.* (1959), p. 235, have made the same suggestion.

6 Exceptions are Schol. *Ap. Rh.* 2. 498 and Pindar cited by Servius Auctus on 1. 14.

7 I owe these two points to Sir Roger Mynors.

8 Anderson, *C.Q.* (1933), p. 40.

9 Callim. fr. 612 Pf.

10 Ap. Rh. 4. 1132 ff.; Diod. 4. 81; Ov. *Ex P.* 4. 2. 9.

11 Schol. Ap. Rh. 2. 498; Klingner (1963), pp. 199–200.

12 There are other Homeric echoes, for which see Otis, p. 196.

13 Pfeiffer, frr. 253. 8 and 260. 17 ff. with commentaries.

14 P. Friedländer, *Johannes von Gaza und Paulus Silentiarius* (1912), pp. 1 ff.

15 On its nature and relevance see F. Klingner, *Sitz. Bayer Akad. München* (1956), pp. 5–92, esp. pp. 66 ff.

16 *Ibid.* pp. 66 ff.

17 Klingner, *Sitz. Bayer. Akad. München*, pp. 71 f. Cf. Alfonsi, *Poetae Novi*, pp. 191–2.

18 Norden, *Sitz. Berl. Akad.* (1934) p. 653 and n.

19 Klingner (1963), pp. 230–1. Photius, *Bibl.* 186 XLV = Conon, *Dihegeseis* XLV = Fr. Hist. Gr. (Jacoby). Vol. 1, 26.

20 4. 25. J. Heurgon, *Mélanges d'archéologie et d'histoire* (1932), pp. 6–66.

21 *Sitz. Berl. Akad.* (1934), pp. 644–5 656.

22 *C.Q.* (1952), pp. 113–26.

23 Outline of supposed contents, pp. 116–17. O. Gruppe also supposed such a poem, Roscher's *Lexicon* (1884–1937), 3. 1159.

24 P. Scazzoso, *Paideia* (1956), pp. 25–8.

25 Note *ad loc.* and Introduction pp. 16–17.

26 See W. Robert-Tornow, *De apium* etc. (1893) *passim.*

27 Paratore, *Virgilio*, pp. 265 ff. Scazzoso, *Paideia* (1956), pp. 5 ff.

28 *Sitz. Berl. Akad.* (1934), p. 673.
29 *R.Ph.* (1930), pp. 246–7.
30 1963, pp. 234 ff.

31 Pp. 186–90.
32 Pp. 212–14.

Chapter VI. *Philosophical, Moral and Religious Ideas*

1 5. 1083 ff.
2 Implied by Arist., *De Gen. An.* 3. 10. 761a5.
3 Carcopino, *Virgile et le mystère*, pt. I (pp. 1–105).
4 Norden, *Aeneis VI*, pp. 20–48 (Posidonius); P. Boyancé, *R.E.A.* (1955), p. 79 (Antiochus).
5 Ovid, *M.* 15. 75 ff.; Lucr. 2. 352–66.
6 Richter on 517 ff.
7 Otis is especially good on all this, pp. 172–4.
8 See Richter's note on 511 ff.
9 Serv. *ad loc.*
10 G. 3. 232–4; *A.* 12. 103–6. See W. Liebeschuetz, *G.&R.* (1965), p. 71.
11 See Richter's note on 2. 350.
12 4. 1045 ff.
13 See Richter's note on 4. 197 ff.
14 Horace, *Epod.* 2. 39 ff. Cf. *G.* 2. 532.
15 *Navicula Chiloniensis*, pp. 165–7.
16 Suet. *Virg.* 35.
17 *Ecl.* 6. 31 ff.; *Aen.* 1. 742 ff. (suggested by Ap. Rh. 1. 496); P. Boyancé, 'Le sens cosmique de Virgile', *R.E.L.* (1954), pp. 220 ff.
18 *Ep.* 1. 1; *Odes* 4. 2.
19 Lucr. 5. 200 ff.; *G.* 1. 237–8; cf. *caeli indulgentia*, 2. 343–5.
20 Lünenborg, *Das Philosophische Weltbild*, p. 47.
21 *Pol.* 272 c.
22 *W.D.* 289; cf. 303–4, 309.
23 See D. R. Dudley, *A History of Cynicism* (1937), p. 33.
24 *Phaen.* 112–13. Macr. *Sat.* 1. 7. 19–26 (apparently following Protarchus of Tralles); cf. Dion. Hal. *Ant. Rom.* 1. 38.
25 *P.V.* 458–522. *Prot.* 321.
26 18 DK; cf. Solon 1. 41–64D³, esp. 1. 64.

27 15. 64.
28 A. Kleingünther, *Philologus, Supplb.* xxvi (1933–4), Heft 1, 1–33.
29 See esp. *Pol.* 267–74; *Laws* 672–82A.
30 See W. Headlam, *C.Q.* (1934), pp. 63–71.
31 Iambl., *Vit. Pyth.* 28. 139; Xen. frr. 10 ff. DK.
32 *Tim.* 29d ff.; esp. 41B. See A. O. Lovejoy, *The Great Chain of Being* (1936), pp. 50–2.
33 *S.V.F.* II, 1172 (von Arnim).
34 Gell. *N.A.* 7. 1. 4 f.; Plut. *Sto. Resp.* 37A; *S.V.F.* II. 1183. E. V. Arnold, *Roman Stoicism* (1911), pp. 203, 206–9.
35 γυμνάσια τῶν τῆς ἀνδρείας ἐν ἡμῖν σπερμάτων. *S.V.F.* II. 1152.
36 K. Reinhardt, *R.E.* s.v. Poseidonios, 807–8; cf. Sen. *Ep.* 90. 7–26; Epict. *Diss.* 1. 24. 1; Sen. *Dial.* 1. 2. 6; cf. 4. 7.
37 Cic. *De Rep.* 1. 19; *D.N.D.* 2. 37–8; *De Fin.* 3. 67.
38 J. Stroux, *Vergil* (1932), p. 14.
39 Lünenborg, *Das philosophische Weltbild*, pp. 8–13.
40 *Antig.* 332–64. Shakespeare, *Hamlet,* II. ii.
41 *Summa contra Gent.* 3. 71.
42 469, 488. See Klingner, *Hermes* (1931), pp. 175–6.
43 Aug. *Civ. Dei* 6. 5. Boyancé, *R.E.A.* (1955), pp. 62–3.
44 G. Wissowa, *Hermes* (1917), p. 97.
45 See Richter's long note.
46 See M. Desport, *L'Incantation virgilienne* (1952), p. 313.
47 Bailey, *Religion*, p. 198.
48 K. Meuli, *M.H.* (1955), pp. 206 ff.
49 Meuli, *M.H.* p. 213. Cf. Bailey, *Religion*, p. 147.

50 For disentanglement of Roman custom from Greek literary tradition in this poem see A. L. Wheeler, *Catullus and the Traditions of Ancient Poetry* (1934), pp. 189–213.

51 See the remarks of Fraenkel, *Horace*, pp. 163–6.

52 G. 2. 49. Posidonius had identified Zeus and nature. Diog. Laert. 7. 148.

Chapter VII. Political and Social Ideas

1 On all this see F. Klingner, 'Italien: Name, Begriff und Idee im Altertum', in *Röm. Geisteswelt*, pp. 11–33. (Originally *Die Antike*, 1941, pp. 89–104.) Serv. on *Aen*. 1.2.

2 1. 6; 13; 2. 14.

3 Klingner, 'Italien', *Röm. Geisteswelt*, pp. 18–9.

4 P. A. Brunt, *J.R.S.* (1965), pp. 101–6, stresses the importance of the vote.

5 Brunt, *J.R.S.* (1965), pp. 97–8.

6 Klingner, 'Italien', *Röm. Geisteswelt*, pp. 24.

7 Brunt, *J.R.S.* (1965), pp. 98–101.

8 *Ant. Rom*. 1. 36–7.

9 Pliny, *Ep*. 8. 8.

10 Royds, pp. 40 ff.

11 *N.H*. 18. 120; 17. 49.

12 See M. P. Charlesworth, *Camb. Hist. Journ*. (1926), pp. 9 ff.; K. Scott, *M.A.A.R.* (1933), pp. 41 ff.

13 Syme, p. 453.

14 App. *B.C*. 5. 14; 53; 58–9.

15 For the events of these years see W.W.Tarn and M.P. Charlesworth, *Octavian, Antony and Cleopatra* (1965), and Syme, chs. xviii–xx.

16 *B.C*. 5. 132. Cf. Dio, 49. 15.

17 Büchner, col. 256.

18 Fraenkel, *Horace*, pp. 287–8; G. Barra, *Ann. Fac. Lett. Napoli* (1957), pp. 39–56.

19 See Klingner (1963), pp. 63–9, against Richter.

20 L. R. Taylor, *The Divinity of the Roman Emperor* (1931), ch. I.

21 L. R. Taylor, *Divinity*, ch. II, and pp. 151–2 for Genius Augusti. But see C. J. Classen, *Gymnasium* (1963), pp. 312–38, for the strangeness of the idea at Rome.

22 Wissowa, *Hermes* (1917), p. 100.

23 See A. Alföldi on the symbolism of Augustus' cuirass on the Prima Porta statue. *Mitt. deutsch. archäol. Inst., röm. Abt.* (1937), pp. 48 ff. Cf. Norden on *Aen*. 6. 794 ff.

24 Ll. 24–8. Pliny, *N.H*. 15. 125; Gell. 5. 6. 20 ff.

25 Suet. *Aug*. 52; Dio, 51. 20. 6–7. L. R. Taylor, *Divinity*, pp. 146–8.

26 *Odes* 3. 5. 1–4; 3. 11–12.

27 Cic. *Ad Att*. 13. 28. 3; 44. 1. L. R. Taylor, *Divinity*, ch. III.

28 *Ann*. 4. 38.

29 Cic. *Tusc*. 1. 34.

30 *Odes* 3. 4; 1. 12. Later, 4. 2 and 4. Cicero quotes Pindar in two letters to Atticus, 12. 5 and 13. 38. 2. Pindar is rarely mentioned by commentators in connection with this proem. Jackson Knight, *Roman Vergil*, pp. 65, 150, Büchner, col. 269, Fleischer, *Hermes* (1960), 281–2, Wimmel, p. 181, are exceptions. But these are little more than passing references; the influence seems to me to be fundamental.

31 See also C. Nardi, in 'Αντίδωρον *U.E. Paoli* (1956), pp. 242–9: (*Aen*. 6. 601–7 and *Ol*. 1. 54–8, *P*. 2. 21–4).

32 *O*. 6. 1 ff.; *P*. 6. 5 ff.; 3. 113; *N*. 1. 8.

33 Dio, 51. 22.

34 *Ibid*.

35 Dio, 49. 15. L. R. Taylor, *Divinity*, pp. 119–20.

36 Dio, 53. 1.

37 E. Norden, *Hermes* (1893), p. 521.

38 Fleischer, pp. 315–16.
39 Fr. 94a Snell. Cf. *N*. 8. 21 ff.; *I*. 2. 43.
40 Horace, *S*. 2. 1. 10–15 (to Trebatius); *Odes* 2. 12. 9–12; 4. 15. 1–2; *Ep*. 2. 1. 250–9. Propertius, 2. 1. 17–26; 3. 9. 1–4.
41 For echoes of *G*. 3. 10–39 in *A*. 8. 675–728 see Drew, *C.Q*. (1924), pp. 195 ff.
42 *Neue Jahrbücher*, VII, (1901), 317–22.
43 Fleischer, p. 328.
44 *S*. 2. 2. 103–4.
45 Very much so, in the opinion of Dahlmann, *Abh. Akad. Mainz, Geistesw. Kl*. 1954, pp. 547–62. But

see the criticisms of Klingner (1963), pp. 243–4.
46 *Odes* 2. 15. 13–14; cf. 3. 1. 33–7; 24. 45–54; *S*. 2. 2. 103.
47 *Epod*. 9. 14–15. *Odes* 1. 37. 9–10.
48 Pliny, *N.H*. 14. 148. Scott, *M.A.A.R*., p. 46.
49 50. 27–8.
50 *Mor*. 319J–320A; cf. *Vit. Ant*. 33. 2.
51 P. 547.
52 P. 213.
53 Oltramare: *Étude sur l'épisode d'Aristée* (1929), pp. 98 ff.; Perret, pp. 84 ff.; Duckworth, *A.J.Ph*. (1959), p. 232; T. J. Haarhoff, *Cl.Ph*. (1960), pp. 101–8.

Chapter VIII. Poetic Approach and Art

1 4. 246; 15. cf. Ovid, *M*. 6. 1 ff.; 474 ff.
2 See Burck, *De Vergilii...*, pts. III and IV.
3 *R.R*. 2. 5. 7–9; *G*. 3. 51–9. *R.R*. 2. 7. 5; *G*. 3. 75–88. Woestjine, *R.B.Ph*. (1931), pp. 911–3.
4 Robert-Tornow, *De apium*, etc. pp. 93, 162 ff.
5 *Terrea* (Medicaeus², Lact. *Inst*. 2. 10) seems a preferable reading to the vulgate *ferrea*. For the history of the conception see Richter's note.
6 See Richter's excellent note on 323 ff.
7 See Wilkinson, *Golden Latin Artistry*, pp. 32, 61.
8 See, for example, Aesch. *Danaïds*, fr. 44 N² and Wil.
9 Büchner, col. 265.
10 Macr. *in S. Sc*. 1. 21. 23 f. Serv. on *G*. 1. 43. Norden, *Geburt*, pp. 16–17.
11 Euseb. *H.E*. 7.32. 369: ἄφεσις τοῦ τῶν πλανητῶν δρόμου. Norden. *Geburt*, pp. 16–17 and n.
12 *Golden Latin Artistry*, pp. 74–83. Some of the examples given below occur in the same chapter.
13 *G*. 2. 402. Varius, *ap*. Mar. Vict. 1, p. 2503; *D.R.N*. 4. 472.
14 Noted by Quintilian, 9. 3. 51.
15 J. Marouzeau, *Traité de stylistique latine* (3rd edn. 1954), p. 314.

16 For six examples from the *Aeneid* see Marouzeau, *Traité*, p. 307³.
17 Büchner, col. 299.
18 'Nove locutus est' (Serv. *ad loc*.).
19 70: sterilem. Richter, *ad loc*.
20 Norden on *Aen*. 6. 78 f.
21 Richter, *ad loc*.
22 For the way Virgil will deal with a Greek original see Richter's note on 1. 231 (Eratosthenes).
23 See Paratore, *Virgilio*, pp. 227–9.
24 See Richter's note.
25 Dio, 45. 17. 6–7; cf. App. *B.C*. 4. 1. 4.
26 Dio, 47. 2. 3; cf. 47. 40. 2 for Rome. 45. 17. 4.
27 4. 1. 4.
28 47. 40. 5. Cf. Horace, *Odes* 1. 2. 13 ff.
29 App. 4. 1. 4; Dio, 46. 33. 4; 47. 40. 4.
30 Dio, 45. 17. 7.
31 Dio, 46. 33. 2.
32 In the Forum itself: App. 4. 1. 4.
33 Dio, 45. 17. 3–4; 47. 40. 2; App. 4. 1. 4.
34 Pliny, *N.H*. 8. 183; 36. 135. Cf. Cic. *De Div*. 1. 97f.
35 Against this E. Burck, review in *Gnomon* (1959), p. 235.
36 Kroll, *Neue Jahrbücher*, pp. 23 ff. See also pp. 43–7 above, and Wilkinson, *Golden Latin Artistry*, ch. 7: 'Architectonics of Verse'.

37 On what follows see Wilkinson, *Golden Latin Artistry*, ch. 8: 'Word-patterns'.

38 Otis, ch. IV (though straining his case somewhat).

39 From Richter's notes I gather that L. Castiglioni in his *Lezioni intorno alle Georgiche di Virgilio* (1947) made some of these points at pp. 132 ff. and contrasted the Homeric *ethos* with the Virgilian *pathos*.

40 Otis, p. 195.

41 *Hymn* 3. 14. See Richter's note.

42 See Richter's note on 336–44.

43 Norden, *Sitz. Berl. Akad.* (1934), p. 636 n. Wilkinson, *Golden Latin Artistry*, p. 38.

44 See p. 44 and note.

45 *Georgica* (1963), pp. 206–11.

46 *Od.* 1. 144 ff.; 4. 52 ff.

47 Cf. 417. Ovid, *M.* 11. 229; 592.

48 For a detailed comparison see Klingner (1963), pp. 211–22.

49 See further Otis, pp. 203–4.

50 Pp. 207–8.

Chapter IX. Agricultural Lore

1 For recent discussions see Perret, *Virgile*, pp. 55–9; White, *Proc. Virg. Soc.* (1967–8), pp. 11–22. Select bibliography in F. Cupaiuolo, *Tra poesia e poetica* (1966), pp. 151–3 nn.

2 *N.H.* 18. 210–17.

3 Getty, *T.A.Ph.A.* (1948), p. 39, and for general criticism pp. 43–5.

4 *R.R.* 1. 11; 2. Introduction 6. For cases where Virgil seems to be introducing details on his own see Burck, *De Vergilii Georgicon partibus iussivis*, part I.

5 W. Mitsdörffer, *Philologus* (1938), pp. 449–75. On Virgil's use of Theophrastus see also P. Jahn, *Hermes* (1903), pp. 244–64; L. A. S. Jermyn, *The Ostrakon*, printed for the Virgil Society (1952).

6 Col. 1. 1. 13.

7 Richter, *ad loc.* For Virgil's use of Varro see Woestijne, *R.B.Th.* (1931), pp. 909–29.

8 For Pliny's criticisms see P. Lejay, Introduction to edn. of the *Georgics* (1914), p. xxxvii; R. T. Bruère, *C.Ph.* (1956), pp. 228–46.

9 Col. 2. 2. 18. White, *Proc. Virg. Soc.* (1967–8), p. 19.

10 *R.R.* 1. 27. Cf. Col. 2. 4. 1.

11 *Proc. Virg. Soc.* (1967–8), p. 14.

12 *N.H.* 18. 300.

13 Long note on 1. 85 ff.

14 5. 519 ff. 'Occultas vires'; 'spiracula' (6. 492); 'penetraleque frigus' (1. 494). *Proc. Virg. Soc.* (1967–8) p. 18. Add 'excoquit' (6. 962).

15 Inverso caespite herbarum radices necantur (Pliny, *N.H.* 18. 176).

16 Macr. *Sat.* 5. 20. 17–18.

17 *N.H.* 17. 14.

18 Theophr. *C.P.* 3.7; Col. 2.2.10; 8.3.

19 1. 271. Not however according to Cato's list, 2. 4.

20 1. 270; 2. 371–9. Col. 2. 21. 2.

21 1. 51.

22 K. D. White, *Agricultural Implements of the Roman World* (1966), pp. 123–45; and as to the Virgilian plough, App. G. 3 (pp. 213–16), against R. Aitken, *J.R.S.* (1956), pp. 57 ff.

23 Varro, 1. 29.

24 Varro, 1. 34; Pliny, *N.H.* 18. 120.

25 Cato, 4. 1; Cic. *De Off.* 1. 18. 59. Billiard, p. 126.

26 Pliny, *N.H.* 18. 260–2.

27 See White, *Agric. Impl.* pp. 154–5.

28 *G.&R.* (1951), p. 50.

29 *G.&R.* (1951), p. 33.

30 Kynaston on Theocr. 3. 57.

31 Royds, p. 40.

32 *G.&R.* (1951), p. 37.

33 383–7; Theophr. 15; Arat. 942–3; Varro of Atax ap. Serv. on 375; *Il.* 2. 460.

95 Royds, p. 81.
96 Von Frisch, *The Dancing Bees*, p. 46.
97 H. M. Fraser, *Beekeeping in Antiquity*, p. 41.
98 Sargeaunt, pp. 14–16.
99 Including Nicander, and most fully in *Geop.* 15. 2 (Florentius).
100 For King Juba of Mauretania's prescription see *Geop.* 15. 2; for

Mago as an authority on it see Col. 9. 14. 6. A. S. F. Gow, *C.R.* (1944), pp. 14–15.
101 C. R. Osten-Sacken, *On the Oxenborn Bees of the Ancients* (1894).
102 A. E. Shipley, 'The Bugonia Myth', *J.Philol.* (1918), p. 98.
103 *Théâtre d'agriculture* (1804 edn.), II, xiv, 106.

Chapter X. The 'Georgics' in After Times

1 Suet. *Gramm.* 16; C. Hardie, *Vitae Vergilianae Antiquae* (1966), Pref. XV–XVI.
2 1. 8. 5.
3 H. I. Marrou, *A History of Education in Antiquity*, tr. G. Lamb (1956), pp. 251–2, 278.
4 1. 4. 4.
5 11. 1. 31; 7. 3. 23.
6 10 Pref. 3–4; *G.* 4. 148.
7 3. 12. 5; *G.* 2. 298.
8 3. 10. 20, apparently referring to *G.* 1. 197–200 (on legume seeds); cf. 2. 9. 12.
9 9. 14. 6–7.
10 On all this see Bruère, *C.Ph.* (1956), pp. 238–9.
11 Noted by F. Münzer, *Beiträge zur Quellenkritik der Naturgeschichte des Plinius* (1897), p. 83.
12 14. 126–7. Bruère, *C.Ph.* (1956), pp. 236–7.
13 *Somn. Scip.* 2. 8. 1.
14 P. 74.
15 *European Literature and the Latin Middle Ages*, tr. W. R. Trask (1953), pp. 201 n. 231, based on E. Faral, *Les arts poétiques du XIIe et du XIIIe siècle* (1924), pp. 87–8.
16 Commentary on *Aeneid* in Cod. Bibl. S. Marc. Venet. ch. XIII (Lat), n. 61, c. 3. Comparetti, pp. 117, 129.
17 *European Literature*, p. 190.
18 *Ibid.* p. 192.
19 *The Monastic Order in England, 943–1216* (2nd edn. 1963), p. 6.
20 *Inst.* 1. 28. 5–6, quoting *G.* 2. 483–5.

21 Knowles, *Monastic Order*, p. 7.
22 *Ibid.* pp. 19–23.
23 *Ibid.* p. 467.
24 Lord Ernle, *English Farming Past and Present* (6th edn.), p. 33.
25 Ed. Lodge and Herrtage, 1873 and 1879.
26 1. 45, cf. *G.* 1. 128; 6. 159, cf. *G.* 2. 30–1. Ed. C. Jessen. *De Animalibus* ed. H. Stadler.
27 Grosseteste and Walter of Henley, ed. E. Lamond (1890). Ernle, *English Farming*, p. 90[6].
28 M. L. Lilly, *The Georgic* (1919), p. 28.
29 7. 9 and 10. Other examples in *Anth. Lat.* ed. Riese: 117; 567–78; 639–40; 864.
30 ἔκφρασις χρόνων, recommended by Hermogenes, p. 22, 14 Rabe.
31 *G.* 1. 65.
32 *G.* 1. 383.
33 *G.* 1. 95.
34 *G.* 2. 520
35 *G.* 4. 563.
36 A. Riegl, *Mitth. d. Inst. f. oesterreichische Geschichtsforschung* (1889), p. 36; also Th. v. Inama-Sternegg, in foreword to German translation by P. Herzsohn, *Westdeutsch. Ztschr.* 1 (1882), 280–8; Manitius, *Geschichte*, I, 558. This is corroborated by the great authority on the Rhine, R. Lauterborn, *Ber. d. Naturforsch. Ges. zu Freiburg-im-B.* (1930), pp. 36–8.
37 *P.L.A.C.*, ed. Dümmler, II, 645.
38 *Praef.*

39 *De Cons.* 3. 12. 52–8.

40 Migne, *P.L.* vol. CXI; Manitius, *Geschichte*, I, p. 292.

41 Text in F. Novati, *Mélanges Paul Fabre* (1902), pp. 265 ff. See further E. F. Wilson in *Speculum* (1933), pp. 358–77.

42 Wilson, *Speculum* (1933), p. 371.

43 Ambrose, *De Virg.* 1. 8. 'Nesciunt concubitus' (apes).

44 15. 22.

45 C. Schaarschmidt, *Johannes Saresberiensis* (1862), p. 98.

46 See most recently P. Dronke, *Medieval Latin and the Rise of the European Love-lyric*, II (1966), 341–52.

47 Nitchie, pp. 39–40.

48 E. Moore, *Studies in Dante*, I (1896), 344 ff.

49 Long recognised, e.g. Moore, *Dante*, p. 21.

50 Ullman, *Stud. Med.* (1932), p. 64.

51 *Ep. Fam.* 4. 1.

52 Zabughin, I, 30.

53 F. Marconi, *Atti. R. acad. Georg. Fir.* (1892), pp. 139–63; P. de Nolhac, *Pétrarque et l'humanisme* (1907), vol. II, exc. II: 'Pétrarque jardinier'. *G.* 2. 315 ff.

54 *Essaies*, II, 10. P. Hensel, *Vorträge d. Bibliothek Warburg* (1925–6), p. 73.

55 W. H. Storer, *Virgil and Ronsard* (1923), lists them on pp. 131–2.

56 Nitchie, p. 69.

57 *Henry V*, 1. ii. 191–6; *Othello*, 3. iii. 330–1. T. W. Baldwin, *William Shakspere's Small Latine and Lesse Greek* (1944), II, 469 ff.

58 M. L. Clarke, *Classical Education in Britain 1500–1900* (1959), p. 11.

59 T. W. Baldwin, *William Shakspere's Small Latine*, I, 321–32.

60 C. Hoole, *New Discovery of the Old Art of Teaching Schoole*, ed. Campagnac, pp. 52, 63, 138, 156.

61 A. Hubelei, p. 62.

62 Van Veen, *De Soeticheydt des Buyten-Levens Vergheselschapt*, p. 167 and p. 238 n. It may have been written earlier.

63 *Ibid.* p. 206.

64 G. R. Hibbard, *Journ. Warb. Inst.* (1956), pp. 159, 165.

65 E. W. Manwaring, *Italian Landscape in Eighteenth Century England* (1925), pp. 134–5. Shenstone's poem *Rural Elegance* appeared in 1750.

66 Hubelei, p. 62.

67 1. 484–510.

68 3. 340–1.

69 2. 206–54.

70 Manwaring, *Italian Landscape*, pp. 98–101.

71 R. E. Tickell: *Thomas Tickell and the Eighteenth Century Poets* (1931), pp. 198 ff.

72 *The Practical Husbandman and Planter*, 2 vols. (London, 1733–4). G. E. Fussell, *More Old English Farming Books* (1950), pp. 1–3.

73 J. Martyn, Preface to edition of 1755, pp. viii, xiii; A. Dickson, *The Husbandry of the Ancients*, 2 vols., very badly edited in 1788, twelve years after his death.

74 *Husbandry of the Ancients*, I, pp. 449, 467–8.

75 *The Life and Labours of Adam Clarke* (1834), pp. 11–12. I owe this reference to Prof. M. L. Clarke.

76 P. Larousse, *Grand Dictionnaire Universel du XIXe siècle*, tome 13, s.v.

77 *Le lac de Genève*.

78 *My first acquaintance with Poets, Essays*, ed. R. Vallance and J. Hampden (1964), p. 19.

79 As does A.-M. Guillemin's *L'originalité de Virgile* (1931).

80 Perret, p. 77.

81 *Summer*, 676–80.

82 *Spring*, 82–5.

List of modern works cited

(N.B. This is not intended to be a full bibliography. For a recent one see G.E. Duckworth, *The Classical World*, II (1957–8), 89 ff. and LVII (1963–4), 193 ff.)

ABBE, E. *The Plants of Virgil's Georgics.* 1965.

AITKEN, R. 'Virgil's Plough', *J.R.S.* 1956, pp. 97–106.

ALBINI, U. 'Struttura e motivi del primo libro delle Georgiche', *Studi Italiani di filologia classica*, 1951, pp. 49–64.

ALFÖLDI, A. 'Zum Panzerschmuck der Augustusstatue von Primaporta', *Mitt. deutsch. arch. Inst., röm. Abt.* 1937, pp. 48–63.

ALFONSI, L. *Poetae Novi.* 1945.

ALTEVOGT, H. *Labor Improbus.* 1952.

ANDERSON, W. B. 'Gallus and the Fourth Georgic', *C.Q.* 1933, pp. 36–45; 73.

ANDRÉ, J. *L'alimentation et la cuisine à Rome*, Études et Commentaires, XXXIX. 1961.

ARNOLD, E. V. *Roman Stoicism.* 1911.

AXELSON, B. *Unpoetische Wörter.* 1945.

BAILEY, C. *Religion in Virgil.* 1935.

BALDWIN, C. S. *Renaissance Literary Theory and Practice*, ed. D. L. Clark. 1939.

BALDWIN, T. W. *William Shakspere's Small Latine and Lesse Greeke.* 1944.

BANNISTER, H. M. 'The Vetus Itala. Text of the Exultet', *J.Th.S.* 1909, pp. 43–54.

BARRA, G. 'All'indomani di Nauloco', *A.F.L.N.* 1957, pp. 39–56.

BAYET, J. 'Les premiers "Géorgiques" de Virgile', *R.Ph.* 1930, pp. 128–50, 227–47.

'Un procédé virgilien: la description synthétique dans les Géorgiques', in *Studi in onore di Gino Funaioli*, 1955, pp. 9–18.

BEDDIE, J. S. 'Ancient Classics in the Medieval Libraries', *Speculum*, 1930, pp. 3–20.

BELLESSORT, A. *Virgile, son œuvre et son temps.* 1920.

BEUTLER, R. 'Zur Komposition von Virgils Georgica I, 43–159', *Hermes*, 1940, pp. 410–21.

BILLIARD, R. *L'agriculture dans l'antiquité d'après les Géorgiques de Virgile.* 1928.

BOLGAR, R. R. *The Classical Heritage and its Beneficiaries.* 1954.

BOLISANI, E. 'Vergilius o Virgilius', *Atti dell'Istituto Veneto*, 1959, pp. 131–41.

BORINSKI, K. *Die Antike in Poetik und Kunsttheorie*, II. 1924.

BOVIE, S. P. 'The imagery of ascent-descent in Virgil's Georgics', *A.J.Ph.* 1956, pp. 337–58.

BOWRA, SIR M. 'Orpheus and Eurydice', *C.Q.* 1952, pp. 113–26. *Pindar.* 1964.

BOYANCÉ, P. 'Le sens cosmique de Virgile', *R.E.L.* 1954, pp. 220–49. 'Sur la théologie de Varron', *R.E.A.* 1955, pp. 57–84.

BRINK, C. O. *Horace on Poetry.* 1963.

BRUÈRE, R. T. 'Pliny the Elder and Virgil', *C.Ph.* 1956, pp. 228–46.

BRUNT, P. A. 'Italian Aims at the time of the Social War', *J.R.S.* 1965, pp. 101–6.

BÜCHNER, K. 'P. Vergilius Maro', *Real-Enzyklopädie* VIIIA. 1955. Separately published 1956.

343

LIST OF MODERN WORKS CITED

BURCK, E. *De Vergilii Georgicon partibus iussivis*. Dissertation. Leipzig. 1926.
'Die Komposition von Vergils Georgica', *Hermes*, 1929, pp. 279–321.
'Der Korykische Greis in Vergils Georgica', in *Navicula Chiloniensis* (Festschrift F. Jacoby), 1956, pp. 156–72.
Review of W. Richter's *Georgica*, *Gnomon*, 1959, pp. 224–38.
CARCOPINO, J. *Virgile et le mystère de la quatrième églogue*. 1930.
CASTIGLIONI, L. *Lezioni intorno alle Georgiche di Virgilio*. 1947.
CESARIO, E. 'Ottaviano nel proemio delle Georgiche', *Athenaeum*, 1931, pp. 223–42.
CHARLESWORTH, M. P. 'The Fear of the Orient in the Roman Empire', *Camb. Hist. Journ.* 1926, pp. 9–16.
(With W. W. Tarn) *Octavian, Antony and Cleopatra*.
(Extracts from *Camb. Anc. Hist.* vol. X. 1934. Re-published separately, 1965.)
CLARK, SIR KENNETH. *Landscape into Art*. 1949.
CLARKE, ADAM. (Anonymous Memoir on Adam Clarke. 1834.)
CLARKE, M. L. *Classical Education in Britain 1500–1900*. 1959.
CLASSEN, C. J. 'Gottmenschentum in der römischen Republik', *Gymnasium*, 1963, pp. 312–38.
COLEMAN, R. G. G. 'Tityrus and Meliboeus', *G.&R.* 1966, pp. 79–97.
COMPARETTI, D. *Virgil in the Middle Ages*, tr. E. F. M. Benecke. 1895.
CONINGTON, J., NETTLESHIP, H. and HAVERFIELD, F. *The Works of Virgil* (edn.), vol. I, 5th edn. 1898.
CRÖNERT, W. *Kolotes und Menedemos*. 1906.
CUMONT, F. 'Les présages lunaires de Virgile et les sélénodromia', *A.C.* 1933, pp. 261–70.
CUPAIUOLO, F. *Tra poesia e poetica*. 1966.
CURTIUS, E. 'Rhetorische Naturschilderung im Mittelalter', *Romanische Forschungen*, 1942, pp. 219–56.
European Literature and the Latin Middle Ages, tr. W. R. Trask, 1953.
CZECH, G. *Die Komposition der Georgica*. 1936.
DAHLMANN, H. 'Der Bienenstaat in Vergils Georgica', *Abh. Akad. Mainz, Geistesw. Kl.* 1954, pp. 547–62.
DALE, F. R. 'Virgil, Georgics IV, 228–30', *C.R.* 1955, pp. 14–15.
DESPORT, M. *L'incantation Virgilienne*. 1952.
DODDS, I. C. 'Dextrae iubae', *C.R.* 1968, p. 24.
DREW, D. L. 'Virgil's Fifth Eclogue', *C.Q.* 1922, pp. 57–64.
'Virgil's Marble Temple', *C.Q.* 1924, pp. 194–202.
'The Structure of Virgil's Georgics', *A.J.Ph.* 1929, pp. 242–54.
DRONKE, P. *Medieval Latin and the Rise of the European Love-lyric*, II. 1966.
DUCHESNE, L. *Christian Worship: its origin and evolution*, tr. M. L. McClure. 5th edn. 1919.
DUCKWORTH, G. E. 'Vergil's Georgics and the Laudes Galli', *A.J.Ph.* 1959, pp. 225–37.
DUDLEY, D. R. *A History of Cynicism*, 1937.
Lucretius (ed.). 1965.
Virgil (ed.). 1969.
DÜMMLER, E. (ed.). *Monumenta Germaniae Historica*, II: *Poetae Latini Aevi Carolini*.
EDWARDES, E. TICKNER. *The Lore of the Honey-bee*. 1923.
ERNLE, LORD. *English Farming Past and Present*. 4th edn. 1927.

LIST OF MODERN WORKS CITED

FARAL, E. *Les arts poétiques du XII et du XIII siècle.* 1924.

FLEISCHER, U. 'Musentempel und Oktavianehrung des Vergil', *Hermes*, 1960, pp. 280–331.

FOWLER, W. WARDE. *A Year with the Birds.* 3rd edn. 1889.

FRAENKEL, E. 'Virgil und Cicero', *Atti e Memorie della R. Accademia Mantova*, 1926–7, pp. 217–27.

'The Culex', *J.R.S.* 1952, pp. 1–9.

Horace. 1957.

FRANK, T. 'Vergil's Apprenticeship', *C.Ph.* 1920, pp. 23–38; 102–19.

Vergil: a Biography. 1922.

FRASER, H. M. *Beekeeping in Antiquity.* 1931.

FRAZER, J. G. *The Golden Bough.* 1890–1915.

FRIEDLÄNDER, P. *Johannes von Gaza und Paulus Silentiarius.* 1912.

FRISCH, K. VON. *The Dancing Bees*, tr. D. Isle and N. Walker. 1967.

FUCHS, H. 'Zum Wettgesang der Hirten in Vergils siebenter Ekloge', *M.H.* 1966, pp. 218–23.

FUSSELL, G. E. *Old English Farming Books, from Fitzherbert to Tull: a bibliography.* 1947.

More Old English Farming Books. 1950.

GARROD, H. W. 'Vergil', in Gordon, G. S. *English Literature and the Classics.* 1912.

GETTY, R. J. 'Some Astronomical Cruces in the *Georgics'. T.A.Ph.A.* 1948, pp. 24–45.

GLOVER, T. R. *Virgil.* 1904.

GORDON, G. S. (ed.). *English Literature and the Classics.* 1912.

GOW, A. S. F. 'Bugonia in Geoponica XV. 2', *C.R.* 1944, pp. 14–15.

GRANT, M. *Roman Literature.* 1954.

GRIMAL, P. 'La "Vme Églogue" et le culte de César', *Rev. Arch.* 1949. (*Mélange Charles Picard*), vol. I, pp. 406–19.

GRUPPE, O. 'Orpheus', in W. H. Roscher's *Ausführliches Lexicon der griechischen und römischen Mythologie.* 1884–1937.

GUIARD, A. *Virgile et Victor Hugo.* 1910.

GUILLEMIN, A. M. *L'originalité de Virgile.* 1931.

HAARHOFF, T. J. *Virgil in the Experience of South Africa.* 1931.

'Virgil and Cornelius Gallus', *C.Ph.* 1960, pp. 101–8.

HARDIE, C. *Vitae Vergilianae Antiquae.* O.C.T. 2nd edn. 1966.

HARDT, FONDATION. *Hésiode.* Entretiens VII. 1962.

HASKINS, C. H. *Studies in the History of Medieval Science.* 1927.

HEADLAM, W. *A Book of Greek Verse.* 1907.

'Prometheus and the Garden of Eden', *C.Q.* 1934, pp. 63–71.

HEINZE, R. 'Ovid's Elegische Erzählung', *Ber. Sächs. Akad. Leipzig*, 1919.

HEISS, H. 'Vergils Fortleben in der Romanischen Literaturen', in *Aus Roms Zeitwende (Das Erbe der Alten)*, 2nd ser. XX, 1937.

HEITLAND, W. E. *Agricola.* 1921.

HEITMANN, K. 'Orpheus im Mittelalter', *Archiv für Kulturgeschichte*, 1963, pp. 253–94.

HENRY, J. *Aeneidea.* 1873–9.

HENSEL, P. 'Montaigne und die Antike', *Vorträge d. Bibliothek Warburg*, 1925–6, ed. F. Saxl, 1928, pp. 67–94 = *Kleine Schriften*, 1930, pp. 342–75.

HÉROUVILLE, P. D'. *À la campagne avec Virgile.* 1930.

Géorgiques I–II, Champs, Vergers, Forêts, 1942.

HERRMANN, L. 'Le domaine rural de Virgile', *Latomus,* 1960, pp. 532–8.

HERZSOHN, P. (With Th. v. Inama Sternberg) 'Rheinisches Landleben im 9 Jahrhundert', in *Westdeutsch. Zeitschr. für Geschichte und Kunst,* I, 1882, 277–90.

HEURGON, J. 'Orphée et Eurydice avant Virgile', *Mélanges d'archéologie et d'histoire,* 1932, pp. 6–66.

HIBBARD, G. R. 'The Country House Poem of the Seventeenth Century', *Journ. Warb. Inst.* 1956, pp. 159–74.

HIGHAM, T. and BOWRA, M. (ed.). *The Oxford Book of Greek Verse in Translation.* 1938.

HOOLE, C. *New Discovery of the Old Art of Teaching School.* Written 1636, published 1659.

HORNSTEIN, F. 'Vergilius Παρθενίας', *W.S.* 1957, pp. 148–59.

HOUSMAN, A. E. 'The Latin for *Ass*', *C.Q.* 1930, pp. 11–13.

HUBAUX, S. (With A. Tomsin) *Les travaux agrestes (Géorgiques)* (verse tr.) 1947.

HUBELEI, A. 'Virgile en France au XVIe siècle', *R. Seiz. Siècle,* 1931, pp. 1–77.

HUDSON-WILLIAMS, T. 'King Bees and Queen Bees', *C.R.* 1935, pp. 2–4.

HUXLEY, H. H. *Virgil, Georgics I and IV* (edn. with comm.). 1963.

HUXLEY, J. *Ants.* 1949 edn.

JACKSON, C. N. 'Molle atque facetum', *H.S.Ph.* 1914, pp. 117–37.

JAHN, P. Articles on sources of the *Georgics* in *Hermes,* 1903, pp. 244 ff.; *Rh.M.* 1903, pp. 391 ff.; 1905, pp. 361 ff.; *Philologus,* 1904, pp. 66 ff.; *Progr. d. Kölln. Gymn. zu Berlin,* 1905.

Jahresbericht über Vergil, 1901–4. Bursian, 1905.

JERMYN, L. A. S. *The Singing Farmer* (verse tr. of *Georgics*). 1947.

'Weather-signs in Virgil', *G.&R.* 1951, pp. 26–37, 49–59.

The Ostrakon (Virgil Society). 1952.

JONES, W. P. *The Rhetoric of Science.* 1966.

KAPP, E. 'Philosophy and History', in *Essays Presented to E. Cassirer.* 1936.

KEATS, J. *The Letters of John Keats,* ed. M. Buxton Forman. 2nd edn. 1935.

KEIGHTLEY, T. *Notes on the Bucolics and Georgics of Virgil.* 1846.

KIDD, D. A. 'The Pattern of *Phaenomena* 367–385', *Antichthon,* 1967, pp. 12–15.

KLEINGÜNTHER, A. *Philologus Suppl.* XXVI, vol. I, 1933–4, pp. 1–155.

KLEK, J. and ARMBRUSTER, L. 'Die Bienenkunde des Altertums', *Archiv für Bienenkunde,* 1920, pp. 263 ff.

KLINGNER, F. (See also *Römische Geisteswelt,* 4th edn. 1961). 'Die erste Hirtengedicht Virgils', *Hermes,* 1927, pp. 129–53.

'Über das Lob des Landlebens in Virgils Georgica', *Hermes,* 1931, pp. 159–89.

'Italien: Name, Begriff und Idee im Altertum', *Die Antike,* 1941, pp. 89–104.

'Virgil' in *L'influence grecque sur la poésie latine de Catulle à Ovide.* Fondation Hardt, Entretiens II, 1953.

'Catulls Peleus Epos', *Sitz. Bayer. Akad. München,* 1956, pp. 5–92.

Virgils Georgica. 1963.

'Die Einheit des Virgilischen Lebenswerkes' *Mitt. Deutsch. Arch. Inst. Röm. Abt.* 1930, pp. 43 ff.

KLOTZ, A. 'Die Umarbeitung von Vergils Georgica', *Würzb. Jahrb.,* 1947, pp. 140–7.

LIST OF MODERN WORKS CITED

KNIGHT, W. F. JACKSON. *Roman Vergil*. 1944.
KNOWLES, D. (M.C.) *The Religious Orders in England*, vol. I, 1948.
The Monastic Order in England, 943–1216. 2nd ed. 1963.
KÖRTE, A. 'Augusteer bei Philodem', *Rh.M.* 1890, pp. 172–7.
Review of W. Crönert, *Kolotes und Menedemos*, in *G.G.A.* 1907, pp. 251–66.
KRAPP, H. 'A source of Vergil, *Georgics* II, 136–76', *C.Q.* 1926, pp. 42–4.
KROLL, W. 'Ciceros Schrift *De Oratore*', *Rh.M.* 1903, pp. 552–97.
'Unsere Schätzung der römischen Dichtung',*Neue Jahrbücher*, 1903, pp. 1–30.
'Randbemerkungen', *Rh.M.* 1909, pp. 50–4.
Studien zum Verständnis der römischen Literatur. 1924.
LAUTERBORN, R. 'Der Rhein', *Ber. d. Naturforsch. Ges. zu Freiburg-im-B.*, 1930.
LEO, F. 'Virgil und die Ciris', *Hermes*, 1902, pp. 14–55.
LEWIS, C. DAY. *The Georgics of Virgil* (verse tr.). 1940.
The Buried Day. 1960.
LIEBESCHUETZ, W. 'Beast and Man in the Third Book of the Georgics', *G.&R.* 1965, pp. 64–77.
LILLY, M. L. *The Georgic.* 1919.
LOVEJOY, A. O. (With G. Boas) *Primitivism and Related Ideas in Antiquity.* 1935.
The Great Chain of Being. 1936.
LÜNENBORG, J. *Das philosophische Weltbild in Vergils Georgika.* Dissertation. Münster, 1935.
MACKAIL, J. W. 'Virgil's Use of the Word *ingens*', *C.R.* 1912, pp. 251–5.
MALCOVATI, E. *Cicerone e la Poesia.* 1943.
MANITIUS, M. *Geschichte der lateinischen Literatur des Mittelalters*, vol. I. 1911.
Handschriften antiker Autoren in Mittelalterlicher Bibliothekskatalogen, ed. K. Manitius. 1935.
MANWARING, E. W. *Italian Landscape in Eighteenth Century England.* 1925.
MARCONI, F. 'Il Petrarca nella storia dell'agricoltura', *Atti. R. Acad. Georg. Fir.* vol. XVI, 1892.
MAROUZEAU, J. *Traité de stylistique latine.* 1954.
MARROU, H. I. *A History of Education in Antiquity*, tr. G. Lamb. 1956.
MENDELL, C. W. 'The Influence of the Epyllion on the *Aeneid*', *Yale Studies in Classical Philology*, 1951, pp. 203–26.
MERRILL, W. A. *Parallels and Coincidences in Lucretius and Virgil.* 1918.
MEULI, K. 'Altrömische Maskenbrauch', *M.H.* 1955, pp. 206–35.
MITCHELL, D. G. *Wet Days at Edgeworth.* 1884.
MITSDÖRFFER, W. 'Vergils *Georgica* und Theophrast', *Philologus*, 1938, pp. 449–75.
MOORE, E. *Studies in Dante*, vol. I. 1896.
MORITZ, L. A. 'Some Central Thoughts on Horace's Odes', *C.Q.* 1968, pp. 116–31.
MORNET, D. *Les sciences de la nature en France au XVIIIe siècle.* 1911.
MÜNZER, F. *Beiträge zur Quellenkritik der Naturgeschichte des Plinius.* 1897.
MUSTARD, W. P. 'Virgil's *Georgics* and the British Poets', *A.J.P.* 1908, pp. 1–31.
NARDI, B. *La Giovinezza di Virgilio.* 1927. Tr. B. P. Rand as *The Youth of Virgil.* 1930.
'La tradizione virgiliana di Pietole nel medio evo', *Stud. Med.* 1932, pp. 104–38.
NARDI, C. 'Reminiscenze pindariche in Virgilio', in 'Ἀντίδωρον U. Fr. Paoli, 1956, pp. 242–9.

NICOLAS, P. A. *Les Géorgiques* (verse trs), *Lettres d'Humanité*, VII, 1948, 22–6.
NITCHIE, E. *Vergil and the English Poets*. 1919.
NIXON, G. *The World of Bees*. 1954.
NOLHAC, P. DE. *Pétrarque et l'humanisme*. 1907.
  Ronsard et l'humanisme. 1921.
NORDEN, E. 'Vergilstudien II', *Hermes*, 1893, pp. 501–21.
  'Vergils *Aeneis* im Lichte ihrer Zeit', *Neue Jahrb. für das klassische Altertum*, VII, 1901, 249–82; 313–34.
  Ennius und Vergilius. 1915.
  Aeneis VI (edn. with comm.). 1907. 3rd edn. 1927.
  Die Geburt des Kindes. 1924.
  'Orpheus und Eurydice', *Sitz. Berl. Akad.* 1934, pp. 626–83 = *Kleine Schriften zum klassischen Alterum*, 1966, pp. 468–532.
NORWOOD, G. 'Vergil, *Georgics IV*, 453–527', *C.J.* 1940–1, pp. 354–5.
NOVATI, F. 'Un poème inconnu de Gautier de Châtillon', in *Mélanges Paul Faure*, 1902, pp. 265–78.
OLTRAMARE, A. *Étude sur l'épisode d'Aristée*. 1929.
OPPERMANN, H. 'Vergil und Oktavian', *Hermes*, 1932, pp. 197–219.
OSTEN-SACKEN, C. R. *On the Oxen-born Bees of the Ancients*. 1894.
OTIS, B. *Virgil: a Study in Civilized Poetry*. 1963.
PARATORE, E. Introduzione alle *Georgiche di Virgilio*. 1938.
  'Spunti lucreziani nelle Georgiche', *A.&R.* 1939, pp. 186–93.
  Virgilio. 1961.
PARKER, C. P. 'Vergil and the Country Pastor', *The Churchman*, 18 April 1914 = *C.W.* 1914, pp. 74–5.
PEARCE, T. E. V. 'Enclosing word-order in the Latin Hexameter II', *C.Q.* 1966, pp. 298–320.
PERRET, J. *Virgile: l'homme et l'œuvre*. 1952. 2nd edn. 1965.
  Virgile (illustré). 1959. *Horace*. 1959.
PIRENNE, H. *Soulèvement de la Flandre Maritime de 1323–29*. 1900.
PRESCOTT, H. W. *The Development of Virgil's Art*. 1927.
RABY, F. J. E. *A History of Secular Latin Poetry in the Middle Ages*. 2nd edn. 1957.
RAMAIN, G. 'À propos de Virgile, Géorgiques III, 416–39'. *R.Ph.* 1924, pp. 117–23.
RAND, E. K. *The Magical Art of Virgil*. 1931.
REINHARDT, K. 'Poseidonios.' *Real-Enzyklopädie*, XXII, I, cols. 556–826.
RIBBANDS, C. R. *The Behaviour and Social Life of Honey Bees*. 1954.
RICHTER, W. *Vergil, Georgica*, (edn.). 1957.
RIEGL, A. 'Die mittelalterliche Kalenderillustration', *Mitth. d. Inst. f. oesterreichische Geschichtsforschung*, 1889, pp. 1–74.
ROBERT-TORNOW, W. *De apium apud veteres significatione et symbolica et mythologica*. 1893.
ROHDE, E. *Der griechische Roman und seine Vorläufer*. 1876. 4th edn. 1960.
ROSE, H. J. *The Eclogues of Virgil*. 1942.
ROSTOVTZEFF, M. *The Social and Economic History of the Roman Empire*, I, 2nd edn. 1957.
RØSTWIG, M. S. *The Happy Man*, vol. I, 1954; vol. II, 1958.
ROYDS, T. F. *The Beasts, Birds and Bees of Virgil*. 1914.

LIST OF MODERN WORKS CITED

SAINT-DENIS, E. DE. 'Une source de Virgile dans les *Géorgiques*', *R.E.L.* 1938, pp. 297–317.

Virgile, Géorgiques, ed. Budé. 1956.

SANDBACH, F. H. 'Virgil, *Georgics* II, 277', *C.R.* 1928, pp. 59–60.

Review of M. Schmidt, q.v. *C.R.* 1931, pp. 140–1.

SANDYS, J. E. *Latin Epigraphy*. 2nd edn. with Campbell, S. G. 1927.

SARGEAUNT, J. *The Trees, Shrubs and Plants of Virgil*. 1920.

SAVASTANO, L. *Studi Virgiliani*. 1931.

SCAZZOSO, P. 'Riflessi misterici nelle Georgiche', *Paideia*, 1956, pp. 5–28.

SCHAARSCHMIDT, K. *Johannes Sarisberiensis*. 1862.

SCHEFOLD, K. *Pompeianische Malerei*. 1952.

SCHMIDT, M. *Die Komposition von Vergils Georgica*. 1930.

SCHUSTER, M. *Tibull-Studien*. 1930.

SCOTT, K. 'The Political Propaganda of 44–30 B.C.', *M.A.A.R.* 1933, pp. 8–49.

SEGAL, C. 'Orpheus and the Fourth Georgic', *A.J.Ph.* 1966, pp. 307–25.

SELLAR, W. Y. *Roman Poets of the Augustan Age*, vol. I: *Virgil*. 1874 3rd edn. 1897.

SERRES, OLIVIER DE. *Théâtre d'agriculture*. 1804 edn.

SHIPLEY, A. E. 'The Bugonia Myth', *J. Philol.* 1918, pp. 97–105.

SLATER, D. A. 'Was the Fourth Eclogue written to celebrate the marriage of Octavia to Mark Antony?' *C.R.* 1912, pp. 114–19.

SLICHER VAN BATH, B. H. *The Agrarian History of Western Europe, A.D. 500–1850*, tr. O. Ordish. 1959.

SNELL, B. *Die Entdeckung des Geistes*, tr. as *The Discovery of the Mind*. 1948.

STANFORD, W. B. *Greek Metaphor*. 1936.

STORER, W. H. *Virgil and Ronsard*. 1923.

STROUX, J. *Vergil*. 1932.

SYME, SIR R. *The Roman Revolution*. 1939.

TARN, SIR W. W. 'Alexander Helios and the Golden Age', *J.R.S.* 1932, pp. 135–60.

(With M. P. Charlesworth) *Octavian, Antony and Cleopatra*. Extracts from *Camb. Anc. Hist.* vol, X. 1934.

Republished separately 1965.

TAYLOR, L. R. *The Divinity of the Roman Emperors*. 1931.

TAYLOR, M. E. 'Primitivism in Virgil', *A.J.Ph.* 1955, pp. 261–78.

TENNYSON, H. *Tennyson: A Memoir*. 1897.

TERZAGHI, N. 'Sulla seconda edizione delle Georgiche', *Athenaeum*, 1960, pp. 132–40.

THIELSCHER, P. *Des Marcus Cato Belehrung über die Landwirtschaft*. 1963.

THOMPSON, D'A. 'The Mole in Antiquity', *C.R.* 1918, p. 9.

TICKELL, R. E. *Thomas Tickell and the Eighteenth Century Poets*. 1931.

TOMSIN, A. (With S. Hubaux) *Les travaux agrestes (Géorgiques)* (verse tr.). 1947.

TOWNEND, G. B. 'The Poems.' Ch. V in *Cicero*, ed. T. A. Dorey. 1965.

TOYNBEE, A. J. *Hannibal's Legacy*. 1965.

TREVELYAN, R. C. *Virgil, Eclogues and Georgics* (verse tr.). 1944.

TUGWELL, S. 'Virgil, *Eclogue* 9. 59–60', *C.R.* 1963, pp. 132–3.

TUSSER, T. *Five Hundredth Good Pointes of Husbandry*. 1573.

ULLMAN, B. L. 'Virgil in certain medieval florilegia', in 'Virgilio nel Medio Evo', *Stud. Med.* N.S., V, 1932, pp. 59–66.

LIST OF MODERN WORKS CITED

VAN VEEN, P. A. F. *De Soeticheydt des Buyten-Levens Vergheselschapt met de Boecken·* 1960.

WEBB, G. 'The Christ of the Trades', *The Listener*, 1967, pp. 12–14.

WELLESLEY, K. 'Virgil's Home Revisited', *Proc. Virg. Soc.* 1963–4, pp. 36–43.

WESTENDORP-BOERMA, R. E. H. *P. Vergilii Maronis Catalepton*, vol. I, 1949.

WHEELER, A. L. *Catullus and the Traditions of Ancient Poetry*. 1934.

WHITE, K. D. 'Virgil's Knowledge of Arable Farming', *Proc. Virg. Soc.* 1967–8, pp. 11–22.
Agricultural Implements of the Roman World. 1967.
Roman Agriculture (forthcoming).

WHITFIELD, B. G. 'Virgil and the Bees', *G.&R.* 1956, pp. 97–117.

WILKINSON, L. P. *Horace and his Lyric Poetry*. 1945.
'The Intention of Virgil's Georgics', *G.&R.* 1950, pp. 19–28.
'The Earliest Odes of Horace', *Hermes*, 1956, pp. 495–9.
'The Language of Virgil and Horace', *C.Q.* 1959, pp. 181–92.
Golden Latin Artistry. 1963.
'Virgil's Theodicy', *C.Q.* 1963, pp. 73–84.
Review of B. Otis, *Virgil*, q.v. *C.R.* 1965, pp. 182–5.
'Virgil and the Evictions', *Hermes*, 1966, pp. 320–4.

WILLIAMS, G. G. 'The Beginnings of Nature Poetry in the XVIII Century', *Stud. in Philol.* 1930, pp. 583–608.

WILSON, E. F. 'The *Georgica Spiritualia* of John of Garland', *Speculum*, 1933, pp. 358–77.

WIMMEL, W. *Kallimachos in Rom*, Hermes Einzelschriften, Heft 16. 1960.

WINBOLT, S. E. *Latin Hexameter Verse*. 1903.

WISSOWA, G. 'Das Prooemium von Vergils *Georgica*', *Hermes*, 1917, pp. 92–104.

WITTE, K. *Die Geschichte der Römischen Dichtung*, Part I, 2: *Vergils Georgica*. 1927.

WOERMANN, K. *History of Painting*, tr. S. Colvin. 1880.

WOESTIJNE, P. VAN DE. 'Haud mollia iussa', *R.B.Ph.* 1929, pp. 523–30.
'Varron de Réate et Virgile', *R.B.Ph.* 1931, pp. 907–29.
'Mécène et Virgile', *Mus. Bel.* 1931, pp. 261–84.

WORMELL, D. E. W. See Dudley, D. R.

ZABUGHIN, V. *Virgilio nel Rinascimento Italiano da Dante a Torquato Tasso*. Vol. I, 1921. Vol. II, 1923.

ZAPPERT, G. *Vergils Fortleben im Mittelalter*. 1851.

Index of Proper Names (Selected)

Figures in square brackets refer to the notes in the Index of References

Boethius, 283n
Bolgar, R. R., 275n
Bolisani, E., 20n
Borinski, K., 283n
Borsselen, van, 297
Boswell, J., 301n, 335 [24], [25]
Bourbon, N., 301
Bourbough, 309n
Bovie, S. P., 72n, 332 [2]
Bowra, Sir C. M., 117, 241n, 325
Boyancé, P., 336 [4], [17]
Bradley, R., 307n
Brescia (Brixia), 40
Brink, C. O., 334 [16]
Britain (-ons), 164, 168
Brown, 'Capability', 299
Brown, E. L., 319
Browning, R., 148n
Brueghel, 13, 295n
Bruère, R. T., 272n, 339 [8], 341 [10],
    [12]
Brunt, P. A., 337 [4], [5], [7]
Büchner, K., 3, 29n, 31n, 72–3, 99n,
    110 and n, 224n, 315, 323, 333 [28],
    [46], 335 [21], 337 [17], [30], 338
    [9], [17]
Burck, E., 59n, 70n, 72 and n, 98, 132,
    314–15, 325, 329, 335 [31], 338 [2],
    [35], 339 [4]
Burns, R., 310
Byrne, P., 301n

Caecilius, 40
Caesar, Julius, 18n, 24–8, 25n, 35, 43,
    52, 84, 130, 154, 159, 164, 179, 204,
    224, 242, 245
Caesar, Octavianus, *see* Augustus,
    Octavian
Callimachus, 17, 34, 40–1, 61, 71, 114,
    164, 171, 216–19, 323–4, 340 [90]
Calvus, 40n
Campania (-ian), 13, 88, 226 and n,
    251, 272
Camps, W. A., 328
Carcopino, J., 334 [28], 336 [3]
Carew, 306
Cassino, Monte, 276
Cassiodorus, 276
Cassius, 20

Castiglioni, L., 3, 339 [39]
Cato, Marcus, 50, 57, 58, 82n, 132,
    147n, 153, 223n, 225, 227n, 228, 247,
    259
Cato, Valerius, 40
Catullus, 19, 22, 25n, 26 and n, 35–8,
    39–41, 43, 45, 54n, 61, 91, 115–16,
    150, 164n, 211, 214, 220, 327–8
Cave, E., 300
Celsus, 253n, 271
Cesario, E., 164n
Charlemagne, Carolingian, 273, 276
Charlesworth, M. P., 337 [12], [15]
Chaucer, 288
Chinese, 242n
Chrysippus, 140
Cicero, 10, 20, 44n, 54n, 61–2, 67n,
    78n, 132, 144n, 164, 187, 224n, 234–
    5 and n, 316, 317, 337 [30]
Cinna, 39–40, 61
Cistercians, 276–7 and n
Clark, Sir K., 290n, 291n
Clarke, A., 309, 342 [73]
Clarke, M. L., 320, 342 [58], [75]
Classen, C. J., 337 [21]
Coleman, R. G. G., 46n, 326
Coleridge, S. T., 15, 183, 310
Columella, 54n, 103n, 135n, Ch. 9
    passim 270–2
Comparetti, D., 273 and n, 341 [16]
Compitalia, 89
Conington, J., 1n, 34 and n, 71, 97n,
    105n, 183, 198, 218n, 231n, 241n,
    246n, 250, 258, 325
Conon (astronomer), 42
Conon (mythographer), 116–17 and n
Consus, 147
Corycian, 54, 68, 70, 102–3, 174, 264
Cowley, A., 298
Cowper, W., 299, 302
Crabbe, G., 302
Cremona, 19 and n, 23–5, 29–31, 40
    and n, 268
Crescentius, 277 and n
Crönert, W., 332 [12]
Cumont, F., 58n
Cupaiuolo, F., 339 [1]
Curtis, E., 274–5, 317
Cynics, 138, 140

INDEX OF PROPER NAMES

Gilmour, J. S. L., 243n, 244n
Gladstone, W. E., 16
Glover, T. R., 1
Goldsmith, O., 301n
Googe, B., 305
Gow, A. S. F., 41n, 341 [100]
Grahame, J., 310n
Grainger, J., 93, 301n
Grant, M., 4n
Grimal, P., 27n, 140n
Grosseteste, 277, 341 [27]
Gruppe, O., 335 [23]
Guarino of Verona, 291
Guiard, A., 310n
Guillemin, A-M., 342 [79]

Haarhoff, T. J., 263, 328, 338 [53], 340
    [60]
Hadrian, 17
Hamilton, J., 306
Hardie, C., 341 [1]
Hardouin, 283n
Harington, Sir J., 296
Haskins, C. H., 288n
Haverfield, 258
Haydn, 304
Hazlitt, W., 310
Headlam, W., 7n, 336 [30]
Hégémon, P., 305
Heinze, R., 151n
Heiss, H., 310n
Heitland, W. E., 49n, 50n, 54, 333 [1],
    [3], [15]
Heitmann, K., 283n
Henry, J., 141n
Hensel, P., 342 [54]
Heresbach, C., 305
Hermogenes, 341 [30]
Hérouville, P. d', 244n, 253n, 263n,
    329, 340 [86]
Herrmann, L., 333 [33]
Herzsohn, P., 341 [36]
Hesiod, 3, 5, 14, 52, 53, 54, 56–60, 67,
    76, 80, 83, 132, 134n, 135–40, 143,
    156, 193, 203n, 215, 217n
Heurgon, J., 325, 335 [20]
Heyne, 229, 240n, 325
Hibbard, G. R., 342 [64]
Higham, T., 6n

Hildebert, 277 and n
Hippolytus, 190
Homer, 4, 59, 68, 114, 126, 204, 213–18,
    230, 238, 241n, 270
Hopkins, G. M., 9, 143
Hoole, C., 342 [60]
Horace, 17, 21n, 23, 49, 51, 53, 56, 70,
    74, 104, 124n, 133, 144, 156n, 163n,
    170, 171, 173, 179, 180, 211, 297, 298,
    314, 338 [40]
Hornstein, F., 20
Housman, A. E., 199n
Hubaux, S., 2
Hubelei, A., 285n, 342 [61], [66]
Huber, F., 266
Hudson-Williams, T., 340 [91]
Hugo, V., 309–10 and n
Huxley, H. H., 1n
Huxley, Sir J., 340 [33]
Hyginus, 224n, 267n, 268n, 270

Inama-Sternegg, Th. von, 341 [34]
Isidore, 284
Iulium Sidus, 27, 33

Jackson, C. N., 22n
Jahn, P., 329, 334 [25], 339 [5]
Jammes, F., 285n
Janus Secundus, 297n
Jermyn, L. A. S., 1, 2, 44n, 234–42,
    249n, 250, 339 [5], 340 [43]
Jerome, 286
John of Garland, 284
John of Salisbury, 286
Johnson, C., 295
Johnson, S., 94, 301 and n, 302n, 311
Jones, W. P., 302n, 305, 310n
Jonson, Ben, 298
Juba, 341 [100]
Julia Augusta, 245

Kapp, E., 333 [46]
Kazantzakes, 317
Keats, J., 7, 9, 310, 332 [4]
Keightley, T., 27n, 78n, 81, 97, 112n,
    236, 237, 240, 246n, 255n, 325, 329
Kidd, D. A., 328
Kiessling, A., 317
Kirchmayer, T. (Naogeorgus), 284

Index of Passages Cited from the Georgics

BOOK II

BOOK III

BOOK IV